Television Drama

Much recent work in television theory has emphasized the active agency of audiences. John Tulloch goes beyond that approach to underline the agency of drama practitioners in their 'readings' of conventional genres and forms. This is the first book to focus on television drama from a cultural studies perspective which examines the active agency of both viewers and media practitioners in this area of popular culture.

Taking examples from US, British and Australian TV drama, Tulloch examines myths and counter-myths as they circulate in popular culture, with illustrations from soap opera, science fiction, sitcom, cop series and 'authored' drama. Working within an ethnographic framework, he looks in detail at both the production and reception of TV drama. He draws extensively on direct empirical research on both audiences and practitioners, observing closely the productions of 'authors' like Ken Loach, Trevor Griffiths and John McGrath, as well as the TV routines of 'ordinary' viewers.

Television Drama will be an invaluable text for students of media, film and television studies, as well as of sociology and cultural studies.

John Tulloch is Associate Professor and Head of Mass Communication at Macquarie University, New South Wales. He has written widely on film history and theory, audience analysis and theories of textual criticism, and has published books on the British science fiction series, *Doctor Who*, and the Australian soap opera, *A Country Practice*.

STUDIES IN CULTURE AND COMMUNICATION

General Editor: John Fiske

Television Drama

Agency, audience and myth

John Tulloch

ROUTLEDGE
London and New York

To Jef

First published 1990
by Routledge
11 New Fetter Lane, London EC4P 4EE
29 West 35th Street, New York, NY 10001

Printed in Great Britain by
Richard Clay Ltd, Bungay, Suffolk

British Library Cataloguing in Publication Data
Tulloch, John
   Television drama: agency, audience and myth. –
   (Studies in culture and communication)
   1. Television drama in English
   I. Title II. Series
   791.45'75

Library of Congress Cataloging in Publication Data
Tulloch, John.
   Television drama : agency, audience, and myth / John Tulloch.
   p. cm. – (Studies in culture and communication)
   Bibliography: p.
   ISBN 0 415 01648 7. – ISBN 0 415 01649 5 (pbk.)
   1. Television plays – History and criticism. 2. Television broadcasting.
   3. Television audiences. 4. Popular culture. 5. Communication. I. Title.
   II. Series.
   PN1992.65.T85   1989
   302.23'45–dc20   89-6325

Contents

Conclusion: comedies of 'myth' and 'resistance' 243

Acknowledgements

I would like to thank the many people who have made the writing of this book possible: John Fiske, who asked me to write it and acted as a helpful and incisive editor; Trevor Griffiths, Ken Loach, John McGrath, the production team of *A Country Practice* who gave so generously of their working time and their hospitality in providing access to their ideas and their productions; the elderly people in Bournemouth (including my parents and family) who allowed me to do an audience study, giving me access to their homes and their pleasures; Peter Holland at Trinity Hall, Cambridge, for his hospitality during part of the research for this book; the many media academics and critics whose work is summarized here; Manuel Alvarado, Philip Bell, Marian Tulloch, and Trevor Griffiths for reading the manuscript and offering critical advice as well as support; Charlotte Brunsdon for insisting so firmly on the gendered politics of academic writing; and Jane Armstrong for being the most well-informed and thus helpful publisher that I have encountered. For the task of typing and re-typing the various versions of the manuscript I have solely to thank Jennifer Newton, whose cheerful contribution to the book went beyond the secretarial to that of the popular drama fan.

To the (no doubt many) academic writers and critics of TV drama not represented here, my apologies; even a book in a series intending an overview of the 'current debate' must be, as I say in the Introduction, subjectively selective in its choices. I have tried to make the basic principles of my selections clear (in relation to producers as well as critics). Other than that, the increasingly 'industrial conditions of production' of writing within tertiary institutions makes any encyclopaedic intent impossible, even if it were desirable.

One significant recent area of research on TV drama is not covered in this book. Originally it was intended to include a chapter (written by Manuel Alvarado) examining Latin American production and theory via a case study of TV Globo in Brazil. Manuel's other commitments made it impossible to include this piece, given pressing publication dates. My view is that some of the Latin American theory (as for instance in Jesus Martin-Barbero's work) takes recent ethnographically oriented audience analysis significantly further – going beyond, for instance, theories of sub-cultural competence, 'gossip', and oral culture to specifically historical and socio-cultural analyses of media, examining the cultural competence of particular classes in particular countries at particular times. Rather than attempt a scant summary of this work in an already over-crowded manuscript, I felt it better to leave this area for another book. But in signalling this omission and the selections made, I hope to encourage readers to tease out their own meanings from the original texts rather than trust, finally, in mine.

John Tulloch

Foreword
Trevor Griffiths

The first plays I ever wrote were for television, back in the early 1960s. I was a liberal studies tutor in a technical college at the time, teaching – among other things – a course on communications with a hefty element of television studies at its core. Listening to day-release apprentices discussing their last evening's viewing merely served to confirm what I'd been learning within my own family and social network for some years: that television was already developing great importance in all our lives; and that it might, with work and will and purpose, prove a major popular educative force for the future.

I learned something about plays and drama, too, from those early encounters; something my formal education at grammar school and degree in English Language and Literature had not really prepared me for. Namely, that plays were genuinely *popular* events, capable of engaging minds and desires and sensibilities *across* the social classes, as well as of exploring social issues, in ways that were both complex and arresting, without necessarily 'losing' the audience at its 'lower end'. When I entered television professionally a couple of years later, it was at least as much out of a need to learn more about television and its workings as to serve the institutional ends of the BBC as a further education specialist.

Something of what happened next, to me and a whole generation of writers as well as to British television drama, is brilliantly charted in the book that follows. For many cultural workers in the 1970s and 1980s, television became the necessary and central site of struggle; and John Tulloch's book, with considerable insight and rich sourcing, offers a powerful account of the aesthetic, political and practical terrains disputed and of the strategies deployed.

This is a book for audiences as well as programme makers, for students as well as teachers, for electorates as well as politicians. The vicious if undeclared *Kulturkampf* still being waged by the British state against independent thought and belief has left its mark on almost every aspect of civil society. The assault on television has been particularly fierce, testimony to broadcasting's inherent capacity to frustrate the triumphant march of capital towards dystopia dressed as liberty, as terminal a view of the future as any historically available. Tulloch's book, in reminding us of who and how we were only yesterday, clearly signals the dangers of today's fevered deconstructions and importantly insists on the need to imagine a quite different tomorrow from the no-alternative film-flam currently on offer.

General editor's preface

This series of books on different aspects of communication is designed to meet the needs of the growing number of students coming to study this subject for the first time. The authors are experienced teachers or lecturers who are committed to bridging the gap between the huge body of research available to the more advanced student, and what the new student actually needs to get him started on his studies.

Probably the most characteristic feature of communication is its diversity: it ranges from the mass media and popular culture, through language to individual and social behaviour. But it identifies links and a coherence within this diversity. The series will reflect the structure of its subject. Some books will be general, basic works that seek to establish theories and methods of study applicable to a wide range of material; others will apply these theories and methods to the study of one particular topic. But even these topic-centred books will relate to each other, as well as to the more general ones. One particular topic, such as advertising or news or language, can only be understood as an example of communication when it is related to, and differentiated from, all the other topics that go to make up this diverse subject.

The series, then, has two main aims, both closely connected. The first is to introduce readers to the most important results of contemporary research into communication together with the theories that seek to explain it. The second is to equip them with appropriate methods of study and investigation which they will be able to apply directly to their everyday experience of communication.

If readers can write better essays, produce better projects and pass more exams as a result of reading these books I shall be very satisfied; but if they gain a new insight into how communication shapes and informs our social life, how it articulates and creates our experience of industrial society, then I shall be delighted. Communication is too often taken for granted when it should be taken to pieces.

John Fiske

Introduction: theories of myth, agency and audience

This book is about television drama, but obviously it cannot be about *all* television drama. Any book, any communication medium, is selective; it has biases, it 'distorts' the field – not only in what it chooses to talk about and what it omits, but also in how it talks about what is selected. The question then is: what motivates the selections made? I'll begin by looking at some principles of selection in other books in the field of TV drama, as a way of introducing the choices in my own.

In his edited book, *British Television Drama*, George Brandt admits to a bias towards the single play in his selection. He claims this is 'more a matter of convenience than of dogma',[1] but in my view his choices are determined by a clear sense of what 'merits critical attention'.[2] He notes, for instance, the mid-1960s development of serials like *Mogul, Dr Finlay's Casebook, The Power Game* and *The Troubleshooters*, 'aimed at the mass viewing public in a ratings game which made it possible at other times to take a chance on the not-so-popular single play'.[3] This is similar to his argument earlier (supposedly aimed at 'high culture' critics of television), that the mass audience appeal of cinema from the 1920s to the 1950s was a necessary 'base' for 'the masterpieces of Chaplin, Ford, Lang, Hitchcock, Renoir and von Stroheim'.[4]

When Brandt does valorize another TV drama form, it tends to be because it allows a writer to learn to do better the things that the single play is already valued for; thus the TV serial gives the writer 'the chance to paint a broader canvas, to develop stories of greater complexity'.[5] That word 'complexity' is crucial to Brandt's sense of critical merit, as is its linking to 'television writers of distinction', since this is what separates British television drama from North American 'machine-made series and serials with high gloss, canned laughter and routine violence'.[6] Brandt is explicit: British TV drama in the 1960s and 1970s owed its excellence 'first and foremost to the quality of the writing'.[7]

What Brandt's book actually gives us is a set of histories, which intersect with and validate each other. Most obviously there is a history of creative individuals – pre-eminently writers, but behind these there are imaginative directors and producers, themselves supported by other individuals like Sydney Newman who 'used his key position' as BBC Head of Drama to promote 'a great many original plays by up-and-coming or established writers that exemplified his policy'.[8]

Secondly, there is a history of TV technology: live studio transmission, monochromic, low definition images, colour transmission, and the coming of videotape and lightweight filming equipment. This history intersects at points with that of Brandt's 'authorial' individuals, since it was their innovative response to the limits of current technology that *made* them 'merit critical attention'; as for instance, in the case of lightweight film equipment:

> The producer most closely associated with the use of film on the *Wednesday Play*, Tony Garnett, worked with authors like David Mercer . . . Jim Allen and Jeremy Sandford. The play that epitomised this veristic trend was Sandford's *Cathy Come Home*. Produced by Tony Garnett and directed by Ken Loach . . . it entered into television mythology instantly.[9]

Intersecting with both the history of technology and the history of creative individuals, there is a history of style; in particular the debate about television naturalism.

> Kennedy Martin demanded two things of the TV play of the future: that it should break away from the theatre and that it should abandon naturalism. Greater camera freedom and release from the constraints of real time would ally the 'new drama' more with the cinema; but he rejected the Hollywood emphasis on the close-up as a 'subjective' device. . . . What exactly did its author mean by the objective use of the camera (other than preferring medium long shots and long shots to coming closer?).[10]

Brandt doesn't take his own question much further, but it is taken up by other contributors to the book: in Edward Braun's reference to Trevor Griffiths' critique of 'sham' objectivity among television presenters in *All Good Men*; in Paul Madden's discussion of Jim Allen, and of John McGrath's rejection of 'bourgeois naturalism'; in Albert Hunt's description of Alan Plater's irreverent reflexivity, as he broke down the boundaries between TV drama and other light entertainment forms (both on and off television); in Philip Purser's discussion of the transmutation between fantasy and fact, objective and subjective versions of events in Dennis Potter; and, perhaps most productively, in S.M.J.

Arrowsmith's analysis of Peter Watkins' engagement with historical discourse, turning 'the technological coding systems of the twentieth century . . . on the hitherto coded history of the eighteenth century'.[11]

Each of these writers in Brandt's book establish, of course, their own trajectory, based on their own notions of significance. But the fact that they are there to speak at all depends on Brandt's fourth (and overarching) history – a liberal history which sets all the others in place. 'Television playwriting will flourish best in an atmosphere of freedom both in choice of subject and in matters of style.'[12] This history relates the spate of historical costume dramas in the 1970s (*The Six Wives of Henry VIII, Edward VII, Edward and Mrs Simpson, Jenny, Upstairs Downstairs*) not only to the invention of colour (Brandt's position is by no means a simple technological determinism); but also to 'a dreamland of stable class . . . relationships as a consolation for the turbulent present'.[13] This sense of the popular historical series as carrier of national myth is countered by Brandt's celebration of the single play as the form par excellence for 'the ventilation of public issues . . . one of the most valuable functions that television drama can perform'.[14] This is why Brandt's emphasis is on the 'artists and intellectuals' of the single play – the Jim Allens, Trevor Griffiths, David Mercers, Peter Nichols, Alan Platers, Dennis Potters, Jeremy Sandfords and Peter Watkins (together with the occasional anti-prejudice series *Till Death Us Do Part* and the odd anti-naturalist serial like *Pennies From Heaven*). It is these that 'merit critical attention'.[15]

George Brandt's criteria of 'significant' TV drama are ones which would be widely recognized and accepted within the TV industry. Speaking of the British soap opera, *EastEnders*, the Head of Series and Serials at the BBC, Jonathan Powell, comments, 'there are episodes of *EastEnders* which I would frankly be very happy to put up as a one-off play'.[16] David Buckingham comments on this: 'Significantly, although popularity is clearly valued, "quality" is still defined here by standards which derive from the "cultural high ground" of the single play.'[17] Many current TV drama writers in Britain bewail both the decline of the single play at the hands of the 'ghastly American mini-series', and the excessive commitment to 'facts' and naturalism in the soap operas where they make their living. The negotiation between creative writers, current technology, naturalism, and the 'ventilation of public issues' that Brandt describes would be regarded by many television workers *as* a definition of their field; epitomized by Dennis Potter's celebrated series *The Singing Detective*, or by Troy Kennedy Martin's *The Edge of Darkness*, and his determination to take on board the technology of rock video by writing four-minute plays which are interrogative both in subject matter and style. As Kennedy Martin put it at a recent television writers' conference,

> One of the few places I think that naturalism is justified institutionally is in things like *Edge of Darkness*, where you have the long form, and there does seem a lot more mileage. . . . This sort of thing is an extension of the nineteenth-century novel. . . . The other way to go is to try and get really short 2-, 3- and 4-minute pieces, where you can't have naturalism because it doesn't really work. One needs to use the small size to actually fragment, interconnect and deconstruct . . . in a way similar to music videos. But these short pieces should actually be inside a new channel which is itself deconstructive . . . of the little proscenium arches we put around each of 'news', 'documentary', 'fiction'. . . . We should have bits of *EastEnders* – all the rows in *EastEnders* – cut into the programmes all the way through the day . . . and also cut in very short ads like 'Don't buy this roof, you know where it comes from', and then you would have these little pieces of drama . . . which cost quite a lot of money and should be obsessional . . . and be looked at time and time again, the way people play records. What we are looking for is a . . . kind of thinking person's *MTV*.[18]

Although there are certainly differences between Troy Kennedy Martin's position and George Brandt's, the very *form* of *British Television Drama* (as an edited book of essays) allows it to represent the liberal/ critical discourse of many television practitioners ('discourse' I define here in John Fiske's sense as communication comprising 'a topic area, a social location, and the promotion of the interests of a particular social group'[19]). Brandt's topic area is television drama; the social location is the alliance between a liberal academia and a 'critical' media practice which allows the 'ventilation' of public issues; and the ideological work of the discourse is in promoting 'creativity' (though occasionally 'politics') to a 'mass audience' by way of, primarily, public service television.

Though no doubt recognizable by many media workers as describing their 'reality', Brandt's discourse was already running against the trend of dominant media theory when he wrote the book. As John Caughie argued in an article published at about the same time, there has been a surprising lack within concurrent media theory of rigorous attention to the single play and 'serious drama': 'the vast majority of politically engaged attention has been directed towards . . . popular genres (soap opera, situation comedy, light entertainment)'.[20] Caughie's own important work notwithstanding, that trend has continued, emblematized most recently by John Fiske's book, *Television Culture*. While sharing Brandt's rejection of high culture put-downs of television, and his belief that 'any portrayal of reality is constructed',[21] Fiske's principles of selection as to what constitutes significant drama are remarkably different. Indeed, it is precisely those 'machine-made series and serials with high gloss . . . and routine violence' which attract Fiske's most dedicated attention.

He too, of course, constructs a history in what he chooses to emphasize – in this case much more openly and reflexively. Like the dominant media theory Caughie describes, Fiske's is a politically engaged position. 'Popular pleasures and politics' is the subtitle of his book, and the politics of feminist, Marxist and post-modernist concepts of pleasure are what prescribe both his choices of TV drama, and how he discusses them. Working through feminist psychoanalytical notions of voyeurism and the fetishization of the female in cinema, Fiske considers their relevance to the more interactive and segmented nature of television reception, and so examines 'the articulation of a specific feminine definition of desire and pleasure' in soap operas.[22] Drawing on Marxist notions of power and social control, Fiske insists on the socially oppositional possibilities of pleasure: 'The pleasure experienced by more liberal or even radical viewers of *Hill Street Blues* or *Cagney and Lacy* is a form of *plaisir* to be found in confirming their social identity as one that opposes or at least interrogates dominant social values.'[23] And accepting a post-modernist refusal of 'the notion of subjectivity as a site where sense is made, for sense-making is the ultimate subjecting process',[24] Fiske argues that however strongly narrative may fight 'to close each episode with a resolution in which sense, control, and masculine closure are all achieved, the style, the music, the look, the interruptions of the narrative remain open, active, disruptive and linger on as the pleasures of *Miami Vice*'.[25] Whereas for Troy Kennedy Martin, anti-naturalist four-minute drama as 'a kind of thinking person's *MTV*' is seen as a *writer's* resistance to standard fare like *Miami Vice*, for John Fiske the fragmentary nature of images, 'their resistance to sense', *within Miami Vice* and *MTV* enable the *viewer's* resistance as 'a postmodernist pleasure'.[26]

The entire structure of Fiske's book depends on the tension between pleasures of power and pleasures of resistance. 'While there's clearly a pleasure in exerting social power, the popular pleasures of the subordinate are necessarily found in resisting, evading, or offending this power. Popular pleasures are those that empower the subordinate and they thus offer political resistance, even if only momentarily and even if only in a limited terrain.'[27]

So whereas Brandt's book is about 'authors', Fiske's is about 'audiences'; where Brandt speaks of 'ventilating public issues', Fiske emphasizes 'resistance to dominant ideology'. My point is, that selectivity and 'bias' are not simply matters of omission and distortion. They are profoundly embedded in our view of 'the real', and deeply determined by one's *own* 'pleasures and politics' – that is, by the amalgam of daily desires, practices, assumptions and discourses which make up one's agency as an author. Inevitably these construct *my* topic area, television drama; socially locate it in terms of the alliances I make (with media theory, with radical TV 'authors'); and promote the interests of particular social groups (within both theory and the media). That *is* inevitable, and it is well to be aware of it. In my case the 'biases' are carried by my own sub-title, 'Agency, Audience and Myth', in a book which will examine resistant practice both among Fiske's viewers *and* Brandt's media practitioners, and which will have a significant focus on both 'machine-made' serials *and* 'serious' one-off dramas and series.

Myth

A myth is a story by which a culture explains or understands some aspect of reality or nature. Primitive myths are about life and death, men and gods, good and evil. Our sophisticated myths are about masculinity and femininity, about the family, about success, about the British policeman, about science. A myth, for Barthes, is a culture's way of thinking about something, a way of conceptualizing or understanding it.

John Fiske[28]

This book is part of a series which aims first to introduce readers to the most important results of contemporary research into communication together with the theories that seek to explain it; and second, to 'equip them with appropriate methods of study and investigation which they will be able to apply directly to their everyday experience of communication'.[29] What the series takes to be 'important' research (and 'appropriate' methods of study) must, of course, also be a matter of interpretation and preferred selection; as must the current debate about TV drama which I was asked to survey and critically engage with as the brief for my particular book. Indeed, John Fiske's concluding editorial remark that 'Communication is too often taken for granted when it should be taken to pieces'[30] itself implies a pattern of relevance and coherence that was initially fundamental in this project, and is still important: that communication is too often taken to be a natural and transparent transaction, when in fact it is a process of myth-making which requires deconstructing. As John Hartley says in his book in the series, *Understanding News*, 'News is a myth-maker' – and he is using 'myth' not in the sense of something that is fake, or pertains only to primitive cultures, but in Fiske's (and Barthes') sense. As Hartley puts it, myth allows a society 'to use factual or fictional characters and events to make sense of its environment, both physical and social'.[31]

In this definition of myth the distinction is not made between 'fictional' and 'factual' (as between 'myth' and 'reality'), but between those 'dominant myths' which are accepted by enough people to seem transparently 'true' (or 'common sense'), and 'counter-myths' embedded, as Fiske says, in subcultures within our society. Science, he points out in the inaugural book in the series, is an area where counter-myths (of science as evil, signifying humankind's selfish materialism) strongly challenge the dominant myth (of science as objective, signifying humankind's beneficial adaptability to its environment). Both myth and counter-myth are circulated very visibly in popular culture: 'the factual side of television, news, current affairs, documentaries, tend to show more of the dominant than of the counter-myth: fictional television and cinema, on the other hand, reverse the proportions. There are more evil scientists than good ones, and science causes more problems than it solves.'[32]

In contrast to science, myths about the police are represented less evenly. In media circulation there are 'a limited number of significantly different ways of photographing the police', and so very few 'myths by which we understand the police force'.[33] In one sense representations of the police do change: George Brandt describes the shift from the myth of the decent, unarmed British 'bobby' (as portrayed in the drama series *Dixon of Dock Green*) to 'the distinctly post-Dixon view of the work of the police in a northern New Town' (*Z-Cars*), 'a view not initially popular with the force';[34] and then later on, a further change in the Gordon Newman/Tony Garnett *Law and Order* series which 'aroused the ire . . . of the Prison Officers Association and the Metropolitan Police'.[35] But (leaving aside for the moment the 'authored' case of *Law and Order* which was denied repeats on British TV as well as sale abroad) in another sense the dominant myths of the British police retain core ('caring' and 'humane') values which do not change, and protect the police from the widespread circulation of counter-myths of the threatening kind we see in the field of science.

The less our dominant myths are publicly challenged by counter-myths, the more 'natural' they appear: not then as *social* constructions at all, but as 'truth'. As O'Sullivan *et al.* argue in another book in this series, myth's 'prime function is to make the cultural natural'.[36] A first criterion of selection in this book, then, is of TV drama within the context of myth as Fiske, Hartley, O'Sullivan and others in this series have defined it (with a particular focus here on science fiction and police genres, Chapter 2).

But these authors' frequent reference to the work of Barthes and to the *semiotic* definition of myth indicates the circulation of a further myth. If myth 'refers to a culture's way of understanding, expressing and communicating to itself concepts that are important to its self-identity as a culture',[37] then 'myth' *as* concept (in its semiotic definition) is itself a way of understanding, communicated during the last twenty or so years as a central aspect of self-identity within the culture of communication scholars and critics. The 'Studies in Culture and Communication' series represents a 'Cultural Studies' validation of this myth (which is dominant within major parts of media studies, but is only a counter-myth within society generally). Indeed, this definition of myth (that 'myth works to naturalize and universalize the class interests of the bourgeoisie'[38]) has *defined* the preoccupation of Cultural Studies; as in O'Sullivan *et al.*'s definition of Cultural Studies in *Key Concepts in Communication*: 'culture is seen as the sphere in which class, gender, race and other inequalities are *naturalized* and *represented* in forms which sever (as far as possible) the connection between these and economic and political inequalities'.[39]

My analysis in this book is embedded in that Cultural Studies myth, and also in O'Sullivan *et al.*'s further definition of culture as 'the means by and through which various subordinate groups live and resist their subordination. Culture is, then, the terrain on which *hegemony* is struggled for and established, and hence it is the site of "cultural struggles".'[40] The emphasis here is on the struggle for meaning between dominant and counter-myths (including that between mainstream media and media studies definitions of the television drama field); but also *within* the institutions of mainstream media, which is why there is an emphasis in this book, in addition to popular genres, on the work of radical 'authors' like Trevor Griffiths, Alan Bleasdale and John McGrath. Again, there is no way of being exhaustive or 'objective' in this choice. For me these TV dramatists are engaging in some of the most important counter-myth struggles within the television institution, which is why there are chapters on them here.

So the selection of both the TV drama significant for analysis and the 'important research' to be surveyed (as a brief of this series) is strongly influenced by work within the 'Cultural Studies' tradition. Until recently a major proportion of English-speaking work in this tradition was British; latterly a lot of it has been from the US and Australia – and this 'bias', too, is reflected in the book.

AGENCY

> The theme of the decentering of the subject . . . should not lead to the disappearance of the self as agent. . . . The consequences of this for social theory . . . involve rescuing the knowledgeable agent as the conceptual centre for social analysis, and situating what 'knowledge-ability' is in the context of the ongoing practices of social life.
>
> Anthony Giddens[41]

If 'myth' is one major influence on the selection and definition of 'TV drama' in this book, 'agency' is another. O'Sullivan *et al.*'s emphasis on the agency of subordinate groups *living* and *resisting* their subordination masks a tendency within cultural and social theory (influenced by structuralism and post-structuralism) to de-emphasize the 'knowledge-ability' of human behaviour. As Giddens says, this is most evident in Levi-Strauss' statement that he is concerned to show 'not how men think in myths, but how myths operate in men's minds without their being aware of the fact';[42] and the same preoccupation with 'de-centring the subject' dominates structuralist and post-structuralist work: in Foucault in relation to history and the end of the 'age of man'; in Barthes in terms of the 'death of the author'; in Lacan's re-working of psychoanalysis. All of these, rightly, reject the 'I' as 'the expression of some continuous selfhood that is its basis'.[43] But they go further.

> All the above authors agreed upon the irrelevance of the author to the interpretation of texts. The writer is not a presence somehow to be uncovered behind the text. Just as the primacy accorded to the author is an historical expression of the individualism of the Age of Man, so the 'I' of the author is a grammatical form rather than a flesh-and-blood agent.[44]

This general 'death of the author' has been exacerbated by a particular concern within Cultural Studies to conflate much recent *radical* author-ship in TV drama with its notion of 'realism' (or in Colin MacCabe's case, with the 'classic realist text'). Raymond Williams has in fact made the point (shared by all the radical dramatists analysed here) that radical realism's *defining* characteristic (in contrast to an empiricist naturalism) is its *explicit* and self-conscious 'knowledgeability'. This immediately draws attention to itself inter-textually as a constructed view – that is, in its relations of similarity and difference with other television dramas. But despite this, radical realism has been accused of empiricism, of a 'transparency' effect, and of repressing 'its own operations', thereby seeking to guarantee 'its truthfulness because it disguises its arbitrariness and therefore its political effectivity'.[45]

So, despite its clear interrogation of the 'common sense' positioning of television's 'subjects', radical realism has, in its turn, been accused of constructing a 'unity in the viewing subject'[46] equivalent to its own unity of view. This *subjecting* view of the 'real' then appears as that kind of 'common sense' that Barthes speaks of, where 'truth . . . stops on the arbitrary order of him who speaks it'.[47] Despite radical realism's very clear determination to situate both ideology and 'common sense' within the workings of a specific society at a particular historical moment (as, for instance, in Ken Loach's *Days of Hope*), it has been itself situated (within the discourse of Cultural Studies) as that 'realism' which is 'the process by which ideology is made to appear the produce of reality or nature, and not of a specific society and its culture'.[48] Radical realism, according to this discourse, has itself become part of dominant myth in the sense of it 'being a discourse . . . that hides its discursive nature and presents itself as natural rather than cultural'.[49] Radical TV dramatists, in this account, are not agents of change at all, but dupes of myth and the 'visual epistemology' of empiricism.[50]

In contrast, this book will work out of a counter-discourse of the real (and 'realism'), as applied to history and textual analysis by Gregor McLennan, to aesthetics and representation by Terry Lovell, to art and literature by Janet Wolff, to radio and television soap opera by Robert Allen, among many other 'realist' theorists in many other discursive areas. Each of these would agree with Giddens that 'an extra-subjective reality exists and that it is describable via social theory'.[51] I will take up their work at several points later, but here want to agree with Giddens – and this marks a second selective principle of what constitutes 'TV Drama' in this book – that 'If we regard language as situated in social practices, and if we reject the distinction between consciousness and the unconscious followed by the structuralist and post-structuralist authors, we reach a different conception of the subject – as agent. . . . Meaning is not constructed by the play of signifiers, but by the intersection of the production of signifiers with objects and events in the world, focused and organized via the acting individual.'[52]

Giddens' work is part of a renewed theoretical reflection on Marx's insistence that people 'make history, but not of their own choosing'. As such it is part of a broad current critique of post-structuralism for its 'linguistic turn'. This, as Paul James remarks, has abandoned the 'over-emphasis on production in the base-superstructure model only to reductively treat the structure of society in terms of language and signification. . . . It has rightly "de-centred the subject", but to the extent that people as knowledgeable human subjects are left out of history.'[53] Giddens' particular contribution to this critique is in emphasizing the agency of even routine social behaviour, and so of *all* human actors (hence of 'audiences' as well as 'authors'). It is, as James says, part of a 'political project to de-centre elitist theories of the subject which reduce people living in day-to-day routines to inconsequential, non-comprehending, Coronation Street dwellers'.[54]

Actually, Giddens doesn't reject the distinction between consciousness and the unconscious. What he does do is insert *between* them another area of 'knowledgeability': practical consciousness.

> As regards the terminology of human subjectivity, it is essential to understand that the fact that the 'I' is constituted in language, and does not 'mean' the body or the acting self to which the 'I' refers, should not lead to a methodological disappearance of the agent. Terms like 'I' and 'me' may not have as their meaning the object (the body) to which they relate, but they nevertheless gain their significance from the context of activities in which human agents are implicated. They are part of the practical mastery of social relations, and of the continuity of social context, which human agents display.[55]

A great deal of screen theory over the last two decades has concerned itself with textual strategies for fixing subject positions. As O'Sullivan *et al.* argue, 'there's a tendency in this area for texts to be privileged as the constructors or producers of our subjectivity, and for individuals to be seen as more or less passive "subjects" in ideology'.[56] Though the main emphasis of this work was on 'readers', this was true also of producers of the text (unless they radically deconstructed the 'realist' form). For Giddens, in contrast, ' "Subjects" are first and foremost agents' (whether 'authors' or 'readers'), reflexively monitoring (and thus 'understanding') their own contextually based actions. This notion of understanding differs in a crucial way from the understanding-as-myth that I discussed earlier. Myth, in its primitive and modern forms is discursive: a culture's 'story', a 'chain of related concepts'.[57] In contrast, our reflexive capacity as agents engaged in the flow of daily social conduct 'operates only partly on a discursive level. What agents know about what they do, and why they do it – their knowledgeability *as* agents – is largely carried in practical consciousness.'[58]

Social actors reflexively monitor their conduct, and are *partially aware* of the conditions of their behaviour. This is partial awareness in two senses: one resting on Giddens' distinction between practical and discursive consciousness; the other on his distinction between mutual knowledge and critique of common sense belief. Most human knowledge 'is practical in character: it is inherent in the capability to "go on" with the routines of social life'.[59] Frequently, this 'understanding' is contained within routine competence, and 'should not be equated with the discursive giving of reasons for particular items of conduct, not even with the capability of specifying such reasons discursively'.[60] Giddens gives as an example here our routine competence in language. 'To speak a language, an individual needs to know an enormously complicated range of rules, strategies, and tactics involved in language use. However, if the individual were asked to give a discursive account of what it is that he or she knows in knowing these rules, etc., he or she would find it very difficult indeed. The chances are that only a very trivial account would be given discursively of what is known in order to speak a language.'[61] The same is often true of soap opera and romance novel fans' ability to explain discursively the very considerable sophistication which (as Robert Allen and Janice Radway have described) they routinely apply to the 'reading' of their favourite books and shows.

However, as Giddens argues, between practical and discursive consciousness there is no bar, as there is between conscious and unconscious; 'there are only the differences between what can be said and what is characteristically simply done'.[62] The division between the two can be altered by all kinds of learning experience, including the producer-audience relationship of TV drama, and the research process itself in the case of audience study. Hence, as one respondent said to Janice Radway during her study of romance readers, 'We were never stimulated before into thinking why we like the novels. Your asking makes us think why we do this. I had no idea other people had the same ideas I do.'[63] The sense of pleasure in knowledgeable solidarity that Radway observed here (and that unemployed viewers of Alan Bleasdale's *The Boys From The Blackstuff* spoke of: Chapter 11) also relates to Giddens' other distinction, between mutual knowledge and common sense.

This distinction is crucial to the 'double hermeneutic': the relation between, on one hand, 'getting to know what actors already know, and have to know, to "go on" in the daily activities of social life',[64] and on the other hand, social theorists' 'second order' concepts describing these activities. Emphasizing the importance of ethnographic work, Giddens argues that we cannot describe social activity at all – whether of primitive cultures, football hooligans, TV producers, soap opera viewers or schizophrenics – 'without knowing what its constituent actors know, tacitly as well as discursively'.[65] Rather than 'objectively' placing any of these as (often 'deviant') 'other', it is important to treat their utterances and behaviour as 'making sense' within their own cultural space. It is precisely this kind of empathy ('mutual knowledge', shared tacit and discursive understandings between observer and observed) which marks Bleasdale's rejection of an 'authorial' socialist reading in *The Boys From The Blackstuff*, and also informs recent analyses of soap opera, as distinct from earlier social scientific studies of the 'problem' of female drama consumption (Chapter 1). It is this sharing of tacit as well as discursive knowledge, I think, that lies behind the often-remarked observation that some of the best analyses of popular culture come from critics who are also fans.

However, as a realist Giddens insists on a methodological distinction between respect for the 'authenticity' of belief as a necessary condition of ethnographic understanding, and a sufficient critical distance to evaluate the empirical justification (and ideological ramifications) of belief. The analytical emphasis here is the realist one of human agents acting in conditions of *bounded* knowledgeability – conditions and consequences of social practice of which they may be partially unaware, and which can only be understood via social theory.

The relationship between 'agency' and the 'bounds' of social structure is always a dynamic one ('subjects' are, in other words, never simply 'positioned' as 'effects' of structure). Giddens, for instance, cites Paul Willis' emphasis in *Learning to Labour* on the *knowledgeability* (at the level of both discursive and practical consciousness) of working-class boys about power relations in school. By way of humour, banter, aggressive sarcasm and classroom 'gossip' the boys could 'knowledgeably' undermine the formal structures of command. Indeed, by their very refusal of school-based definitions of what *is* discursive (such as propositional statements) they were resisting the 'subject' positioning of the school's formal and hidden curricula. Similarly, Alan Bleasdale's 'boys' undermine the bureaucratic discourse of the DHSS office via Liverpuddlian humour; as in Chrissie's 'Let me know when you're coming and I'll bake a cake' in response to the unemployment sniffers' suspicion about *why* he was out when they visited.

On the other hand, in both cases 'the boys'' rebellious attitude (to the school and its curricula, to the unemployment bureaucrats and their routines) was bounded by the social structure. Bleasdale's unemployed remained unemployed; and in the case of Willis' boys, the unintended consequences of their rejection of school was their fate in unskilled, unrewarding jobs, 'thus facilitating the reproduction of some general features of capitalist-industrial labour. Constraint, in other words, is shown to operate through the active involvement of the agents concerned, not as some force of which they are passive recipients.'[66] The boys' fate was something about which they would become only too well aware (practically and discursively). The theoretical 'knowledgeability' about this in terms of the systemic and structural properties of capitalism, however, is made available via Willis' social theory.

The analytical relationship that Giddens is describing here is between knowledgeable actors and knowledgeable observers, as he maps one set of distinctions ('mutual knowledge' versus 'common sense') over another ('discursive consciousness' versus 'practical consciousness'). Human beings as agents are knowledgeable by way of *routine* daily activity (which gives them a sense of 'ontological security', a sense of trust in who they are); they may also be knowledgeable *discursively* (as in the wide discursive repertoire of 'irreverent marauding behaviour' among Willis' 'lads'); and they may be knowledgeable in the *theoretical* manner that can 'understand' this behaviour in the context of social reproduction and transformation (through, for instance, Willis' theory).

This approach to agency via the notion of stratified *layers* of consciousness offers the opportunity to re-think questions of authorship, adding an emphasis on the socially oppositional possibilities of media practice to Fiske's emphasis on audience pleasure.

One of the significant features of all the TV 'authors' I focus on in this book is precisely their understanding of the mutable relationship between these different strata of consciousness, and so between active agency and the 'boundedness' of structures – not only in the human beings that they observe, but in their *own* practice. This has to do with their sense of themselves as 'surveillant' social observers in relation to 'knowledgeable' social subjects. It has also, in their own practice, to do with the necessary relationship between (to use Trevor Griffiths' terms) the 'innocence' of asserting human agency and the 'guilt' of being determined by institutional structures. One of the notable features of Ken Loach's work in film and television, for instance, has been the public circulation of the daily routines (of solidarity and dissension) and the discursive practices (*both* as 'mutual knowledge' and 'common sense') of the working class. What has often been taken by critics as a naive naturalism in Loach, has been an attempt to engage with that deeper (routine) reflexivity of practical consciousness which Giddens is describing: and it is by way of that background (of working-class work and non-work routines, hobbies, social rituals and arts) that Loach speaks with knowledge of subordinate groups who 'live and resist their subordination'. As he says of *Fatherland*, which he made with Trevor Griffiths,

> The call for optimism that we felt in the film was the fact that, as the father says, people fight back. He called them . . . 'people of innocence'

who, when they find themselves in a situation they can't put up with, will fight back, whether they are people on strike or people opposing nuclear weapons or whatever. People will fight back against all the odds – *that* is the innocence that the father feels he has betrayed and so becomes obsessed by. History shows that it always happens – people will fight back, and we need to have respect for that fight back and join it.[67]

The resistances that Loach describes here (strikes and anti-nuclear demonstrations) are critically discursive ones, counter-myths of science and the labour movement. But as often in his work he engages with what Terry Lovell has described as the *pleasures* of resistance, 'pleasures of common experiences identified and celebrated in art, and through this celebration given recognition and validation; pleasures of solidarity to which this sharing may give rise; pleasure in shared and socially defined aspirations and hopes; in a sense of identity and community'.[68] These are the kinds of pleasures Loach represents in the penultimate sequence of 'Lock Out' in *Days of Hope* when the miners and their families engage in rituals of solidarity (dancing, brass bands, beer drinking, Geordie folk singing) deeply embedded in their *normal* living routines; pleasures which then swell out – more critically – in the pub singing and poetry of *Which Side Are You On?*, as working-class children's favourites like the 'Laughing Policeman' are given a new inflection during the British miners' strike against Thatcher.

As a writer who wants 'my socialism to be upfront in everything I do',[69] Trevor Griffiths is more overtly theoretical (Chapter 3), centrally concerned in his work with the social reproduction of dominant cultural myths and with the historical conditions of counter-myths which promise the utopian 'innocence' of social transformation. He is also more concerned than Loach with the implications of 'bounded knowledgeability' for his own practice – formally and collaboratively. Griffiths is a theorist who is 'not interested in endless disquisitions on the politics of form, but . . . in form . . . as part of my process of working'.[70] The counter-myths he describes are as frequently found in the practical consciousness and daily routines of his characters (for instance, in Amundsen's team in *The Last Place On Earth* who themselves represent models for collaborative *television* practice, Chapter 3) as in their other kinds of knowledgeability. Griffiths' critical concern with the surveillant powers of the media (as in his representation of the 'neutral' TV documentarist in *All Good Men*), his rejection of genres like news and current affairs for their 'bracketed, catalogued and categorized understandings',[71] and his insistence as a dramatist that 'while I'm in the business of persuasion I'm not in the business of propaganda – I don't want to agitate people out of their understandings'[72] are based on his probing of the relationship between authorship, knowledgeable actors and knowledgeable observers.

As a writer of comically irreverent 'marauding behaviour', Alan Bleasdale represents the bounded knowledgeability of Willis' 'lads' (Chapter 11). Out of the bleak pessimism of a dominant Thatcherism in contemporary Britain, Bleasdale has forged his own ironic resistance through popular series like *The Boys From The Blackstuff* and *The Monocled Mutineer*, where the restrictive implications of ironic resistance are themselves made critically discursive (via the series, and then in the audience). Bleasdale's authorship is in dramatically juxtaposing 'mutual knowledge' with reflexive critique, in drawing attention to a potential role of TV drama in not only making practical consciousness discursive, not only bringing to knowledgeability the restrictive implications of ironic resistance itself (in the absence of available alternatives among the Liverpool unemployed), but also throwing into disrepute his own 'knowledgeable' rationality as socialist author. Unlike Willis (and Griffiths), Bleasdale in the end relies on the power of carnival rather than theory for his resistance.

The social sciences, Giddens notes, 'draw upon the same sources of description (mutual knowledge) as novelists or others who write fictional accounts of social life', and so introduce 'forms of meaning associated with certain contexts of social life to those in others'.[73] The relationship between knowledgeable observer and knowledgeable observed is in both cases an ethnographic one: though the distinctions between *kinds* of observer (as between social scientist and TV dramatist) are important too. In the case of TV dramatists, their relationship with the audience is already in place (via, among other things, notions of genre) in a way that is not usually the case with the social scientist observing another culture. Audiences *and* authors reflexively monitor their understanding of reading and production practice in this regard. As Giddens says,

> Most of the remarks about understanding the production of texts in relation to the reflexive monitoring of action also apply to reading. No text is read in isolation; all reading occurs within frameworks of 'inter-textuality' as well as in settings involving drawing upon mutual knowledge. . . . We must know what readers understand of the particular genre within which the work is written. We have to know about the reader's knowledge of previous texts similar to the one in question. . . . Since all authors are also presumably readers, such discussion has to be closely integrated with explication of the production of texts.[74]

There are also similarities between textual practice and ordinary day-to-day activity. Both are grounded in conventional routines and practical consciousness, the products of which 'escape the intentional input of its creators' (raising important questions of inter-textual meaning, Chapters 3, 5, and 9). But, as Giddens notes, there is also a significant distinction between a text and routinized daily practice in that 'the creation of form is known to the agent to be constitutive of what the work is'.[75]

'Authors', then, are both social observers and audiences. As we will see, a significant difference among the radical 'authors' discussed in this book is the degree and kind of their penetration of the nature of that task of 'creating form' – and its relation to theory, routine knowledge-ability and discursivity. But whether it is Trevor Griffiths engaging with the genre of historical adventure (Chapter 3), John McGrath's negotiating with the mini-series form in *Blood Red Roses* (Chapter 7), Michael Brindley's attempt to enlarge the politics of prime-time soap opera (Chapter 7), or Alan Bleasdale's playing between realism and the grotesque as a denial of political authorship in the 'mad black farce' that is Thatcher's Britain (Chapter 11), that working through of generic form is crucial to their consciousness, as writers, of how their readers may *make* the text as an inter-textual practice and as a collaboration of mutual knowledge.

Agency, as Giddens has reminded us, has to do with power; and power inheres in much more than the top-down structures of social control. 'Power and freedom in human society are not opposites; on the contrary, power is rooted in the very nature of human agency, and thus in the freedom to act otherwise.'[76] Like the 'readers' Giddens describes, radical 'authors' are constrained by both mutual knowledge and generic expectation. But they also assert in those areas 'the freedom to act otherwise' as 'mutual knowledge' becomes 'common sense', and as generic expectation promotes the deconstruction of dominant myth. It is in this dual sense of power (as constraining and emancipating) that Janet Wolff has argued for the retention of notions of authorship and agency.

> The author as fixed, uniform and unconstituted creative source has indeed died. The concept of authorial dominance in the text has also been thrown into question. But the author, now understood as con-stituted in language, ideology, and social relations, retains a central relevance . . . in relation to the meaning of the text (the author being the first person to fix meaning, which will of course subsequently be subject to redefinition and fixing by all future readers).[77]

In *Television Culture* John Fiske cites Foucault in support of his argument for 'bottom-up' (audience) power.

> The pleasure that comes of exercising a power that questions, monitors, watches, spies, searches out, palpates, brings to light; and, on the other hand, the pleasure that kindles at having to evade this power, flee from it, fool it or travesty it.[78]

The point is, of course, that we are, all of us (TV dramatists, media academics, adult members of the television audience) necessarily engaged in *both* the pleasures of knowledgeable observers (questioning, monitoring, watching, bringing to light) *and* the pleasures of knowledgeable actors (evading, fleeing from and fooling this power). We need to be aware of both pleasures in *all* the institutional and agentive situations to which we customarily relate.

AUDIENCE

> The 'sociological' direction of modern philosophy involves a recovery of the everyday or the mundane. . . . All social analysis has a 'hermeneutic' or 'ethnographic' moment.
>
> Anthony Giddens[79]

> Commodities like mass-produced . . . texts are selected, purchased, constructed, and used by real people with previously existing needs, desires, intentions, and interpretive strategies. By reinstating those active individuals and their creative, constructive activities at the heart of our interpretive enterprise, we avoid blinding ourselves to the fact that the essentially human practice of making meaning goes on even in a world dominated by things and by consumption. In thus recalling the interactive character of operations like reading, we restore time, process, and action to our account of human endeavour.
>
> Janice Radway[80]

The 'New Tendencies in Television Research', as the title of a recent conference in Germany confirmed, are especially about 'Re-thinking the Audience'.[81] Audience theory has currently reached an ethnographic moment, focusing on the meanings and pleasures generated through popular texts by particular audience members who are situated *actively* in a field of inter-textual and interdiscursive relations.

A particularly relevant interdiscursive space for TV audience analysis is the context of domestic leisure. For David Morley,

> Given that television is a domestic medium it follows that the appropriate mode of analysis must take the unit of consumption of television

as the family or household rather than the individual viewer. This is to situate individual viewing within the household relations in which it operates, and to insist that individual viewing activity only makes sense inside of this frame.[82]

In calling for an ethnographic focus on varieties of audience positioning, Morley concludes that to make these points is:

> to argue ultimately for the return of the somewhat discredited discipline of sociology to a central place in the understanding of communication. In this connection . . . Richard Nice . . . in a commentary on the significance of Pierre Bourdieu's work argued . . . in my view correctly, that 'those who seek to expel sociology . . . in favour of a strictly internal analysis of what happens on the screen, or how the viewing subject is articulated can only do so on the basis of an implicit sociology which, in so far as it ignores the social realities of the differential distribution of cultural competences and values is an erroneous sociology, the more insidious for being unrecognised'.[83]

In particular, as Janice Radway argues, a sociology which interprets readers and audiences as passive consumers of dominant ideological meanings 'does so by reifying human process itself and by according extraordinary and pre-eminent power to the commodities produced and used within such processes rather than to the human activities themselves'.[84] Indeed, there is the real danger of the critic completing capitalism's fetishizing process itself by 'automatically assigning greater weight to the *way* a real desire for change is channelled by a culture into non-threatening form than to the desire itself. To do so would be to ignore the limited but nonetheless unmistakable and creative ways in which people resist the deleterious effects of their social situation.'[85]

The focus of this book is in the direction of the return that Morley describes, to a sociology of agency and an ethnographic account of human semiosis: though with some cautions (to summarize what has been said so far) to Morley and other ethnographically inclined researchers. The first is that though the household may be statistically the most representative and visible unit of consumption of television (and also a major site of patriarchal control and resistance), it is certainly not the case that individual viewing activity *only* makes sense within this frame. 'Individual' viewing encounters a variety of institutional practices, from the director watching back-episodes of a soap opera before plotting his first block, through the producers watching the first assembly of an episode, to school children in the playground competing to retell the previous night's story.[86] Further, as television studies increasingly penetrate the formal education system, as soap opera is 'taught' in schools, new kinds of audience space are constructed, contained on one hand by the 'teacher-talk' of school staff, contested on the other hand by students' own 'irreverent and marauding' spaces (through the sub-text of silences, glances and laughter which 'leak' the discourses of playground and fan letter). As James Anderson says, 'Meaning construction . . . is an ongoing process which reaches well beyond the moment of reception. . . . Further interpretation awaits an occasion in which media content is seen to have some utility.'[87]

The second caution is that Radway's insistence that popular texts are selected, constructed and used 'by real people with previously existing needs, desires, intentions and interpretive strategies'[88] is as true of *producers* of texts as of their audiences. Recent ethnographic accounts have been slow to extend analysis to the 'creative ways in which people resist the deleterious effects of their social situations' *within the media industry itself*. This is surprising, given the concern (as in Radway) for encouraging protest 'in such a way that it will be delivered in the arena of social relations rather than acted out in the imagination'.[89]

Radway perhaps undervalues the importance of the politics of the imagination here. As Cora Kaplan has argued, women can read and watch popular romance as a form of psychic power: 'Still excluded in major ways from power (if not labour) in the public sphere, where male fantasy takes on myriad discursive forms, romance narrative can constitute one of women's few entries to the public articulation and social exploration of psychic life.'[90] Nevertheless, to concentrate *only* on readings determined by domestic consumption is also a misconception, since it tends to reify the media industry (and many other institutions as well), denying analytical space to oppositional workers in these spheres. It is, then, as important to conduct empirical research into the reflexive constructions media workers place on their own behaviour ('into the nature of the assumptions they bring to the texts, and into the character of the interpretations they produce'[91]) as, Radway rightly insists, it is for their audiences. The importance of ethnographic analysis is in its taking human actors' (whether 'performers' or 'audience') self-understandings seriously. Each of the features – reflexivity, contextuality, meaning system explication, and theory development – which Lindlof and Meyer point to as integral within ethnographic research, is as relevant to 'authors' as to 'audiences'.[92]

So my argument is for an *extension* of the ethnographic approach from the domestic sphere into strategic conduct in all those institutional, professional, industrial, educational, and leisure spaces where pleasures and meanings contest in the construction of TV drama 'texts'. This should always be an examination of 'structures' in so far as these interdiscursive spaces (production offices and studios, magazines and fanzines, school classrooms and playground, and family living room) are sites of hierarchy and power. But it will also be a description of 'agencies', as these relate to routine and discursive practices. A major feature of Radway's analysis of the romance audience is the (sometimes guilty, always ambiguous) pleasure derived by married women in their *act* of reading, as well as in their *identification* with the 'independent' heroines of the fiction. The very duplicity of this pleasure (at one and the same time resisting and reproducing the patriarchal order) confirms the inextricable relationship of structure[93] and agency.

If ethnographic analysis needs always to be placed in the context of both structure and agency, a third caution must be to examine the 'power' and 'fantasy' of the ethnographic observer him/herself. Morley, Ien Ang complains, has not reflected upon his own position as a researcher in his audience studies. 'How did the specific power relationship pervading the interview situation affect not only the families, but also the researcher himself?'[94] As Ang says, these are problems of conducting ethnographic research which are difficult to unravel. In particular, there is the positivist tendency Ang notes of relegating the audience 'to the status of exotic "other" – merely interesting in so far as "we" as researchers use "them" as "objects" of study, and about whom "we" have the privileged position to know the perfect truth'.[95] One of the reasons that Dorothy Hobson's *Crossroads* research[96] still stands up as a pioneering ethnographic study is in her conscious identification with her audience as exploited members (by gender and age) of a patriarchal culture; and work by other feminists on soap opera and romance novels since then has deliberately rejected the 'otherness' relationship of researcher and audience. Janice Radway's book on the romance reader, for instance, has been exemplary in establishing *both* a relationship of mutuality with her audience as women *and* a critical distance as feminist, thus calling for strategies that 'we might join hands with women who are, after all, our sisters and together imagine a world whose subsequent creation would lead to the need for a new fantasy altogether'.[97]

Valerie Walkerdine's work on video fiction and fantasy has taken this further, going beyond Hobson's too easy identification with her audience to examine her *own* power and fantasy in the observation situation. Walkerdine calls for recognition of our fantasied positions when we engage in 'mutual knowledge'. This, as she argues, is 'an important step beyond assertions that academics should side with the oppressed, that film-makers see themselves as workers or that teachers should side with their pupils'.[98] Such rhetoric may represent little more than our 'wish-fulfilling denial of power' as the kinds of surveillant 'authors' (asking questions, monitoring, 'bringing to light') that Foucault describes, whose knowledge brings both power and pleasure. Returning to Paul Willis' *Learning to Labour*, Walkerdine observes that it *could* be interpreted as 'the story of an "earhole" who wants to become a "lad", a male academic vicariously becoming one of the boys'.[99] It is precisely this *surveillant* identity with 'the boys' which, I have argued, Alan Bleasdale avoids in *The Boys From The Blackstuff*.

Walkerdine's analysis signals a much-needed return within ethnographic audience work to psychoanalysis. But, as she says, this is a psychoanalysis which is cautious of its use in much screen theory 'to explore the relations within a film rather than to explain the engagement with the film by viewers already inserted in a multiplicity of sites for identification'.[100] In Walkerdine's account, the ethnographic observer is herself one of those viewers, 'voyeur' of both the film *and* the audience watching it, and playing out her desires and fears in relation to both.

Some of the most interesting feminist work on popular cultural texts is reflexive in this way: not the *inscribed* self-reflexivity of film texts so valued by radical screen theorists in the 1970s (with their distancing and élitist tendencies as regards a mass audience), but a self-reflexivity which takes account of both the personal history and social role of the observer. Thus Cora Kaplan speaks of her secret pleasures reading *Gone With The Wind* 'with heart pounding and hands straying' as an adolescent in a 'bookish, left-wing but rather puritanical household';[101] of her problem in reading a book which promoted her sexual fantasies but was for her parents (and for her) ideologically unsound, especially during the McCarthy era. 'For me personally it was a resonant and painful text, for I was engaged in a long and bitter struggle with my father in these years, for my autonomy, for his love and approval.'[102] Similarly, Valerie Walkerdine seeks to describe her initial horror at the violence and sexism of a working-class family's response to *Rocky II* in terms of her own fantasies: as a child to be the 'small, protected, adored, and never-growing-up'[103] object of her working-class father's gaze; and as an adult, to escape (through the mind rather than the body) that gendered and class-determined fantasy by way of becoming, in her turn, a 'Surveillant Other'.

Work by male academics has not been so reflexively honest or insightful in this area. Middle-class male academics analysing soap audiences must necessarily set up a different relationship; and there is always the risk (I felt this acutely in studying an elderly audience), that however much mutual understanding and empathy with the restricted conditions of living, is achieved (in my case by way of including close family members in the elderly group), the gap (in age, resources and power) between researchers and researched still makes of the latter little more than a suitable case for treatment; observed, recorded and then replaced by some other 'other'. Dorothy Hobson has written honestly about this problem, where, in her case, elderly viewers to whom she had become a friend, were surprised and disappointed when the research process finished and deprived them of an important additional resource in their lives.

On the other hand, the male left-wing academic is, like the socialist dramatists he analyses, both in a position of some discursive power and, increasingly, social and intellectual marginality – which perhaps offers some ground for the avoidance of 'otherness' in the research process that feminists have found in different ways. This is particularly the case where the researcher believes, as I do, that the Griffiths, McGraths and Loaches have been treated, at best, minimally by left-wing academics.[104] It is important, I repeat, to take serious account of these dramatists' own construction of their practice, and not simply reduce them to a reified effect of a de-historicized 'realism'.

Raymond Williams has been consistent (and almost alone) in his determination to analyse 'significant realist works and the quite unresolved problems of this kind of work'[105] by tying it to specific social and historical rather than to formalist analysis. It is in this sense of *analytical* support that Williams refuses the 'otherness' of the research relationship. As he says of the work of Loach and Garnett, 'It is in that sense, feeling very much on the side of the makers of this film – that is to say sharing with them evident general political values, general dramatic intentions' that 'problems within the realist and naturalist modes and the problems of consistency within them' deserve critical analysis.[106]

So as well as 'mutual' relations of sharing and empathy, it is important to locate these professional practices (as Radway does with her romance readers) in terms of their covert procedures and unintended consequences; to try to achieve sufficient critical distance to examine *their* different accounts of 'good' and 'bad' practice in relation to conditions of 'bounded knowledgeability', to dominant ideological and aesthetic structures.

For that reason I quote Loach's frustration with left-wing academics on the BFI board, while, like them, sometimes being critical of his formal practice. The importance of radical TV workers like Loach (whom I choose as a particularly extreme case of left-wing television workers being constructed as 'other' by left-wing academic writing) is in being the very opposite of the romance readers that Radway describes. She argues that their 'oppositional act is carried out through . . . the fundamentally private, isolating experience of reading', so that these women 'join forces only symbolically and in a mediated way in the privacy of their individual homes and in the culturally devalued sphere of leisure activity'.[107] Loach, in contrast, shares his experience publicly through a whole range of variously valued television genres (drama, documentary, arts programme), thereby reaching a variety of audiences. He also (to a degree undreamed by most left-wing academics) becomes, in *his* oppositional act, his own ethnographer, giving the same due respect to the voiced construction of behaviours by his audience of workers that Radway gives to her female audience.

We live, Raymond Williams argues, in a society which is

> rotten with criticism, in which the very frustrations of cultural pro-
> duction turn people from production to criticism, to the analysis of
> the work of others. It is precisely because these makers are contem-
> poraries engaged in active production, that what we need is not
> criticism but analysis, and analysis which has to be more than
> analysis of what they have done: analysis of a historical method,
> analysis of a developing dramatic form and its variations, but then I
> hope in a spirit of learning, by the complex seeing of analysis rather
> than by the abstractions of critical classification, ways in which we
> can ourselves alter consciousness, including our own consciousness,
> ways in which we can ourselves produce, ways in which indeed if we
> share the general values which realism has intended and represented,
> we can ourselves clarify and develop it.[108]

The 'complex seeing', the analytical *mutuality* which Williams is describing here, is directly relevant to the relationship between left-wing academics and left-wing producers like Ken Loach (as it also is, of course, relevant to the relationship between Loach and the working-class subjects of his films).

This sense of analytical mutuality has as clearly influenced my choice of realist 'authors' in this book as feminist writers' choice of soap audiences. And inevitably in this regard, part of *my* fantasy of 'surveillant voyeurism' as Walkerdine describes it – my 'set of desperate desires for power, for control, for vicarious joining-in' – will have to do with the relationship between these choices, ethnographic research and the broader politics of academic writing, set within changing historical conditions. It is no doubt as part of these desires that I argue that John McGrath is pointing (in Chapter 5) to a problem for left-wing academics as well as for his own TV practice when he explains his move away from overtly self-reflexive to a less avant-garde realism in terms of the historical decline of working-class politics. This relates in important ways to Richard Dyer's belief that 'faced with the cynicism of liberal culture and the widespread refusal in contemporary left culture to imagine the future, we would do well to look at the utopian impulse however and whenever it occurs in popular culture';[109] to Terry Lovell's recognition that 'the oppositional valences of popular culture are not treasure buried in the depth of the text, and recoverable only with the aid of the right kinds of readings which are the exclusive preserve of a highly educated elite';[110] and to Adrian Mellor's concern over the 'long era of Kuhn, Feyerabend, Althusser, Lacan and Derrida'.

> In their collective evolution these new perspectives have issued in ways of seeing the world which, by and large, militate against our acting in it. . . . Despite their self-proclaimed radicalism . . . the characteristic mode of these new perspectives is one of contemplation: in their relativism and in their obsessional epistemological ambivalence, in their rejection of historical modes of analysis, and – at their termini – in their embrace of intellectual nihilism and irrationalism, they opt for non-involvement, for social abstention, for an inner emigration from an unbearable present and a problematic future.[111]

Dick Hebdige argues similarly:

> the varieties of postmodernist critique which abjure all hope might be said to presage the historic decline not of politics, or meaning in general, but rather of a specific professional intellectual formation. What is perhaps most clearly intimated in such accounts is the impotence of negative critique. Rather than surrender mastery of the field, the critics who promulgate the line that we are at the end of everything . . . make one last leap and resolve to take all – judgement, history, politics, aesthetics, value – out of the window with them.[112]

The pleasures of contemplation that Mellor and Hebdige are alluding to here – whether in the 'democratic' diversity of gratificationists[113] or in the more current 'play' of meanings (endlessly *voiced* by, and so in the control of, individual academics) among post-structuralists – are closely related to questions of academic surveillance, power and politics: to having a controlling voice in the world of 'reading' when there is no control in a world of acting. Bob Connell, too, points to a turn in ·radical intellectuals' thought in the 1970s,

> first signalled by the popularity of a linguistic version of psychoanalysis . . . then followed by the conversion of the theory of ideology into an

analysis of discourses; a massive preoccupation with semiotics and its application to such enterprises as film criticism; a turn in feminist thought from analyses of practices of oppression and the mobilisation of resistance to discussions of language, discourse, speaking. . . . Its main practitioners have been the new Left and feminists. For both groups the second half of the 1970s was a period of disillusion after the worldwide radical upsurge of 1965–75. In the second half of the 1970s it was increasingly clear that the masses weren't following. It was perhaps natural that a good many intellectuals should then discover that the masses weren't necessary, and that their own speciality – discourse – was at the heart of things.[114]

But we should equally beware the extent to which current *ethnographic* theories of popular cultural 'resistance', linked to theories of audience 'pleasure, semiosis and difference' lead, despite their own intentions, to precisely those same pleasures of contemplation that Mellor and Connell describe, at the expense of *other* 'somewhat discredited' sociological theories: of structure, monopoly control, cultural imperialism, etc. Further, radical academics may write about others' 'resistance to the dominant ideology' while, in their practical routines as 'Surveillant Others' (as Foucault would say, asking questions, monitoring and 'bringing to light'), they reproduce 'new' interpretations of 'old' media texts as part of the conventional academic process. Might not, Paul James asks, 'Giddens, and Polity Press, despite their honourable belief that critical theory is "a practical intervention in society, a political phenomena in a broad sense of that term" be taken up within the academic world as merely *entrepreneurs* of social theory' (my italics)?[115]

In this regard, Radway's account of romance readers is particularly valuable because it relates the oppositional tendencies of their textual encounter not only to the socially reproducing *structural principles* of both their act of reading and the narrative itself, but also to Radway's own position as researcher. And, in a different way, Kaplan examines the relationship between her own fantasies, the psychically liberating quality of *The Thorn Birds* in speaking 'powerfully to the contradictory and unreconciled feelings about femininity, feminism and fantasy'[116] *and* its structurally reactionary assumption that 'women readers have become progressively reflective about sexuality, but remain conservative, uninterested and unreflective in their thinking about other political and social concerns'.[117] In addressing the area of popular fantasy, Kaplan answers Connell's over-generalized critique of recent tendencies within the New Left and feminism, while, like him, warning us 'away from those half-baked notions embedded in certain concepts of "post-modern" culture and "post-feminism" which see the disruption of subjectivity and sexual difference as an act which has a radical autonomy of its own and a power to disrupt hierarchies beyond it'.[118]

The same kind of analysis of the intermeshing of radical authorship, fantasy and myth, of oppositional practice (including academic practice) with the reproduction of social order needs, as I have said, to be extended to areas of social control other than sexuality, patriarchy and the domestic household; not least to the media industries themselves. In Radway there is a tendency to see mass mediated fictions as mythical effects of social order, somewhat similar to Will Wright's understanding of the Western as myth, where the genre works to reconcile the contradiction between capitalist values of possessive individualism and its ethic of 'shared social needs, goals and interests'.[119] Radway goes much further than Wright both in emphasizing the radical potential of the genre and in examining the active reproduction of order by the audience; but Wright and Radway tend to lose to view the media industry itself as a site of transformative practice.[120] The same is true of John Fiske in *Television Culture*. Fiske argues that 'The unequal distribution of power in society is the central structuring principle in understanding the relationships of any one group to others, or to the social system as a whole',[121] yet he is coy about accepting this as a *real* statement about the capitalist world. He also insists that 'Pleasure for the subordinate is produced by the assertion of one's social identity in resistance to, in independence of, or in negotiation with, the structure of domination',[122] yet does not extend this understanding to the producers of TV dramas, nor to our relationship as academics with them.

'Intellectuality', Paul James says in his critique of Giddens, 'is seductive as a retreat from practice. The reconstitution of practice will, perforce, only begin and develop as a transitional project. And it has to begin in practice not just in theory.'[123] A final (and perhaps fundamental) 'bias' of this book is to bring together in dialogue critical theory (such as Giddens') with that of radical practitioners (such as Griffiths), in the context of different layers of 'knowledgeability'. So, for instance, the analytical survey of 'Popular TV drama: ideology and myth' which is the focus of Part 1 is followed by a much closer engagement with the thinking and practice of radical practitioners like Trevor Griffiths, John McGrath and Ken Loach in Part 2, 'Authored drama: agency as "strategic penetration"'. Here notions of 'serious drama' are reconsidered in terms of media structure and radical agency – in particular the nexus of these dramatists' political theorizations with the various formal and institutional processes (naturalism; television as 'Art' or 'leisure'; 'creative' versus 'controllers' orders of discourse; performance as a semiotic 'thickness' of sequential and simultaneous practices, etc.) which facilitate, ambiguate or control their 'strategic penetration'. Behind this section there lies an 'ethnography of production', based on time spent observing the production practices of Trevor Griffiths and Ken Loach. Here the analytical voice is less that of the 'surveillent other' of Part 1 and more, I hope, in the spirit of Raymond Williams' 'analytical mutuality' – both Griffiths and Loach were, for instance, asked to comment on what I have written about their work.[124] As with the various 'ethnographies of audiences' which are surveyed in Part 3, Part 2 does not claim to be 'representative' (writers with different theoretical preoccupations from mine might, for instance, have said much more about Dennis Potter, less about Griffiths and McGrath than I do). Rather, the dramatists were chosen for analysis because of *my* critical assumptions, which lead me to emphasize *their* importance as a case study of 'strategic penetration'. (However, I have tried to be representative in the various TV genres covered in the book – science fiction and cop shows, soap opera and 'authored' drama, historical mini-series and spy-thrillers – ending with a case study of humour in both sitcom and 'authored' drama which tries to bring together the various approaches covered here.)

In the last resort, ethnographic study of day-to-day life in all its institutional settings is important because, as Giddens says, daily routine and consciousness are integral to the active reproduction of *all* institutionalized practices. Otherwise the risk is of losing sight of society as an historically positioned and differentiated formation, in which knowledgeable actors struggle in every institutional arena (in the media industries and in academia as much as in the domestic household) to make their meanings.

Part One

Popular TV drama: ideology and myth

1 'Soft' news:
the space of TV drama

There in the middle of the news bulletins, the ads, the sports, entertainments and party politicals, there in virtually every home in the land, seen with the social guard down and the texture of the modern world all around it, is a precious space for *drama*.

Dennis Potter[1]

In the Introduction I discussed my criteria of relevance and significance in positioning 'television drama' in this book. Clearly, though, 'TV drama' is situated differently in other discourses: those of other media academics, TV critics, fans, television controllers, and so on. The 'precious space for drama' that Dennis Potter speaks about will have shifting configurations and boundaries in those different discourses. It is 'precious' in different ways for different social groups. But in each of those discourses it is positioned in terms of its *margins*, in relations of similarity to and difference from the other genres that surround it. In this chapter I want to begin by examining that 'space for drama' in the context of its relationship to other TV forms – particularly as it impinges on the working practices and daily routines of TV practitioners and audiences, as well as in the theoretical 'knowledgeability' of media analysts and critics. Finally I will consider the spaces and margins of TV drama in terms of the particular critical theory I am adopting.

Regulating discourses: the 'important' and the 'trivial'

In his book, *Speaking of Soap Operas*, Robert Allen tells a cautionary tale:

In the 1950s my mother occasionally talked with my Aunt Helen about the soap operas they both watched, while at the same time writers and editors at *Time* magazine also occasionally 'spoke' to their readers about the same soap operas. However, the discourse of professional journalism could impose itself upon the meaning of soap opera in other discourses in a way and on a scale my mother's discourse could not.[2]

Allen's point is that 'serious' media voices that discuss 'important' political and world events, like *Time* magazine, have a greater regulatory power in speaking to us about our culture than his or any other average mother. In setting this 'importance' agenda, news media and politicians relate symbiotically. As the *Sydney Morning Herald* said of the history of Australia's most prestigious current affairs programme, *Four Corners*: 'Every politician had to watch it', and 'Practically anybody who's anybody in Australian television today has worked there at some time.'[3]

On the same day, there was an article by Peter Luck on the history of Australian soap opera, which he likened to 'swimming through slowly setting cement'.[4] Popular TV drama does not generally attract politicians to watch or appear in it; nor is it normally the career goal of 'anybody who's anybody' in television. So, rather grudgingly excepting 'issues' dramas like *A Country Practice* (which *was* seen as sufficiently 'serious' to attract an appearance by the Australian Prime Minister in an anti-nuclear story) or *The Flying Doctors* (first in the soap field in Australia to tackle AIDS), Luck only found soaps interesting if they sent themselves up ('*No. 96* was a very funny spoof').

Luck's history of soap operas was dismissive (he called *Certain Women* 'Cretin Women'), in marked contrast to the high-tone respect in the *Sydney Morning Herald*'s other television history that day ('anything that was talked about was talked about on *Four Corners*'). This kind of positioning of 'trivial' drama in the context of 'politically serious' news and current affairs is quite typical, and itself has a long history. As Allen says, our current response to soaps comes 'always-already-read' as a result of fifty years of dismissive criticism. Social scientific research beginning in the 1940s has left the lasting idea that whereas the appeal of news is self-evident, the typical soap opera listener has been 'an intellectually and imaginatively impoverished "lower-class housewife" whose interests extended only as far as her own front door'.[5]

In the light of this, it is probably not surprising that Elliott, Murdock and Schlesinger point in 1983 to the 'orthodoxy' of media sociology that it is news and current affairs rather than popular drama which provide analysts with 'crucial social maps' of the national culture.[6] Recent work in media theory has begun to demand a greater centrality for TV drama study. But even inside the academic community resistance to 'studying soap operas' is strong; and certainly beyond it the 'seriousness' of news/current affairs and the 'triviality' of soap opera still represent widely held generic *margins* of the 'always-already-read' aspect of television drama. TV drama is 'serious' if it handles AIDS or nuclear current affairs, 'trivial' if it is about gossip and (as Luck says of 'Cretin Women') 'people drinking tea'.

Not everyone would agree, of course, either within the TV industry or the TV audience. To the extent that this book is ethnographic in approach, I will be examining the 'meaning' and positioning of TV drama within the organizational culture of programme makers and within audience sub-cultures. These are embedded in the flow of television as industry on the one hand, television as reception on the other. In particular I want to bring out from behind journalistic and other (male-dominated) regulatory discourses, the 'mother's' discourse that Robert Allen recalls. In so doing I will underline Elliott *et al.*'s contention that neither news/current affairs nor TV drama can be (nor are taken to be by audiences) 'virtually self-contained areas', either in relation to each other as TV genres, or in relation to the commercials which are inserted within them.

The 'space' for TV drama, then, is a shifting one, in so far as what counts as 'significant' drama is constituted by the various organizational, sub-cultural and critical discourses which represent it. Some of these discourses are more powerful than others. So, necessarily, this chapter will raise questions of both structure and agency; structures of commercial scheduling and domestic routine, and the agency of both 'authors' and 'audiences' within those. On the one hand, I will look at the commercially ordered flow of television, the predominance within it of the dominant culture's discourse, and TV drama's potential for releasing 'authorial' voices which challenge the orthodoxies of the powerful. On the other hand, I will be concerned with domestic habit, and with audience definitions of drama deriving in particular from the traditionally less powerful definers of media significance and 'reality': like homemakers and the elderly.

Ideological spaces: official, alternative and oppositional discourses

TV drama has been typed and differentiated by media academics in a number of ways,[7] but seldom in ways helpful in considering it as Dennis Potter's 'precious space' in the field of *other* TV forms like news/current affairs. One typology which does contextualize TV fiction in terms of TV 'actuality' has been outlined by Elliott *et al.* Like Allen, Elliott *et al.* are concerned with the work of regulatory discourses (and the concomitant suppression of less powerful voices) in defining the

Figure 1

	Intended audience		
	Maximum		*Restricted*
Actuality programmes	news magazines, e.g. *Nationwide*	current affairs e.g. *Panorama*	'authored' documentaries, e.g. *Heroes*
Fiction programmes	action-adventure series, e.g. *The Professionals*	serials, e.g. *Blood Money, A Spy at Evening*	single plays, e.g. *Psy-Warriors*
Programme structure	relatively 'closed'		relatively 'open'

agenda for debate and the definition of significance. Their focus is on the representation of violence and terrorism in news and drama since these pose 'a fundamental threat to the stability of society' and raise in an acute way questions about access to a media voice. Elliott *et al.* compare these representations as between series, serials and single plays, making the important point that television drama 'is able to depict two key groups of political actors who almost never appear in current affairs and documentary programmes – the terrorists themselves and the members of the military and intelligence service'.[8]

Series

It is not only the discourses of the weak but also the 'secret state' that are generally denied direct access to television production. However, the battle for mass audiences (via 'ideological themes that are most familiar and endorsed by the widest range of potential viewers'[9]) leads to the 'official' discourse of the powerful being represented anyway, especially in the drama series.

A series like *The Professionals* (with a stable set of characters over different self-contained episodes), aims at an international market drawing heavily 'on elements from the official discourse, since these are the most pervasive and best publicized'.[10] This 'ensures a product that is readily intelligible in any culture familiar with American shows, and because it centres on action (chases, fights, escapes) rather than dialogue, it saves the buyer the cost of extensive dubbing or subtitling.'[11] 'Alternative' discourses – just because they are not 'common sense' or part of the dominant myths in a culture – require space for elaboration and dialogue. But this is denied them in the action-adventure series where 'the upholders of order and the agents of disruption are always unequally represented. . . . Usually we know next to nothing about the villains.'[12]

Serials

Because the plot develops over several weeks 'the more relaxed pace of the serial provides opportunities to develop more complex characterizations of terrorists and their motivations and space to interrogate the nature and operations of the "secret state"'.[13] Alternative discourses do appear in drama serials, but here the 'contrast between the depiction of terrorists as fanatical and inhuman on the one hand and as human but politically motivated on the other is never resolved and remains a permanent tension within the text'.[14] Still larger and 'more significant fissures open up around the presentation of the forces of law and order'.

The single play

Here, because of less pressure from ratings, 'authors' are expected to 'express their own particular viewpoints and commitments in their own distinctive voice and style'.[15] Because they are 'not in the front line of the battle for audiences or programme exports and so . . . are not under the same pressure to work with the most prevalent ideological themes', and because the transmitting institution distances itself from the play by signifying its individual authorship, this kind of drama is 'given a licence to raise awkward political questions and to do so in forms that may disturb or even overturn the audience's expectations'.[16]

These distinctions between series, serials and single play, Elliott *et al.* similarly make between mass audience oriented news magazines, 'quality' current affairs programmes, and 'authored' documentaries, such as Pilger's critiques of US imperialism in Latin America. Thus:

(a) The *official discourse* is most familiar on news and action-adventure series, with stereotyped character types (the terrorist as extremist or psychopath) and standard narrative resolutions (gunning down of terrorists by state agents).

(b) An *alternative* perspective (surfacing in 'serious' current affairs programmes like *Panorama* and *Four Corners*, and some drama serials) derives from civil libertarians, critical academics, opposition politicians and the like. This discourse questions the use by the state of violent means even against violent opponents, reminds viewers that some of the worst world violence is committed by the state, and calls for social engineering to deal with the oppressive conditions that engender the fanaticism of terrorism. Because of the ambiguity and tension generated for the narrative where this discourse enters the popular drama serial, Elliott *et al.* make a further distinction:

> A 'tight' format is one in which the evidence and argument is organized to converge upon a single preferred interpretation and to close off other possible readings. A 'loose' format, in contrast, is one where the ambiguities, contradictions and loose ends are not fully resolved within the programme, leaving the audience with a choice of available interpretations.[17]

The 'tight/loose' distinction cuts across the dichotomy between 'open' and 'closed' presentations, since a programme can be 'open' in providing space for anti-official elements, but 'tight' in the way the material is mobilized on behalf of a particular reading.

(c) *Oppositional discourse.* An 'authored' serial like Ken Loach's *Days of Hope* which adopts an oppositional discourse (to the degree that it advocates the complete overthrow of the state and its political and economic system) is 'open' because it offers a strong critique of official (*and* reformist/alternative) discourses. But it is also 'tight' in mobilizing its narrative for a particular reading; which is why it was heavily criticized by left-wing screen theorists in the 1970s.[18] Soap operas, on the other hand, may be 'open' in offering space to anti-official discourse (e.g. the *EastEnders* doctor who says, with obvious reference to Mrs Thatcher, 'What I'd like is a Prime Minister who stands up and condemns racism as strongly as she condemns terrorism'), but are 'loose' in narrative organization, which, as we shall see later, is one reason why many feminists like them.

In the area of popular TV drama genres, then, we can add to Elliott *et al.*'s model to suggest a contrast between action-adventure series which are 'tight' (and 'closed' around the official discourse) and soap operas which are 'loose' (and usually contain an 'open' mix of official and alternative discourses). As for oppositional discourses, Tania Modleski has argued that these are as unlikely to appear in soaps as in action series.

> As a rule, only those issues which can be tolerated and ultimately pardoned are introduced on soap operas. . . . An issue like homosexuality, which could explode the family structure rather than temporarily disrupt it, is simply ignored. Soap operas, contrary to many people's conception of them, are not conservative but liberal.[19]

However, recent production and recent theory both speak (to an extent) against Modleski's point. The English soap *EastEnders* does introduce homosexuality in a central and non-threatening way (though it also prioritizes the family structure), and in *Television Culture* Fiske argues that even as ideologically conservative an action-adventure series as *The A-Team* offers spaces for 'oppositional or resisting stances'[20] in terms of class, race, or age (though not in terms of gender). Fiske also points to the commonness of incest as a topic in soap operas and its absence from more 'masculine' television genres, suggesting 'that women find more pleasure in interrogating the system that has set them in place'.[21]

Nevertheless, Modleski is right to the extent that these 'resisting stances' are rarely, if ever, articulated as oppositional discourse in Elliott *et al.*'s sense. Buckingham notes of *EastEnders* that though class difference is certainly emphasized in many of the key relationships, 'the explicit discourses of class politics are . . . rarely visible';[22] that though the serial often takes an explicitly didactic stance on race, it 'rarely makes reference to broader structural inequalities – in this case, to institutional racism';[23] that by 'marginalizing and undermining explicit feminist politics . . . the serial effectively confines women's "protest against aggression" to the level of interpersonal relationships with men';[24] and that though *EastEnders* 'has consistently posed masculinity as a problem',[25] the serial 'cannot be said to have provided many significant alternative definitions of masculinity'.[26] What we can say is that in the action-adventure 'terrorist' serials it is the legitimacy of the state that comes under most pressure, whereas in the soap opera the authority of the family and marriage is consistently tested (which is why incest and homosexuality become problems). The major public and private institutions of our society (the state and the family) are scrutinized by two of our most popular cultural forms, and the statements they make vary from the conservatism of the *Professionals*, operating firmly within the terms of the official discourse, to the 'loose' liberalism of *Crossroads* and daytime soaps. To find 'tight' *radical* positions one generally has to look to authored single plays and the occasional authored serial: Jim Allen's *United Kingdom*, Loach's *Days of Hope*, Trevor Griffiths' *Country* and *Bill Brand*, Alan Plater's *A Very British Coup*.

Elliott *et al.*'s analysis suggests that space for oppositional discourses in both news/current affairs and drama is ghettoized as the 'personal vision' of 'creative' authors (often carrying a disclaimer that these views are those of the channel – as in the case of Pilger's 'bicentennial' series in Australia). However, differences (in the potential for alternative and oppositional discourses) between popular genres also need noting, particularly in relation to both 'authorial' and audience agency. Elliott *et al.*'s typology, while a useful starting point, tends to be too economistic and schematic here. Top-rating series may offer institutional spaces for alternative or oppositional production voices; and action-dramas may carry an official discourse but be *read* differently. Fiske argues that conventional action-adventure series like *The A-Team* certainly have no 'socialist motivation of helping the weak as a class';[27] they do, nevertheless, in the hero team have a dramatic figure that 'provides the viewers with multiple points of entry for their identification with the hero'.[28] As Fiske says, what is needed is an analysis which relates these textual characteristics to alternative (male) audience positions – to 'the denial of social power to some working-class men or to those of "devalued" races, or the lack of physical and social power in boys'.[29]

Overall, though, Fiske would agree that television narrative forms are relatively 'closed' or 'open' according to the 'gender' of the genre: soap operas differ from action dramas in avoiding narrative closure, in emphasizing the process of problem solving, intimate conversation and the feelings that people experience (exploring these across multiple characters and plots), and in establishing as close a correspondence as possible to real time. It is these formal characteristics of soaps which open up challenges to official discourses, appealing to women and (I shall argue in this chapter) to the elderly.

Scheduling spaces: paradigms and syntagms

If traditional academic discourse has tended to contrast single-play 'seriousness' with soap-opera 'triviality' in positioning TV drama, *scheduling* is central to its positioning inside the organization of the TV industry. Scheduling television drama involves making choices according to two sets of relationships. First, there is the choice of *which* TV genre – soap opera, current affairs, news or action-adventure – to place (or view) in any one time slot. Secondly, there is the choice of the *sequencing* of programmes: news at 6.00 p.m., current affairs at 7.00, followed by soap opera at 7.30 and action-adventure at 8.30. Speaking about the replacement of the declining current affairs show, *Willesee at Seven*, a Channel 7 executive in Australia said:

> The Willesee programme having gone, there was a need for two half hours. We cast about to fill that gap. It wasn't however, a current affairs timeslot that we had to fill. It was a timeslot that needed *some* entertaining programme in there. At that time, of the programmes we were looking at, the most appealing happened to be these two serials *A Country Practice* and *Sons and Daughters*. We saw them as an answer to our problems. And they worked.[30]

'*Some* entertaining programme' meant one that would appeal to a generally young age group. The particular genre did not matter (indeed, as *Sons and Daughters* declined in ratings, it in turn was replaced by a different Willesee current affairs show) provided that it delivered the target audience. 'Get the kids in at 6, 7, or 7.30 and the parents will watch too. Older people will watch shows for younger people, but not vice versa.'[31] In Queensland, 'at 6.30 on Sunday we are very successful with *The Wonderful World of Disney* . . . a very large family audience. We felt that *A Country Practice* would attract a very similar style of audience. So now the audience flow-through from Disney to *A Country Practice* is quite strong.'[32]

On the one hand, there is the notion of delivering audiences from one show or genre to another on the same channel by careful sequencing. On the other hand, there is the importance of out-rating competing shows in the same slot on other channels in order to deliver those audiences to advertisers. In this regard, 'Programmes are either strong ones that can go on against tougher opposition or perhaps need a softer time slot. *A Country Practice* was seen as a programme that could hold its own. And it's done that'[33] against high-rating US dramas like *The A-Team* and against Australia's top-rating show, *Sixty Minutes*, a current affairs programme.

All of this matching and mixing of TV genres is, as the Channel 7 programme development manager put it, 'part of the menu'; which is a relevant description because, like TV scheduling, a menu consists of two planes. For Roland Barthes, the menu 'paradigm' consists of that 'set of foodstuffs which have affinities or differences within which one chooses a dish in view of a certain meaning: the types of entrée, roast or sweet'.[34] The equivalent in commercial television terms is the ratings-determined choice of genres that can be placed in any one time-slot: so, for instance, Philip Hayward describes how the reflexive show *Moonlighting* was introduced on the ABC as 'a direct competitor to *Remington Steele* (based around a similar male/female detective duo)', before being moved back an hour to compete with NBC's action-adventure *Riptide*, 'calculating that *Riptide* had a largely male audience and could be beaten with a show with mixed gender appeal'.[35] The menu 'syntagm' is the 'real sequence of dishes chosen during a meal'.[36] The television equivalent is the sequential 'flow-through' of genres during the channel's transmission time (e.g. the 'family' orientation of the sequencing of *The Wonderful World of Disney* and *A Country Practice*).

As with the food system, so with television, the set of choices and vertical sequencing is culturally determined; in the latter case in quite precise industrial terms, usually according to demographics and ratings.

High-rating ('strong') shows like *A Country Practice* (in Australia) or *Moonlighting* (in the US) can be used to 'hang' less popular shows on either side of it to try and ensure sequenced viewing on one channel; a 'weaker' show may be introduced in a non-ratings period, when competition is less strong, to give it a chance to build up a following, and may be 'hammocked' by high-rating shows on either side of it.

In addition, in commercial TV organizations, there is another syntagmatic set of relationships. As well as the flow-on relationship between TV genres, there is the flow-on effect *within* programmes between the drama itself and the advertisements placed in it. My emphasis in the next part of this chapter will be on how the construction of the TV menu – paradigmatically and syntagmatically – relates to audience agency. I will consider how the organizational space that TV drama occupies (soap opera in this time slot in opposition, say, to news, or quiz show, and flowing on from current affairs; in prime rather than day time; broken into by advertisements) may effect audience meanings. As such, I hope to take further the discussion of 'official' and 'alternative' discourses of the last section. I will begin by reporting on two pieces of ethnographic audience research, one in Australia, one in England.

'Normal, everyday things': choices of paradigm

It was Sunday in a Queensland household, and the Brown's were arguing over which prime-time show to watch. Bill Brown intended to watch *Sixty Minutes*. His wife Mary and her teenage daughter Susan preferred Australia's top-rating TV drama, *A Country Practice*. Since there were both colour and black and white TV's in the house, this debate wasn't about which show would be missed; but which one would be seen in the main living room on the colour set, and which on black and white in a bedroom.

Here TV drama was engaging with the world of domestic politics, and its meaning had as much to do with those family negotiations over choices of generic paradigm as with its own subject matter. Bill's argument for 'lobbing in' to current affairs and news programmes in his leisure time was symptomatic of ones that researchers have heard many times.[37] Current affairs shows helped him 'become informed', whereas the soaps that the rest of the family watched were just 'garbage . . . gossip that you can pick up anywhere around the place'.[38] In contrast, the Brown women felt that the 'exact-same-thing' news portrayals of major disasters, ritually consumed by their menfolk, were pointless and much less interesting than discussing soap events. As Charlotte Brunsdon notes, soaps call up the traditionally feminine competencies associated with the responsibility for managing the sphere of personal life;[39] and it was in this sense that Mary Brown said she valued the 'gossip'.

In an old people's housing complex in Bournemouth, England, I encountered a different age group discussing their TV watching. Again it was males, like Harry Savage who preferred the news, whereas his wife Ivy liked musicals and films 'with a bit of romance in them'. But there was a slightly different emphasis here, because both Harry and Ivy explained that they were left feeling powerless and vulnerable by the content of news and current affairs.

I: 'I can't – I won't watch anything with violence. . . . I can't stand it. It turns me right off. . . . We don't see the news very often, do we now, because of it. . . . If a serial like *A Country Practice* was on and the news was on, we wouldn't trouble about the news, we'd watch that.'

H: 'Well, it fits in with our life better. . . . We've had so much of violence in recent years that we've got a little bit sickened by it all. And it's not our way of life, so we obviously don't want to know about it.'[40]

At their stage of life, they argued, there was nothing they could do about this unpleasant world of politics, so 'We'd rather watch something that will give us a bit of pleasure. . . . The dramas don't push things down your throat – it's ordinary, everyday things.' Not only current affairs, but even 'Question Time' programmes were infected with 'politics', where, they complained, left-wing Labour people like Derek Hatton made everything political, 'even if the question isn't political', and tried to 'push their point of view down your throat'. In contrast, even though *A Country Practice* raised social issues, 'it's normal, everyday things. You're not being brainwashed. We've reached the stage now that's what we want.'[41]

In both the Australian and English households a distinction between TV genres was being made. This was not always a simple matter of distinguishing between 'information' and 'entertainment' genres (since even the information-oriented Bill Brown 'lobbed in' to current affairs quite haphazardly as part of his entertainment pattern after work, and the women were informing themselves, through discussing soap characters, about perceptions related to domestic management). Rather, the distinctions were varied inflections of the notion of 'hard' and 'soft' news, between 'tight' and 'loose' formats, between 'brainwashing' and 'ordinary, everyday things' in Harry Savage's words, or between 'issues' and 'gossip' in Bill Brown's.

In professional newsgathering terms, a clear distinction is often made between 'hard' and 'soft' news. As John Hartley points out, a 'hard' story is based on 'facts', and relates to 'important' sectors like the economy, politics and foreign affairs. A 'soft' story is a 'human interest' angle on an area *not* seen as 'important', but describing individual experience.

> These [news values] have been developed, of course, by white, middle-class men, generation upon generation of them, forming opinions, imposing them, learning them and passing them on as Holy Writ. We have inherited a *hierarchy* of news values.[42]

In the interviews I did, it was generally the men who accepted this 'man-made' hierarchy between 'hard' and 'soft' (though not so clearly among the elderly). As one man said, 'I watch . . . shows like *Nationwide* and *Pressure Point* that stimulate conversation . . . about topical issues, not what's happening to Vera in the next episode?' Hartley notes that the news does have its 'soft' human interest stories; however, these are 'offbeat', 'off-centre', often defined as 'having a woman's angle' and occupying 'the tailpiece of news bulletins, where the newsreader settles more comfortably, smiles, softens his or her tone and perhaps even goes as far as to make a joke'.[43]

For the old people in Bournemouth, however, the distinction between 'hard' and 'soft' news was not to do with 'important' versus 'off-beat', with *scale* of significance in life and death terms, but rather in what could and could not be controlled. The routines of external violence and death in news and current affairs were beyond their grasp, and frightened them so that, as Harry Savage said, they 'didn't want to know'. But the routines of *personal* sickness and death *could* be negotiated with, by way of visiting professionals, and by their own long-term skills in caring. 'With so much violence outside, we're very lucky in here', one elderly lady said, mentioning the warmth of their flats, and the protective warden who would come at the press of a bell, and who organized excursions for them. Their feeling of security flowed to the outside world through friends (who took them shopping) and professional workers (who took them on trips); and similarly the events of the outside world flowed in to them by way of TV friends and TV professionals (in shows like *A Country Practice*).

In Bournemouth, Mr and Mrs Mallard's preference for medical soaps illustrates how TV drama is part of a daily life pattern, of ageing and illness.

> Mrs M: '*A Country Practice* is our favourite. . . . The doctors are interesting in the various complaints they have to see about the

hospital, and – I don't know – there's something in it that keeps you going.'

Mr M: 'I listen because I've got diabetes, and on there they talk about it.'

Mrs M: 'We always did like the medical stories.'

Mrs Mallard went on to talk about *her* experience of the medical routine: how she would lie on the bed next to her sick husband, reading a medical history between his 9.30 bedtime and 10.30 Complan; how on Tuesday mornings she would be taken shopping by her younger friend from upstairs, returning for lunchtime when both Mr Mallard's prescribed meal time *and* the medical soap, *A Country Practice*, called.

For these old people soaps were firmly placed in a daily routine of organization and caring, as well as their favourite programmes being *about* professional organization and caring. Such things were of no less life-and-death significance than the information on the news; simply more immediate and more manageable. For these people, then, the 'soft' news of soaps is neither 'offbeat' nor trivial. The younger male's put down of 'what's happening to Vera in the next episode' tells us little about the significance of this genre in much of its audience's experience. The quiet dedication of Mrs Mallard demonstrates that.

My point is that soaps are positioned and absorbed pleasurably by the old people I studied (as 'ordinary, everyday things' in contrast to the uncontrollable 'violence' and 'brainwashing' of news and current affairs) because there is a homology of fit between what Hartley calls their worlds of 'experienced' and 'mediated' meanings.[44] The experienced world of these old people reaches out to issues of life and death by way of a known community of friends and professional care; and the mediated world of social issues ranging from nuclear war to care of the elderly reaches inwards by way of that self-same (but fictionalized) personal/ professional community. In this way the narrative protagonists of soaps are *known* to the elderly viewers; they dramatize (across a number of conflicting discourses) the practical agency of their audience. Soap operas are 'open' and 'loose' – they don't, as Harry Savage said, push their politics 'down your throat'; they explore the daily problems and intimate concerns of a wide range of viewers; and they not only engage closely with 'real time' but are intimately interwoven into their *audience*'s real time.

'Hard' and 'soft' information (focused generically as 'news' and 'soap opera' in the sense that the 'centre' of each is determined by the 'off-centre' or absence of the other) features, then, in a number of discourses.

(i) In professional media discourse, 'hard' and 'soft' are often determined by being 'important' as against 'offbeat'.

(ii) In the eyes of academics and soap opera critics they have traditionally been contrasted as 'serious' (and healthy) versus 'impoverished' (and noxious).

(iii) Yet, among the elderly, as Mr and Mrs Mallard demonstrate, those items of 'gossip' that for critics extended only to the viewer's front door (and not to the 'significant', 'public' world beyond) were, in a very real life-and-death sense, matters as important as the political events outside. The companionship of quiet, daily caring based on a coherent and loving routine (parallel to the caring routines of the medical soaps they enjoyed) could in no sense be described as 'impoverished'. Indeed, because soaps articulated the skills and concerns of their own practical consciousness, they were real in a way that the other world of 'news' violence was not.

The relationship of these old people with the outside world was a mediated one, routinized (as in Mrs Mallard's case), *negotiated* with, and not entirely beyond their control. In *Coronation Street, A Country Practice, Crossroads, Sons and Daughters*, the world out there was not 'escaped', but *focused* according to human-scale values and practical competences, through characters who could be identified as extensions of themselves. For Harry Savage, Frank, the policeman in *A Country Practice*, was 'a man after my own heart: he doesn't say too much', and the events of the narrative always 'come back to him and his wife Shirl'.

This relationship between an elderly man and a fictionalized cop by way of practical consciousness is very different from that of the audiences of many cop shows. Keith Windschuttle has argued that whereas soap opera audiences 'are constantly engaged in checking the plot and characters against their own experience',[45] in 'social explorer' genres, like cop shows, there is a tendency to tell the audience that 'they cannot hope to solve the problems of their time, and that they still need parent figures like supercop Kojak, or super-detective Ironside. We are presented with a world in which social collapse is always pending but which is prevented by super-brave and super-talented authority figures who are specially set apart from society for this purpose.'[46]

This world of violence and social collapse, precisely, is Harry Savage's news world, outside his control and his pleasure. Not surprisingly, Hartley sees definite similarities between the narrative structure of news and cop shows.

It is normal for the 'heroes' like Regan and Carter in *The Sweeney* or Starsky and Hutch . . . to survive as characters from week to week, series to series. Their antagonists, the villains – on the other hand . . . are positively required to efface themselves (i.e. be defeated by the heroes) in each and every one. Only their *function* survives. . . . In the news, similarly, the cast of newsworthy 'characters' is different from day to day, whilst on the contrary the institutional presenters are always there to guide us through their otherwise mysterious doings. . . . The accessed voices in the news, which do not survive the individual episode, only achieve continuity through their function.[47]

In contrast to this 'authoritarian' narrative of news and cop shows, the narrative of soaps is looser. As Modleski says, 'Soap operas invest exquisite pleasure in the central conditions of a woman's life: waiting – whether for her phone to ring, for the baby to take its nap, or for the family to be reunited shortly after the day's final soap opera has left *its* family still struggling against dissolution.' In Mrs Mallard's case waiting (between her husband's bed-time and his Complan) is her resistance against the personal dissolution of ageing and death. 'Soap operas do not end. Consequently truth for women is seen to lie "not at the end of the expectation", but *in* expectation, not in the "return to order", but in (familial) disorder.'[48]

Modleski has noted that soap operas 'present the viewer with a picture of a family in which the mother is a permanently needed confidante and adviser'.[49] Harry and Ivy Savage would have agreed. For them *The Sullivans* had 'gone off since the mother died'.

I: 'There's no story there now, really. She kept it together.'

H: 'She reminded me of normal family life. The family drifts apart when the mother dies.'

The sickness or death of elderly soap characters has a special significance for this audience.[50] So, for these old people, 'having a woman's angle' (and particularly the mother-figure's angle) was not 'off-centre' as in the news, but crucial to the 'ordinary, everyday' (and 'loose') plotline. One group of old people after another complained to me that *Coronation Street*, *Crossroads* and *The Sullivans* had 'gone off' after the matriarchal figures left the show.

The soap opera mother, Modleski notes, is central and 'ideal', but not a victor. Her 'sympathy is large enough to encompass the conflicting claims of her family (she identifies with no one character exclusively)',[51] but by that token she can establish no certain normative claims of her own. 'By constantly presenting her with the many-sidedness of any question, by never reaching a permanent conclusion, soap operas undermine her capacity to form unambiguous judgments.'[52] The soap opera mother is both token and guarantee of the genre's liberal plurality of discourses.

By the time old age impinges, the elderly audience has an often poignant memory of this 'mother' role. It was Ivy Savage's mothering role that had led her to the old people's centre in Bournemouth in the first place.

> 'Been here two and a half years. We're Londoners . . . but unfortunate circumstances – my daughter-in-law moved down here and was taken ill; having a baby. So we gave our place up and came down to look after her. But she died within six months and then we looked after the baby for a while. And that's why we're down this end.'

As Mrs Mallard's routine suggests, this 'mothering' activity never ends. But in old age, the energy diminishes, and greater daily store is set on family members with cars, on friends who are fifteen years younger, and on professionals who extend the security of the inside world to trips outside.

Among the elderly, perhaps even more than younger women, soap opera is likely to appeal to what Ien Ang has called the tragic structure of feeling, with soap's 'melodramatic imagination' called up as a psychological strategy to offset 'the impossibility of reconciling desire with reality' – in their case, reconciling resistance with 'dissolution'.[53] The exaggerated events of soap opera are, Ang argues, narrative metaphors which raise the half-understood, unspoken tragedies and banalities of daily life to a special plane.

> There are no words for the ordinary pain of living of ordinary people in the modern welfare state, for the vague sense of loss. . . . By making that ordinariness something special and meaningful in the imagination, that sense of loss can – at least for a time – be removed.[54]

But this is not 'escape' in the sense that term is usually used. Rather, soaps draw on the repertoire of skills, values and resistances located in the practical consciousness of people who reproduce the world manageably in their own sphere, in the absence of power in the public sphere.

News and soaps are TV genres determined in part by the other's symptomatic absences: in the structural relation of 'hard' and 'soft' news which TV's paradigmatic differentiation of the social world establishes. But their particular generic meanings are finally established by *specific* audience experience and location. Among the elderly, the 'familial disorder' of Modleski's housewives has been replaced, necessarily, by the intimately precise routines of *their* mothers. Among younger women viewers, Seiter *et al*. point out, 'the experience of working-class women clearly conflicts in substantial ways with the soap opera's representation of 'a woman's problems', problems some women identified as upper or middle class'.[55] And the fact that many of the elderly men admitted 'switching' from news to soaps only recently is, I would suggest, a mark of their own decline from the competitive work force and the masculine myths of news journalist and social explorer.

I will take further this question of audience readings in a later chapter. My emphasis so far has been on the paradigmatic possibilities of programming, the choice between 'hard' and 'soft' TV genres, the potential implication for audience 'information' of selecting certain kinds of TV drama for a particular time slot rather than news/current affairs, and the practical and discursive inflections of these positions by different age and gender groups. These scheduling choices are not taken casually by television executives, and the type of genre that a particular channel *doesn't* choose for a time slot, but which another channel does, itself has implications for programme construction. For instance, in Australia, when ATN 7's top-rating drama, *A Country Practice* began to slip in the ratings after a number of its cast left, other commercial channels attacked its crucial under-18 audience by re-scheduling *The A-Team* (appealing to teenage boys) and *It's a Knock Out* (appealing to female as well as male under-18's) against it. *A Country Practice* hit back by making a stronger appeal to teenage girls with more romance, as well as 'serious' school stories such as teenage sexuality and the 'anti-nuclear' story that brought in Prime Minister Hawke. Some of this may have proved disturbing to the show's elderly audience – certainly Harry Savage was one among a number in Bournemouth who said he had 'gone off' *EastEnders* because of its sexual emphasis.

Schedulers juggle audiences according to this paradigmatic range of possibilities. As ATN 7's programme development manager said, 'The mix of programmes across the five television stations in the market at any one time is probably more important than the mix of programmes running from start to finish in the day on one station.' But though this kind of competition between channels (and TV genres) within time slots is fundamental, as we have seen it *is* complemented by a concern for programme flow. So TV drama is also part of a defined syntagmatic space; that is, it takes its place in a sequencing of programme genres.

TV drama and programme flow: syntagmatic spaces

On ATN 7, the early evening news bulletin at 6.00 p.m., followed by the current affairs programme *Terry Willesee Tonight*, played an important role in building and holding a mass audience through the prime-time period. As Elliott *et al.* point out, this sequencing in itself has implications for a programme's meanings, since the strategic position of news and current affairs in the ratings battle 'pushes the programme towards populist forms of presentation and discourse which work with the most widely held images and assumptions in the interests of mobilising the largest possible audience'.[56] There was a tendency for this populist mode of address to run over from current affairs shows like *Terry Willesee Tonight* to the following peak-time drama *A Country Practice* (where, for instance, the composer of the musical score for an 'especially hard-hitting' AIDS story was asked to 'balance' his 'menacing' AIDS theme with a 'lighter' theme for the 'G audience'). Alternatively, on a number of occasions, social issues exposed in *A Country Practice* have been taken up by *Terry Willesee Tonight* or the earlier news bulletin, without any clear shift in tone or focus.

This breaking down of closure between genres is emphasized by the segmentation of television which, as John Ellis has pointed out, tends to broadcast its various programmes in relatively short and discrete packages of 'sequential unities of image and sound'.[57] The news typically works this way, but, Fiske argues, 'Even drama series and serials, where the narrative requires the principle of logic and cause and effect, may be segmented into short scenes with logical links omitted.'[58] Television segmentation and populist mode of address together work to break down the paradigmatic differentiation of the world that television genres in other ways establish.

In addition to this relationship of flow and interruption between programmes, TV drama's own sequencing is frequently interrupted by advertisements; and the relationship between commercials and drama is crucial, both to the general (paradigmatic) placing of types of programme in this daily schedule, and in the meanings a drama generates sequentially within any one time slot. As we saw, industry notions of who controls the TV set at any one time are important in decisions about the sequencing of shows ('You wouldn't change from a teenage oriented programme at 7 p.m. . . . .'); and they are also important in deciding when to schedule shows (and advertisements) targeted at particular audiences.

Recently, for instance, advertisers and programmers have challenged the assumption that the career woman 'is too busy to watch TV and can be reached only by alternative media' like women's magazines. The television industry has begun competing for the 'working housewife':

> By providing new initiatives and an aggressive programming devel-
> opment policy, the working woman is still as viable a marketing

proposition as her stay-at-home sister. Among these initiatives in recent years have been: a 6 p.m. news service to allow for earlier viewing if other household duties require attention later in the evening; introduction of news at other periods to give more frequent opportunity of viewing (for example, during the day and late evening). The development of breakfast television is emerging as one of the most significant vehicles for targeting working housewives.[59]

Earlier, daytime soap opera owed *its* origins to advertisers' targeting of the 'stay-at-home sister'. During the Depression, the major soap company Proctor and Gamble increased its advertising budget on the assumption that in a period of reduced consumer buying-power, advertising efforts had to be stepped up if sales levels were to be maintained. Daytime network radio was cheap compared to prime time, housewives listened to it in vast numbers, and P & G's customers were overwhelmingly female. The first soaps were aimed at this audience. P & G directly sponsored thousands of hours of daytime soaps, and early female soap writers 'kept uppermost in their minds the function of their stories as advertising vehicles'.[60]

Scheduling *types* of programme in particular time slots (breakfast news, daytime soap, prime-time series) for particular audiences depends, then, on economic imperatives. On commercial TV, the ordering of programmes, their sequencing through the day, their type and composition is primarily determined by the varying needs of delivering targeted audiences to advertisers.

But what is the effect of these advertisements placed sequentially within the programmes themselves? As Fiske says, the *effect* is not necessarily economic, even if the motivation is: 'many more viewers gain pleasure from advertisements than buy the products being promoted'.[61] What is the relationship between the 'orthodox' commercial messages and the 'alternative' discourses of their targeted audience in this interrupted flow of advertisements and drama?

Tania Modleski has written interestingly about the interactive relationship between the 'stay-at-home sister', daytime soaps and the advertisements that address them during these shows. Above all, 'at home' motherhood means being responsive to interruptions, and 'daytime television plays a part in habituating women to distraction, interruption, and spasmodic toil.'[62] The script writers, 'anticipating the housewife's distracted state, are careful to repeat important elements of the story several times.'[63] And the sequential switch in daytime TV from, say, quiz shows (with their clear sense of winning and narrative closure) to soaps is also a kind of interruption, just as the housewife is required to endure monotonous, repetitive work but to be able to switch instantly and on demand from her role as a kind of bedmaking, dishwashing automaton to a large sympathising consciousness. . . . Quiz shows present the spectator with the same game, played frenetically day after day, with each game a self-contained unit, crowned by climactic success or failure. Soap operas, by contrast, endlessly defer resolutions and climaxes and undercut the very notion of success.[64]

So, for Modleski, 'the flow . . . between soap operas and other programming units reinforces the very principle of interruptibility crucial to the proper functioning of women in the home'.[65] This function, and this central television experience of flow-as-interruption, is 'a profoundly decentring experience'.[66]

Moving from the sequencing of programme genres to the sequencing of advertisements and drama *within* the soap opera, Modleski takes the 'principle of interruptibility' and the notion of switching between 'success' genres and 'deferred resolution' genres further. Within soaps,

Revelations, confrontations, and reunions are constantly being interrupted and postponed by telephone calls, unexpected visitors, counter-revelations, catastrophes, and switches from one plot to another. . . . Like the (ideal) mother in the home, we are kept interested in a number of events at once and are denied the luxury of a total and prolonged absorption. Commercials constitute another kind of interruption, in this case from *outside* the diegesis. Commercials present the housewife with mini-problems and their resolutions, so after witnessing all the agonizingly hopeless dilemmas on soap operas, the spectator has the satisfaction of seeing something cleaned up, if only a stained shirt or a dirty floor.[67]

What seems, on the surface, to be an antithesis between the commercial's resolution of trivial chores (saggy nappies, carpet stains) and soaps' *lack* of resolution of the 'large problems of human existence' (love, death, dying) in fact, says Modleski,

embodies a deep truth about the way women function in (or, more accurately, around) culture: as both moral and spiritual guides and household drudges: now one, now the other, moving back and forth between the extremes, but obviously finding them difficult to reconcile.[68]

As with Mrs Mallard (but in a different way) there is an experiential relationship between these women's practical consciousness and the daytime shows they watch. But the emphasis in Modleski's analysis is on the space for the play of discourses *between* TV genres (quiz/soap; soap/advertisement) set in train by their sequencing. This is in contrast to Budd, Craig and Steinman, who, in analysing the advertisements transmitted during an episode of *Fantasy Island*, emphasize the dominance of 'official' discourse. They explain the relationship of apparently disconnected segments in terms of commercial and ideological *closure*, as 'commercials respond fairly directly to the problems, desires and fantasies articulated in the program's narrative by promising gratification through products'.[69] Thus a drama sequence focusing on a mother's worry about her child is followed immediately by a cereal commercial showing happy children. Modleski, however, discovers an '*alternative*' potential in this sequential play (in the 'decentring' challenge to narrative closure), even though the subject matter – particularly of the advertisements – is conservative.

Advertisements certainly do act out their own dramas, and establish their own 'official' mythologies. Sandy Flitterman has observed that there is a distinction between day and prime-time advertisements. Not only is there a tendency for 'men's' advertisements (cars, business machines, investment firms, banks) not to be seen during daytime soaps, but even advertisements addressed at women differ as between day and prime time. 'While the evening programme advertisements for such products as perfume and alcoholic beverages . . . offer an image of the liberated, sexually sophisticated and glamorous woman . . . independent of domestic surroundings',[70] the emphasis of daytime advertisements is on cosmetic improvements that can be made (reducing weight, disguising ageing) *while* running the home.

Yet, while not denying the profoundly conservative nature of these advertisements, Flitterman, like Modleski, is concerned to show how they *work* as television, as part of the programme sequence. Advertisements – these '*real*' soap operas' – offer that promise of richness and plenitude that the soap always defers. In this sense their meanings relate to soap narratives in a way similar to quiz shows: as (narrative) flow, but also (for their audience) as perceptual contradiction. In form advertisements are richer than soaps, with a far greater variety of narrative styles, more elaborate camera technique, and optical and musical innovations virtually unknown in the generally low budget dramas. In content, the advertisement offers that consensual plenitude of the ideal family that the soap opera constantly sets up and consistently destroys. 'To the soap opera's conventional and consistent fare of illegitimacy, rivalry, false parentage, adultery, secrecy and betrayal, the commercial offers the happy family, the good mother, the affectionate

companion and the conscientious housewife.'[71] So advertisements –
like the temporary resolutions of happy marriages in the soaps themselves
– function as lures in the narrative of deferment.

Flitterman's emphasis is on the interactive function of commercials
and drama, the nexus of interruption *and* flow, the continuity *and*
conflict between them: on the one hand, advertisements operate as a
key part of capitalism's 'equation of material consumption with well-
being',[72] on the other hand they partake in that play between genres
that makes women's pleasure narratively 'off-centre', and potentially
critical of dominant patriarchal modes. In this way the segmented flow
of TV drama may challenge official discourses.

Robert Allen also points to the structural interaction between 'determinacy' (of the advertisement) and 'indeterminacy' (in the relation of
advertisement and soap opera). The value systems of the show and the
sponsor must, at the very least, he says,

> not be contradictory; at best the former supports and encourages the
> reader's acceptance of the latter as valid. But the two must not
> appear to the reader to be identical; otherwise the 'author's' (sponsor's)
> true intent is laid bare and the fictional narrative becomes nothing
> more than a parable in a marketing sermon. The message must be
> kept apart from but ultimately reassociated with the fictional world
> of the show. . . . the former must supply a degree of indeterminacy to
> compensate for the absolute determinacy of the latter.[73]

In fact, it *is* possible for advertising and drama values to be contradictory. As Douglas Kellner points out, 'its profit-imperative . . . render
networks unreliable defenders of the existing order'.[74] In Australia,
Singapore Airlines sponsored both Trevor Griffiths' *The Last Place On
Earth* and *Land of Hope* (an Australian 'high class soap opera' which
carried a Left/Labour critical history of capitalism and corporate profit-
making). And as Allen himself points out, an important consequence of
the removal of the authoritative narrator from the narrative world of
TV soaps (concomitantly with a tendency to disperse the narrative
perspective as soaps got longer and characters multiplied) was the
opening up of the soap opera text to a greater variety of views and
norms. It was this openness that enabled the TV soap opera to give the
appearance of normative daring (the liberal rather than conservative
attitude to social issues that Modleski describes) while seldom straying
far from the consensus.

The narrative indeterminacy of modern-day soaps allows them to
widen their audience range – more men, adolescents, college students –
with minimal risk, allowing,

for a sort of feedback mechanism, through which the fate of . . . perspectives at some distance from the core values . . . can ultimately be decided. If network, sponsor, or viewer response indicates the perspective to be too far from the normative 'centre' and thus threatening or destabilizing, the character and plot line containing it can be dispensed with. . . . Or the new perspective might be attached to a character on the margins of the soap's core value system and thus kept 'at the edge' of the soap's normative territory. Finally, the new perspective might over time be absorbed within the dominant value system, as that system itself changed.[75]

As a result, contemporary soap opera narratives are able to 'accommodate a far greater range of "negotiated" readings than other, more normatively dominant forms of fictive narratives', and, in this way, are counterposed to the 'perspectival determinacy of its commercial messages'.[76]

Soaps and ads: normative margins

Most of the analysis of generic flow and segmentation on TV has focused on audience positioning, textually or ethnographically. What has been almost entirely missing from television analysis (except in the case of 'single-play' authorship) has been a textual or ethnographic account of flow and contradiction in popular serials in respect to television practitioners. Yet this feature of the soap/audience relationship within commercial television must depend on the agency of production practices within quite specific institutional structures. To take an example of 'authored' drama first, an 'up-market' channel like England's Thames Television may be prepared to risk a 'radical soap' like Trevor Griffiths' *Bill Brand*, provided, of course, it is clearly authored by Griffiths rather than the channel. More interestingly (in relation to my discussion of popular serials and flow/segmentation), a channel such as ATN 7 in Australia (which traditionally has seen itself as a 'half-way house' between the 'quality' ABC and the other 'ordinary soap' commercial channels) can provide institutional space for a quite focused 'alternative' critique of the 'official' discourse of its own commercials.

I have described elsewhere how the agency of a radical producer/ script editor at ATN 7's *A Country Practice* transformed a 'Romeo and Juliet story designed for the mums' into an anti-sexist, anti-'multiculturalism-as-exotica' challenge to the commercials transmitted during the show. On the one hand, the advertisements built up through their sequencing the 'model qualities' of the show's variously targeted (yet composite) female audience: woman as mother, nurse, cook, shopper, housekeeper, sex object and competent professional. The advertisements also inflected this 'model' woman multiculturally: as the oriental 'impulse exotique' of a body spray advertisement, or as the dark 'excitable' Italian and blond Nordic 'cool' of a Kraft cheese advertisement. On the other hand, 'Australianness' advertisements (such as the Paul Hogan tourism commercial) ritually repeated and re-worked in different combinations the same dominant cultural myth: of the active but stoically irreverent *male* Australia. As I have argued more fully elsewhere, there is a 'resisting' relationship between the drama and advertising sequences.

> The Hogan tourism advertisement works so well because it is hedonism which in the end *provides* work; it is *leisure* which is active. So the site of production (work) is displaced by the site of active consumption (tourism, sport), and questions of class, ethnic and gender exploitation are displaced by images of human and socio-natural reciprocity. Advertisements, Judith Williamson points out, 'obscure and avoid the real issues of society, those relating to work: to jobs and wages and who works for whom'.[77]

> Yet television does, as Rowse and King say,[78] construct its audience in contrasting ways, even if mainly favouring the hedonistic. *A Country Practice* is a top-rating prime-time drama, and in 'A Touch of Class' it does quite specifically deal with issues of class, and who works for whom. Further, it emphasises that leisure time is something that significant sections of the population *do not have*. It strips away cultural stereotypes to expose difference rather than multicultural uniformity (that 'new Australianicity'); and cultural difference is related structurally to social exploitation rather than to the plenitude and symbiosis of cultural or natural exotica.

> Cultural difference, in other words, is seen less as a commodity to be exchanged, but as part of a global system of exploitation. . . .

> This *A Country Practice* episode *links* and systematises the extremes of soap representation that Modleski refers to, between the 'large problems of human existence' and the daily chores. 'A Touch of Class' makes the 'foreign' stereotype work to expose a woman's daily labour as an *effect* of, and contributor to, those 'large' problems – here given a clear economic dimension. Mrs Belotti's exploitation and 'bounded knowledgeability' is marked both in class terms (it is her labour which pays for Ashleigh's car, house and clothes), and ethnic/gender terms (as she seeks to reproduce her own culture's patriarchal codes in her son).[79]

Gaps, spaces and margins

My argument for flow and contradiction in the construction of 'Australianness' in a sequence of *A Country Practice* and its advertisements is not intended to mark a clear distinction between a 'progressive' drama series and 'conservative' advertisements. In fact, in discussing 'A Touch of Class' I have, firstly, privileged a particularly 'radical' episode in a generally consensual series, and secondly, explicated certain dominant storylines in that episode at the expense of other much more conservative (even if more minor) ones. Moreover, it might well be possible to select a sequential relationship which works the other way: where the commercial is potentially more disturbing to hegemonic ideology than the drama. John Hartley, for instance, discussing a Del Monte Orange Juice commercial, argues that advertisements are sometimes 'outrageously honest about the relations of production' telling us 'the blatant truth about capitalism'.[80]

Hartley's argument – that critics should concern themselves with the dangerous *margins* of television, as well as its hegemonic centrality – is an important one. As he says, 'Even if television, like formal education, tends to work in the interests of the efficient development of capitalism and despite its undoubted success in popularizing hegemonic consciousness, the fact remains that, like schooling, it produces more knowledge than such "functions" require.'[81] In its very process of constructing clear, unambiguous boundaries of acceptable knowledge and behaviour, television,

> *over-represents* the marginal, ambiguous, scandalous areas of society. Action series, drama, news and movies alike are founded on violence, murder and criminality; on deviance, dissidence and pathological behaviour; on illicit, over-displayed or 'abnormal' sexuality; on breakdowns, break-ups and break-ins . . . in order to limit meanings, it must first produce *excess*.[82]

As I have argued, TV drama sometimes interrogates the 'scandalous' at the very heart of capitalism's central institutions: the state (and terrorism), work (and unemployment), the family (and incest). Hartley notes that this danger of excess lies in both the structural marginality of television (the relation between its different genres, as well as between its programmes and its scheduled 'gaps' – advertisements, promos, time checks, announcements, etc.); and in its representational marginality (its peopling of soaps 'by widows, divorcees, remarriages and relationships that border on the incestuous', and its 'decentring' of these characters into adolescent preoccupation).[83]

Hartley's plea is for a critical discourse which both accounts *for* these areas of marginality and brings them *to* account, since otherwise 'both capitalism and popular consciousness continue to develop and change *unaccountably* in the margins of television'.[84] The *kind* of critical discourse adopted will, as I said in the Introduction, influence the nature of that 'account'. Fiske's discourse in Television Culture, drawing on post-modernist theory, is one kind of 'accounting' for the 'dangerous margins' of television; my discourse in this book, drawing on a realist epistemology and arguing for an ethnography of production, is another. Our differing notions of what is 'marginal' or 'de-centred' from the dominant ('official') myth need noting here, because they also flow through some of the analytical work surveyed in this chapter. I will conclude by focusing this difference around the use of cars in the dramas that Fiske and I analyse. Fiske refers to the Ferrari in *Miami Vice* as 'excessive'.

> It is more car and more style than police officers normally need or have. Its excessiveness extends its meaning beyond the ideological domain of masculinity and into that freer, less controlled one of style . . . its style is that of consumption for pleasure. . . . Flaunting the lack of use-value is 'criminal' in capitalism. Commodities of pure pleasure, pure waste, question the norms of the commodity itself, and crack the alibi that late capitalism tries to establish for itself in the ideology of consumerism. . . . However hard the narrative fights to close each episode with a resolution in which sense, control, and masculine closure are all achieved, the style, the music, the look, the interruptions of the narrative remain open, active, disruptible, and linger on as the pleasures of *Miami Vice*.[85]

Fiske's emphasis on the excess of style in *Miami Vice* – the deadpan wit of the Chandleresque dialogue, the 'excessive stylishness of Crockett and Tubbs' which arguably 'sets up contradictions between the excessively macho behaviour and speech of the pair and the feminized style of their clothes',[86] the 'voluptuous visuals' that represent (like oil paintings) 'the tactile uniqueness of objects which positions the spectator as sole possessor of them'[87] – is based on the belief that it is 'a style that is readily accessible to all'.[88] This will be inflected in different ways according to the class, gender and ethnic practices of different audiences, but it is a general quality of the text that opens the viewer of even the 'closed' narratives of action-adventure series to 'a post-modernist pleasure'. Fiske here is mapping a political aesthetic of reception over the open/closed, tight/loose categories of production that I discussed earlier.

In my analysis I began to examine the representation of the Alfa-Romeo in 'A Touch of Class' both in terms of sets of similarities and differences made available by television's segmented mode of representation (a central project of Fiske also) and in terms of producer Michael Brindley's understanding of the place of 'Australianness' within a global system of exploitation.

This seduction performance by Ashleigh in front of her friends is also contained within a discourse about 'Australianness'. Lorenzo is a 'spunk', a beautiful Italian whom, like her equally beautiful Italian car, Ashleigh wants to possess. 'Italianness' is conceived here as an exotic national product, an export which, together with other foreign cultures, make up Australia's 'multi-cultural society'. As such, Ashleigh's discourse equates with those of a number of advertisements that went to air during 'A Touch of Class'. . . . . In an Impulse Exotique body spray advertisement, 'foreignness' signifies oriental charm and sexuality, and its narrative is played out between Asian female (*her* red sportscar reproducing Ashleigh's) and Australian male. So here foreignness and Australianness come together in a different way, typical of the representations of women Flitterman points to in prime-time advertisements. . . . Fulfilment lies in the blending of the Australian with the foreign, as multiculturalism is commoditised.[89]

It was the mobilization (*within* that segmentation) of oppositional discourses of image and sound that I dealt with. My emphasis there was on the politics (as agency) of both audience and production, set within daily domestic and professional routines. Whereas Fiske's post-modernist emphasis is 'loose', stressing 'ambiguities, contradictions and loose ends', my own realist emphasis is 'tight', a relationship of critical mutuality with those particular television workers' own 'preferred' and systemic explanations of class, gender and ethnicity within capitalism. That 'tight/loose' distinction is part of a broader current debate between 'modernist' and 'post-modernist' positions, between a 'unified epistemological project'[90] and 'difference theory'; and my own position in that debate will certainly influence what kind of 'bringing to account' of the dangerous margins of television I emphasize in the pages that follow. In the following chapter I will explore the notion that the 'ambiguity of marginality' is a central feature of television myth-making itself.

2 Genre and myth: 'a half-formed picture'

The key to the myths . . . of our own powerlessness . . . is that we've been robbed of our visionary ability. It's something that's taken away from us very early on by such concepts as 'Oh, it's only human nature', 'boys don't cry', 'girls don't do that kind of thing', 'it's always been that way', and other such . . . illusions, snares and traps, which both rob us of our history in terms of ways of . . . living that have been different, and also rob us of our ability to dream about the way that we think things could be.

Sally Potter[1]

Myth as the social construct of instrumental reason must be pierced and exploded by the powers of the imagination which maintains a use value.

Jack Zipes[2]

The 'ordinary, everyday' domestic intimacy that the elderly audience liked about soap operas is not a 'natural' feature of the genre. It has a long history of being worked for. The emphasis on the domestic immediacy of the soap form, on a performance style that seemed to address each member of the audience individually, and yet placed women in a special listening position as privileged consumers, was already an integral part of the development of radio as a popular cultural form. The construction of special 'managerial' or 'active' audience positions was also part of the broader development of generic myths in the 1930s.

Modern myths, as Fiske says, are a culture's way of conceptualizing 'about masculinity and femininity, about the family, about success, about the British policeman, about science'.[3] In this chapter I will examine the way in which these myths – about femininity and the family, about the police, about science – have been conceptualized in radio and TV drama to provide social order at times of cultural crisis. I will look as well at points of conflict and ambiguity within these myths themselves. In the next section I will examine the construction of myths of the family, science and individual success at an historical crisis point in the growth of modern capitalism, the Depression.

Depression genres: myths of science and the family

The 1920s saw a marked shift in the dominant discourses about radio. Initially it was celebrated as 'wireless science', the *active* preoccupation of small groups of technical 'experimenters' who built their 'own apparatus, dismantling it after one experiment and reassembling it for the next'.[4] But with the rapid development of radio as a consumer durable, the emphasis changed to radio as the simpler and more passive furniture of everyday domesticity. Now depicted as 'listeners-in' rather than 'experimenters' audiences were inscribed in a different way by the myth of '"science" as product rather than practice'.[5]

This new 'scientific' commodity inscribed the family within the world of *modernity*, supposedly available through the market. The radio (together with the vacuum cleaner and oven) composed the 'modern electrical household' – which was coming to determine the image of the family as *consumers* of social and scientific change. These other domestic commodities were said to free the modern housewife *from* the drudgery of endless chores and *for* the leisure of listening-in.

As Lesley Johnson says, it was a targeted leisure, freeing women to hear the advertisers. 'Detailed cooking information, fashion talks, health programmes, the promotion of electricity and/or gas in the home, all worked to produce an orientation to the market. Women were being taught to be efficient managers of the consumption activities of the home.'[6]

At the same time, programme schedules and generic formats were devised to make it 'easy for the housewife to combine her work and her listening interludes'.[7] Daytime advertising could be attracted by the idea of controlling the listening habit. 'On the hour the GPO chimes would be heard to let the housewife know that she was entitled to sit down for fifteen minutes.'[8] Scheduling campaigns transferred notions of 'labour processes closely regulated by time from the outdoor world of work . . . to domestic existence, in particular to women's existence'.[9] Radio (and later television) asked women to forget that 'listening-in' was in fact *work* (part of the task of purchasing) but rather was 'just entertainment'.[10] Women listeners were being situated as receivers of the efficiency function of a modern, technological world 'beyond' the family, but which defined their place *within* the family as special.

> The housewife . . . was being addressed as a controller of the family's purse strings by advertisers; she was being addressed by the new professional groups as manager of the home and controller of child care practices; and she was being addressed as the heart of the new family turned inwards upon itself, preoccupied with its private consumption activities.[11]

At the same time, as Virginia Nightingale argues, the development of brand-image advertising on radio, along with the shopping complex as a 'free of obligation' environment for 'impulse buying', created the 'predictable, programmable "mum"' who knew the lifestyle meanings of branded products for each different member 'of the family destined to consume her purchases'.[12] To be 'feminine' within the family context was to be manager and mediator of this modern, 'scientific' commodity flow.

Though the flow was to be one-way (from a central source to a mass but privatized audience), the rhetoric surrounding this new cultural form suggested a two-way relationship, a sharing of everyday intimacy via the extended family of radio. The trade press emphasized the importance of radio personalities playing 'themselves' as ordinary people; to give the feeling of chatting with someone in the same room, rather than lecturing to a hidden audience.

This personal mode of address was resisted by 'quality' stations (like the ABC in Australia) since it seemed to threaten the gentlemanly and distanced 'aura of culture' which they cultivated. But it was enthusiastically embraced by the commercial radio stations. It not only determined preferred forms of programming (the chatty, interpersonal interview rather than the formal talk), but also activated new genres (family dramas and soaps).

As Johnson says, this 'member of the family/chatting over the backyard fence' mode of performance inscribed a particular ideology. 'Through the very preoccupation with the ordinary, the everyday, the mundane daily occurrences of domestic life, programmes . . . constructed a reality bounded and consumed by these very concerns.' The family hearth 'became the world, the authentic or "real" of listeners' lives'.[13] Radio advertisements pictured its 'family' of listeners clustered around the radio and the fireplace, together forming the heart of the 'home'.

The emphasis on a 'family' of listeners and broadcasters, working together through the daily problems of the Depression, also infused radio's dominant generic styles; as in family serials.

> With titles such as *People Like Us*, *One Man's Family*, *Fred and Maggie Everybody*, *Those We Love*, their preoccupation with the everyday-

ordinary as a shared-in-common of broadcasters and listeners was explicit.[14]

So, as well as having the economic function of inserting particular commodities (chewing-gum, soap powder, etc.) into the daily lives of its family audience, the new radio genres also worked ideologically to emphasize this cultural 'shared-in-common' of daily problems across an entire community in the Depression. But, always, 'sharing' was *spending*.

Cars, house mortgages, new domestic appliances, gadgets, clothes, all formed part of the plots of these serials. The family functioned as a consumer unit.[15]

Allen has shown how the perspectival hierarchy of radio soaps worked to establish a fusion of worlds: advertiser's, character's, audience's. He quotes the *Ma Perkins* announcer:

> And so Ma Perkins . . . realizes what mothers have found since the world began: that you can't run other people's affairs for 'em. . . . You've just got to help 'em. And speaking of help, there's no household job that needs outside help more than washing clothes. . . . [16]

By intervening in the storyline, and mediating between characters and listener, the (usually male) announcer's voice established itself at the top of the soap's perspectival hierarchy. Next in importance was the perspective of one dominant character, usually female. This pyramidal structure (in which the female protagonist was authorized in her dominance of the narrative and domestic spheres by the 'male' economic discourse) was homologous with the real situation of women in the private sphere. She dominated the management of affairs there; but was placed in that situation by economic and 'professional' advice from outside. The effect was to legitimize the advertiser's voice, more readily to penetrate the domestic sphere. Together, these advertising and narrative strategies established a preferred position in which the female listener was passive recipient of expert advice and exhortation (to buy), but was herself the actively dominant agent within the household.

The comforting, motherly *Mrs Dale's Diary* character sitting atop soap opera's narrative hierarchy, intimately revealing to the listener her interpersonal skills, has, then, a deep (formal and economic) generative structure.[17] Other determinants, operating in the same period of the Depression, had other generative effects on other genres. If soap opera turned the listener's gaze inwards to the private sphere where the woman was manager, science fiction directed perspectives outwards, to other worlds where rational/technological *men* were explorers, and managers of the future. Klein and Mellor have argued that the effect of Depression and war on the aspiring (male) technical middle class who made up a major section of SF's readership, was the belief in

> the coming of a rational, technologically oriented 'organisation society', to be built on the ruins of the waning, liberal bourgeois order. . . . Just as the SF fraction anticipated that a benevolent US imperialism could . . . export a new reign of Reason to those countries as yet denied its benefits, so in science fiction, science and rationality built new empires among the stars.[18]

The private and the colonial spheres, the intimate and the 'outer' space, were both significant areas for commodity penetration and, analogously, sources for generic myths of science.

Between the home and these other worlds, though, there was the public sphere itself; the centre of the crisis. Ariel Dorfman points to the origins of yet another popular genre during the Depression. The Lone Ranger radio programme (soon 'to be followed by other superheroes like Superman, Batman and Flash Gordon) 'appeared between 1932 and 1933 in the midst of the greatest crisis that capitalism has ever endured'.[19] For Dorfman, the superhero represents a novel alibi for a modern 'scientifically' organized and interventionist state:

> Day after day, the reader must put up with the State's remoteness . . . its limiting (and frightening) force, the incommunicability and hermeticism of political phenomena. . . . The superhero is able to carry out all these functions of law and order, but without . . . the barriers . . . that antagonize and separate the State from the people it claims to represent. . . . The individual, the persona, the loner . . . appears in the story as active . . . and a source of real power.[20]

Here again, as in the case of the managerial woman at home and the technocratic male in space, the myth was of the active subject; but individualized (at an historical moment which in reality had considerable potential for *class* change), it had a powerful mythic effect in implicitly denying collective aspirations.

> When faced with the collapse of the market economy, drastic solutions are necessary. The newly created superhero naturalizes the social forces to which monopolistic capitalism readjusts, . . . the cautious but decisive intervention of the State; military and moral expansion of the system; total participation in social benefits; fiscal assistance for technical progress and projects for the public welfare. . . . It was necessary for the average citizen . . . to find in works of entertainment

a brand-new, mythical, up-to-date person who would act out the solutions of the dilemmas.[21]

Management, organization, 'scientific' rationality were a central theme of each of these genres – yet they also had to re-affirm dominant cultural beliefs in choice and individuality. As Umberto Eco points out in his 'Myth of Superman',[22] it is the retelling of the known tale which is central to myth's function in ritually reaffirming basic cultural beliefs. And as Radway points out of the romance novel, the repeated emphasis on individual power and choice is central to myth's naturalizing function as ideology.

> While the act of romance reading is used by women as a means of partial protest against the role prescribed for them by the culture, the discourse itself actively insists on the desirability, naturalness and benefits of that role by portraying it not as the imposed necessity that it is but as a freely designed, personally controlled individual choice.[23]

These genres implied that science, rationality, technocratic and managerial skills, were freely and individually chosen. It is the combination of this consumed and consuming generic retelling with the 'realist' effect of a unique individuality and historical contemporaneity that makes myth a powerfully adaptable ideological force. In each of these 'Depression' genres 'science' is both 'naturally' superior and at the same time offset and contained by the myth of active individual agency.

Theories of popular drama as myth: the 'specialized' and the 'nonsensical'

It should be clear from these examples of 'Depression' genres that a focus on ideological manipulation (as myth construction) has been integral to media critics' analysis of the packaging of audiences as commodities. Though tending to underplay resistances to media control within the existing structures of capitalist society, this 'critical theory' position remains important. Indeed, as Robert Dunn summarizes it, the theory becomes even more important for television, which exemplifies the mass media's commodification of culture.

> As a commodity form, television seeks to organize the viewer's relationship to cultural meanings according to the dictates of the role of the consumer. Television attempts to constitute this role at two separate but interrelated levels: given television's economic imperatives, the viewer is constituted abstractly as a consumer in the larger socioeconomic order of capitalist goods and services; more

importantly, given its technological and organizational structures, television attempts to constitute the spectator as a consumer of television as a cultural commodity. . . . In effect, television appropriates the 'free time' of the individual in order to carve out of the private realm of leisure a space in which to produce economic value. . . . Just as the early factory system commodified the labour capacity of the worker, the system of modern broadcasting commodifies the very symbolizing capacity of the privatized viewer, objectifying and quantifying it for the advertising market.[24]

On the one hand, modern media convert subjects (who are potentially active, and, during the Depression, at the fault lines of society) into *privileged* purchasers of commodities. On the other hand, the displacement into privatized (soap) and 'other' (science fiction) spheres deflects attention from the particular historical conjuncture. Social action is replaced by myth (defined in Roland Barthes' sense) as history is transformed into nature, into the common sense of 'it's always been that way, and it'll always be that way' of individual 'choice' – as in the feeling of human intimacy and 'naturally' chosen togetherness which the family serial invoked in the 1930s. This, as Barthes would say, promoted for daily listeners 'a rich, fully experienced, spontaneous, indisputable image',[25] a *facticity* drawing on their own 'ordinary-everyday' lives, and indicative of the 'naturally' good social order which is bedrock and basis for the concept of social change as commodity change.

However, not all theorists of TV drama have accepted this 'cultural studies' definition of myth, or seen this myth-making as a problem specific to a particular capitalist order. Roger Silverstone has argued that television performs a *necessarily* mythical role in binding the 'ordinary, everyday' community together against its unfamiliar margins. The unfamiliar, as he argues, is of two kinds: the *specialized* (those esoteric areas of knowledge about science, art and politics produced and maintained by specialist, exclusive groups), and the *nonsensical* (the areas rejected by a culture as phony, alien, distorted, fearful, unacceptable). 'Between these two forms of knowledge, the one super-cultural, the other pre- (or anti- or even non-) cultural, lies the world of the everyday and the modes of communication which articulate everyday concerns, formally and functionally identically placed to the mythic in primitive society.'[26]

Television, because it is not written, does not communicate fixed and recoverable texts. Like ancient oral myth forms, the potentially endless play of generic formulae create a memory.

Television . . . communicates . . . the endless play of the formula. In drama, news and documentary, success consists in the grafting of the novel onto the familiar, and it is through the familiar – the formula – that the experience of television is grounded in the experience of the everyday.[27]

Fiske, too, stresses the similarity between television and oral culture, in the sense of its closer, more empathetic, more communal identification with the viewer's daily 'knowledgeability' than writing which distances 'the knower from the known'.[28]

For Silverstone, myth is necessarily both adaptive and conservative: 'To be effective conservative thought needs to be able to maintain harmony with the new, and the mythic does this by processes of adjustment and cooperation wherein its structures are preserved.'[29] In his emphasis on the cultural 'control' aspects of myth, Silverstone is close to critical theorists like Dorfman and Wright. Dorfman, for instance, points out that while the Lone Ranger superhero myth adjusts to environmentalist issues in the 1970s and Indian minority rights issues in the 1980s, 'the way in which the hero defeats the contradictions, the means by which he restores the destroyed equilibrium' remain the same.[30] Will Wright looks more systematically at this relationship between structural continuity (of character types) and narrative ad-aptation in the Western, arguing that narrative sequencing 'varies in accordance with changing social actions and institutions' (the shift, for example, from entrepreneurial to 'scientific' capitalism with different mixes of possessive individualism and 'social good'). But the binary oppositions which define social types remain the same: 'for them to change, the society itself must change to such a degree that it would essentially be a new society, which would consequently need a new myth'.[31]

Dorfman and Wright, though, are concerned with the particular historical variations of the Western myth as it encounters, in a particular (capitalist) society, specific crises (such as the Depression, and the change from a competitive market to a planned, corporate economy). Silverstone is more interested in the universal aspect of cultural forms, in how 'the present and the ideological is grafted onto the persistent and the cultural'.[32] If, then, for Silverstone 'television does not deny history or naturalise it' (as cultural theorists think) 'but makes it *bearable*',[33] how does TV drama *differ* from ancient oral myth forms? The difference lies in its *focus* (on cognition and science).

We are much less concerned by the facts of birth, marriage or death . . . in contemporary culture, because, it might appear, we have forms of knowledge which have allowed us to deny or minimise the dangers associated with them. We are, however, much more concerned with that knowledge itself, and with the dangers that it poses to our security. Culture is itself, in its cognitive or aesthetic aspects, in need of mediation, and television . . . is a central instrument of that mediation.[34]

Radway's work on the romance novel suggests that modern audiences are, in fact, very much concerned with matters of marriage. But this supports Silverstone's point, since she argues that this includes a cognitive engagement with 'supercultural' *ideas* (such as feminism) that have impinged upon domesticity: 'For them, the romance is . . . a cognitive exploration of the possibility of adopting and managing some attitude changes about feminine sexuality by making room for them within traditional institutions.'[35]

As a result of this concern with the cognitive, with the dangers of *knowledge* about death and living, TV drama has shown a special concern with social roles (such as doctors and other 'scientific' helpers) that tame and naturalize the supercultural. For Silverstone doctors 'act as mediators, placed on the boundary of nature and culture. . . . Their capacity to intervene between life and death makes them potentially and actually powerful figures.'[36] Similarly, Tulloch and Alvarado have suggested the centrality of the 'good' and 'mad' scientist in SF as marking the boundary between the social and the insane.[37] Soap operas, of course, abound in doctors and as one writer for *A Country Practice* remarked, an occasional distinction of this show from the 'average soap' is to go beyond the 'margin' to focus on the 'nonsensical' in the scientific knowledge system itself. 'It's daring to write about a man whose brother chained him up in the cowshed at certain times of the moon because he went completely mad, and it's daring to suggest that in the end that might be better for him than being carted off to a mental home, to different sorts of chains – the chain of drugs.'[38]

The difference between Silverstone and recent cultural theorists is in their different emphases on the cultural logic of the familiar/unfamiliar relationship – on whether to emphasize cultural 'adaptation' or 'ambiguation'. We could (following Silverstone) argue that popular science fiction and soap opera domesticate, *contain* and 'make bearable' the 'superculturally' unfamiliar (such as technology, medicine, etc.) within the safer world of common sense. In the case of the elderly, for instance, one could argue that 'the mythic' represents that coming together of the different temporal positionings that Giddens speaks of,[39] where the trust in 'the longue durée' of 'caring' institutions like medicine intersects with the inevitable crisis of a closing life cycle by way of the medical preoccupations and repetitions of 'ordinary-everyday' soap opera. But we could equally argue (following Hartley) that soap opera and science fiction ritually *expose* and ambiguate the 'excessive', 'nonsensical' margins (of identity, accepted sexuality, etc.) that define our culture. The 'chain of drugs' example from *A Country Practice*, for instance, *ambiguates* the separate identity of medical science as 'super-culture'.

Silverstone's emphasis, in contrast, in his analysis of the drama series *Intimate Strangers*, is on the universally *adaptive* (and so conservative) function of myth. 'Television, above all, is a machine for the reduction of the ambiguous and uncertain.'[40] The mythic, Silverstone argues, grows out of our fear of chaos, establishing social solidarities and 'making sense' out of the panic engendered by the unknown. As in the case of oral myths described by Levi-Strauss, concepts like 'garden', 'city', 'country', 'kitchen', 'bedroom' become concrete categories to think with, to order the world's contradictions. In *Intimate Strangers*, they re-order the altered relationship of masculinity and femininity caused by changing demands of work in a post-industrial society.

> Predictably enough, the answers . . . are conservative. . . . Despite his various trials, Harry remains master of the household. His position as culture-hero is restated in his plans to build their new house, and his cultural centrality is reaffirmed in the way that the various women who surround him continually act as mediators. The women are marginal beings. . . . Seduction and cure both involve negatively and positively an attempt to de-culture man, to bring him closer to nature. Correlatively these women who seduce or cure, define for man the limits of his world, the world of the masculine, the world pre-eminently of culture. . . . In every way . . . the narrative suggests withdrawal, a withdrawal above all from the extremes of city and garden, a withdrawal from nature and from super-nature and from the margins. . . . Work in terms of production is denied; women's naturalness is denied; it is in a real sense, therefore, a petit bourgeois, not to say Victorian, solution to a contemporary problem.[41]

Like Goodlad, who also equates myth and popular drama in performing 'a cognitive function in informing the members of a community about social structure',[42] Silverstone sees TV drama as acting adaptively to define a culture's boundaries. Despite his apparent rejection of Goodlad's functionalist position, and despite the undoubted usefulness of his emphasis on the symbolic structure of social existence in terms of its 'supercultural' and 'nonsensical boundaries', the problem I have with both Goodlad's and Silverstone's analyses is that the emphasis on a society speaking to itself through television draws attention away from the specifically ideological, historically located work of TV drama, and so away from its specifically controlling *and* ambiguating role. On the one hand, I would argue that in our search for ontological security the new forms of making sense are often *ambiguated*, as in the anti-positivist 'medical chains' example above, or in Radway's example of romance and female sexuality. On the other hand, I would argue that Silverstone's 'Victorian solution' is also a very particular *capitalist* and *patriarchal* solution. In *Intimate Strangers* the privileging of 'culture' (as an authentic place of withdrawal situated between 'nature' and the city as 'super-culture') defines spheres of activity – of *action* – according to gender, and in terms of consumption. As Silverstone admits 'in the home woman is the cultural producer and man is the natural consumer'.[43] Certainly, by re-stating contemporary 'industrial' problems of work and gender in terms of familiar oppositions (city/garden, male/female, culture/nature) the drama ties 'the apparent uniqueness of the moment to the substantial continuity of traditional narration'.[44] But the 'universal' opposition of nature/culture marks out, in *our* society (as Johnson argues), the 'natural' domestic priority of female production and male consumption as an alibi for social action; just as (as I have argued elsewhere) in Australian films of the 1920s, the 'country' (situated between the unproductive 'bush' and the parasitic, 'supercultural' city) marked the 'natural' site of Australian production for *English* consumption in a powerful myth of Empire.[45]

Silverstone's choice of the series *Intimate Strangers* was itself a function of his theoretical aim of relating TV drama to 'universal' categories of narrative and myth: 'this series, concerned as it is with the details of personal relationships much more than with the unequivocal action of say . . . a detective drama, might be expected to be less overt in its narrative structuring. . . . If it can be shown to be relevant to a drama series of the order of *Intimate Strangers* then that demonstration could well be expected to have greater significance.'[46] In contrast, cultural theories emphasizing the ideological function of TV drama have, not surprisingly, focused on a central state apparatus of social control: the police. By analysing the police series, this work has also been able to examine the role of particular genres in the articulation of contemporary myth.

Myth and social control: the police series

Geoff Hurd, John Dennington and John Tulloch analysing *The Sweeney* examine a similar nexus of TV drama/myth/cognitive tension as Goodlad and Silverstone. But they historicize their discussion, situating the show in terms of specific ideological work.

Hurd argues that, given the increasingly fragmented and sectionally differentiated nature of contemporary capitalism, we need something to fill in our 'half-formed picture' of how we (and others) relate to the social totality: 'the drama series, by completing the half-formed picture the viewer has of often unfamiliar sections of society, apparently resolves or disposes of contradictions within society in an acceptable manner, deploying the constituent elements of the series at "points of tension"'.[47] By 'preferring' certain narrative closures of an audience's half-knowledge over other (more subversive) ones genre, as Fiske says, 'attempts to control its polysemic potential'.[48] The half-formed picture that underpins *The Sweeney*, Hurd argues, is (i) public awareness of a rising rate of violent crime and the police's inability to contain organized crime, and (ii) an unclarified awareness of some relationship between the crime rate and police corruption.

The Sweeney relates to a very particular period of British police history and public concern 'surrounding the prosecution of the Krays, Richardson and Tibbs gangs in the sixties and the appointment of Sir Robert Mark as Commissioner of Police on an anti-corruption ticket'.[49] Dennington and Tulloch point to the close parallel between *The Sweeney*'s emphasis on the cumbersome, ineffective nature of lawful police practice, and Sir Robert Mark's public pronouncement that 'Unwillingness to make the law more effective will inevitably . . . increase the pressures on the police to use more arbitrary methods.'[50] In this situation of public concern and half-knowledge, *The Sweeney* (as a programme about the most secret aspect of the police force, the flying squad) proclaims its intention to reveal and disclose. At the same time, Hurd argues, it papers over contradictions:

> Meanings of words like corruption are redefined. . . . Society is a state of war. There is no society without law. The war is to defend the law. . . . If the law is inviolable, as Haskins states, the rules are not and the viewer is presented . . . with a context in which the police are absolved from normal rule-governed behaviour.[51]

Just as the romance cognitively explores and manages new ideas within feminism, so the police genre explores and legitimates new ideas of policing. Regan has a *mandate* for his 'entrepreneurial' violence and rule-breaking. His (tragic and partial) corruption is the price the 'good' society pays for its protection from chaos.

The Sweeney narrative positions the individualist/entrepreneurial Regan in terms of a series of oppositions that describe the current 'problem' of the police as one largely of inflexibility and bureaucracy rather than corruption. These oppositions (Police *v* Crime, Law *v* Rule, Professional *v* Organization, Authority *v* Bureaucracy, Intuition *v* Technology, Masses *v* Intellectual, Comradeship *v* Rank) not only provide the series with rich bundles of 'realistic' characterization, and justify a certain bending of the rules, but also displace analysis of real social contradictions. Divisions of class are replaced by a 'myth of classlessness':

> It is sometimes argued . . . new dividing lines of cultural distinction are coming to the fore which bear no relation to the old divisions of economic class or social status: for instance, between adults and adolescents . . . the latter inhabiting a distinctive 'teenage culture'; between 'high-brow' . . . and the 'masses'; between the retired . . . and earners; between professionals and 'organisation men' in both private and public administration; and so on.[52]

As 'professionals' (intuitive, entrepreneurial, comradely, plebeian) working against the 'organization' (both of villainy and of the police bureaucracy itself) Regan and Carter 'articulate this myth compulsively, simulating the division of a world along lines not derived from class and thereby divorcing the issues surrounding crime from any class analysis'.[53] By separating the police from any representation of the class relations of power, by denying the role of the police as an institution in the *maintenance* of those relationships (in contrast, say, to Ken Loach's representation of the police in *Days of Hope*) the cop genre does its ideological work as an agent of social control.

Genre, history and myth

One especially valuable feature of theoretical work on the cop series is the analysis of genre as a mediating factor between historical moment and social myth. As Alan Clarke argues, *The Sweeney* is certainly a child of its time, marking a shift from earlier crime series which still consensualized crime as part of the 'unusual' disruption of post-war reconstruction, to the more confrontationist politics and increasing para-military function of the police from the late 1960s on.[54] Similarly, Andrew Ross argues that '*Miami Vice* and its moment in American TV history comes at the end of a decade of attempts to reconstruct the credibility of male institutional authority from the vacuum created by Vietnam – a process of reconstruction that has, in a sense, been concomitant with the rewriting of the history of that war.'[55] But *Miami Vice* and *The Sweeney* refracted, rather than reflected, their time and, as James Donald argues, operated as an integral *part* of that historical moment 'working its ideological tensions, anxieties and fantasies into fictional forms'.[56]

Clarke points out that *The Sweeney* relates to a public's *already discursive* knowledge of the police: knowledge conveyed in other police series, in news reports and in the much publicized views of senior policemen like Sir Robert Mark. A cop series takes some of that public knowledge (carefully selected to deny the outrageous – with little or nothing about racism in the police force, or deaths in police custody) and refracts this through generic conventions, which are themselves subject to change.

Hurd, for instance, distinguishes the *centred* biography of *The Sweeney* (deploying the anomic, isolated, violent cop-as-hero in an alienated world) with *Z-Cars'* *decentred* biography (deploying a world of extended relationships, collective police work and small-time criminals). Nevertheless, these shifts in generic convention are distinct ways of handling the *same* social contradiction: the separation of the majority of people from the outcome of their actions within the social division of labour. *The Sweeney* implicitly dismisses collective (class) aspirations by way of positing effective individual action; *Z-Cars* subsumes that collective solidarity within the world of the police-station. In both cases the major contradictions faced by police (conflict with organized labour and racial groups, which are antagonisms inherent in the relations of production characterizing contemporary capitalism) are displaced to the non-structural oppositions described above.

By way of, for instance, the opposition 'masses *v* intellectual' the 'specialist' *super*-cultural world is rejected for common-sense understandings. Yet, as Silverstone says, myth must always seek accommodation between new forms of making sense and the conservative (populist) resolution. In one *Sweeney* episode ('Country Boy', which focuses centrally on the clash between street-wise 'plebeian' cops and university-educated technocrats imposed by the bureaucracy of 'the fifth floor'), the specialist policeman's knowledge is vindicated only after he has proved himself (by his intuition and personal courage) a professional cop after all.[57] 'Science' is posed ambiguously as both threat to the established (police) order and as necessary accommodation to change. The argument here, as in Silverstone, is the 'making bearable' of the threatening 'supercultural' knowledge of science. But in this case, science is related to a very specific time and genre.

The police in the 1970s and 1980s have certainly come to terms with high-tech changes, most notably in the areas of surveillance and riot control. 'Country Boy' raises and displaces problems of new technology and policing, resolving them within the continuity of core values (of police honesty, fairness and firm protectiveness) which, as Clarke points out, binds together in one genre series like *The Sweeney*, *Z-Cars* and *Dixon of Dock Green*, despite their significant differences.

Genres: binding and differentiation

1. On the one hand, TV drama, having worked to bind together the fragmented social order by completing its 'half-formed picture', then re-divides the social totality across differentiated bundles of genres. Hurd points to the way in which the police series excises two-thirds of the legal apparatus (the courts and prisons), confining these to separate genres. This has the ideological effect of inscribing police *within* the genre as agents of an immediate and self-sufficient justice. It separates representations of different institutional spheres, so decreasing the possibility of socially systematic cognition (in contrast, the controversial Australian series *Scales of Justice*, worked *out* of the first episode 'cop genre' to connect – by way of overlapping characterization – the institutional spheres of politics, law, commerce, media and crime).[58]

Because of this excision of significant logical and structural *relations* within the state apparatus, our knowledge of the real world of interlinked institutions and power is reduced. To achieve a 'reality effect', however, a heavy weight of authenticating naturalism is carried in the police series by the individualizing *psychologistic* characterization of the 'frustrations' of central heroes (of which the 'alienated' existential condition of Regan is only the most marked feature). At the same time, it is *only* the police heroes who are given this dense psychological characterization: women tend to be typed, with an emphasis on the sexual predator in *The Sweeney* and the innocently uncomprehending victim in *Z-Cars*.[59] Arguably, this *both* enables the police series to map out male fantasies central to upholding the patriarchal order, as Donald argues (in which female sexuality is presented as both a threat to purity and the purity that is threatened),[60] *and* displaces by excision (as with the case of the court-room and prison excisions) the daily 'existential' world of women into a different genre: the soap opera.

2. On the other hand, the cop genre is differentiated *within itself*. Neale argues that narrative is more than a single discourse moving from equilibrium through disturbance to new equilibrium.[61] Rather, the narrative process within any one genre simultaneously inscribes a number of discourses, and narrative equilibrium/disequilibrium is a function of the *relations of coherence and contradiction* between the discourses involved.[62] Differences generated by social change are mediated by production values: as in the appropriation of feminism as a new 'angle' of interest' for police series like *Charlie's Angels*, *Police Woman*, *Juliet*

Bravo, The Gentle Touch, and *Cagney and Lacey* with women in active or senior positions. The 'caring', social conscience discourse of these series marks a return to an earlier representation of the police, as in the late 1960s episodes of *Z-Cars* and *No Hiding Place*.[63] But at the same time it ambiguates and threatens their 'masculine' action-as-power pleasures. As Fiske argues, 'The A-Team is challenged by the admission of feminine values . . . strongly in *Remington Steele* and very threateningly indeed in *Cagney and Lacey*.'[64]

Clearly, the discourses of the 'alienated' and the 'caring' police are both available within the cop genre, to contest and contend, and be inflected by other social discourses (of welfare statism, feminism, Thatcherism, etc.) as these are appropriated by professional production values. This is probably only possible because, as Clarke says, there is a core of 'human' values that prevents the genre from splitting apart. But it is in the contestation between core discourses and contradictory ones (representing police corruption, the threats of high technology, feminist critiques of a patriarchal culture, etc.) that the narrative trajectories of equilibrium/disturbance/new equilibrium are played out, and in this way the genre is kept fresh and 'socially responsive'. It is by way of discursive tensions *within the developing genre* that the exploration of the ambiguities of social boundaries proceeds. And it is in this generic contestation of social discourses that the historical moment is refracted rather than reflected, with the possibility for 'outrageous' or 'excessive' shifts in the generic paradigm always remaining open, with series like *Law and Order* and *Scales of Justice* concentrating on the corruption of the police, and leading to major police protests.

More often, though, this refraction is a re-working of dominant myths. Bennett and Woollacott point to the way in which the James Bond novels work (for a British audience) *out* of the imperialist spy-thriller (equating 'nation' with the ruling class) which it complicates with 'a number of overlapping disequilibrating/equilibrating tendencies'.[65] Whereas the spy-thriller novels of Buchan and McNeile 'reconfirm effortlessly a substantially uncontested ideology of Englishness', James Bond works to *reconstruct* 'Englishness', as Britain slips from world power status after the Second World War. By positioning the English 'nation' under the sign of a new 'professional' (*worked-for*) competence, the Bond novels promoted 'a certain ideological shift in facilitating an adjustment from one mythic representation of Britain's ruling elite to another, and from one mythic conception of Englishness to another'.[66] At the same time, in putting his 'girls' back in 'place' in a 'patriarchal order defined, socially and sexually, in relation to men', Bond novels 'do not simply confirm established ideologies and fictional representations of femininity but reform them, fashioning a new construction of femininity tailored to the requirements of a promiscuous male sexuality' in a newly 'liberated' era.[67]

In this view *genre* itself operates at the fault-lines of society, so that, just as the popularity of the police genre relates to dominant 'law and order' discourse of the 1970s, so too,

> The Bond films operated in a similar fashion in the early 1960's . . . both to shift and stabilise subject identities at a time when existing ideological constructions had been placed in doubt and jeopardy, when . . . the articulating principles of hegemony were in disarray and alternatives had not been successfully established.[68]

So the 'professional', 'liberated' Bond was captured for new 'meritocratic' principles in the detente 1960s, but could still be '"floated" from this textual and ideological base' to be given a 'law and order' inflection in the 1970s (together with the 'Bondian' *Doctor Who* of this same period),[69] then to be 'pushed into an increasingly comic mode'[70] (again paralleling *Doctor Who* in the late 1970s), before being 'reactivated in relation to the re-emerging Cold War of the 1980s and the flickering reawakening of British post-imperialist ambitions'.[71]

In Bennett and Woollacott's view 'periods of generic change and innovation in popular fiction often coincide with those in which the ideological articulations through which hegemony was previously secured are no longer working to produce popular consent'.[72] The 'refraction' of history in which genre engages can be defined more precisely as 'the services it performs . . . acting as a catalyst enabling other ideological forms to be rearticulated in a new configuration'.[73]

Thus the complexity of discourses within genres allows the 'excessive' to be exposed and contained at the same time, in the process of rearticulating ideological forms. Two further points are worth making here, prior to elaboration later. The first is that the relationship between 'outrageous' and 'contained' within popular culture cannot be mapped onto a simple distinction between 'progressive' and 'reactionary'. As Bennett and Woollacott point out, since the Bond 'girls' have always functioned as objects of male desire, they have never represented a 'free' female sexuality. 'Nevertheless, in the light of the harshly constrained sexuality of women in earlier British films, tutored into submission to duty, the family and domesticity or to a career ending in punishment and death . . . the guilt-free but purely sexual relationship between Bond and the girl could be seen as a welcome break with past conventions.'[74] Drawing on notions of 'reading formations' that I will consider later, they comment that 'the space of popular fiction possesses an ideological economy which is more complex . . . and ambivalent, than some orthodox Marxist approaches imply'.[75] Rather than simply imposing dominant ideologies (as earlier analyses in this chapter tended to suggest), popular fictions ambiguate while they also control, articulating 'the relations between a series of ideologies (subordinate as well as dominant), overlapping them . . . so as to bring about certain movements and reformations of subjectivity'.[76]

The second point is that which I refer to later as the semiotic density of performed texts further enables the 'outrageous' and 'contained' to cohabit. Gillian Skirrow points to the tension in *Widows* between discourses carried by performance and *mise-en-scène* on the one hand and those carried by violence and action on the other, so, she believes, instituting a different kind of pleasure for women viewers in the close relationship of the female characters. Though reactionary in its representation of homosexuality, *Widows'* use of the *mise-en-scène* of film noir (where women were active and ambitious), and its self-referential stress on performance (as women *learn to act* as male gangsters, leading to 'a de-naturalisation of the signifier of male sexuality'),[77] means a use of *and* questioning of the conventions of the male crime series.

In analysing *Minder*, Michael Winterbottom relates this generic organization of 'repetition' and 'difference' (again, a decentring of crime action, this time through a comic blurring of the crime series' rigid opposition between criminal and police) to professional practice at Euston Films. What is interesting in his analysis is the discursive play between *organizational* elements of repetition (the continuity of technical and production personnel; the generic typing of writers) and difference (the greater autonomy of a highly demarcated film production, and particularly of freelance writers and directors) in enabling an 'implied critique of Arthur's comic Thatcherism'.[78]

The analysis of complexly *contending* discourses (as a definition of genre) opens up, for the first time in this chapter, a systematic way to examine the ambiguating (as against socially controlling) aspect of TV drama. Potentially, too, it restores active human agency to drama-as-myth analysis, as particular audiences (Skirrow) and production personnel (Winterbottom) take their place in the transformative *process* of genre. These analyses of genre suggest that no TV drama (even a genre as tied to notions of 'law and order' as the police/crime series) is as uniformly successful in ideologically closing off the 'half-formed picture' as some critics suggest. Further, as Fiske points out (see Introduction), in contrast to myths about the police, representations of science on television allow stronger challenges to dominant myth. In the final part of this chapter I will return to analyses of science fiction to focus on theories which re-open *viewing and production* as two potential spaces for a resistant agency.

Science fiction and audience pleasures: *plaisir* and *jouissance*

Like other theorists we have discussed, John Fiske, in his analysis of science fiction, points to the ideological work of the popular TV series, *Doctor Who*, in resolving social contradictions. *Doctor Who is* composed of a number of contending discourses that define how it is told: a political discourse which sets the values of liberal democracy against those of totalitarianism; an economic discourse that naturalizes free trade as the obviously 'right' system in contrast to the villains' monopolization of mineral resources; a discourse of individualism that softens the authoritarianism of science; a discourse of morality which humanistically (perhaps religiously) establishes the Doctor as 'good'. Not all of these discourses are inevitably closed off in favour of capitalist democracy. In Australia, for instance, a story emphasizing the villainy of 'alien' monopolization of mineral resources might be received and articulated within an already circulating counter-myth (of environmentalism).

But Fiske's emphasis here (like Silverstone's) is on the controlling rather than ambiguating nature of popular genres. In general it is the multiple interweaving of discourses which *saves* the text for the status quo.

> The discourse of morality functions to close off those other discourses whose values are more open to question, particularly those politico-economic ones that are specific to a western industrialised democracy.[79]

Fiske argues that the effect of the popular TV narrative on the viewer is conservative, occluding potential knowledgeability about contradiction and exploitation arising from the viewer's own social experience. It is social experience rather than the text that is composed of contradictory discourses.

> Our social experience is . . . harder to read than a text, because it is fraught with . . . internal contradictions and sites of ideological struggle. . . . Reading a text . . . is easier by far, and the greater closure within it is constantly working to reassure and convince us that this easy reading is . . . totally adequate.[80]

For Fiske (in this analysis), texts are popular precisely because they obviate that uncertainty about the adequacy of the discourses we use to understand the world. The text is believable – and also confirms our social experience as believable – 'because its discourses are part of the ideology of common sense'.[81]

Popular TV drama is 'not escapist but mythic: . . . it enables and encourages the reader to make a particular kind of sense of . . . existence. The reader and the text are both active and the text becomes popular only when the two activities are mutually supportive, and when they can be replicated to make sense of that much broader, more open text that is our social experience.'[82]

In his textual analysis of *Doctor Who* Fiske finds no answer to his concluding question: 'how can popular art be other than reactionary?'[83] However, in his more recent work, Fiske has shifted his emphasis from textual analysis and the 'conforming spectator' to *audience* 'pleasures of subversion'. These pleasures are available as a condition both of the text (even in the most reactionary of genres, such as the police series) and of audience sub-cultures. While I have insisted on the central importance of critical theory's stress on ideological control, I have also suggested at various points in this chapter the ambiguating nature of popular genres. Fiske in *Television Culture* takes this further, drawing on Barthes' distinction between '*plaisir*' ('a mundane pleasure that is essentially confirming, particularly of one's sense of identity'[84]) and '*jouissance*' ('a pleasure of the body, experienced through heightened sensualities that relate it to human nature rather than culture'[85]) to argue that popular genres generate pleasures beyond and against the bounds of myth.

While Silverstone may be right to argue that the narratives of TV drama investigate cognitively (and conservatively) the boundaries of culture and nature (of 'common sense' and 'non-sense'), the material *body* of popular texts (in Fiske's view) may contest that closure. In an extension of Skirrow's argument, Fiske suggests that the close-ups of soap opera work against narrative closure. The 'intense materiality of emotion in the magnified quiver of the mouth's corner, the narrowing of the eyes, the breathy wetness of the voice may produce tears in the viewer quite independent of, or even counter to, the narrative of what is said, of what is felt and the way they work on subjectivity'.[86] This *jouissance* 'of reading with the body, of establishing a presence that is outside culture, outside ideology because it is not concerned with meaning (either of self or of the world) but with presence and intensity'[87] is available, Fiske argues, in even the most conservative of police series, where 'the fast editing, the dislocation of narrative sequence, the disruption of the diegesis may produce the sensation of fragmentariness . . . of the physical uniqueness of experience rather than its meaning'.[88] Fiske doesn't discuss science fiction in relation to *jouissance*, but one is reminded of SF experiences like *2001* when he speaks of fast editing, narrative dislocation, the sensation of fragmentariness and the *physicality* of experience. In *2001* (and its spin-offs) future technology and massive, uncontrolled speed establish their own eroticism and sensuality – certainly in the view of audiences that return to the film again and again for its 'psychedelic' kick (*Doctor Who*, of course, draws on *2001* for the 'vortex experience' of its opening).

The world of outside or 'anti-culture', which is exposed but contained (according to Silverstone) by the cognitive preoccupation of modern myth, returns as physicality. In Fiske's analysis, the cop show's 'sensuality' of playing with gold and flicking through banknotes, and its 'eroticism' of loading, checking and feeling the weight of gun in hand, certainly promote the confirming '*plaisir*' of the dominant myths of patriarchal capitalism, but they also (in Baudrillard's sense of the term) 'seduce' it.[89]

> Their sensuous imperative is so strong they *are* our experience . . . *our* pleasure. Denying the narrative domain of these objects dislocates them from the ideological one as well. The pleasure here is not in resisting ideology, nor in challenging it with a 'better' one, but in avoiding it, in liberating oneself from it.[90]

Fiske acknowledges his debt to Baudrillard's notion of the 'hyperreal' here: the endless world of simulation which isolates and privatizes individuals in a closed circuit of images where it is impossible to distinguish between the spectacle and the real – indeed, in which there *is* no real. Baudrillard's theory, however, ludicrously reduces the power of agency. As with the most reductive of critical theory, Baudrillard's 'hyperreal' is a condition of mass 'hyperconformity'. 'Messages are given to them, they only want some sign, they idolize the play of signs and stereotypes, they idolize any content so long as it resolves itself into a spectacular sequence.'[91] What saves Fiske from this over-emphasis on media manipulation is his insistence on the *agentive* mobilization of pleasure in relation to counter-myth. Despite his comments about pleasure 'not resisting ideology', it is, in the last resort, crucial to Fiske that even '*jouissance*' operates within the *social* context of audiences. Thus the hegemonic distinction 'between the public-political world of the man and the private-domestic world of the woman' which, as we have seen, has generated separate popular genres, is itself mobilized for the resistant pleasures of '*jouissance*': 'The privatization of pleasure allows for its articulation in the body and the senses, and its feminization allows it to be articulated with the culture of the repressed.'[92]

Fiske's later emphasis, then, is on *audiences*. He does examine TV drama texts for signs of generic conflict.

> In *Cagney and Lacey* the masculine 'end' of the narrative is often neglected in favour of a feminine emphasis on the process by which that end is achieved. . . . *Hill Street Blues* with its multiple plots and characters, its rapid switching from plot to plot, its sense that characters live between episodes, its 'memory' from episode to episode combines many of the elements of soap opera with the action and achievement characteristic of masculine narrative. It is, significantly, one of the most popular cop shows with women.[93]

But the focus is still on audiences, with a relationship suggested between form (male narrative 'closure' versus female narrative 'openness') and gendered distinctions of sexuality within the audience (male 'climax' versus female 'process').

The representative genres (of 'climax' and 'process') that Fiske considers here are cop shows and soap opera – with their various degrees of hybridization (as in *Cagney and Lacey* and *Hill Street Blues*) seen as the articulation of the 'culture of the oppressed' among women. Significantly, he pays no serious attention to science fiction (as another 'male' genre). What then of his earlier discussion of the counter-myths of science? His emphasis on '*jouissance*' in 'male' and 'female' genres takes us no closer to understanding why in SF 'There are more evil scientists than good ones and science causes more problems than it solves.'[94] To understand how popular science fiction 'can be other than reactionary'[95] we need also to examine (as Winterbottom's analysis of *Minder* suggests) the hybrid and contradictory aspects of popular series in terms of *production* ambiguities and conflicts.

Counter-myth and ambiguity: science fiction in production

In contrast to Fiske's study, Tulloch and Alvarado's analysis of *Doctor Who* is a production study which examines production ambiguities and conflicts as inflections of deeper discursive tensions situated historically within the popular genre itself. For them *Doctor Who* is neither simply conservative (as in Fiske) nor is it a hybrid form simply because of current ratings needs (as in Fiske's analysis of *Hill Street Blues*). Tulloch and Alvarado point also to a dual potential for progressive meanings in SF in general (and *Doctor Who* in particular), depending on two historically dominant myths operating within the genre.

  (i) On the one hand, there is the SF genre's epistemologically realist potential to construct other worlds ('absent paradigms') which challenge the common-sense paradigms of our own. In this respect SF as a genre is 'super-cultural' and conjectural, estranging the reader from the 'ordinary-everyday' of common sense.

> Potentially this 'other' world of science fiction is, as Angenot points out, a place that (though 'fictive' and 'delusive') offers a coherent and utopically estranging light on the audience's empirical world . . . in order to see beneath its surface more 'realistically' – a tendency which is compounded by the anti-individuating and 'epic' character of science fiction, its desire to speak about entire cultures and worlds. . . .[96]

Tulloch and Alvarado examine the allegiance of SF's alternative utopias to the Positivist tradition of scientific realism, as represented in literature by Zola, Chekhov and Wells. This 'supercultural art', they argue, was 'captured, in terms of authorship, product and audience, by the fraction of the middle class whose wealth consisted in their education, and who were by no means always in accord either with owners of capital or with the proletariat'.[97] The scientific-realist tradition put its faith, as Elliott *et al.* note, in 'alternative' discourses (the counter-myth of social engineering among critical professionals and academics) to oppose the excesses of *both* capitalism and revolution. This was always a counter-myth of intellectual professionals: 'The hero is now a doctor, a scientist *in* the world and *in* the universe.'[98] The 'utopic' strand of SF, then, originally represented the identity confirming '*plaisir*' of a social group which saw itself as marginal to *both* the dominant ('official' and 'oppositional') myths of the late nineteenth century.[99] This degree of ambiguity between the owners of financial and cultural capital (the capitalists and the intellectuals) needs noting, for instance, in relation to my too easy identification earlier in this chapter of the technical middle-class SF audience with the ruling class.

(ii) On the other hand, there was a different intellectual tendency, the mad 'hero' of Romanticism, working beyond the *other* (distorted, unacceptable, anti-cultural) boundary of common sense. This was the central character of Victorian Gothic, the strangely experimenting outcast standing for the human spirit against the dull, 'ordinary-everyday' and consensual state of social contingency. In so far as this outcast rejected the reifying masks of social role and conditioning to release the 'true', active self, he was a hero; but in so far as he left the status quo for the solipsism of the laboratory he was a villain. In this way the Romantic-Gothic text both exposed and contained the 'nonsensical' margins of common sense, marking and ambiguating the boundaries of forbidden sexuality and the anti-social. The Romantic project deployed the hero-as-villain, and contributed in important ways to the fantastic which flows through the history of popular SF.

The fantastic opposes the entire game of knowing, and of possessing by naming. . . . The demonic is no longer that which threatens the hero, but that which threatens the concept 'hero' by threatening the *difference* between it and the image of the character it is opposed to. . . . The demonic is that which dissolves the certainty of 'reality' by destroying the system of differences of the language which constitutes it.[100]

A central feature of the narrative equilibrium/disequilibrium of popular SF has been, Tulloch and Alvarado argue, this tension between scientific cognition and romantic difference.

This ambivalence is played out across the syntagmatic and paradigmatic planes of the narrative – which we can now define as between the quest for nomination (through cognition, control: 'knowing') and the madness of 'un-knowing'. . . . *Doctor Who* as science fiction must be understood in terms of both: (i) its drive towards the coherent, signified as a verifiable empirical world . . . and (ii) its recognition of incoherence in the fictionality of 'naming' the ego (. . . the constantly regenerated selves, the doppelgangers).[101]

Science fiction is determined as a genre in the dangerous play between its two 'margins': of cognition (superculture) and incoherence (anti-culture). Popular science fiction habituates but never denies the possibilities (and pleasures) of the unfamiliar, the margins beyond common sense of the 'specialized' and the 'nonsensical'. Both these 'margins beyond' common sense (of a politically estranging realism, and of meaning-disrupting fantasy) are constantly available for inflection within TV science fiction; and this is where Tulloch and Alvarado's production study relates to their analysis of generic ambiguity. They point to the way in which *both* these different oppositional possibilities are called up by specific production workers at certain moments in the show's institutional history, despite its general tendency to an habituated naturalism and the 'empiricism of robot-spotting'.

For instance, the tradition of scientific realism was drawn on in different production eras of *Doctor Who*: 'The Robots of Death' (produced by Philip Hinchcliffe) 'in which an effete profit-hungry ruling elite is decimated by a robot revolution' and 'the Doctor represents the "middle class" resort to humanity against "alienation" and "revolution"';[102] and 'The Sun Makers' (produced by Graham Williams), an Orwellian-type critique of a capitalist world dominated by one trans-global company.[103]

Between the Hinchcliffe and Williams production eras, however, lay the very damaging public attack on *Doctor Who* for violence and horror by Mary Whitehouse's National Viewers' and Listeners' Association. The Gothic Horror signature of Hinchcliffe's period (which had allowed the series most consistent and successful deployment of the Doctor/doppelganger theme) was, as a result, replaced by comedy under Williams, and by a heavily signposted inter-textual signature intended to appeal to a 'bonus' film-buff audience ('The Sun Makers', for instance, played on the theme and *mise-en-scène* of *Metropolis*). Both production factors (Hinchcliffe's 'Gothic' signature, Williams' 'comedy' one) and audience factors (Hinchcliffe's turn to something ' a little bit more scary . . . to try and win over more adults',[104] Williams' use of inter-textual references to capture a 'bonus' audience 'by tapping into various popular areas'[105]) mediated these 'utopic' stories.

In contrast, Fiske's understanding of syntagmatic dominance (and audience pleasures) in *Doctor Who* seems altogether too cosy, ignoring both production history and the dialectic of 'unspeakability' and consensus (mapped out across syntagmatic and paradigmatic planes of the narrative) that constitutes popular culture. Arguably other 'male' genres are informed by similar narrative tensions. Donald, for instance, argues that *The Sweeney* works through narratives hostile to 'bisexuality and its implicit subversion of the order of fixed sexual identities'.[106] Like *Doctor Who*, it plays with fears at the loss of difference – in this case between genders. 'It is this entertaining fear that is the investment made by the audience. As Moretti observes of the monstrous terrors of Frankenstein and Dracula, "it is a fear one needs: the price one pays for coming contentedly to terms with a social body based on irrationality and menace".'[107]

Similarly, Bennett and Woollacott say of James Bond, that 'M represents the phallus as the privileged signifier in relationship to which sexual difference is defined just as he represents the authority of the Law and of Knowledge.'[108] In contrast, Dr No is a doppelganger for Bond's rebellious tendencies, 'in . . . that his biography usually evidences a complete lack of respect for the father and . . . all forms of authority'.[109] Further, like the 'girl', the villain is sexually aberrant. The villain threatens Bond's understanding of the difference between 'good' and 'evil', 'threatens to de-centre him, to pull him out of the ideological places into which he has been stitched . . . in the service of England and the patriarchal phallus'.[110] The 'girl' requiring to be 're-positioned' correctly by Bond in compensation for the absence of her own father, 'threatens to divert the phallic power Bond needs in his contest with the villain'.[111] Hence the 'crisis' of the narrative.

To Bennett and Woollacott's analysis I add two further points. First, the aberrant Dr No (as doppelganger) carries within himself the long-history of Romantic discourse challenging Identity, Law and Cognition. Second, because the (aristocratic/amateur) M himself represents the 'outmoded' hegemonic principle of the Bond texts, the novels can never completely re-establish clear distinctions of 'hero' and 'villain'. 'Father', 'Law' and 'Knowledge' have lost their uniquely privileged status in defining 'difference'. The long history of Romanticism within English popular culture and the historical moment of transition to 'professional-meritocratic' capitalism conjoin: a narrative crisis indeed. The class/culture of M's England has become as dully laughable as Doctor Who's world of Gallifrey,[112] and *some* of that laughter is at the behest of popular forces and social change. It is in that play between historical change, generic inflection and production history that 'popular art can be other than reactionary'.

Folk and fairy tales: signs of Utopia

Tulloch and Alvarado relate the historical shifts and retrogressions of realist, reflexive, fantastic and naturalistic SF in *Doctor Who* to the particular institutional history of the BBC, to its location as popular drama between 'quality' and 'mass' notions of public service, to its construction of SF 'mystery' as an absence of television's habitual 'here-and-now' actuality, to its susceptibility as 'children's TV' to powerful public pressure groups, as well as to the different professional discourses within the production team and the generic play within the narrative. They attempt, in other words, to examine genre in the context of industrial agency and process. A more general attempt to examine questions of control and resistance in terms of production agency and the operations of the culture industry itself, is Zipes' analysis of folk and fairy tales within modern media forms. For Zipes,

> Once there was a time when folk tales were part of communal property and told with . . . fantastic insights by gifted storytellers who gave vent to the frustration of the common people. . . . Not only did the tales . . . help bridge a gap in their understanding of social problems . . . but their aura illuminated the possible fulfilment of Utopian longings.[113]

Zipes does not take the populist view that because they emerged out of the 'people', folk tales were inherently progressive.

> Here the notion of the *folk* should not be glamorized or mystified as an abstract concept representing goodness or revolutionary forces.

Sociologically speaking the folk were the great majority of people, generally agrarian workers, who were often illiterate and nurtured their own forms of culture in opposition to that of the ruling class and yet often reflecting the same ideology, even if from a different class perspective. . . . These classes had practically no opportunity to resist the increasing exploitation. . . . Thus they could only conceive a Utopian image of a better life for themselves.[114]

In this sense they were like Radway's romance readers. But crucially, for Zipes, the potential for change was an *interactive* one.

Gifted narrators told the tales to audiences who actively participated in their transmission by posing questions, suggesting changes and circulating the tales among themselves.[115]

This volatile, interactive relationship was lost, Zipes believes, as first the expansion of publishing, and then the electronic media, led to a culture industry and the instrumentalization of fantasy.

The emphasis on play, alternative forms of living, pursuing dreams and daydreams, experimentation, striving for the golden age – this stuff of which fairy tales were (and are) made challenged the rationalistic purpose and regimentation of life to produce for profit and expansion of capitalist industry.[116]

Experiences of contradiction, desires for security and social solidarity, were subtly transmuted (as in our family serials example earlier) into commoditization. 'The narrative voice is no longer responsive to an active audience but manipulates it according to the vested interests of the state and private industry.'[117]

The contrast Zipes makes is between fantasy (as a *use value*) and myth, which is a product of instrumental reason.

As Walter Benjamin has emphasised, 'a great story-teller will always be rooted in the people, since he or she has the practical task of communicating wisdom as a use value to the people, and such mediation can effectively bring audiences closer to nature and endow them with a sense of possibilities for self-realization. . . .'[118]

So Zipes asks, 'Given the extent to which the state and private industry have collaborated to increase their power to administer and bureaucratize our public and private lives through technology', has reason 'become so instrumentalized for the purpose of capitalist realization that human beings have become depleted of their inherent creative and critical potential to shape the destiny of humankind?'[119]

Zipes tends to over-emphasize the 'regimentation' of audiences by television. Fiske, for example, would insist that television *is* an interactive medium, and that the active 'gossip' of audiences around TV drama *is* a way of 'posing questions, suggesting changes and circulating the tales among themselves'. Nevertheless, while underestimating audience agency, Zipes' theory is important in pointing to pockets of radical agency within the 'culture industry' itself. Following Negt and Kluge (against the pessimistic view of the Frankfurt School about the culture industry) Zipes puts his hopes in the possibility of a 'consciousness industry' to reproduce and circulate the genuinely liberating fantasy of the folk tale. Like Lovell, Negt and Kluge posit the existence of 'blocks of authentic needs and wants of human beings which are reflected in the use values produced by humans and which resist total commod-ification'.[120] Even mass-produced commodities like *Snow White and the Seven Dwarfs* and *Star Wars*, despite their conservative ideological function at specific historical moments, still contain a positive glimpse of Utopia. 'In *Snow White* . . . the little people and the frail Snow White unite to overthrow the oppressive rule of the evil queen.'[121]

Radway also, of course, finds positive glimpses of Utopia even in the privatized reading situation of the romance novel. But, as Zipes rightly argues (and Radway also admits), 'folk and fairy tales *per se* have no actual emancipatory power unless they are used actively to build a social bond through oral communication, social interaction, dramatic adaptation, agitorial cultural work, etc.'.[122] Hence he affirms Negt and Kluge's notion of a plebeian public sphere (including service workers, intellectuals, marginal and oppressed groups, in addition to the tradi-tional working class) constructing a consciousness sector within the interstices of the culture industry. Working out of 'the very collective nature of the technological mass media', these might then mobilize, interactively, those 'blocks of real life' which contain a complex of contradictory tendencies against the instrumentalist tendencies of capitalism.

It is to that area of potential collective action at the very heart of the culture industry – in popular TV drama – that I will turn in the next chapters by looking at Trevor Griffiths' and Ken Loach's work. On the one hand, Loach does engage, as story teller, with workers in an attempt to interact with and mobilize them in a new actualization of history; on the other hand, Griffiths argues for a collectivization of TV production against TV's 'controllers':

What one looks for is a working process which involves everybody . . . who works on a piece and involves them totally. . . . This is a huge conglomerate of different sorts of craft skills and talents and histories. As they are presently constituted within the TV industry, they are all isolates. . . . When you have tasted the other, when you have embraced the always messy but rewarding collective process as for example we began to achieve on *Bill Brand* . . . then you begin to sense what is possible working in TV.[123]

In focusing on myth and genre (particularly the 'masculine' genres of science fiction and cop series) in this chapter, I have wanted to give due weight to critical theory's emphasis on media control, conservative ideology and the commodification of culture. At the same time, though, I have wanted to point to the ambiguating quality of myth-construction; and in particular to emphasize the potential for resistant discourses *both* in production and in reception. The following chapters will take this emphasis on agency further. Myth, Barthes argues, is the process of transforming historical agency into the 'it's always been that way' of 'human nature'. Myths, Sally Potter says, 'rob us of our history'; in contrast, I will look in Chapter 3 at representations of historical agency as a way of 'reperceiving the world', of 'dreaming about the way that we think things could be'.

Part Two

Authored drama: agency as 'strategic penetration'

3 'Reperceiving the world': making history

I try to occupy the space provided by character and terrain . . . and to get inside that sociologically, psychologically and politically – and *historically* . . . opening up categories of understanding that are not available in news and current affairs items, where things tend to be bracketed and catalogued and categorised in fairly narrow definitions. I think drama is a perfect space to find ways of understanding and reperceiving the world.

Trevor Griffiths[1]

Most of the analysis of the 'space' of TV drama in the book so far has been of popular works. As I pointed out in Chapter 1, in the area of television analysis until recently most attention was given to 'serious' (i.e. news, current affairs) genres over TV drama. But *within* the study of TV drama itself there has been a different picture, since in this case it is the 'serious' or 'quality' product that has had the least attention. John Caughie argues that part of the hesitancy of theorists in engaging with this area 'may come from a reasonable suspicion of the way in which the cultural prestige of "serious drama" is used by television and television reviewing'.[2]

This emphasis on the *appropriation* of drama by conservative controllers and critics is an important one. Sylvia Lawson quotes one critic from the quality Australian newspaper, the *Age* discussing *The Dismissal* (a highly regarded dramatic reconstruction of the sacking of the Australian Prime Minister, Gough Whitlam, by the Governor-General, Sir John Kerr):

Its success will depend on whether Australians will want to sit down and watch six hours of stuff which is . . . not *Sons and Daughters*. It will require concentration.[3]

It is this familiar 'high culture' discourse (positioning 'serious drama' as *other* than 'mindless soap') that radical theorists have recently been challenging.[4] But in its turn this new polemic on behalf of popular television has frequently been just as quickly dismissive of 'serious' or 'authored' drama (for representing 'élite' high culture). In fact, as Elliott *et al.* point out, the area of authored drama is potentially a space for alternative or even oppositional discourse. On the face of it, it seems curious that radical critics who would welcome an authored documentary from, say, John Pilger on CIA and MI5 involvement in the sacking of Whitlam, are often more hesitant about welcoming an authored drama on the same theme. The reason for this, as Caughie says, is partly radical critics' questioning of the notion of authorship itself as part of their 'assessment of the increasingly marginal place which theatre and theatrical forms occupy in present culture';[5] and partly because 'quality' drama on TV *has* had a tendency to represent an élite and ideologically conservative culture.

Sylvia Lawson, commenting on the *Age* review of *The Dismissal*, argues that the critic's frequent references to Greek tragedy and *Hamlet* 'collaborate with the implied concept of the audience as one which would pack out a visit of the Royal Shakespeare Company, an audience accustomed to, and requiring, the classic narrative in which the pivots are not politics, but fate and destiny'.[6] Further, the *mise-en-scène* of *The Dismissal* itself locates *which* 'fate' quite clearly:

> grand room sets with attendant butlers, full-length drapes, chandeliers and cut-glass; beyond them, manicured gardens. These place the series, and us, in the discourses of quality TV as elaborated in many years of BBC practice; the audience is positioned as one which seeks to be regaled by tales from above . . . for the noblesse oblige of *A Horseman Riding By*, for *Upstairs, Downstairs* (with its aborted politics) and of course for *Brideshead Revisited*. . . . The notion of an audience which has to be ritually admitted to the corridors of power (again *Upstairs*) is also that of an audience which is by definition quite powerless.[7]

The Dismissal, according to Lawson, inscribes a variety of audiences: a high-culture audience more at home at 'serious' theatre; the 'watching audience for magnificent weddings and funerals'[8] vicariously admitted to the homes of the élite; and Zipes' 'instrumentalized' media audience as *represented* in the series, 'the population whose lives are presumed to be flat and colourless', needing the shocks and shots of media hype 'in indefinite succession' to arouse it out of presumed passivity.[9]

In Lawson's analysis (as in George Brandt's), 'quality' historical series operate mythically: how can they then work as 'dreams about the way things could be', a genre for 'reperceiving the world'?

The historical series

As Stuart Cunningham argues, television typically represents history either as nostalgia or as epiphenomenon: 'on the one hand, history as radically other, the sealed past – a lost Eden of traditional values (e.g. *The Sullivans*) . . . on the other hand, history as utterly familiar, the banal quotidian (e.g. news and current affairs programming)'.[10] Both 'comforting nostalgia' and 'superficial nominalism' obscure history as a *relationship* between past and present – and not simply in news and historical soap opera. As Crofts and Craik say of *The Dismissal*, though both the CIA and the media are mentioned as part of the tapestry of power in 1970s Australia, their role as historical *agents* (in the continuing context of Chile, Nicaragua and elsewhere) is either underplayed or obscured, and politics is recast 'from institutional practices to individual behaviours (ideas, whims, lobbying, etc.)'.[11]

Nevertheless, as Cunningham rightly says:

It would be a mistake . . . to position *The Dismissal* wholly within this field. . . . The excessively hybrid form of the text renders it difficult to place simply within established conventions of television drama. The excessiveness of the prologue establishes a difficult stylistic asymmetry with the rest of the material: Gotterdammerung sequences lifted by Dr Miller from Mad Max 2. . . . A left Labor stance, tantamount to calling for a radical reform of the Constitution . . . tacked on at the end in the midst of further metaphysics about time's winnowing.[12]

The hybrid nature of *The Dismissal* as history, and its willingness to engage with questions *concerning* historical reconstruction, Cunningham argues, relate to its non-unitary sources. Drawing on books by both Whitlam and Governor-General Kerr, *The Dismissal*'s sources are 'an open field of contestation'.[13] However, most radical critics have argued that its generic interpellation of the audience for *Brideshead* (by way of *mise-en-scène* and tragic theme), its use of documentary-style voice-over whose 'sonorous tone . . . underscores the dramatic irony of Whitlam as a tragic hero',[14] and above all its *appropriation* by TV journalists in terms of arguments about historical veracity and the ethics of doco-drama, have tended to drown out its debate about historical reconstruction and the relationship between past and present. In the end, Cunningham agrees, *The Dismissal* appropriates recent history for a primarily fatalistic, individualistic and élitist view of human action;

and here the mini-series takes over from the Australian period film of the 1970s in signifying 'taste, quality and (national) culture'.[15]

In a later article, however, Cunningham is more positive about the 'textual innovativeness' of the Australian historical mini-series as compared with the Australian period film, suggesting that other series (*The Last Bastion, The Cowra Breakout, Vietnam, Bodyline*) share *The Dismissal*'s ' "hybridization" of documentary and dramatic modes' and its 'multi-perspectivism'.

> Almost half of *Cowra Breakout* is spent on the Japanese 'side', encouraging empathy with their point of view. . . . *Vietnam* . . . insists on Vietnamese perspectives and shows them to be as fraught with divisions as Australian positions with regard to the war and the personal tensions it provoked. Further, it is arguable that these mini-series took seriously the radical historiographical dictum that 'the past is only interesting politically because of something which touches us in the present'.[16]

These mini-series, Cunningham argues, unlike Australian period films, deal with the *makers* rather than the fated victims of history. Moreover, because of their 'multiplication of authorizing perspectives' and their insertion into an often 'known' history (as in the case of the Whitlam sacking), 'far from being lulled, many viewers regard mini-series as significant – verifiable or falsifiable historical *arguments*, if the amount and nature of public correspondence generated around them is taken into account'.[17] Hence the mini-series displaces '*events* by *causation* and *consequence*', and invites the viewer into the text 'as knowledgeable citizen, rather than distracted consumer'.[18]

Cunningham intends his arguments to apply to the mini-series form in general, its 'hybridization' creating as many 'definitional problems' (despite its 'quality' signature) as, for Fiske, there are in *Cagney and Lacey* and *Hill Street Blues*. However, it is not clear how *Cowra Breakout* and *Vietnam* differ significantly in their 'multiplication of authorizing perspectives', in their multiculturalism, or in their invitation to viewers 'as knowledgeable citizens' from the 'A Touch of Class' episode of *A Country Practice* that I discussed in Chapter 1. How, in other words, do these features differentiate the mini-series from soap opera?

A lot of weight here rests on Cunningham's claims that the hybridization of form in historical mini-series creates an excess, as 'drama comments on the archive, and archive comments on drama', thereby weakening the usual use of archival footage as a naturalistic 'recognition effect'. Yet the same 'fastidious attention to historical verisimilitude' which Cunningham sees as part of the mini-series' institutional signature (as up-market, 'quality' product) invites the invocation of an *empiricist* history which works quite against any 'definitional problems' its hybridization might provoke – as a significant part of the public communication around both *The Dismissal* and *Days of Hope* attest.[19]

I will take up this problem of empiricist historiography and the 'authorizing' use of archival sources later, particularly in relation to Trevor Griffiths' *The Last Place On Earth*, which focuses quite directly on the problem of historical reconstruction. Here I would suggest that the qualities of mini-series which Cunningham draws attention to themselves need to be given a cultural and historical location. The *particular* Australian mini-series he discusses, taken as a cluster, do propose a re-reading of Australian history; and they have done so at a time when many Australians (in the period from Whitlam's 'new nationalism' to the Bicentennial) *have* become uneasily 'knowledgeable citizens'. Reporting the Bicentennial Australia Day celebrations under the page 1 headline 'Day of contradictions', the *Sydney Morning Herald* said:

> Descendants of the Europeans celebrated 200 years of settlement, while descendants of those who had been here 200 times as long looked on. . . . Such are the contradictions of Australia. A new society in an old land; an old people living on the fringes of the new society.[20]

At a time when the original white invasion and appropriation of aboriginal land has become a high profile media event nationally and internationally, Australian mini-series have constructed a history where the imperialism to be resisted is British or North American (*The Last Bastion, Bodyline, Anzacs, Land of Hope, Vietnam, The Dismissal*) rather than 'white', and where military, economic and political events are mediated by a liberal ('multi-perspectival') multiculturalism (*Waterfront, The Cowra Breakout, Vietnam, In Between*). Taken in this inter-textual context of other Australian mini-series, *The Dismissal*'s invocation of a 'past that is only interesting politically because of something which touches us in the present' reads now as an early call *for* multiculturalism (in its representation of the Cairns/Morosi affair) and *against* British imperialism (in the Governor-General's sacking of Whitlam). The cultural crisis which Australian mini-series address is one *contained* within the new national imaginary of 'multiculturalism'. The problem they address is 'How to invoke "Australianness" as *different* from British and US imperialism, given *white* Australia's own imperialism and genocide?'. Historical mini-series have been working to re-articulate and reconstruct 'Australianness' – a re-working of dominant nationalistic myths.

Cultural crisis, history and myth

Sylvia Lawson's examples of British historical dramas (*Upstairs, Downstairs, Brideshead Revisited*) suggest that they reach back further and less problematically into the nostalgia of history than Australian mini-series. Colin McArthur points to *Edward the Seventh, The Forsyte Saga, The Duchess of Duke Street*, as representing 'a more direct form of quite a common phenomenon in television – the recurrent return to the late Victorian, Edwardian and Georgian periods as milieux for drama'.[21] Nevertheless, this 'recurrent return' is, as in the Australian historical mini-series, evidence of a culture in some kind of crisis.

> For post-war Britain, faced as it is with adjustment to being a post-colonial power, a mediocre economic performer, a multi-racial society and a society in which the consensus of acceptable social and political behaviour is fragmenting . . . what better ideological choice, in its art, than to return to the period of the zenith of bourgeois and imperial power or to immediately succeeding periods in which the facade of that power appeared convincing.[22]

McArthur's point is speculative, but it gets some support from my own audience research. For instance, a contemporary 'downstairs' worker (a housekeeper at a Cambridge college) commented on *Upstairs, Downstairs*.

> It's very sort of English – you know, sort of what Great Britain was all about, I suppose. . . . I mean, servants in them days, they used to be sort of retainers. They used to let them work there, and when they retired they'd make sure they were alright in their retirement.[23]

The facade of power and moral harmony of that earlier period only appear convincing, however, in hindsight. The times themselves needed their own myths; hence their historical *connection* with the present. In the Edwardian period *contemporary* figures like Scott 'of the Antarctic' were constructed as legends of a British Empire *already* under threat. Quoting Kipling's 'all our pomp was yesterday', Roland Huntford argues 'These intimations of decline seem curiously personified in Robert Falcon Scott. . . . Within the edifice of Imperial grandeur, the structure was beginning to rot.'[24] Out-traded by Germany and the US, with most important inventions being made abroad, and industry and the military stifled by a rigid and uncreative discipline, 'Britain was forgetting how to think, how to compete and how to adapt'.[25]

For Trevor Griffiths, writer of the TV mini-series about Scott, *The Last Place On Earth*, it is the case that 'the past is only interesting politically because of something that touches us in the present'. He sees an ideological *liaison* between that period and our own:

> The myth had to be created to justify the war that followed. And it's because we live in times that are themselves not very different that I wanted to write *The Last Place On Earth*. Because myths are being conceived and constructed . . . inside the organs of the state. . . . It's possible to see it as a myth to cover up imperial decay from here, or from post-1918. The myth was that the decay was a moral decay. . . . Everything was collapsed into 'Englishness' or 'Britishness'. It was like we were losing our contact with the breed, with the race – that was the problem. The race wasn't throwing up the great, spectacular stars, who secured the empire in the first place, put us where we are, top of the league of nations, champions of the first division.[26]

Griffiths argues that 'since 1979 and Thatcher coming to power . . . there's been a deliberate attempt by government and state to foster the notion that we are still a great British people'.[27] He cites the following instance of a politician celebrating the Falklands victory as an example of the way that contemporary myths liaise with the past:

> Ladies and Gentlemen, we meet on the morrow of a national triumph in the South Atlantic. It recalled a former fellow of this society, Sir Arthur Quiller-Couch, on another memorable episode in the same area of the world, exactly seventy years ago. Let us keep our language noble for we still have heroes to celebrate.[28]

On the one hand, this myth-making directly links the British imperial present (the Falklands War) with its past (Scott of the Antarctic). On the other hand, the *location* of this discourse at the Royal Society of Literature reminds us that the great tradition of British 'quality' (leading from Shakespeare to the present) can be invoked for political as well as high cultural purposes.

'Classic' historical dramas can, McArthur notes, regenerate for contemporary audiences myths of heroism and militarism, while naturalizing real and (in the England of Thatcher) ever more visible social divisions. He cites a character in *Upstairs, Downstairs* commenting on the General Strike:

> It was a fair trial of strength. Both sides kept their heads. There was loyalty, self-sacrifice, very little anger. I think the whole nation can be proud. . . .[29]

Pride in the consensus of sacrifice (whether in the 'domestic' history of *Upstairs, Downstairs* or in the 'exploration' adventure of the Scott myth) obscure social differentials of power behind notions of a 'caring' and co-operative humanity. Together, McArthur argues, historical series like *Upstairs, Downstairs* and *Edward the Seventh* represent comparable ideological strategies. 'The humanization of the British monarchy and the valorization of Social Democracy constitute the best available terrain in which to fight for the maintenance of the socio-economic status quo.'[30]

It would be a mistake, though, to encapsulate these dominant myths too simply into a homogeneous 'ruling' or 'official' ideology. The differences between a Thatcherite militaristic/heroic myth (as in British tabloids' coverage of the Falklands War) and that of a social democratic 'caring monarchy' (as in *Edward the Seventh*) need also to be recognized, and sometimes themselves surface forcibly in the media (as instanced in the thinly veiled threats to the monarchy which appeared in conservative magazines as a result of the Queen's resistance to Thatcher's South African policy). The 'caring state' and the 'nationalist populist state' represent, in fact, different dominant phases in the British national imaginary as it shifted from the consensus of state welfarism to Thatcherism. Whereas it was the 'social democratic myth' that Ken Loach and Jim Allen challenged in *Days of Hope*, it was the heroic/militaristic re-construction of history which Griffiths addressed in *The Last Place On Earth*.[31] I will turn next to a study of the recent works of Trevor Griffiths to examine the way that the two dominant world myths of our time, capitalism and socialism can be deconstructed in dramas which *make* history and so 'reperceive the world'.

History and empiricism

In addition to their specific ideological functions at particular historical moments (as I have suggested for Australian and British series), TV histories have more deeply based and systematic connections with conservatism, in that they reproduce an empiricist notion of history. McArthur quotes E.H. Carr as a rare critic (within British historiography) of empiricism:

> First ascertain the facts, said the Positivists, then draw your conclusions from them. In Great Britain, this view of history fitted in perfectly with the empiricist tradition which . . . presupposes a complete separation between subject and object. Facts, like sense impressions, impinge on the observer from outside and are independent of his consciousness. The process of reception is passive: having received the data, he then acts on them.[32]

These 'facts, like sense impressions . . . independent of consciousness' are part of a 'visual epistemology' that supposedly makes the historical observer as passive as one of Lawson's *Dismissal* viewers. In this history 'sources' are fetishized as the legitimate *basis* of historical knowledge, 'documents' like diaries, blue-books, rent-rolls and private letters offer evidence that is 'visible and tangible as befits the Anglo-American philosophic disposition'.[33]

Further, as McArthur argues, the primacy given to sense data as perceived by individual consciousness[34] established the 'ideological category of *the individual*'.[35] This is one of the key categories for understanding both the dominant forms of history-writing in Britain and the forms of television programmes about history'.[36]

In the writing of empiricist history 'facts' and 'the individual' have been conjoined within (as Griffiths noted) a moral history of 'Britishness'.

While leaning heavily on the positivist notion of 'facts', British historians rejected the positivist impulse to formulate general laws when the facts were gathered, preferring rather to exercise moral judgment. History thus conceived therefore focused on observable phenomena like the British Constitution and Great Men and was incapable of dealing with non-sensible realities such as class and mode of production. Similarly, the ideas of progress and continuity favoured a kind of linear narrative history whereby 'facts' and 'great men' were assembled in chronological order and suitable moral judgments made about their interrelationship.[37]

It was within this empiricist ('facts'/'great men') historical tradition that the original media myths about Scott were constructed. For instance, a contemporary British newspaper wrote of Scott's expedition, 'It may be that . . . we are a race of degenerates, living in a flabby age. But at least there can be no degenerates aboard the Terra Nova. . . . These men are the spiritual sons of the great Elizabethans . . . where a Shackleton fails gloriously, a Scott is found ready.'[38] And writing his own history, Scott made the moral relationship between 'facts' (in this case the necessary death of dogs on Polar expeditions) and great men especially clear.

In my mind no journey made with dogs can approach the height of that fine conception which is realised when a party of men go forth to face hardships, dangers and difficulties with their own unaided efforts, and by days and weeks of hard physical labour succeed in solving some problem of the great unknown. Surely in this case the conquest is more nobly and splendidly won.[39]

As McArthur perceptively argues, television has adopted the empiricist tradition in *its* narratives of the past, systematically overlaying earlier media conjunctions of 'facts' and 'great men' with its own. It has its own fact fetish analogous to the historian's 'source'. 'Just as the bourgeois historians of the last century pinned their faith on *documents* . . . so do the tele-historians of the twentieth century pin their faith on actuality film or, when that is not available, on the next best thing, reconstruction film, and the return to the "actual scene" where particular historical events occurred.'[40] So, for instance, the TV documentary *In The Footsteps of Scott* has its protagonists re-treading Scott's exact route, like him pulling their sledges without dogs – camera and sound emphasizing the individual sensations of exhaustion, pain and heroism in the trek to the Pole. This fetish for the naturalistic view of the 'actual' event (usually associated with 'great' individuals and at the expense of a complex understanding of the real social forces determining it) has become part of the practical consciousness and routine practice of TV's history makers.

In contrast, when the camera in *The Last Place On Earth* moves in on the *process* of history-making (as Scott writes his diary, and visual and written records contradict each other), attention is focused on myth construction – Scott's *and* Griffiths'. The distinction here, Trevor Griffiths would argue, is between a naturalism based on sense experiences and a realism which examines the underlying social forces; between a history that is written according to 'a materialism of detail' and one that examines the 'materialism of forces'.[41] *Event*, in Cunningham's words, is replaced by '*causation* and *consequence*'; and 'cause' is defined in realist terms, proposing

> models of real structures and processes which lie at a 'deeper' level of reality than the phenomena they are used to explain. The theory explains the phenomenon because the phenomenon and the 'deep structures' are causally connected.[42]

Myths of empire: *The Last Place On Earth*

The Marxist realist philosophical tradition to which Trevor Griffiths belongs rejects empiricism, and with it conventional forms of television history. As Gregor McLennan points out, realism as a philosophical position certainly acknowledges 'the theoretical moment in science' (i.e. the discursive position of the observer), but always *together with* 'an emphasis on the independence of empirical evidence'.[43] This distinguishes it from the conventionalist view that the historical world of people and events can *never* be known as a world independent of the discourse of the analyst. As McLennan argues, it is because of its concern for the causal relationship between surface appearances available as sensory data and systemic 'hidden' determinants, that a realist theory

> cannot be cognitively assessed primarily on empirical evidence, though realism must explain empirical phenomena. Realism is the philosophical view that knowledge is knowledge of objects or processes that exist independent of thought. In the terminology of one of its prominent spokesmen, Roy Bhaskar, science discovers the 'generative mechanism' that, when known, causally explain phenomena. . . . Marxism postulates generative mechanisms at the level of the mode of production, which help to explain the development of historical and empirical problems or phenomena. Social forms, conjunctures, and strategies are to be understood in terms of theoretically expressed tendencies that have a real, structural status but are not empirically transparent.[44]

As a critical realist, Trevor Griffiths exposes 'generative mechanisms' so challenging the individualistically based narratives which assemble 'facts', 'great men', and conventional moral judgements. Here, for example, is a speech from *Bill Brand*, with Brand speaking against the 'Further Prevention of Terrorism' Bill. As a politician of the Labour Left, he challenges the conventional morality that denigrates individual terrorists, and exposes the 'generative mechanisms' underlying a *system* that creates terror:

> When honourable gentlemen on both sides of the aisle talk about these 'men of blood', let them consider all the men of blood, not just those who murder with bombs and guns. . . . Currency speculators for example who murder by telephone, who bring the pound down until a Labour government sees sense and gives cast-iron guarantees that it will carry out their policies which inevitably include extended wage standstills, vicious cuts in social spending and a huge increase in the reservoir of the unemployed. Old people will die this winter – thousands of them, of hypothermia – as a direct result of those telephone calls. Let us have laws against capitalists and the employers who have engineered the largest investment strike over the past few years as a means of clubbing a socialist government into accepting capitalist policies. These men kill facelessly, with pen and ink, with telephones and telex machines, but they are men of blood none the less.

Similarly, in *The Last Place On Earth*, Griffiths wanted to challenge the individualistic myths of those characters most distinguished from terrorists in the public mind, British military heroes and explorers like Scott, by locating them in an international web of power and capital. Here Scott represented the contradictions of 'an imperial class in action'. The differences in achievement between Scott and Amundsen reflected not so much personal idiosyncrasy (and still less 'luck') but rather the effect of nations at different stages of development in the historical conjuncture of a globally competitive capitalism. So, for instance, Amundsen's secretiveness about his expedition is (in Griffiths' original intention) stripped of its individual motivation.

> Norway . . . was in a different historical conjuncture as a nation, an extremely young nation, relatively powerless. There was a power game being played between Germany, France and Britain as to who will rule the roost, and they needed allies. And Nansen's role [as Norwegian ambassador in Britain] in this . . . is not to tweak the lion's tail. That's why Amundsen couldn't disclose that he was taking on the British in the South, because Nansen would have said, forget it. Because the Germans wanted Norway reconflated into Sweden again. It didn't serve their grand design for Europe . . . to have an independent state there.[45]

Fundamentally, the difference between conventional television histories and Griffiths' depends on differences in notions of 'the real' and historical representation. For Jerry Kuehl, whose empiricist understanding of history is reflected in the massive 'archivalist' narrative of his *World at War* series, TV is a sequential and non-reflective medium, 'ideally suited to telling stories and anecdotes' of great men and nations. 'It is difficult to use it to relate coherently complicated narrative histories, and it is quite hopeless at portraying abstract ideas.'[46] For Trevor Griffiths, television cannot tell the true tales of history *unless* it uses ideas to reveal the real (but not directly observable) deep structures.

> I have a terrific passion for ideas. Ideas are concrete. . . . I'm not interested in work that is only sensuous.[47]

By 'sensuous' Griffiths is referring to the naturalistic details that are readily available, as sense data, to us as experiential phenomena. These are no more than surface effects, causally connected to 'deep structures'. As he said of the transmitted form of *The Last Place On Earth*, 'There is a way of doing realist texts which denies what they are about and simply celebrates their effects.'[48] This is to turn critical realism into naturalism, analytical history into celebration of the 'timeless presence' of Britishness – and so to reinforce rather than critique the Scott myth we learned from our school books.

When we come to Scott . . . still taught in schools . . . we are talking about a piece of the country's history that has become mythologized into a timeless presence. . . . The spirit of Scott is with us today. Palpable, breathing, in the way we perceive the world, the way we seek to change it or retain it.[49]

The school book 'Scott' is a myth of heroic dying. 'You've read . . . those deaths a thousand times . . . vainglorious, heroic, rhetoricized death in British imperial legend.'[50] And Griffiths' aim was to confront such empiricist myths (and those of the Falklands War with which the series was intimately related) with a history focusing not on heroism and 'bad luck', but on 'maladroitness and incompetence, stupidity, hierarchy'.[51]

Scott, in Griffiths' history, is both agent and victim of British hierarchy, in class terms and in imperial terms – a necessary hero (however unwilling and sensitively ill-equipped) for a nation in crisis. In our first view of him (in the television text)[52] he is reprimanded by an admiral for his inefficiency while in command of his ship, and is literally coerced into becoming an expeditionary hero. The admiral is at play (at a snooker table), easily aware of his class, irritably quick in his power, constructing out of this meeting a potent combination of gamesmanship, adventurism, amateurism and hierarchy that is emblematic of the British imperial dream. Our first view of Amundsen (and this is the opening sequence of the series) is very different. Amundsen sits with Eskimos (himself 'a European Eskimo'), learns their culture, their geography, their survival skills in the ice. There is no hierarchy here, except in environmental understanding. Its transmission is democratic.

As Griffiths points out, in the British schoolbook myth of Scott, that *other* expedition, 'the one that got to the pole and came back without losing a life' is 'carefully filleted out'.[53] By looking 'at the story again with that included' Griffiths is able to compare not only historical but also *potential* political systems: authoritarian and democratic.

For too long any view of Amundsen and the Norwegians was one of banal professional hacks. Spoilsports, liars, cheats, freebooters. Nothing could be further from the truth. These people believed in doing things well, and not losing their minds in vainglorious, rhetorical gestures. . . . The way they turned back for instance, was a democratically arrived at decision because they had started too early, because

it was too cold, and because it was no fun anymore. Compare that
with the absolutely autocratic power wielded by . . . Scott. . . . There
is not the slightest fragment of even relative autonomy for these
people.[54]

Inside this British hierarchy, as Griffiths presents it, there are the
further contradictions of class. Within the ruling class itself, there is
Oates who is socially superior to Scott, and despises his aspirations.
His life has been determined by Scott's vainglory. So he refuses Scott
his death, crawling out into the snow for a 'call of nature', thus
demystifying the heroic words and manly, upright action of the schoolbook story. Bowers is Scott's social inferior, irredeemably loyal to the
point of ritualism, and thus unaware he is marching to death. As
Griffiths says, 'that's another kind of subordination'.[55]

Griffiths' history in fact challenges each of the conventional categories
of empiricist television history that McArthur points to.

The category of the individual and authority of 'actuality'

McArthur notes the foregrounding in empiricist historical dramas of
individual heroic action and the *testimony* of individual men and women
(in even those historical series criticized by some for 'anti-imperial
bias', like *The British Empire*). In *The Last Place On Earth*, in contrast, the
'hero' is located in his class, and that class placed (in Griffiths' writing
at least) in the history of imperial struggle. Further, the central focus of
the narrative is reflexive, pointing to the construction of history as myth
by way of individual testimony.

Let's look at all the evidences including Scott's own testimony . . .
including the 60 pages of journal which had been carefully filleted
from the received version that we all know and love. . . . The central
aim of the project as I perceived it . . . was the nature and genesis of
historical distortion.[56]

Out of the concatenation of British imperial power needs and the
inefficiencies of ruling-class, gentleman amateurism, Scott (and then
others) constructed an historical 'source': the Scott diaries. Griffiths
argues that *only* an heroic death rather than a professional victory at the
Pole could provide the myth of suffering and dying that Britain needed
for the coming First World War; only a *legendary* Scott not a returning
hero, could conjoin these contradictory demands of British economics
and British culture. Scott, in Griffiths' view, consciously wrote himself
(in his diaries – written for publication) as legend; and any signs of
inefficiency and failure in human management that he left in, were

removed by his family and members of the ruling class after his death. In this sense Scott's mythically necessary death was a 'calling to account' in the Lukacian sense,[57] revealing the social contradictions of his class and time as a convergence of character and social collision, rather than a personal failure.

Chronological monism

On the one hand, the contrast between Scott and his more professional rival, Amundsen, clearly represents the crisis of a certain kind of expansionist impérialism, which is a recurring feature of Britain in decline. Griffiths makes the parallel between Scott and the Falklands War clear in this respect, disagreeing with Poole and Wyver's view that 'in the one we were underprepared, stupid and so on, in the other we were massively prepared and effective'.[58]

> I think this is a deep misreading of what actually went on . . . in the campaign. . . . The story we have of the Falklands is not what happened at all. . . . We know that with a tiny accidental beaver one way or another there could have been a totally different outcome. . . . It's bizarre that when the Falklands came up and I was writing the piece, I was still a long way away from the end, but somehow it seemed clearer and clearer. . . . It confirmed the project for me. . . . I called the final episode REJOICE, because it was so neat . . . because here we were on another crazed, impossible, vainglorious venture, and . . . we were being instructed to approve. Our whole Britishness, our status as Britons depended on our approval. . . . This thing has simply resurfaced, it has never gone, it's always there.[59]

On the other hand, though, Amundsen represents an alternative to this unspoken problematic of Britishness. Griffiths gives an indication of this when he compares the different historical developments of Norway and Britain, and hence their different place in early twentieth-century capitalist expansionism. In this sense, *The Last Place On Earth* challenges what McArthur calls chronological monism. Writing of the contrasted portrayal of 'British' (humane) and 'foreign' (totalitarian) monarchy in *Edward the Seventh*, McArthur points out that

> What is wholly repressed in the programme . . . is that these diverse forms of monarchy took their highly individual character from the fact that they constituted different stages of development in relation to the transition from feudal to bourgeois society within their own concrete social formations. Characteristically in this

bourgeois television drama, these structural differences between British constitutionalism and the Russian and German absolutisms are repressed and displaced to reappear in the form of personality differences . . . with the added suggestion that the constitutional reasonableness of Edward VII is a reflection of the innate decency and good sense of the British people.[60]

In Griffiths' text the structural differences between different kinds and chronologies of bourgeois nationalism are fundamental. Norway's place in the international power struggle could not be, as Griffiths says, in any way jingoistic. Hence the discourse of exploration could never be flag-waving or expansionist. For Griffiths, 'the flag isn't the heart of that journey in any way. It's like a formality. . . . That journey is about getting it right, doing it properly, doing it well.'[61] Different discourses of exploration rely on different phases of nationalism.

Griffiths also makes the Norwegians emblematic of 'underdevelopment' in a broader sense. The opposition, between their skis and dogs and the British fiascoed mix of foot-slogging and mechanical sledges, represents a contrast between Amundsen's openness to the environment and the British reliance on moral superiority and industrialism. Griffiths makes this clear when explaining his own relationship with Marxism, and his enthusiasm for practical consciousness.

I'm talking about folk ways, peasant practices, third world, traditional approaches to questions of medicine. . . . I think a Marxism that inflexibly excludes the knowledge of the people is pointless and self-defeating. John Berger, a very important Marxist writer in my view, has . . . almost single-handedly sought to refute the crude Marxist idea that the European peasantry . . . is to be rescued from 'rural idiocy', which is a Marxist phrase. . . . Berger, by . . . living the life of the people at a very simple level, has written a series of books that show, very clearly and very precisely, what has been learnt by the common people about life and death, about the importance of things, about humorous resistance. . . . Marxists' . . . whole notion of rural idiocy, that electrification, organization and industrialization will eliminate it immediately and create the new man, is deeply troubled. . . . We just think of . . . the life of people at a very simple level . . . as quaint and charming and passé, overtaken by history. As a Marxist I don't do that. For example in *Last Place On Earth*, the first image is Amundsen sitting in an igloo with three Eskimos, learning to live the life of the people in ice and snow.[62]

Hence, Amundsen's journey is representative of the practical consciousness of another, more 'primitive' stage of history, where cultures
are unsentimentally attuned to nature. As a 'European Eskimo', his
'doing it properly, doing it well' *depends* on 'what has been learnt by the
common people about life and death'. Learning (without pride of
jingoism) from the Eskimos, Amundsen stands before his task, as
Griffiths describes:

> The Norwegians see the mountains for the first time. . . . Now they
> have to solve this problem, 12,000 feet of transarctic mountains.
> They're trying to work out how many dogs they are going to need,
> how long it's going to take, and so on. And they stand in this kind of
> misty hollow base of the mountain, little wisps of questions and
> answers just dotting around these people. . . . It's like how craftsmen
> tackle problems. Compared with which nothing about Scott's journey is
> of any value at all.[63]

This craftsmanship is, in Griffiths' view, related to a quasi-democratic
decision-making process, as evidenced by the Norwegians' decision to
turn back (against Amundsen's wishes) 'because it was too cold, and
because it was no fun anymore'. Again one should compare this with
Griffiths' view of a North African tribe's use of fun and play, in a village
where they send children away for three years to learn both craft and
decision-making.

> Their children . . . make the huts from branches and leaves, they
> make their own cooking pots, they elect a chief and a council, they
> take wives and husbands. . . . Just look at the elements in that, of
> preparation, of democracy. . . . It's there to be seen and yet we don't
> see it. We erase all of that inside our general Western urbanite
> industrialized sensibility.[64]

From this perspective, Griffiths' determination to present the *two*
journeys as 'the real history of that expedition and that period' is not
an archivist's concern to put the record of the past straight. The
'juxtaposed expedition' presents, within the format of a popular action-
adventure storyline, a contrasting politics and a contrasting technology.

The influence of the Marxist aesthetician, Georg Lukacs, which is
fundamental in Griffiths' critical realism, is evident in this 'clash
between two social orders' conveyed by their representative 'world-
historical-individuals'.[65] When Scott leads his party of walking men
and tractors out from the base camp, with flags and banners fluttering
in the wind, the action in the TV text is *imaged* as another Crusade. The
British present (and, as we know, its Falklands future) is given this

feudal underpinning, while paradoxically Amundsen's 'primitive' craft and proto-democratic procedure presages the possibilities of the future.

Myths of socialism: *Fatherland*

That Griffiths' concern for the alternative cultural and political spaces of the Third World is by no means romantic nostalgia is clear from *Fatherland*, his next work after *The Last Place On Earth*. The script that Griffiths wrote for this film, made for British, French and German television, and directed by Ken Loach, is again the story of a journey, as the East German *émigré* and *liedermacher*, Klaus Drittemann, moves from East to West Berlin, and from there to Cambridge in England to search for his father.

The old man, Jacob Drittemann, is a legend of socialist dissidence, and, as in the Scott work, the narrative deconstructs a dominant myth as Klaus discovers at the end that his father was turned by the Fascists in Spain, used by the Nazis to betray members of the Dutch resistance during the Second World War, and then lifted back into East Germany by the CIA. Now, old and hunted both by state security agencies and by a young Dutch journalist, Emma De Baen, who works for an organization tracking down Nazi war criminals, Jacob Drittemann spends his time photographing in a long lens the faces of women protesters at an American airforce base, and converting the photos into obscenely grimacing paintings.

In these works he too, like Scott, constructs a history. As he tells his son when finally traced:

> I've seen these faces all my life: in Hitler's Germany, in Stalin's Spain, in Roosevelt's America, in Ulbricht's Democratic Republic; it's the face of innocence, it's the face of the drinkers of blood. There *is* only power. . . . It's the first law of humankind. The innocent think there is a choice. . . . We have both learned the second law of humankind: any life is better than no life. Later still, you learn the third law: it's all one, life is nothing.

For Griffiths, Jacob Drittemann's greatest betrayal is in denying human agency.

Soon after this Jacob Drittemann is murdered, probably by the Americans. His death, hanging from a beam in his Cambridge kitchen, is not 'noble' like Scott's. But it is, as surely, embedded in myth-making. Klaus Drittemann's journey is into the history and myth of socialism, which his father represents. Jacob Drittemann refutes the socialist wager, refutes all human choice. He speaks to his son about his wife, Rosa:

> Met her in Spain, you know . . . red red Rosa, in the full . . . obscene bloom of her innocence, 'wading through slaughter like Stalin's daughter'. . . . I was . . . a child too, 19, 20, seeking the ancient battleground between right and wrong, but I glimpsed what she would never see: the hand of the puppet-master, controlling the dance. . . . Why should this interest you? You're a functionary, a thing of the state. . . .

But, in fact, Klaus is not an agent of the Stasi; and nor will he become a puppet of the capitalist music industry in West Berlin in return for wealth and an American passport. In contrast to Jacob's pessimistic deconstruction of socialism, Griffiths constructs an alternative possibility, even while accepting the force of that Stalinist betrayal.

Griffiths' narrative of *Fatherland* represents human relationships in three spaces. The first is emblematized in East Berlin by the final night's love-making between Klaus and his former wife, Marita. Her new husband, Hans Peter, accepts their need for this kind of parting, and offers to look after the child so that they can sleep in together. They make love, 'direct, honest, unsentimental, pleasures voiced openly in the empty room, sliding and dipping in folds of custom and trust'; while elsewhere in the flat, voices can be heard, 'a low-tone discussion of the Polish question . . . it's serious, wide-ranging, well-informed; men more than women, but not exclusively; the thrust and tenor of argument are socialist rather than "dissident", anti-party not anti-DDR'.[66]

There is a mutuality here, at the private and public level, informed and underpinned by the beliefs of socialism. In contrast, there is the later love-making of Klaus and Lucy Bernstein (who works for the West German Taube Records, recently taken over by a US multinational). 'Drittemann and Lucy Bernstein fight naked on the bed, attempting love. They address each other in their respective languages occasionally, deep breathy barks, but mostly they bruise each other in silence. A bad fuck: trustless.'[67] The debate just before this commodity-fucking is at a party for Klaus given by Rainer Schiff, another East German *émigré* who, as Griffiths says, is 'paddling in the shit', making money, laying out 'lines of cocaine with a pen-knife' while 'people sit or kneel around the Chinese carpet, waiting to snort'.[68] This is a culture of hedonism and manipulative competitiveness, in contrast to the mutuality of the previous love-making.

Yet each culture has its quotient of innocence and guilt. The East German group is as subject to the myth of socialism in Jacob Drittemann as Klaus is; and, in West Berlin, Lucy has her own version of innocence.

> Lucy's sin is no more than that in order to work professionally and commercially in Europe, as an American in West Berlin, she has to become imbricated to some extent with American foreign policy as prosecuted through the CIA. These . . . are the choices for a woman like that, since she's basically a-political.[69]

Lucy's life is a set of contradictions across a narrow scenario of choices. As Griffiths sees it, 'I think increasingly all lives are that – in Europe; all lives lived relatively consciously.'[70]

In the third geographical space of the narrative, 'Fortress Britain', Emma de Baen has her own quotient of innocence and guilt. Here Klaus Drittemann has his third relationship with a woman. They lie in bed in a Cambridge boarding house, but not sexually. For Griffiths,

> That lying naked together is another kind of respect and trust. . . . The problem with that relationship is that it is still manipulative, in the sense that . . . she needs him not to know what the hidden agenda is vis-a-vis why she is looking for his father, because he would hardly be complicit in her object if she told him up-front. . . . There is this idea of 'West-women'. The way in which personality and character as shaped . . . in Western societies and cultures, has a high degree of manipulation built into it, so that relationship becomes about power . . . about getting the other to do things that serve you. And Emma's quite cool about this. Drittemann's relations with oppositionists inside his own society are very different. They're not power relationships at all. They're about love and comradeship. I didn't want Emma and Drittemann to be a sexual relationship; I wanted it to be a man–woman relationship that approached comradeship but never quite made it. . . . I think I've been shaped sufficiently over the last fifteen years by feminism to realise that there are many, many relationships available to men and women that are not . . . to do with overt sexuality. . . . But there is a great fondness and affection . . . glimpsed, between these two as they gain more experience of each other, and a deeper relationship is not denied them. It's just that the job ends as it were, and then choices have to be made. The choice that she makes is to go back, re-group and get on with the next task. I think it's very important to see not only men but women too who know their project and are not deflectable from it.[71]

Emma goes on with her fight against Fascism; Klaus refuses a lucrative music tour that Lucy and the record company have planned for him, and sings instead at an unheralded concert of 20,000 young people in Zurich.

Begins to sing . . . 'Fatherland'. Complex, hard, affirmative: a celebration of necessary innocence. The first half of the song is a modern history of white Europe and its horrors, in the pure German liedermacher style of early Konstantin Wecker. The song breaks in the middle . . . Drittemann's piano turns electric, as the second half affirms the necessity of innocence in rock. Fireworks lay out peace symbols across the sky. Long white candles light in ones and dozens and hundreds all round the stadium. Faces gleam at the future from the darkness.[72]

This is Griffiths' 'dream about the way we think things could be'.

In both *The Last Place On Earth* and *Fatherland* Griffiths reports a twentieth-century history of power and competition, and sets a dream of comradeship in opposition to it. As he says, 'When Amundsen at the South Pole addresses his fellow workers as comrades, I get the sense that the term has been earned in some important way.'[73] Similarly, the faces gleaming at the future from the darkness of *Fatherland* are celebrating the 'innocence' of comradeship. 'Innocence', in *Fatherland* is 'Unschuld' – *un*-guilt, a necessary wager that there are 'cracks and spaces' against oppression that we can work with and mobilize.

That's the fervent hope. That's the desire of the text. Jacob Drittemann and a great segment of the audience, I suspect, would absolutely deny that they are anything except self-delusory spaces, that they don't actually exist – it's just that we are driven so crazy by the absence of comradeship that we invent them. But this is not what I feel. . . . It's such a problematic concept, the concept of comradeship in the West. . . . To find it in a deep sense, in a common struggle, is I think, inordinately difficult.[74]

The 'innocence' of comradeship is not an abstract Utopianism: it is Griffiths' demand of politics *and* his demand of his daily workings in the television industry. As he says of *The Last Place On Earth*, 'what one looks for is a working process which involves . . . everybody who works on a piece and involves them totally, so we are not just talking about a director's response to the text on which he bases his creative interpretation. We are also talking about actors and craftsmen of all kinds, researchers, costume people and wigging and make-up. This is a huge conglomerate of different sorts of craft skills and talents and histories.'[75] The comradeship of crafts, talents and friendship which took Amundsen's team to the Pole, the sense of 'fellow workers as comrades' transferred to the TV industry, is one of those 'cracks' that Griffiths seeks to mobilize. It is, in its collective efforts at social organization, precisely that proletarianization of the public sphere that Negt and Kluge call for in their challenge to the myths of the culture industry. As a result of this daily grounding of politics in professional practice, Griffiths' sense of identification with the Greenham women, with affirmative rock and other 'spaces' of resistance is unsentimental.

I find *Fatherland* a very hard piece . . . unsentimental. . . . It says . . . that the mythography of socialism from the Bolshevik Revolution onwards, is something that has propped us all up in our socialist beliefs at one time or another. I think it's increasingly important . . . for socialists to confront that history, as I think Drittemann is forced to. This is very much a play about Europe – the rottenness of Europe. . . . Not just the rottenness of capitalism and imperialism, but the rottenness of a particular kind of deformed socialism. And if we're going to have a socialism for the future, I think it's got to be aware of its history. When Drittemann says at the end of the play, 'Maybe innocence is all that we have', I see the play as a meditation on the notion of innocence and guilt; and there are different sorts of innocence and different sorts of guilt. Rosa's innocence/guilt quotient, for example, is very complex. I personally have a tremendous amount of admiration for certain sorts of socialism inside East European countries like the DDR. There is the line about Rosa in the play that 'She fought at Stalingrad, and that makes the difference', and it certainly makes the difference vis-a-vis Jacob Drittemann whose life has been one long journey into nothingness, into puppetry. At another level, the piece is about human agency and power, and finding that relationship in one's own life is inordinately difficult politically. The extent to which one's field of action is proscribed by party, or by history, or by tradition of doing things in certain ways, the extent to which one can actually innovate, create, reimagine . . . these are densely difficult questions I think for political beings in Europe to answer. We *all* suffer from the sense that the modern state is pretty well all-powerful, certainly all-pervasive. But this is not a jaded or a tired piece. It actually comes out with a kind of hard affirmation of a future, but I don't think it's done with any sense that the youth movements and the peace movements of Europe are single-handed going to solve the problem.[76]

The trajectory of the drama is away from the sense of patriarchal and state control implied in the title *Fatherland*. 'We are not responsible for the sins of our fathers, but we have to be aware of them, and part of Drittemann's journey in the play is to become aware of them.'[77] When at the end, Emma tells Klaus that 'fathers are men's necessary fictions', and he replies 'I had imagined we were comrades somehow', the sense is that the authoritarian myths and fictions of family, class and nation are (tentatively and imperfectly) to be challenged by the kind of colleagueship that Amundsen had with his men at the Pole. But it is an imperfect relationship. As Griffiths argues, 'the opportunities to experience colleagueship, comradeship . . . I think are diminishing in Europe. . . . I see more comradeship in South Africa than I see here.'[78]

The contrast Griffiths feels between the 'rural idiocy' of Africa and the 'rotten' organization of Europe is clear in his comparison of two of his works that take a particular moment of historical opportunity as a theme: *Occupations* (about Gramsci and the 1920 Turin factory occupations) and *Acts of Love* (about contemporary South Africa and the black/white relationships and work of a white, US-educated, radicalized South African woman in the black townships).

> The difference is a matter of where the text intervenes in the historical development. From the time I visited South Africa on the research trip at the beginning of 1985, I felt that I was walking the fault lines of that society, and that the fault lines had developed into uncoverable cracks that would simply go on getting wider and wider until the thing fell apart. That was not the historical moment that I began to write *Occupations*. . . . The major wave of occupations in Western Europe had begun in '67, and had pretty well fallen back by '70–'71 when I began to work on *Occupations*, and that's probably why I sought some kind of historical correlative for what was going on at some earlier point, in some earlier period, and came up with the occupation of factories in northern Italy, which had been a *defeat*. I don't smell defeat about the South African situation at the moment, and at the moment of writing the text of *Acts of Love* I didn't feel it. . . . It's a text about a concrete and graspable future. The text itself is prefaced by . . . the ANC statement, about what South Africa could be . . . as a way of totalising an opposition to apartheid and racial capitalism.[79]

Near the end of the work, the white radicals visit a black festival in a neighbouring state, where, as at the beginning of *Fatherland*, there is a concatenation of love-making, political discussion and sensuously affirmative music. But this time it is part of that 'primitive' knowledge 'learnt by the common people about life and death . . . about humorous resistance'. This quality of black affirmation is not confined to the flats of intellectuals, as it was in East Berlin. It encompasses '*jouissance*' as well as '*plaisir*'. It is a combination of musical skills, human sensuousness and comradeship among men, women and children, black and white together; and it is at the front line of power politics. The festival is blasted by South African jets, and most of the participants killed. Yet, the power of the scene carries over to the end, overwhelming the individual defeats of the jailed whites.

> Utopian? Well, I don't know. I mean, it's this old dialectic of Gramsci's, that we have to show at one and the same time pessimism of the intellect but optimism of the will. . . . So that while . . . all the elements of state surveillance, state control . . . objective suppression of the individual as agent of his or her own destiny . . . are set intellectually in place in *Fatherland*, we still find these spaces for . . . something oppositional to emerge that may carry a seed of the future. Now, it seems to me irresponsible *not* to embrace that, and not to embody that in the text, otherwise I think we all become Beckett, I think we all become terminal. . . . In *Fatherland* there is a resonance throughout the piece about faces. In my original text . . . you see the Molesworth women singing a peace song . . . the whole perimeter fence of this place patrolled by cops and soldiers. . . . We then pick up the photographs of those faces. We've seen those faces directly, we've seen them through the old man's lens, we now see them as photographs on the canvas that he's painting, and then we see the paintings themselves all around the house. Now this is all one deeply pessimistic meditation via Jacob Drittemann on the theme of innocence. But by the end of the play, we see (at the concert) those faces again. And this time they're not distorted, and they're not the 'drinkers of blood'. There is an innocence, an unschuldig quality, *un*-guilty.[80]

Griffiths' concern with the politics of representation here indicates (as in all his plays) a constant reflexivity about his own place as an artistic worker in the politics of innocence and guilt. As he says, 'Klaus Drittemann's confidence is also an artistic confidence, a belief in his own ability to make relevant and persuasive and important music';[81] and his song 'In Praise of Nicaragua' amplified over the party in West Berlin, contrasts both with Western hedonistic decadence and also with the 'terminal' art of his father.

Griffiths admits that there is a strong autobiographical element in Drittemann the artist:

> The trouble for Drittemann is there is nowhere else to go. If he can't stay inside the DDR, he's got to come out. And the only passport he

can get is a West German one. . . . For me, the problem is whether to stay in the First World or whether to get the hell out of it . . . and start writing about the First World from the Third World, which is the only political standpoint . . . about the First World now. That's *my* problem. So there is an equal dissatisfaction, though its location is slightly different in each case.[82]

For Griffiths, the trip to South Africa for *Acts of Love* was a step towards standing deeper in those 'uncoverable cracks'. But even if he does move to black Africa, the economics of international media flow will still force him to *make* his works for US or European production. There, in that precise area of control and resistance, Griffiths works out his own dialectic of innocence and guilt.

People ask me quite frequently how it is that I can work with Hollywood, and 'how can you write a full bodied text when you know that it's going to be macerated, stretched, rubbished and re-assembled by lunatics?' . . . But there is a necessary innocence about doing a work like *Acts of Love*. I'd had the most appalling row of my life with the producer of this South African project in advance of writing the piece. I was contractually *obliged* to write the piece by the time I sat down to write it. . . . It was the hardest text that I've ever created, because my *innocence* about making the best and most persuasive text that I could had been very severely fractured by this exchange. . . . When I wrote *Reds* I had to protect that small quantum of innocence about what would happen to it when I wrote it, and then fight like fuck to defend as much of that text as it was possible to defend. . . . With *Acts of Love* I just hope I can be strong enough, because I don't need my innocence any more. I've written the text. Now I need all my guile, all my wisdom about what happens to texts, and all my anger to defend what I've written . . . from these people who want . . . to make a film that will cost as little as possible and make as much as possible. . . . I suppose the craft of what I do with Hollywood is to seek to persuade to other views these people who are up to their necks in the shit of Hollywood wisdom, Hollywood convention. . . . It's like chess now, because they want to win, and they *will* win. But they'll win at cost. The cost to them will be that maybe 50% or 60% of this text will be lodged inside the final version.[83]

The innocence and guilt that Griffiths works through – as different moments of each project are part of *his* journey, *his* expedition of craft and endurance, *his* dialogue of theoretical consciousness and daily routine – make works like *Bill Brand* (about the struggle between radicalism and compromise in a Left/Labour politician) deeply self-reflexive. The institutions (of parliament, of TV industry) are different; but the fight between human agency and organizational power is the same. The often noted opposition in most of Griffiths' works between reformism and revolution, between 'soft' and 'hard' characterization (which he constantly negotiates by positioning in historically changing spaces, forces and mythologies) is as much a theoretical method as a matter of ideological content. Bill Brand, a compromised radical, is even more problematic in his gender relations, and the project of this work is to confront an audience, as it confronts Griffiths himself, with their own contradictions. As Griffiths says of *Fatherland*:

It's a play of contradictions, and it's not a programmatic play in political terms. It doesn't come out with a thick residuum of meanings and values and prescriptions for action. . . . It asks questions, and it demands to be tested against the terrains of choice that its readers or its watchers operate within.[84]

Equally, he says of *The Last Place On Earth*:

You live their dying moment by moment in what I believe to be a wholly proper way. And you see their contradictions, and you see them seeing their contradictions, like Oates, like Wilson. Nobody can respond to that by feeling that these people are being brutally shovelled out of the way in order for some schematic, political agitprop notion to be inserted into contemporary consciousness.[85]

In Griffiths, in his audience, in his characters and their historical myths, in his class, gender and culture, there are contradictions. While on the one hand in Griffiths' works there is a strong sense of the constraining power of structures like class, race, gender, culture and nation, there is also a stress on human agency in its ambiguities and complexity. The play between innocence and guilt is the necessary interrelationship of agency and constraint, process and structure, in a reality which, like his plays, is there to be used, its deep structures revealed in order to be worked on and, one way or another, transformed.

Griffiths' historiography, to use McArthur's words, 'is not a process of reconstructing the past but of acting upon it – through the traces of it which remain – for the present, of producing a theorized awareness of the past which will shape action in the present'.[86] So the task of *The Last Place On Earth*, as Griffiths sees it, is not just the demystification of the Scott legend.

There's a whole garden laid out there in 1912–14 and every single plant is growing now inside Britain, British consciousness and the subconscious of this society. The Scott myth is not the only thing growing there. There are plants to do with democracy, to do with equality, to do with commonness and fraternity that are also there.[87]

But drama's task of 'rooting out the weeds'[88] of class myth, and innocently exposing these potentials of comradeship, has still to be achieved *through* the public and commercial communication industries of the state, the problems of which I will consider next.

This chapter has related to the previous one in being about the construction of history as myth, and (in Griffiths' words) finding 'spaces for something oppositional to emerge that may carry a seed of the future'. As in the previous chapter there has been a tendency to move from a stress on cultures constructing their own myths at the beginning of the chapter to emphasis on resistance and agency at the end. But this chapter differs from Chapter 2 in going further into the ethnography of production that I argued for in the Introduction. Inevitably, too, there has been a difference in the positioning and tone of my authorship, a shifting from the more distanced 'overview' (of my brief for this book) in Chapter 2, to (I hope) the sense of 'analytical mutuality' I described earlier.

I have chosen to stress Trevor Griffiths' own theoretical 'knowledge-ability' about history and myth, authorship and institution, resistance and control (together with his understanding of the agency of practical and discursive consciousness) as part of my emphasis on *knowledgeable* actors struggling in every arena of the TV communication system. It is because I agree with Douglas Kellner (in his critique of Baudrillard) that

> while it could be conceded that we are living in an age of transition and rapid change, it is questionable whether we have gone beyond modernity, class politics, labour and production, imperialism, fascism, the phenomena described by classical and neo-Marxism[89]

that I have chosen to focus on Griffiths' view of the changing socio-historical conditions of both our current 'totalizing' systems, socialism and capitalism. As Kellner says, 'Baudrillard's radical critique of the categories of political economy, marxism, sociology, etc. . . . ends up in a cul de sac where he denies the very possibility of social theory or social transformation'.[90] With Griffiths, I want to insist on the 'innocence' of 'resistance, struggle, or refusal'.[91]

4 'Serious drama':
the dangerous mesh of empathy

In the case of *Bill Brand* we have the curious anomaly of an oppositional message encoded in a dominant aesthetic language, naturalism. Griffiths criticizes government in Britain in a way that questions the foundations of parliamentary democracy. Yet, particularly because of the overwhelming emphasis on a single individual's experience . . . a possible audience response is to sympathize with Brand's personal problems and regard him as just another individual in a difficult situation. . . . Brecht long ago pointed to the dangerous mesh of empathy.

Jim McGuigan[1]

The previous chapter strongly emphasized the theoretical 'knowledge-ability' of an important TV drama writer, Trevor Griffiths. *Time Out* has argued that Griffiths (with John McGrath, David Edgar and Jim Allen) is the best representative of a band of socially critical writers that the conservative '80's has shoved . . . up against the wall'.[2] But as left-wing media critics have argued, Griffiths *et al.* are 'up against the wall' already, in so far as the *forms* they use, the social and performance *spaces* which they seek to mobilize, and the *television institutions* that commission their work, already make 'compromised writers'[3] of them. Television drama for these socially critical writers is a collaborative (and contestive) practice, not the simple translation to screen of radical theoretical ideas.

In Chapter 1 I touched on the relationship between regulatory discourse and 'serious drama'. In this chapter I will take the analysis of radical authorship and regulatory discourses further, expanding on work by John Caughie who makes a number of valuable points about the political importance of 'authored' drama. These have mainly to do with its historical associations: with naturalism, with the theatre, and with contemporary social events. In the following three chapters I will take up each of these theoretical issues within an ethnography of production.

Naturalism

Naturalism has been criticized by theorists like Lukacs for its 'passive capitulation' to descriptive method and empiricism: 'in . . . seeing the results but not the struggles of the opposing forces'[4] within capitalism. Naturalism has also been consistently attacked by television writers like John McGrath and Troy Kennedy Martin for its formal characteristics, which 'simply followed the characters rather than expressing a view of them'.[5] But Caughie reminds us that naturalism has also been associated historically with political progressivism (in, for example, Zola's novels), and that on television, despite their ready appropriation by an 'apolitical' reformism, works like *Coming Out* (gay men in bed), *Cathy Come Home* (the homeless), and *Culloden* (the lost history of Scottish feudalism and English genocide), have served 'within a politics of radical humanism to introduce . . . an element (the working class, women, social justice) which previously had been excluded'.[6] Caughie argues against the 'a-historical formalism' of recent theoretical critiques of naturalism, and a concomitant tendency to celebrate 'an "avant-garde" with Dennis Potter at its head'.[7]

> What I think has to be considered for television – for its mode of circulating, for its institutional determinations, for its conservatism – is the possibility of a debate within naturalism as well as a struggle against it.[8]

Like Caughie, Raymond Williams points to progressive features distinguishing the growth of naturalism and realism from earlier dramatic forms, such as the emphasis on contemporaneity, secular causality and social inclusiveness in human relationships. He also notes an emerging difference between naturalism and realism in the nineteenth century, opening up the possibility of a debate about 'naturalist' methods.

> Naturalism as a doctrine of character formed by environment could emerge . . . as a passive form: people were stuck where they were. . . . A counter sense of realism, mainly within Marxism, insisted on the dynamic quality of all 'environments', and on the possibility of intervention to change them.[9]

This is, of course, Trevor Griffiths' 'materialism of detail/materialism of forces' distinction, and in Williams it underpins a further contrast: between 'high' and 'habituated' naturalism. Modern TV drama's tendency is to emphasize the 'unconnected and inconsequent impressions of a mind or a world that is mobile and dynamic at the surface only, the larger world view which contains them being again and again the static properties of the "human condition" or the symbolic or archetypal permanences of a universalist psychology or a permanently alienated civilisation'.[10] Callan and *The Sweeney*'s Regan are examples of this alienated and psychologized 'existential' hero.[11] This, Williams argues, represents an habituated naturalism which has long since jettisoned its overt relationship with 'scientific' theories of evolution and degeneration (high naturalism as in Zola), but which still traps character and events within the individualism and 'plausibility' of common-sense views.

In contrast, 'progressive realism' may set in motion an 'experiment', an 'as if' narrative situation, to trouble the common-sense surface of events. Trevor Griffiths' 'innocence' in reconstructing Amundsen's expedition as an example of radical primitivism is arguably one such experiment. And Raymond Williams points to other examples in the Tony Garnett/Jim Allen work, *The Big Flame*:

> a certain dramatic, but also political, hypothesis is established. What would happen if we went beyond the terms of this particular struggle against existing conditions and existing attempts to define or alter them? . . . What would happen in specific terms if we moved beyond the strike to the occupation? Thus if we are establishing the character of realism in *The Big Flame*, we have to notice the interesting combination . . . and . . . a certain fracture, between the familiar methods of establishing recognition and the alternative method of a hypothesis within that recognition, a hypothesis which is played out in realistic terms but within a politically imagined possibility.[12]

Williams points to specific techniques in *The Big Flame* which carry this tension between naturalism and realist hypothesis: the shift within the narrative 'from the rather ragged discussion which is done within naturalist terms to the conscious voice-over presentation of an alternative point of view';[13] the satiric representation of the media's construction of events, which draws attention to the problems associated with naturalist techniques within *The Big Flame* itself; the reversal of conventional point of view by placing the camera systematically behind the workers rather than behind the police; the Brechtian device of the judge moving well beyond the conventions of the naturalist method in saying 'that it's all right for students to have these ideas, but if working men get them it's very dangerous';[14] the use of the 'Ballad of Joe Hill' which introduces the *connections* of a wider working-class history, and so a 'consciousness, classically defined as realism in contrast with naturalism, of the movements of history which underlie the apparent reality that is occurring'.[15] Together these techniques which generate 'a certain fracture' within the text signify the 'authorship' of realism, defined by Williams as 'the consciously interpretive in relation to a particular political viewpoint'.[16]

Television and theatre

As with naturalism, Caughie extends a cautious recognition to the radicalizing influence some forms of theatre have had on TV drama. In the main, the 'high culture' influence of theatre has been conservative. Nevertheless,

> The relation of television to theatre may also help to explain the drama producer's anxiety that they should be seen to be controversial. What has to be preserved . . . is the memory of the key position which theatre occupied in the left-liberal cultural revolt in the period immediately after 1956, a year which was marked not only by Hungary, Suez, and the splits within the British Communist Party, but also by the Royal Court production of *Look Back in Anger* which initiated critical and popular discourses in which the renaissance of British theatre was associated with protest.[17]

Not only were young dramatists like Trevor Griffiths influenced by this movement, but the institutional impasse which the 'Angry Young Men' of the theatre encountered became part of Griffiths' theoretical understanding. The 'combination of individual mobility with the stability of institutions'[18] that Raymond Williams (who was influential on Griffiths' thinking at this time) described as a politically nullifying practice for young playwrights, became both a common theme of Griffiths' work and a reflexive concern of his own practice. Thus, for instance, *Comedians* describes the attempt to generate a non-racist, non-sexist comic practice within commercial light entertainment, *Bill Brand* examines the fate of a radical young politician inside parliament, and in *Country* Griffiths displays a concern for his own separation from his working-class origins (especially after his greater affluence following work on the Hollywood film, *Reds*). The 'innocence' which Griffiths clings to, the question about moving to the Third World, are features of his concern to resist that absorbing British structure of individual mobility and stable institutions.

But, as Caughie points out, the television institutions themselves are not monolithic 'sets of controls, determinations and easy appropriations'.[19] One of the 'cracks or fissures' (to use Griffiths' term) in the institution is precisely *at the meeting point of theatrical and television values of practice*. As Griffiths says, 'TV is run by controllers, and controllers are so called . . . because they seek control over the form and content of the material they transmit. Theatres are on the whole cottage industries at a quite different level of capital development. They are fairly openly dealing in ideas with less capital at stake.'[20] Yet when it comes to 'authored' TV drama, that theatre quality of 'dealing with ideas' is at a premium. 'Theatre' legitimizes the TV institution in terms of *its* 'quality', in the sense that TV's 'balance' between informing ('leading' society) and entertaining ('serving' it), is seen as a balance between 'art' ('dealing with ideas') and commerce.

There is a continuous negotiation at the 'controller' level between television drama which 'pushes back the boundaries' and work which goes too far into 'excess'. The negotiating discourses here are, Caughie notes, not radical: official (controllers') discourse speaks of 'provocation' and 'offence'; creative discourse talks of 'conviction' and 'talent'. The ambiguity is generally patched over by labelling the 'excessive' dramatists 'untalented'. But at least there is enough play and uncertainty within the institutional discourse to allow controversial documentary dramas like *Days of Hope* or *Law and Order* to be 'commissioned, made, shown, celebrated and condemned, then withheld despite protest, then reshown in apparent deference to the protest'.[21] It is this ambiguity within institutional discourse which allows the progressive aspect of the naturalist tradition to surface in TV drama from time to time.

Television as social event: factions and documentary drama

TV critics often equate 'serious drama' with the 'gritty realism' of documentary-drama. Caughie argues that, unlike American 'factions' such as *Holocaust* (which are firmly melodramatic, without a mixture of narrative and documentary forms), and documentary reconstructions like Granada's *Three Days in Szczecin* (which prioritize the journalistic over the dramatic), drama documentary works according to the formal articulation of two 'looks' – the look of the documentary and the look of the dramatic fiction.

The dramatic look is 'the rhetoric . . . of narrative realist film: eyeline match, field/reverse-field, point-of-view. This rhetoric . . . orders the world into a readable hierarchy.'[22] Caughie's analysis here draws on the screen theory tradition, exemplified by Colin MacCabe's attack on Ken Loach's *Days of Hope* as a 'classic-realist text';[23] in other words, as a work which conceals its own conditions of production, claiming a transparency of vision when in fact its narrative is determined by a controlling discourse. In this way, MacCabe argued, *Days of Hope* resolved contradictions rather than opened them up for interrogation by the spectator.

When Colin McArthur responded that *Days of Hope* did expose the contradictions of social democratic institutions at certain '*obviously* structured moments' (as for instance 'in the scene in which Pritchard, the gentlemanly Northern coal owner, lectures Ben and the three arrested Durham miners on the excellence of the British tradition of peaceful, gradual and constitutional reform while, in the background, the soldiers brought in to suppress dissent in the coalfield indulge in bayonet practice'[24]) MacCabe replied that McArthur's example was in fact 'exactly the classic realist form which privileges the image against the word to reveal that what the mine-owner says is false. In this matter our position of knowledge is guaranteed – we may choose to disagree with what the narrative tells us but if it has already placed us in the position where we are sure we are right, it has not questioned the very construction of that position.'[25]

MacCabe's work here itself draws on a theoretical tradition which, as Dunn argues, sees visual media as

> the cultural homologue of modern positivism, collapsing knowledge and experience into the category of visual sense perception and elevating sensory experience to the place of dominance.[26]

We have seen that McArthur himself is critical of TV history's empiricist tendency to privilege 'facts like sense impressions'. But MacCabe is taking the argument further as part of wider theories of the 'visualization of culture'. He argues that in its 'congruence of realms of truth and vision, *Days of Hope* adopts an empiricist attitude to knowledge in which the process of the production of knowledge . . . is elided into the instantaneous moment of sight'.[27] This 'visual epistemology', theorists like Debord argue, is closely tied in with the commoditization of the viewer, since the capitalist 'degradation of *being* into *having*' is followed by 'a generalized sliding of *having* into *appearing*'.[28] The meanings objects have for us inhere not in their use value but in the *image* of what their possession will bring – i.e. further possessions (of power, sexuality, etc.), which themselves are further images.

In Baudrillard's work, this critique of the visualization of culture reaches an extreme, where there is no longer any distinction between image and reality. For Baudrillard, as Kellner says, 'As simulations proliferate, they come to refer only to themselves: a carnival of mirrors reflecting images projected from other mirrors onto the omnipresent television screen and then to the screen of consciousness which in turn refers the image to its previous storehouse of images also produced by simulatory mirrors.'[29] So for Baudrillard, the Vietnam War and *Apocalypse Now*, 'reality' and image, implode on each other: 'War as a trip, a technological and psychedelic fantasy; war as a succession of special effects, the war become film well before it was shot.'[30] Similarly, in its 'logic of the extermination of its own referent, a logic of the implosion of meaning in which the message disappears on the horizon of the medium',[31] the television series *Holocaust* 'telescopes' into the actual extermination of the Jews.

> The same process of forgetting, of liquidation, of extermination, the same annihilation of memories and of history, the same inverse, implosive radiation, the same absorption without trace, the same black hole as Auschwitz. . . . Properly speaking it is *Holocaust* the television film which constitutes the definitive holocaust event.[32]

By the time we come to Baudrillard's argument that the Harrisburg meltdown was a simulation of *The China Syndrome*, 'the anticipation of reality by images and media',[33] that 'the real core of the affair' (the reactor core) is 'like the real; buried and indecipherable, ultimately of no importance' so that the television event has 'supremacy . . . over the nuclear event which itself remains . . . in some sense imaginary',[34] it is clear that theories of the visualization of culture have reached a very different concept of 'the real' from that of Raymond Williams and Trevor Griffiths. In their work it is precisely that hidden 'core' which must be revealed if we are to avoid the naturalism of appearances. Baudrillard's is a theory where, as Kellner argues, '"Implosion" collapses social phenomena into each other, so that it is impossible to distinguish between media and reality, classes and masses, simulations and realities, forces and relations of production, etc.'[35] Hence, it seems, there *are* no causal 'generative structures' of social control and so (unlike in realist theory) nothing to socially transform.

Various radical theorists have tried to find ways out of this impasse: Fiske by trying to combine theories of the visualization of culture with theories of the active audience; Cunningham by emphasizing the 'excessive' discursivity of hybridized visual forms, so that, as 'drama comments on the archive, and archive comments on the drama' in mini-series, the *process* of knowledge production (which MacCabe argues is missing from visual forms like *Days of Hope*) is revealed.

Caughie's analysis of the 'two looks' in drama-documentary gestures in this direction. As well as its dramatic look, *Days of Hope* also relied on the documentary look, which Caughie defines as 'the system of looks which constructs the social space of the fiction'.[36] As Caughie argues, a fundamental feature of the documentary look is the rhetoric of the 'unplanned' shot; the 'easily visible but unsteady' representation of 'unproblematic fact', 'the hand-held camera, the cramped shot, natural lighting, inaudible sound' and the 'camera surprised by the action'.

In relation to this Caughie quotes Ken Loach's concern to 'let the conversation call for the cuts, rather than the camera knowing who was going to speak next'.[37] Potentially, then, there will be a hiatus between the 'ordered hierarchy' of the dramatic look and the 'unplanned' documentary look, drawing attention to the work's conditions of production. But, although apparently spontaneous, within Ken Loach's 'process' this appearance of the 'unplanned' has its own form of premeditation, as Trevor Griffiths describes:

> What the naturalist director seeks to reproduce . . . is the actual conditions of the meeting of two or more people. . . . The performers . . . shouldn't know in advance what's going to happen. And, of course, the way to prevent them knowing, to deny them knowledge, is to deny them the text. And then to get them to improvise the text, the idea of the text . . . via the director's spoken word, via his account of it. He will have strategies for stimulating particular responses at particular times, which will be secretive by and large.[38]

When Loach does this, it is because he has already chosen cast who have more experience of what they are portraying than he has, as director. As he puts it, 'the characters they are playing are themselves, as near as possible';[39] hence actors become the 'experts' in their own emotions and reactions, which it is the task of the director to release.

In this 'process', careful selection of the main actors is central. Theirs are the privileged experiences. So, Caughie argues, because the dramatic look privileges the main protagonists with whom the audience is invited to identify, whereas the documentary look tends to fix its object as static victims who 'are looked at and look on', in the end there is no contestation of visual discourses:

> the dramatic narrative will impose its resolutions on the documentary disorder, and the drama will end up being about the privileged, centred individuals. . . . What documentary drama offers (like naturalism) is the experience of the drama rather than the analysis of (or 'scientific experiment' on) the document. . . . Thus *Days of Hope* offers the experience of history – memory – rather than its analysis.[40]

Yet *despite* all this, Caughie does not dismiss the progressive potential of TV drama. On the one hand, there are those (rather rare) cases like McGrath's *The Cheviot, The Stag, and the Black, Black Oil* where the documentary discourse (a touring theatrical performance in the

Highlands of Scotland) *does* radically separate itself from the dramatic one (a Highlander being chased by a redcoat soldier), so that the history of exploitation in Scotland is analysed and interrogated rather than romantically experienced. On the other hand, Caughie rightly insists on the insertion of documentary dramas into *current* history; and here Caughie shifts from critiques of the visualization of culture to a realist theory of history as a *process* of structure and agency.

> Thus, however much the ideology within which it operates may be characterised as reformist, the screening of *Cathy Come Home* is an event with material effects within the history of British social work; *Law and Order* is an event within the history of the relations between the police and one of the major media; the screening of *The Big Flame*, coinciding with the Devlin report on the docks and the Upper Clyde Shipyard sit-in, occurs within a particular conjuncture of events and forces which makes the identification of its political effectivity more complex. . . . Within the social space of television, within the politics of its institutions, and within the way it circulates, television programmes have the capacity to be events as much as to be texts.[41]

The 'events' which Caughie is referring to here are not the continuous events of image and spectacle in Baudrillard's 'hyperrealism of simulation', but events with real 'material effects' in the various histories of social resistance.

In this context, Ken Loach can point out (despite MacCabe's claims to the contrary) that *Days of Hope*, far from being 'the experience of history – memory – rather than its analysis', was part of the contemporary struggle of the miners against the Heath Conservative government. Like his later documentary, *Which Side Are You On?*, the film was taken around unions, trades councils and coal fields during the strike. As Loach says, the process of information flow here was two-way. Miners could criticize the film's analysis from their own experience; and the film could sharpen up a growing awareness that 'the police are integrated into the rest of the state machine. . . . Police are political; this was only triggered by the film.'[42]

This existence of TV drama as event as well as text also has, Caughie notes, the potential of confirming social identity. The 'dangerous mesh of empathy' may in fact help the growth of solidarity among the oppressed groups; though this can work in contradictory ways, as the much-debated reception of *Holocaust* in West Germany suggests. On the one hand, tapping into the growing Nazi nostalgia in Germany of the late 1970s, *Holocaust* enabled political and media figures who had 'gone along' with Fascism to make 'honest' confessions thus, Zielinski argues, achieving a curious kind of honour in struggling with their conscience. 'It was not the resistance fighters nor the victims who were now put forward as an example but instead, the pitiable fellow-travelers.'[43] The 'massive positive echo' this evoked in the general public was due, in Zielinski's view, to the fact that these public figures shared their biography 'with the majority of German men now over 50',[44] thus providing 'the exemplary model for identification'. On the other hand, though, '*Holocaust* awakened another, positive, variety of new self-awareness in those social minorities who were also victims of the Nazi regime of violence. They are still suffering in the present day because of their identity – Gypsies, homosexuals, the politically persecuted. For the first time in the history of the Federal Republic, their voices have been heard loudly and frequently in public demanding recognition, ideological and material redress.'[45]

The most valuable part of the critical debate about *Holocaust* as social event has been the careful analysis of the discourses carrying Right, Left and Centre ideologies, before, during and after the transmission. These have focused debates about aesthetic forms, political facts and pedagogical strategies, and extended the media critique of Fascism beyond the high culture forms in which it had circulated before. As Markovits and Hayden point out, until *Holocaust* anti-Fascist texts aimed at a small élite audience were more than offset by the 'penny detective novels which celebrated fascist tendencies, such as a strong death wish, a desire to sacrifice oneself for one's country at all costs, militant anti-communism, and the glorification of heroes and supermen'.[46]

This point about *Holocaust* illustrates Caughie's argument that the politics of a TV drama must be seen both in terms of 'the place which it occupies within the political forces and contradictions which are current at the time of its screening', and in terms of its relationship to the other representations predominantly circulated within popular culture. Hence it is unrewarding to establish the conditions for 'progressive' TV drama by way of formal analysis alone. 'The conjuncture in which programmes are screened has to be critically identified; and because the programmes are made within basically conservative institutions which are both highly determined and highly determining, their place within the politics of the institutions has also to be brought into consideration.'[47]

The case of *Holocaust*'s reception aside, however, work on the 'conjuncture in which programmes are screened' within the politics of media institutions has hardly begun. The critical and emotional furore around *Holocaust* as 'a portrayal of ontological horror' have tended to draw attention away from the quite *continuous* operation of TV drama as social event. To take the analysis of TV drama as social and institutional event further, I will return to Trevor Griffiths' *The Last Place On Earth* and *Fatherland* in the next two chapters to see how works even by the same 'author' are situated in complex and different ways according to the particular formal, social and institutional field they inhabit.

5 TV drama as social event: text and inter-text

There was something about a man's world and Edwardian days . . . you know, the old blood comics. And I wasn't sure that I could find a politics within this piece that could be inserted into a contemporary discourse and the present struggle.

Trevor Griffiths[1]

In her analysis of *The Flame Trees of Thika*, Tania Wollen is one critic who does address the specific social and institutional 'event' of TV drama:

In the late summer and early autumn of 1981, the production of a memory in which a white middle-class family brought control and government to an unruly land inhabited by black, unpredictable people, was of no small significance. . . . Only months before the first episode of *Flame Trees* was broadcast, Britain's inner cities flared. The riots of 1981 were class riots in that those on the streets (and on television) were the young unemployed, the new dispossessed. They were race riots in that of those dispossessed, black people constituted the majority and in that the police oppressed them most severely. . . . The riots were constructed as 'race' riots by the media and so the history of a particularly subjugated part of the working class was repressed. As 'race riots', the disaffection of a whole class could be minimalised, limited to particularly 'black' areas of the inner cities.[2]

Flame Trees reproduced (in 1981) the long-term image of 'Africa as a dark and devious threat',[3] welding it so successfully to myths of benevolent and patiently enduring colonialism, that the *Daily Mail's* review could welcome it as real and comforting history:

Today, when we hear nothing but abuse about the whites in Africa and their wicked colonialism, it is refreshingly new for many of us to learn how life was really like for so many of those Europeans. . . .

Many, like Elspeth Huxley's family, brought work, medical advances and, above all, agricultural husbandry, to areas that were a wilderness.[4]

While *Flame Trees* re-worked a long history of racist texts, and itself was re-worked by secondary texts like the *Daily Mail*, institutionally it was part of a culturally prestigious flow of TV drama events which were circulating a particular (élite) view of British society. *Brideshead Revisited, The Far Pavilions, Jewel in the Crown* were together producing a sumptuous memory of Britain's colonial past. *Flame Trees*, Wollen notes, was 'not a memory produced as spectacularly' as these others, but 'it preceded these . . . and constructed audience expectations for bigger and better'.[5] As the final credits were rolling on screen, the continuity announcer told viewers that *Brideshead Revisited* would 'be taking the place of the "truly lovely" serial that *Flame Trees* had proved to be'.[6]

The particular value of Wollen's analysis is in locating *Flame Trees'* 'quintessential Britishness' as part of a wider spectrum of Euston Films TV product. Euston makes the contemporary 'male-macho' *Minder* as well as the wistful, 'female-autobiographical' romance of *Flame Trees*. Yet the 'memory of a colonial history . . . was in fact no great departure from the company's construction of an urban present'.[7]

> Euston Films, by combining in its project the dramas of street violence with an account of how a wild open space was tamed, refreshed a national identity. Britishness, now represented by the ruthlessness of working-class heroes, was once represented by the courage and fair play of the more genteel middle-classes abroad. Where there is grit, there was pluck.[8]

Indeed, one could argue that the ideological work of Euston product is (i) precisely in *separating* its images of street violence, black territory, and working-class solidarity across different TV genres; and (ii) in promoting the myth of history as *developing* democracy, from imperial 'pluck' (as colonial 'service') to Cockney 'grit' (as ironic 'resistance').

It was *Flame Trees'* kind of 'quintessential' (but actually class-, gender- and race-based) Britishness that Trevor Griffiths wanted to challenge in *The Last Place On Earth*. In the Scott series British pluck and 'spunky courage' were shown to be ludicrously inappropriate to the task at hand. More, they were part of the process of ideological reproduction and myth-making which constructed 'Britishness' from the Boer War to the Falklands campaign. If the 1981 'race riots' were the historical moment for *Flame Trees*, the Falklands War was the moment for Griffiths'

Scott story. Originally Griffiths had refused the offer to do a TV version of Roland Huntford's book on Scott as too 'Boys' Own'. But a year later, when the offer came again, he changed his mind. 'We were a year closer to Falklands . . . and maybe one could see the . . . recrudescence of imperialist ideology, feeling, silliness.'[9]

Part of his reason for accepting was that at that stage the piece was going to be shot by Roland Joffe, whom Griffiths finds 'politically very interesting' and had worked successfully with on *Bill Brand*. In the end, Joffe did not shoot *The Last Place On Earth*, but whoever the director, there were likely to be problems. As Griffiths points out, a TV contract is very clear:

> Any writing, notes for a character, notes for a sequence, images, jottings, draft treatments, sub-structures, all characters created, all language used on a page, including dialogue, stage directions and so on . . . belong to the producer. They don't belong at any point . . . to the person creating them. Now I'm not arguing that they should belong to the individual person; that isn't my thrust. My thrust is that they belong to somebody else, and that they belong basically to the agents of capital.[10]

In this relationship, the director is himself the agent of the producer. Directors are not dealing 'with the creative interpretation of the text, because they are dealing with . . . the problem of there being no snow there when they get there, and they are supposed to do the polar ice-cap in the next three days. They are dealing with problems of dogs and dog handlers. . . . They are dealing with logistics.'[11]

In *The Last Place On Earth*, because of overspending, a new producer was appointed who listed 112 scenes for omission. Griffiths told Central he was pulling out. Then director Ferdi Fairfax helped him get much of it reinserted. But at cost:

> Since tendentially TV drama series are implacably about narrative, about action, about carrying the story on, a lot of the stuff that I wrote, e.g. the dream sequences, the social and historical context of imperial Britain at the beginning of this century, certain relationships within the text, Kathleen Scott and Nansen for example, these things tended to represent areas of provocation and danger, or areas of massive resource use, expenditure. These disappeared without trace.[12]

In the final product, there were about 80 scenes missing; and, Griffiths added, some of the scenes that remain have had elements, contexts, and signs relocated within them from scenes that have been dropped. And quite often it doesn't work.[13]

But Griffiths' screenplay *itself*, of course, 'relocates elements, contexts, and signs' from a previous text, Huntford's *Scott and Amundsen*, itself a major social event in its time. A TV drama is *inter*-textual, a dynamic succession and synchrony of other texts, other social events. Later in the chapter I will discuss the way in which *The Last Place On Earth* was appropriated and made to circulate as social event by way of secondary texts (particularly newspapers and magazines). But before that, I will look at an earlier stage of the inter-textual process, as Huntford's book re-worked the Scott legend, then became the Griffiths screenplay, which in turn was re-worked in the transmitted text, *The Last Place On Earth*. I will focus on one short sequence in each of the texts: the discovery of the bodies of Scott, Wilson and Bowers by Atkinson and the rescue team.

The Last Place On Earth: transformation and transcodification

Keir Elam has recently addressed the problem of a semiotics of production-as-process (from text to theatricalization). This arises out of his dissatisfaction with an earlier tendency of performance analysis 'not only to semiotize (textualize) the performance but also to . . . reify it (precisely as aesthetic object)'.[14] Elam criticizes here his own (earlier) academic relationship to drama performance as one of 'surveillant/ other' analysis,[15] which took no account of performers' knowledgeability and so reduced performance as a phenomenological, cultural and agentive experience. By examining the 'processual' nature of dramatic and theatrical production as a project of *narrativization*, Elam focuses on the '*work* or *production* (rather than product), ever in progress and ever in process'.[16] The narrativization project goes through 'procedures of *dramatization* (e.g. the adaptation of a narrative text . . .) and *theatricalization* (the quest, common to all productions, for effective spatial, scenic and corporeal vehicles for the showing forth of the dramatic narrative)'.[17] Thus Trevor Griffiths' screenplay (published by Verso as *Judgement Over The Dead*) is a dramatization of Huntford's biography *Scott and Amundsen*, and the transmitted TV series *The Last Place On Earth* is a theatricalization of *Judgement Over The Dead*.

The narrativization process (the production 'story') from biography to screenplay is one of 'transformation' – the preliminary selection and adaptation of existing narrative material. The process from screenplay to television series is one of 'transcodification' – the passage 'from the diegetic codes of prose narrative to the mimetic codes of dramatic theatre'.[18] Of course, in the case of *Scott and Amundsen*, this was itself a transformation of an earlier diegetic narrative: Scott's own account of his expedition.

Scott and Amundsen

The most significant transformation made by Huntford is the *expansion* of his source material by the addition of Amundsen's story, dislocating the original diegesis in order to mesh two adventures. This process of expansion, dislocation and meshing is what structures the Huntford narrative. The following are just a few examples of this process of narrativization:

> Amundsen, so far as we know, wrote no letters at all. Scott seems to be looking over his shoulder at an unseen audience, concerned more with his reputation than his actions.[19]

> The all-pervading sense of urgency at Framheim was little in evidence at Cape Evans. Winter passed in leisurely, amateur, almost dilettante fashion.[20]

> Scott's biscuits . . . contained white flour, with sodium bicarbonate as leavening. Amundsen's, on the other hand . . . were based on wholemeal flour and rolled oats, with yeast as the main leavening. Yeast and whole grain are potent sources of Vitamin B. The biscuits symbolize two different worlds.[21]

Huntford's narrative of 'two different worlds' is primarily an individualistic contrast between Scott as 'one of the worst of Polar explorers'[22] and Amundsen as 'the supreme exponent of Polar technique'.[23] Although Huntford does situate Scott in his class as 'a suitable hero for a nation in decline',[24] his main concern is with Amundsen as 'Napoleonic figure' and 'genius', whose 'masterpiece' journey to the Pole was 'the culmination of the classical age of Polar exploration and, perhaps, the greatest snow journey ever made'.[25]

The endings of the Huntford and Griffiths texts are symptomatic of their different projects. Griffiths cuts from Buckingham Palace, where the survivors of Scott's expedition ('the last of these English – or so it once seemed') meet the King, to the 'artillery flashes and cannonades' of the First World War. The 'ritual dance of class and Empire' at Buckingham Palace fades, and 'another dance begins, in grisly slow-motion, men dying by the millimetre in their millions'.[26] The last words of the screenplay are a woman's, as she anchors the visuals of mud and blood:

> If nothing else, Scott showed his countrymen the way to die. We have so many heroes among us now, so many Scotts, holding sacrifice above gain . . . and we begin to understand what a splendour arises from the bloody fields of Flanders and Gallipoli. . . . [27]

Huntford, in contrast, concludes his book with the final chapter of a biography: 'The Last Adventure' of Amundsen as tragic hero. Amundsen in this narrative is 'the personification of a national genius', whose fate of being misunderstood was the price of his own hubris. The author's admiration for 'great men' and national victory is clear, as he compares Amundsen's secret change from the North to the South Pole with 'the Drake touch; the Nelson stratagem. The main thing was, he *won*.'[28]

Huntford is relentless in his hounding of Scott as everything Amundsen was not – incompetent, authoritarian, self-pitying and, above all, not 'a natural leader of men'. *Scott and Amundsen* is a biographical narrativization of Scott's diaries; in particular one which partakes of the genre's familiar 'deconstructing the legend' strategy. However, it is also a particular version of this formula, since the legend itself was constructed *as* narrative by its author, Scott. Here too, Huntford expands on his original source by meshing it with the story of Amundsen: 'Amundsen followed the time-honoured practice of letting his men tell their own tales when they had a tale to tell . . . Scott does not allow his followers to tell their own tales; he tells them himself, and does so in such a way as subtly to disparage their achievements in order to enhance his own.'[29] Whereas Amundsen, for Huntford, was the 'last of the Vikings' who 'expected his deeds to speak for themselves . . . Scott, by contrast, seemed to have sought experience as . . . the raw material for writing'.[30] Whereas, then, for Huntford, Amundsen is legitimized by the empiricism of transparent deeds, Scott is guilty of *textualizing* history.

Consequently *Scott as narrator* is a major actant (and villain) in *Scott and Amundsen*, where Huntford *calls up* Scott's followers to tell their own tales (via diary extracts etc.). But the tales are told as part of the meta-discourse of a new narrator. Huntford is the narrator at what Genette calls the 'extradiegetic level', in relation to whom Scott and his followers construct second-degree narratives.[31] Authorial authority 'proves' Scott's story wrong to the implied reader. Narrative hierarchy places Huntford (as extradiegetic narrator) 'above' Scott (as diegetic narrator). Narrative omniscience gives Huntford apparent access to Scott's innermost thoughts and feelings ('Scott would have to answer for the men he had lost. Shackleton would have the last laugh. That was something Scott could not face. It would be better to seek immolation in the tent.'[32]). Narratorial commentary – in particular interpretation (as in his explanation that Scott persuaded Bowers and Wilson, in order that his diary be found, to die in the tent rather than on a last quest for One Ton Depot), judgement ('Scott was a heroic bungler'[33]), and generalization (Scott as 'a suitable hero for a nation in decline'[34]) – establish the perceptibility of Huntford's position.[35] Above all, his *reliability* as narrator is established by careful 'scientific' analysis.

Biggest and heaviest of the party, Evans nonetheless had to make do with the same rations as the others. He was, therefore, starving more, deficiencies were accelerated, and his condition grew proportionately worse. . . . The wound that refused to heal, also suppurating cuts and continual nose bleeds, all suggest that after leaving the Pole Evans was suffering from advanced Vitamin C deficiency, and may have been in the early stages of scurvy. One of the effects of the disease is to make blood vessels fragile. In that condition the normally insignificant shock of falling waist-deep into a crevasse, as Evans did, could be enough to injure a blood vessel within the skull and cause a slow brain haemorrhage. That would explain what was happening to him.[36]

The description of the discovery of the bodies of Scott, Wilson and Bowers is brief: Wright finds the tent, Atkinson enters, and, prior to sitting alone 'for hour after hour' with Scott's diary, insists 'on everybody going in one by one to look'.[37] Later, Atkinson tells the tale of disaster to 'the little company gathered around him', and Huntford suggests that 'the shock of discovery was overlaid by a sense of unease'.[38] He calls up their diary extracts: of Gran who wonders whether 'Scott himself is most to blame'; of Cherry-Garrard, haunted by the idea that, had he done the navigation course which Scott denied him, 'he might have saved his friends. In the end, his reason was to be clouded by the thought.'[39] One certainly might make other interpretations of these letters – of, for instance, Gran's 'Perhaps Scott himself is most to blame. He did not want to risk others' lives to save his own.'[40] But all of these extracts are *anchored* by Huntford's scurvy theory, as he describes the thirty pounds of rock they had dragged on the sledge to the very end, 'to show themselves martyrs to Science; a pathetic little gesture to salvage something from defeat at the Pole. . . . Half the weight in seal meat would have saved them.'[41]

Huntford's intrusive authorial voice now contextualizes Atkinson's reading of Scott's 'Message to the Public'.

The effect was immediate. 'Of their sufferings, hardship and devotion to one another (wrote Williamson), the world will soon know, the deeds that were done were equally as great as any committed on Battlefield and won the respect and honour of every true Britisher.' Thus did the legend take root so swiftly and naturally. Scott had known how to speak to his countrymen.[42]

Scott in this scene completes his journey, closes *his* authorial account. The myth is not actively constructed (as in Griffiths' text) by the ruling class; and the 'Battlefield' is not specified as the intra-class imperialism of Griffiths' 'Great War'. We do hear about the later editing of the diaries, but this is done as the 'tacit agreement' of a nation caught in the throes of romantic idealism, hiding its own 'muddling through' from itself. The First World War too is mentioned, but as the mark of British decline for which Scott was the 'necessary myth figure', turning death and failure into heroism.

When the issue of class is raised by Huntford, it is by way of nostalgia for an earlier period of 'great' British history.

Oates . . . was the representative of the old order; one of the landed gentry, an eighteenth-century squire, among a lot of Edwardian bourgeoisie and, on the other side of the partition, the working class. He stood for a doomed world among the inheritors of the new. Most of his companions appreciated his aristocratic virtues; his detachment, tolerance and disdain for petty social conventions.[43]

In this narrativization, Oates and Amundsen are natural companions in the 'era of terrestrial exploration that began with the explosion of the human spirit during the Renaissance'.[44]

Thus gaunt, hungry, frostbitten, Oates with aristocratic detachment stands at the end of the earth, weighing up the commander who has led him to inevitable defeat, and the opponent, who has just as inevitably triumphed. He takes a rational pleasure in seeing that the best man won; standing apart with quiet scorn for an incompetent leader.[45]

'Detachment' and 'rationality' are Huntford's empiricist *markers* of that post-Renaissance 'explosion of the human spirit'. Against it he sets the cramping *Zeitgeist* of 'ideology': not only the 'romantic idealism' of Scott, but also the socialism of Griffiths. Amundsen, says Huntford, unlike Scott, has not become a socialist hero. 'He was too much an individualist, too rational and detached to be harnessed to a barbaric ideology; indeed, ideology of any kind.'[46]

Yet, much earlier in his biography Huntford *had* described a major ideological difference between Scott and Amundsen.

> Although 'Discovery' was technically a merchant vessel, Scott . . . ran her under naval discipline with rigid segregation of officers and men. This is a far cry from Amundsen's 'little republic' on 'Gjoa', his 'spontaneous discipline' and absence of formal hierarchy and rank.[47]

It was this *particular* meshed detail of Huntford's historical fabula, and not his heroic 'post-Renaissance' ('individualist', 'rational', 'detached') world view that Griffiths extracted in transforming *Scott and Amundsen* into *Judgement Over The Dead*.

Judgement Over The Dead

In Griffiths' screenplay the discovery of the bodies is part of a necessary inter-textual journey from ancient Viking folklore to contemporary British myth. In an early scene Amundsen asks Nansen to recite a Viking poem to British journalists.

> Cattle die
> Friends die
> Thou thyself shalt die,
> I know a thing
> That never dies,
> Judgement over the dead.[48]

Griffiths traces the British recontextualizing of that poem, in which the journalists play an important part. Schoolboy essays, newspaper editorials and various Lords' speeches repeat the refrain: that the deeds of Shackleton and Scott prove 'that the manhood of the nation is not dead',[49] that 'British pluck can still triumph over all adversity',[50] that each man is 'willing to spend his life, if need be, in the cause'.[51]

Some of this is in Huntford's narrative too, but in Griffiths' text the process of diegetic (Scott's diaries) and mimetic (British newsreel) myth-construction is always related to matters of class and ideology. There is indeed a 'cause' for these deaths in *Judgement Over The Dead*. In Britain militant trade unionists picket Scott's fundraising:

> Banners proclaim their cause: Jobs not Glory; Why go to the South Pole, there's a wasteland on your doorstep called Lancashire; Not a Penny for the Pole; Send an expedition to Manchester to discover Poverty.[52]

The connection with the Falklands War and Thatcher's England is implicit and intended; though we are reminded that Norway, too, is a capitalist country. A socialist MP speaks against further grants to Amundsen in the Storting:

> Thousands living in squalid and miserable shacks and we say there is nothing we can do to help. Sick people wanting for medical care, the needs of the old and the impaired ignored. . . . Yet here we are again being asked to put a further 25,000 kroner into the pocket of the brave but impudent Mr Amundsen. . . . [53]

In Norway, Amundsen's change of plans (after the North Pole is 'taken'), is connected with 'the press barons and the industrialists and the politicians' who 'want a coup' before they will fund his serious exploration in the north. 'So we'll give them one. . . . We . . . take the South Pole.'[54] In Britain, Scott's supposed interest in scientific exploration is given its economic underpinning, as he tells financing Liverpool manufacturers 'of precious industrial ore discoveries (pitchblende for radium) that would restore British industrial pre-eminence'.[55]

This conjuction of labour and capital, in which the different historical moments of Britain and Norway are set, is Griffiths' context for 'Pole seeking'. Symptomatically, Griffiths meshes an apparently personal letter from Amundsen (telling Nansen he is including Johansen in his team) with this broader historical context:

> Images of Europe – Caption: March 1910 – establishes the essential character of the continent's historical conjuncture, on the last throb of one revolutionary wave, on the verge of another. . . . Militarism, nationalism, chauvinism, industrial militancy, the political mobiliza- tion of women by women, all imaged, the essential context from which this particular narrative is abstracted. The last image, on the mix, is a vast expanse of white – empty, ominous with the sound of dull rumbling machinery.[56]

The following sequence introduces the machinery – the motorsledge. This will be an integral part of the Scott narrative (the 'dance' of failure and death); just as the Johansen letter (which is in fact to buy more time for Amundsen's secret plans) is part of the Amundsen narrative of deception.

These narratives of death and deception dramatize Griffiths' 'images of Europe' and also historicize the 'psychological' states of the two leaders. Scott's 'dance' is underpinned by his dreams and premonitions of death, and by a deep fear of his inadequacy for leadership. His mother, Kathleen Scott, and 'Uncle Bill' Wilson successively become *his* leaders – alter egos in the construction of 'greatness'. Amundsen is no less obsessive, his 'comradeship' with his men masking sexual repression. His dreams bring fear too: as he is chased by 'his demons' (Nansen and Viking past, King Haakon as Norway's newly nationalistic present, Frederick Cook as American competitor in Pole seeking); and as he himself chases but cannot catch Scott's driverless motorsledge.

In both cases these are dreams and fears connected with nationalism. But whereas Scott's dreams *are* premonitions, Amundsen's are not. The difference lies in the professional and historical quality of Norwegian nationalism. As a 'European Eskimo' Amundsen continues the Viking tradition, but in a spirit of comradeship, not militarism. In his pre-titles prologue, Griffiths has his 'European Eskimo' attuning to ice-culture in the Arctic north, while in contrast Scott, Wilson and Shackleton almost die of scurvy on the 1902 Antarctic Expedition.

These two 'Worlds Apart' continue to structure the narratives of 'deception' and 'death'; so, for instance, Part 4 opens with contrasting activities at the base camps of Framheim and Cape Evans. The Norwegians are adapting the environment to their needs, building an ice-tunnel for sauna and workshops. 'All have thick beards, long hair; in fur, they seem like natural beings, perfectly adapted.'[57] The British are playing football, class divided, 'gentlemen versus players . . . a sort of dance of the dead'.[58]

Adapted to their class and culture but not to nature, the British can only *struggle* to the Pole. Griffiths' descriptions are pointed: his screenplay calls for montage of Amundsen's four-day climb to the Polar plateau as 'a mainly wordless narrative of co-operative and highly dangerous action',[59] while Scott's 'ponies are belly-deep and desperate. Forward progress is minimal . . . Scott calls forward. The murderous trudge continues.'[60] Meanwhile the myth is being constructed. British newsreel film introduces 'the mighty motorsledges', 'the intrepid leader' and wishes 'Godspeed' to the 'boys of the British breed. They will do their duty.'[61] Griffiths juxtaposes this media celebration of Scott with Oates's comment on the ludicrous 'circus' that the expedition has become – a direct analogy with the media's construction of the Falklands War which is missing both in *Scott and Amundsen* and in *The Last Place On Earth*.

In Griffiths' text, the discovery of the bodies of Scott, Wilson and Bowers is a necessary symbolization of place (of nature as exploration and suffering) which connects the *structure* of Europe in 1910 with the *agency* of the British ruling class in constructing myths of dying. Griffiths composes a 'funereal montage of images of the discovery and disposal' as 'Lashly gazes gravely at the tent's contents; Atkinson gathers books, papers, effects; Wright stares in horror, fascination at the condition of the dead.'[62] Wright's appalled 'So this is scurvy' is silenced by Dr Atkinson, in the first stage of the latter's successful attempt to prevent 'doubt being cast on the whole organization and conduct of the expedition'.[63] Atkinson, alone in the tent, reads Scott's diary, 'the myth already gripping'; and then conveys Scott's 'Message to the Public' to its first audience.

The scene is of rhetoric and crushing triviality as the message (first in Atkinson's voice, then in Scott's) is 'ground out remorselessly over the tiny British huddle in the vast white plain'.[64] Yet the British, though physically crushed by the landscape, reclaim it in myth. Scott's voice, blaming the weather and his sick colleagues for the disaster, turns 'these rough notes and our dead bodies' into the necessarily continuous history 'which has shown that Englishmen can endure hardships, help one another, and meet death with as great a fortitude as ever in the past'.[65]

Unlike Huntford's narrative, it is not Scott but his class which is prime author of these events. 'Had I lived, I should have had a tale to tell . . . '; but what is needed is his death – and the *continuing* 'dance' of British people on the fields of Flanders and Gallipoli. Whereas Huntford's history connects 1912 with the past (of Renaissance individualism), Griffiths' history connects with the future (of Falklands militarism and news management).

The Last Place On Earth

The militant union pickets, the socialist Norwegian MP's talk about 'thousands living in squalid shacks', Scott's address to the manufacturers of Liverpool 'over shots of port passing at table and cheque books being flattened for the pen', the 'images of Europe's historical conjuncture', the monochrome film of Scott's departure from Cape Evans: all these are missing from the television version of *The Last Place On Earth*. As Griffiths notes, the dreams are missing, too. In the screenplay, the dreams establish character complexity in terms of the psycho-social history of Britain and Norway. In the television text, character 'density' is carried differently – via the naturalism of Martin Shaw's performance as Captain Scott.

Shaw told journalists that he experienced temperatures of -30° F on location, and compared this with Scott's 'temperatures of -77°, without a warm hotel to go back to each evening'.[66] He was quite public about his sympathy for Scott. 'I feel enormous admiration for his achievement, but at first I was quite baffled by his sudden changes in character.'[67] In the absence of some of Griffiths' socio-historical markers, Shaw's performance is a personally 'sensitive' one – Scott as hauntingly uncertain behind the class facade, deeply dependent on Kathleen and 'Bill' Wilson, driving his few talents relentlessly to their end.

This performance is particularly marked in the scene where Atkinson reads Scott's 'Message to the Public'. The TV text abandons Griffiths' 'funereal montage' for Huntford's scene where Atkinson calls each rescue party member in turn to see the bodies. Wright's comment about scurvy and Atkinson's rejoinder are followed by 'Atch' beginning to read Scott's message 'at the express wish of the Captain'. The opening words are accompanied by a camera tilt down Scott's dead body. It reveals the diary, still clutched, pen poised, in his frozen hands.

The diary, as 'source' of the myth, initially anchors the 'Message to the Public'; but as Scott's voice takes over from Atkinson's, there is a paralinguistic change in terms of voice tone difference, not only between Scott and Atkinson, but also between this narratorial Scott and the dramatis persona of the Scott who was earlier seen *composing* the words. Then Martin Shaw's voice had been in two modes: the rasping, laboured words of the dying Scott; and the inner monologue, also slow and impeded, matching naturalistically the pace of Scott's writing movements and mouth action. But in the discovery scene, Shaw's voice is different again; no longer slow and harsh but soft, gentle and appealing – not at all the voice 'ground out remorselessly over the tiny British huddle' of Griffiths' screenplay.

Nor are the British 'tiny' and 'huddled' in the 'vast white plain', as in the Griffiths text. As Atkinson and then Scott speak, the camera pans in slow celebration, picking out, one by one (and monumentally within the frame) this first 'Public' for Scott's message. The camera moves on, passing a final figure (backed by a fluttering Union Jack, and overlaid by Scott's words, 'Englishmen can endure hardships, help one another and meet death with as great a fortitude as ever') to the cairn and its cross. Cross and flag are then combined as the camera pulls out, dissolves to a sweep of the 'vast white plain' from above, travels over the Cape Evans hut, and comes to rest on the huge cross (of Scott's premonition) on the mountain beyond.

All this is overlaid by the slow-rhythmed Elgar-style score which has been Scott's 'pomp and circumstance' theme music. Mike Poole has rightly commented on a 're-working of reality' via the 'repeated use of the dramatic device of having Scott's diary entries heard in voice-over immediately after the events they describe' – a discrepancy 'cleverly underlined by Trevor Jones' score, which is a sort of mock-heroic "Elgarian" parody'.[68] On this occasion, though, the combination of Shaw's sympathetic performance, the monumentalizing (and symbolizing) camera style, and a sound score synchronous with the rise in emotional intensity and volume of Scott's voice, works against Griffiths' 'reworking of reality' sound/image effect. The scene certainly *can* be read ironically – especially as it is marked at one end by Scott's diary, and at the other by Atkinson glancing (arguably) at the central sign of Scott's failure, his huskies. But Martin Shaw's gently emotional 'Surely, surely, a great rich country like ours will see that those who are dependent on us are properly provided for', spoken to an intensifying musical theme and visually marked by the huge cross (as symbol of spiritual *conquest* of the landscape beneath it) works against irony. One suspects that a Bristol schoolgirl's response in 1913 on first reading those words was replicated in many British households in 1985:

> those men had wives and children at home and Captain Scott's last wish was that the people at home should be cared for. This will be done.[69]

The later emphasis on the doctoring of Scott's diary by 'the ruling class' recaptures the narratives of *The Last Place On Earth* for Griffiths' discourse. But arguably this is itself countered by the 'tragic' ending. Griffiths' Buckingham Palace/Great War 'dance of death' conjuncture is omitted; and the narrative closes with a different, more 'angst'-ridden meeting. Two tragically isolated heroes, Cook and Amundsen, meet briefly in prison, and it is there, finally, that Amundsen hears the news of Johansen's lonely suicide. As in Huntford's book, the text ends with the isolation and death of heroes. *The Last Place On Earth* ends as a fractured text, in which *both* the tragic/heroic Huntford biography *and* the critical realist Griffiths screenplay continue to work.

The narrativization process we are observing here is of 'theatricalization' (the television 'showing forth' of the Griffiths text). As Elam says, a familiar problem that adapters of narrative 'source' texts face is 'that of eliminating or delegating or otherwise hiding the intrusive narrative voice, and thus of finding non-diegetic modes of presenting or representing the events of the énoncé'.[70] Since Huntford's book was itself a transformation of an earlier narrative (Scott's diary) Griffiths could ostensibly hide Huntford's 'Boys' Own' voice by offering an 'authorial' position to Scott and Amundsen (as running voice-overs). These 'authors' were themselves positioned in the text (by Griffiths as extradiegetic narrator) by a series of standard and canonical performance techniques: delegating judgement of these narrators to other speakers (Meares, Oates, Johansen); use of syntactical devices (establishing contradictions between 'official' discourses – as in Scott's words and archival film footage – and the events they describe); and 'Big Print' narration, as Griffiths contextualizes the action – not only by his 'Images of Europe' history, but also by 'funereal montage', by shots of picketing workers, speeches in the Storting, concluding archival footage of the First World War with voice-over, etc.

However, many of these canonical markers of authorial perceptibility and reliability were missing from the television version. The television text transcodified Griffiths' screenplay, translating it via what Elam calls a multiplicity of axes of represented and representational space: 'discursive (the dramatic speaker's "I here"); proxemic (spatial relations between speaker-actors: "I here/you there"); topographical-objectual (spatial relations between actor-speakers and the specific features of stage and dramatic world with their objects: "this here/that there"); and metadramatic-metatheatrical (the overall dialectic between the dramatic-theatrical representation ("all this") and the audience and its world ("all that"))'.[71]

In the 'Message to the Public' scene, Griffiths' diegesis of defeated, 'tiny' and 'huddled' British in a 'vast white plain' is 'mimeticized' via each of these axes. The dramatic speaker is, in effect, doubled as Atkinson's message ('ground out remorselessly') changes to Scott's uplifting call to the best human qualities of the British nation (as carried by numerous other 'domestic' historical texts, like *Upstairs, Downstairs*). The 'huddled' proxemic relations of Griffiths' group is transcodified as a series of individual, heroic figures in mourning. These are presented in an almost hieratic, severely planar topography, the 'vast white plain' now acting as no more than backcloth for the accompanying objects of their struggle: a sledge with its measuring wheel, a husky, pairs of ski embedded, points up, in the snow. The camera movement encourages an 'across the page' reading of the images – towards the flag, cross, and upturned sledge-runner of the cairn shot. The mimetic space is, first *symbolized* (in relation to the dramatic action), secondly *identified* (in terms of suffering and spiritual achievement), and, thirdly, subjected to spatial and temporal ellipsis,[72] as the 'vast white plain' becomes a simple *conductor* (via camera dissolve and pan) from burial cairn to the vast cross above Cape Evans. While never breaking with a naturalist form, the *relationship* between the represented world ('all this') and the audience's world ('all that') is invoked more strongly here, as Martin Shaw's quiet emotion speaks directly to the public of post-Falklands Britain, calls up a different Scott from the 'essentially little man' of Griffiths' text, and interpolates a quite different ('Boys' Own') reading formation, which has had a long and continuing history. As early as 1913, the Bristol schoolgirl's 'audience world' of caring domesticity invoking a 'sadder day for some women', was embedded in 'the valiant efforts of Captain Scott and his 4 other brave men to . . . give Britain a proud day'.[73] And seventy years later the public discourses circulating around the series still invoked patriotism and heroism. Significantly, too, Martin Shaw was singled out for his 'excellent performance' in the strongly worded criticism of the series sent by Lord Kennet to the chairman of Central TV (which I will discuss in the next section).

As Elam says, the process of dramatizing and theatricalizing is 'a continuum which can start out indifferently from dramatist or director or designer or actor'.[74] I am arguing that the semiotic density of the performed text empowered, in this case, the actor as 'extradiegetic' narrator, to confuse the stratification of narrative levels and contradict the authority of the writer.[75] However, at most this *ambiguated* the structuring of reading positions within the text. Elam stops his 'rhetoric of dramatic and theatrical production' too early: I will look next at secondary[76] transcodifications of *The Last Place On Earth*.

The Last Place On Earth as social event

The omission of the Kathleen/Nansen scenes in *The Last Place On Earth* reduced the resonances between gender and international power politics that *Judgement Over The Dead* contained, where Mrs Scott used her 'woman's' resources (her body and her child) to further Scott's 'greatness'. But had the scenes remained, another production problem Griffiths encountered would certainly have been exacerbated.

The Scott family (in particular Lord Kennet and Peter Scott) quickly became a critical pressure group, impinging on the production. There had already been attacks against Huntford's book (notorious for its 'breaking' of the supposed affair between Kathleen Scott and Nansen while her husband was on expedition). But, as Griffiths saw it, this was a limited mobilization because the book, as a cultural object, was containable. 'TV has educative and re-educative functions because of its reach, whereas a book of history simply won't reach much of an audience.'[77]

In May 1984, John Hemming, Director of the Royal Geographical Society wrote to the chairman of Central TV, noting the advance publicity for the series:

> It is most regrettable that such a series should have been based on a book by Roland Huntford that was severely criticised for slanderous inaccuracy. . . . If it is not too late, we in this Society or the Scott Polar Research Institute could arrange for unbiased expert appraisal

of your scripts, to try to avoid any factual errors. If this is not done, there is a danger that the programmes will damage your company's reputation more than that of the people they seek to belittle.[78]

Given that prestige productions like this one are aimed at the time when a commercial TV company re-negotiates its contract with the IBA, Hemming's threat to Central was not a trivial one.

In Griffiths' view:

I believe that there was a more or less serious attempt to co-opt certain key personnel involved in the production to a different way of making it from the one that the text suggested. . . . There was also . . . a concerted attempt by those interest groupings to prevent production taking place. There were approaches to the board, to the IBA, and people were enlisted in these approaches, the Royal Geographical Society and others, to seek to have this piece shelved.[79]

Central privately gave this group an undertaking that they would see the finished work before transmission, indeed even before the press showing. Griffiths opposed this, unsuccessfully.

You don't show work to interested parties who might . . . be in a stronger position to frame the public response. And they did . . . to some extent because of their friends in other media . . . prime the press. They did frame the way in which this thing would be treated. There was a very powerful attempt to discount . . . the historicity of the piece. Not with evidence but with authoritative statements that simply went uninspected. . . . A lot of such people in the media wanted to see it as a knocking job. . . . So ultimately . . . things were . . . reduced to . . . the historical authenticity of the characterization of Scott.[80]

Griffiths in fact was not concerned with the 'accurate', 'authentic' Scott, but with the way in which his character

gathers at an important point of confluence all the contradictory social forces of a particular society in a particular period. That goes for nothing in naturalism, because that's . . . about materialism of detail . . . which answers the question, 'Is this what would happen?' But the critical realist text is not necessarily about 'is this what would happen?'. Quite often it is taking the tendency to a much further conclusion than you can habitually measure in observable behaviours within any society at any one time. It's an essentialising, a compressing, a compacting;[81]

and another example of Raymond Williams' 'as if' hypothesis.

As a critical realist, Griffiths was rejecting the empiricism of the 'true' Scott as documented 'objectively' by this testimony of 'experts', the *legitimized* Scott of the Hemming letter. And his recognition that history *must* be a selection (inevitably with political ramifications), that dramatic characterization is a matter of sociological extrapolation and typing, rather than a scientific measure of 'observable behaviours', left him unimpressed by Kennet and Hemming's letter to Central's chairman after the special advance screening of *The Last Place On Earth*. It wasn't relevant to Griffiths that (as they complained) there was evidence of 'Scott's kindness, patience, willingness to take advice'; that the remark 'just showing them who is in charge' could not, in principle, have been said by *any* British naval officer, let alone Scott; that as well as Oates' letter to his mother in which he inveighs against Scott, there is another retracting what he said 'because it was written at close quarters and under stress'.[82]

Kennet and Hemming's reading of Griffiths' work was dominated by a psychologizing and individualizing of historical events, propped up by their own notions of what it was 'inconceivable' for British naval officers to say or do. Yet that individualizing interpretation, as well as the authority of 'scientific expertise' to which Kennet and Hemming appealed were, as I have suggested, already determining narratorial discourses of the *Huntford* text. The prior circulation of *Scott and Amundsen* as a public event clearly influenced the Kennet/Hemming interpretation, and their subsequent agenda-setting performance for the press. Missing Griffiths' emphasis on the myth-making function of Scott's death in relation to the coming war, they ascribe to him Huntford's so-called 'morbid fantasy . . . that Britain was in some sense suffering from a death-wish just before the First World War. . . . His "Scott" is shown in some sense to embody that death-wish in heroic form.'[83] Missing Griffiths' emphasis on the *social* contradictions that Scott played out, Kennet and Hemming read Griffiths' Scott as 'a contradiction of human nature. No such man as that portrayed could have held a polar expedition together in circumstances of such adversity. . . . This "Scott" would certainly have had a mutiny sooner or later, probably before he started on the polar journey itself.'[84]

The production and screening of *The Last Place On Earth* was not stopped, though Griffiths complained that his attempt to re-edit and salvage episode one (which suffered from having three different directors) was lost in the scramble to get 'the thing ready to show to the Scott/ Kennet axis . . . weeks . . . before it went out, because of some chairman of the board's private, gentlemen's agreement with these people'.[85] The struggle for 'Scott' went on primarily not over whether the series should be produced or transmitted, but over the *circulation* of its meanings as history.

Immediately prior to transmission there were a number of discourses circulating in the press about the production. There was the Kennet/ Hemming empiricist history which sought to refurbish British legend and 'patriotism'. There was the quieter response of Central, who retreated to a 'creativity' discourse by labelling the series 'Fiction based on Fact'. This description was criticized by the director but it clearly relied on public knowledge (as quoted in Hemming's letter to the *Observer*) that Griffiths was 'Britain's most prominent Marxist playwright'.[86] Finally, Griffiths himself went stridently public, insisting that his 'fiction' *revealed* the real.

> If Lord Kennet does indeed have such passionate regard for 'history' and 'truth', perhaps he could explain why it took 55 years to make his non-relative's last journals available in full to the public and the community of historians; and why his mother's diaries remain unpublished in full until this day. . . . The evidence I've seen – and it's a lot – persuades me that the Scott I wrote . . . is inestimably closer to the 'real' Scott than anything offered us by the Official Mythography. . . . I found an essentially *little* man . . . trapped inside a particular class-specific Englishness, unequipped, uncharismatic; a man who became, almost literally, other people's projects. . . . Neither villain nor hero: victim. . . . For millennia, playwrights have used the terrains of the past to construct, together with audiences, contemporary social, political and moral meanings.[87]

In this letter to the *Observer*, Griffiths made no secret of his socialist commitment, nor of the politics which Kennet (*and* Huntford) tried to disguise behind empiricism.

> I do not require, nor can I value, lectures on patriotism from such people. If the time should ever come when a Briton will have to call right wrong, bad good, oppression liberation, capital labour, imperialism internationalism, exploitation assistance, racism and sexism human nature, mythology history and falsehood truth, in order to pass the test of patriotism, I may have need of his advice. But we are not in this Britain yet; the passage to Thatcher's desperate dystopia is generating its own intensifying resistance and the lies are slowly beginning to get nailed. I trust 'The Last Place On Earth' is helping to nail a few more.[88]

The circulation of these discourses to the public by way of the press and publicity became a power struggle. Kennet failed in his attempt to persuade the IBA to require Central to 'describe the series as "fictional drama" . . . in the credits'.[89] He did, however, manage to circulate his detailed letter of criticism of the series (written to Sir Gordon Hobday) at the press preview, and this became important in setting the agenda for a number of popular news stories criticizing the series. The *Sunday Express* preview story, 'The debunking of Scott: This dishonest TV mix of fact and fiction'[90] was, for instance, based on Kennet's letter in detail. This is a clear instance of Kennet 'priming an eager press . . . that wants controversy', and 'framing the way in which this thing would be treated'[91] which Griffiths complained of.

Griffiths, in contrast, was less successful in circulating his interpretation of the work through Central's official press publicity pack, which omitted his comparisons of 'news management' over the Scott fiasco and the Falklands War. However, if we look at the press preview coverage of *The Last Place On Earth* in early to mid-February 1985 (immediately prior to transmission of the first episode on 18 February, and so potentially setting agendas for interpretation), the issue of whose voice dominated at this stage becomes less clear-cut.

Certainly, in the conservative newspapers, Kennet's press release, focusing on unpatriotic debunking and scientific/historical inaccuracy, set the tone. The *Sunday Express* TV editor began his piece, 'We live in an age of debunking and it comes as no great surprise that television is about to undertake the task of cutting down to size Britain's great hero, Scott of the Antarctic.'[92] The article not only cites Kennet's letter in detail, but also used the authority of Martin Shaw to emphasize his scientific and human achievement in terms of the moral of 'facts' and 'great men': 'We English prefer to do things the hard way.'[93] The *Express* insists that 'In the name of decency . . . Central . . . should make it clear to viewers in the opening titles that this is a fictional interpretation of the Scott legend. The family seems profoundly hurt, and they have a right to have their views registered in the series.'[94] The more upmarket and therefore more 'responsible' and cautious *Daily Telegraph*, 'objectively' ascribed its comment by way of quotation to Sir Peter Scott ('The portrayal of my father is manifestly not the historical Scott, but a more lurid version'[95]), to Lord Kennet (Central 'deliberately avoided any contact with institutions and individuals who would have been able to give constructive help'), and to Lady Kennet (who 'claimed yesterday that when her husband offered to help, he received a solicitor's letter by return'). But the entire piece is determined by the family's view of the series, and the heading and subheadings of the article ('Capt Scott family attacks Central TV series', 'Paranoid martinet', 'Psychological sadist') clearly indicate the 'controversial', psychologizing slant.

The quality press conducted a gently ironic engagement with Griffiths as a 'political' artist. The *Observer*'s piece, 'Griffiths of the Antarctic', developed a discourse on the individual strengths and weaknesses of the writer to point to as many contradictions in *this* man of the Antarctic as the previous one.

He works mainly at night in a large study complete with video, stereo and, at the moment, a painting which announces: 'Profits are unpaid wages.' The ironies of his position are not lost on him. . . . 'If you can fake it,' he said in 1981, 'you can still write about the working class as if you were having that experience.' . . . But Griffiths has been much less of a threat to society than he would have liked. He plans to write about and even live in the Third World – his allergy to mosquitoes allowing – but increasingly he talks of 'political' struggle within his own, less tolerant industry, such as 'defending a text in Hollywood' . . . hardly one to inspire the masses to . . . the barricades.[96]

Griffiths deals with those kinds of personal contradictions very publicly – in works like *Bill Brand* – and one is reminded in this *Observer* article (by, for instance, the superior irony that extends from the opening 'Griffiths of the Antarctic' to that concluding 'mosquitoes allowing') of the smoothly 'neutral' and 'professional' interviewer Griffiths himself portrayed doing a hatchet job on a compromised Labour peer in *All Good Men*.

The *Observer* followed this with a piece, 'The "truth" of fiction is stranger than the facts', which carefully negotiates the rather unstable institutional space of 'official' and 'creative' discourses that Caughie describes. A former head of Independent Television News is cited as insisting that television organizations have a duty to historical truth, even in TV drama since many people look to it 'for their knowledge of the past'.[97] This is contrasted with the eminently authorial artist, John Osborne, who concludes that 'Whether the facts are right . . . doesn't seem very important if the result is good art. "Shakespeare got away with it."'[98] Within this familiar control/creativity discourse, the antagonists, Kennet (suspecting Marxists) and Griffiths (anxious to 'illustrate how history was made, or how the news is managed') are made to contest, but without serious interrogation of their ideas. 'He freely admits that he invented scenes that never took place. . . . This, he says, was "an essential truth" as distinct from a "necessary truth". Here I lost him.'[99]

By and large, Griffiths' own interpretation surfaced most clearly in the up-market weeklies. Mike Poole had extended pieces in the *Listener* and *Media Week*[100] which arguably went further than the transmitted series in setting the imperial context, and so restoring to the public debate much that had been lost in the production:

> Threatened by the rise of Germany abroad, troubled by increasing industrial unrest at home and faced with the prospect of the end of empire, Edwardian Britain desperately needed a positive image of itself – and Scott was determined to provide it with one.[101]

In these articles by Poole, and by Geoff Dyer in *City Limits*, Griffiths' concern for media management and the construction of history, his linking of this to post-imperial engagements of the present, such as the Falklands, the invasion of Grenada, and the shooting down of the Korean airliner, are made very clear, and ascribed in quotes to him.

> 'In the suppression of evidence, missing diaries and so on, there are obvious parallels with the Belgrano and one day someone will try to write the true story of *that* episode. Here, one of the principal aims is to show the way that a myth is built.'[102]

Given that the series was broadcast soon after the Clive Ponting trial for leaking documents about the Belgrano, here was television drama inserted into public discourse quite consciously as 'event'. And it was inserted in terms of Griffiths' *own* interpretation of the Scott/Amundsen opposition in the narrative. *City Limits* quoted him:

> 'Dramatically I try to present two processes of leadership: one hierarchical, hieratic and trailing clouds of imperial glory; the other practical, comradely, unidealistic, unrhetorical, co-operative and collective. So the British quarters are divided into officers' quarters and mess deck and this is visually contrasted with the Norwegians who are seen sitting around a table, planning, working, discussing.' . . . 'Here', says Griffiths, 'I am trying to show the development of a more socialist approach to leadership. To call it actually *socialist* would be too much of a propaganda overlay – just as it would be a distortion to see Amundsen as a model socialist hero.'[103]

Griffiths' voice, then, was by no means suppressed in the media agenda prior to transmission of the series. But it was largely available only to up-market readers of weeklies, while the popular dailies gave greater space to the Kennet controversy. In Australia, where the 'Art' discourse of Kathleen Scott (with its 'life of steel, fever and pride' Futurist tendencies) was edited out of the transmitted series, newspaper previews and reviews focused on the psychological relationship of Scott and his wife ('Scott . . . in the Svengali-like grip of a strong and attractive woman'; 'Scott . . . driven by his unpleasantly argumentative and vainglorious wife'; 'Scott as the persecuted victim of a relentless and domineering wife').[104] Social context was restored inter-textually in terms of recent *Australian* 'knocking Britain' film and TV histories (like *Breaker Morant, Anzacs* and *Bodyline*), as in Richard Coleman's review: 'At times, its efforts to knock this British hero off the perch he has occupied for so long was so full-blooded that you might have been excused for thinking it was made by Australians.'[105]

The main point to make here is that TV drama's meanings are inter-textual; both in the transcodification process that takes place between (in this case) myth, biography, screenplay and TV text, and in this television text's circulation by other media forms which celebrate it as TV event, and in so doing, help place it as *social* event in the public discourse. To the extent that the Australian critic's reading of *The Last Place On Earth* was as a *simulacra* of earlier Australian films, Baudrillard is right to speak of the 'drama being acted out on the screens'[106] within a universe of simulation and spectacle. Yet, as I have argued, this 'hyperreality of simulation' is working within a very particular crisis in Australian culture (itself struggling with myths of imperialism); and moreover, the critic's reading is in part determined by a process with very particular material effect – that of editing out Griffiths' historically contextualizing scenes. Further, in this *process* of reproduction it is possible for critical positions that are partly closed off in production (like Griffiths' use of *Last Place On Earth* to reflexively interrogate *television* as myth management) to be re-opened – as in the British up-market weeklies. The universe of simulation is certainly not a closed one.

The Last Place On Earth: audience

How the series was actually received would be a matter for audience research, which I haven't done. However, my audience work among elderly soap watchers in Bournemouth did reveal one interpretation of *The Last Place On Earth*. The family of seventy-eight-year-old Mr Tulloch had been imperial 'pioneers' (as civil servants, planters, etc.) over a long period. Sent from India at the age of seven to a top English public school, he was inscribed at source within that 'Boys' Own'/colonial service reading formation which the Scott myth reproduced. He encountered the myth at boarding school in its first years of circulation. Now, in old age, he subscribed to the *Sunday Express*. His comment on Griffiths' series came out of complaints he had been making that *Coronation Street* and *EastEnders* were not 'real', and 'why can't they have something that is middle class, that is sort of decent English?'. *The Last Place On Earth* was, he felt, more middle class and 'real'; 'though I think the real Scott was a bit different from the one portrayed. . . . I would never follow a man like that.' The mediation of the Kennet discourse by the *Sunday Express* came through clearly.

> Now Churchill, to my generation anyway, was a wonderful man, but there are already people who write about Churchill . . . and weren't born, when he was at his height, who belittle him. . . . Whatever person becomes . . . successful . . . there's always somebody who is going to debunk him. . . . So, as far as I can see, one shouldn't have any pride in our past heroes any more.[107]

Mr Tulloch would certainly have agreed with Lord Kennet who (in a letter to *The Times*) bracketed *The Last Place On Earth* with two other 'unpatriotic' plays: 'In one, Winston Churchill was shown arranging the murder of General Sikorsky, the leader of the Polish Army in Britain during the War. In the other, Queen Victoria was having a lesbian affair with Florence Nightingale. *The Last Place On Earth* is best viewed as an expensive contribution to this tradition.'[108]

I am not arguing for an unmediated transmission of TV meanings from print media (as opinion leaders) to audience, any more than I am arguing for a controlling inscription of the social audience by the TV text. Meanings (TV *and* newspaper) are negotiated across a range of discourses and reading positions which construct the viewer as social subject. This particular man had been the *only* male in a very macho/imperialist family *not* to serve in the empire, and *not* to have a war record fighting in India and Burma. He was also the only male in a large family not to have excelled in sport at his public school. And while being conservative, his non-macho background had led to a greater interest in ideas than his older brothers had, even a hesitant toying with socialist views. Consequently, he also referred to Stalin as someone currently debunked. For him, Stalin's 'main object was to build a country up that was in a very poor state, into a great country, which he did; and you cannot do that in a kindly way'.[109] Mr Tulloch's negotiation of politics, and of *The Last Place On Earth*, was by way of authority figures (Churchill, Stalin, Scott, Nelson) that, one suspects, he felt he could never be; and significantly, when he spoke of 'the Scott that I imagine . . . whom one would follow, at least I would',[110] he compared him to his own eldest brother.

I have suggested that this identification with authority figures is a reading made *available* in the work by performance and biographical texts; and this was encouraged by features of transmission, such as the mini-series 'action-adventure' format in Australia where even more of the social background was edited out, and the voice-over announced the series as a contest between 'a dreamer dominated by his wife' and the 'ruthless but practical' professional. Indeed, I was watching the series with a group of radical feminists who simply discontinued viewing because of what they saw as the series' investment in 'macho male rivalry'. But clearly, too, certain press agendas' *focusing* on Scott's qualities of leadership, encouraged readings around issues of individual authority and patriotism which were 'always-already-read' within the Scott legend. Press previews and readers were being co-produced within the 'Boys' Own' reading formation that Griffiths was challenging.

6 Authored drama: 'not just naturalism'

Naturalism wants what it thinks of as free space for social *being* to occur, and for meaning to attach to it.

Trevor Griffiths[1]

As a TV dramatist, Trevor Griffiths has been particularly aware of the ways in which texts are appropriated: by critics, and by the rules of practice of the TV institution itself in its division of works into genres. For instance, his version of Chekhov's *The Cherry Orchard* challenged a dominant critical interpretation that had stripped the work of so much of its class content that

> the play's specific historicity and precise sociological imagination had been bleached of all meanings beyond those required to convey the necessary 'natural' sense that the fine will always be undermined by the crude and that the 'human condition' can for all essential purposes be equated with the 'plight of the middle classes'.[2]

As such, *The Cherry Orchard* had circulated as 'fine theatre', 'art television', a foundational naturalist text in the politics of 'discrimination' and nostalgic regret which found its television apotheosis in *Brideshead Revisited*.

In *Country*, which continued Griffiths' analysis in *The Cherry Orchard*, and was transmitted by the BBC the week after, the 'country house' genre itself was interrogated to expose the 'universalist psychology' of its habituated naturalism.

> One of the things which is never discussed in country house drama is the economic base of the class portrayed, and its exploitation of other classes. What we're asked to see as the truth is that the rich, powerful people share a common humanity with those who are less rich and less powerful. . . . *Country* deals centrally with the question of succes-

sion, with wealth and the perpetuation of wealth and privilege. So it challenges the inbuilt but never spelt out assumptions of a genre.[3]

Brideshead, as a major television event, celebrated all of those generic values, and Griffiths had wished that the BBC would hold *Country* back to show at the end of the *Brideshead* run, as a comment on it. But the BBC didn't 'have the courage';[4] *Country* went out opposite (and was swamped by the media hype around) the second episode of *Brideshead*. Much of Griffiths' reflexive work commenting on the class implications of 'quality drama' is also deeply concerned with questions of 'Britishness'. But in *Fatherland*, which looked for German, French and British co-production money, the social myths and conventional aesthetics to be challenged were broader. Hence the deconstruction of English history and legend in *The Last Place On Earth* would be followed by a 'European piece' which made socialists confront a wider history. Further, the 'source' text which brought Loach and Griffiths together was historically and idiosyncratically 'authorial': Milan Kundera's *The Book of Laughter and Forgetting*. What is notable about Griffiths' version of *The Cherry Orchard* is less its release of 'the play's specific historicity and precise sociological imagination'[5] than its transformation procedures in terms of Griffiths' own historicity. Similarly, the transformation and trans-codification from *The Book of Laughter and Forgetting* to *Fatherland* is revealing of *authorial* appropriation, and particularly of the processual strategies of radical authorship in European film and television today.

Fatherland: screenplay

In *Fatherland* we still find . . . spaces for . . . something oppositional to emerge that may carry a seed of the future. Now, it seems to me irresponsible *not* to embrace that, and not to embody that in a text, otherwise I think we all become Beckett . . . we all become terminal.

Trevor Griffiths[6]

Through his novels Milan Kundera has encountered the twin boundaries of the 'esoteric' and the 'nonsensical' in a very specific historical sense. The Russian invasion of Czechoslovakia (with its 'supercultural' imposition of 'Real Socialism') represents for Kundera 'the laughter of angels'.

Their laughter has nothing to do with jokes or humour; it is the *serious* laughter of angels expressing their joy of being . . . the enthusiastic laughter of angel-fanatics, who are so convinced of their world's significance that they are ready to hang anyone not sharing their joy.[7]

The basic event of the novel, Kundera argues,

> is the story of totalitarianism, which deprives people of memory and thus retools them into a nation of children. All totalitarianisms do this.[8]

Thus, the young Pioneers with their red kerchiefs smile and sing blissfully before the Communist Party leader.

> 'Children, never look back,' he cried, and what he meant was that we must never allow the future to collapse under the burden of memory. Children, after all, have no past whatever. That alone accounts for the mystery of charmed innocence in their smiles.[9]

Kundera's novel form – a polyphony of variations in which 'various stories mutually explain, illumine, complement each other'[10] – reflexively challenges that forward trajectory of a life without memory and the 'innocent' closure of childhood. The novel's priority is not epic advance but variation, not childhood's future but the questions and memories of the author's father. 'In a world built on sacrosanct certainties the novel is dead. The totalitarian world, whether founded on Marx, Islam, or anything else, is a world of answers rather than questions. There, the novel has no place.'[11] For Kundera, the novel of variation pursues memory internally in opposition to a political order where memory is obliterated – the communist world of 'organized forgetting'. Memory is agentive – and the basis for another kind of laughter: that 'contrary kind of laugh, the kind heard when things lose their meaning'. This is the laughter of variation: 'It has a certain malice to it (things have turned out differently from the way they tried to seem), but a certain beneficent relief as well (things are looser than they seemed, we have greater latitude in living with them, their gravity does not oppress us).'[12]

The 'truth' that the author's father reveals at the end of his life is nothing other than variation itself – the privileged and 'infinite possibilities' of the mature Beethoven standing against the 'collective passion' of the electric guitar; the privileged love of Tamina for Mirek standing against the sexual 'brotherhood' of sharing her body with the 'charmed innocence' of children.

Deprived by exile of his nation and history, acutely aware of the fragility of personal identity and cultural memory, Kundera writes from the sense of how 'infinitely little' it needs 'for a person to cross the border beyond which everything loses meaning: love, convictions, faith, history'.[13] Kundera's self-reflexive and 'cataclysmic Devil's laughter' is a precarious identity beyond the borders of the 'nonsensical' – and so, in Griffiths' view, is 'terminal'.

The extent of Griffiths' transformation of the 'terminal' Kundera text will be clear from my discussion of his screenplay in Chapter 3. In particular, in Griffiths' screenplay the themes which are central to both texts – the contrast of different kinds of lovemaking, the search for one's father and memory, the political emphasis on innocence and youth – all 'carry a seed of the future' far beyond the confines of Kundera's reflexive irony.

Some of Kundera's main themes resonate in Griffiths' screenplay (for instance the image of childhood and totalitarianism, of the young Pioneer and the 'inner life that gets so flattened and bleached out in social living'; and also the photographic image of a circle of protesters at a military base confronted by a line of police). But they are relocated. Griffiths widens the focus. The children who dance to Soviet puppet masters are now found in Britain too. A child's voice sings 'Happy land! Happy land!' as King's College choristers make their way past 'paired police; NF slogans; dole queues; banks, churches; bad TV in pubs; dossers and dogs picking a decorous way through the Bentleys and Mercedes'.[14] And fathers are contextualized more precisely than in Kundera's text. Jacob Drittemann himself has a history – not of variation, but betrayal. Indeed, it is Jacob Drittemann who carries *Kundera*'s perspective on the obscenity of innocence, 'wading through slaughter like Stalin's daughter'.

In contrast, as Griffiths stresses, his screenplay 'actually comes out with a . . . hard affirmation of the future'.[15] At the end he 'affirms the *necessity* of innocence' as young people's faces 'gleam at the future out of the darkness'.[16] This contrasts in his text with the reflexive irony and sensual hedonism of the expatriot East European poet, Schiff (representing Kundera?), as clearly as it does with the 'terminal' art of Jacob Drittemann. But, rejecting the 'nonsensical' irony of Kundera, Griffiths' text still had to encounter the 'common sense' of Ken Loach.

Fatherland: film

> You do the research . . . the characters grow in your mind, and you connect them with the events, and try to be authentic and significant. And then, if you've done the job well, it reverberates with people in their own experience.
>
> Ken Loach[17]

As a European film and television project, *Fatherland* faced a different set of problems from *The Last Place On Earth*; though, as myth deconstruction it also encountered some difficulties which were, symptomatically, the same. As a co-production (of the German ZDF channel, Britain's

Channel 4, and French television) *Fatherland* was made on 35-millimetre film for cinema distribution, prior to TV showing. But Griffiths' interest in it was because of the 'cultural penetration' that only television could give. Pressures on the production quickly became apparent. Loach rejected a Berlin Grant because of 'political' demands. The financial interest of the French government, through Minister of Culture Jack Lang, led to a requirement that the Dutch journalist, Emma, become a French character played by a French actress. Griffiths fought this, and lost. Even more significantly, the French distributor challenged the portrayal of Jacob Drittemann. Here, from the Left, was an interesting parallel to the conservative criticisms of Griffiths' deconstruction of the Scott history.

> The whole idea that there could have been a comrade in Spain who was turned by the Gestapo. . . . He said there is no evidence that anybody ever did that.[18]

Griffiths regarded this as 'an insulting intervention' in 'a piece of imaginative fiction'. But Ken Loach worried that it might leave them 'open to the charge of rewriting history',[19] and suggested that they ask the French distributor (whom Griffiths believed to be a 'Stalinist') for evidence from authoritative sources that no communist betrayed the resistance. If this was forthcoming, he suggested that they change the script. Griffiths' reply indicated a basic theoretical difference between the two men.

> More than 40,000 foreigners fought for the Republic in the International Brigades in Spain. . . . Of those who failed to get out after Catalonia and Madrid, several thousand were captured by fascists, either to be summarily executed or to disappear into gaols. No one knows what happened to many of them. . . . My fiction imagines one of them, frail with disillusion, doing a deal to save his skin. . . . The instant, like the film itself, is a fiction, and like fiction, seeks to interpret reality, not simply reflect it.[20]

With *Fatherland*, Griffiths was entering a different social and institutional field than with *The Last Place On Earth*, where similar criticisms (the charge that he was inventing history) coming from different quarters (European Left, not English conservatives), were mediated through different media/professional sources (in this case the director, Ken Loach, rather than the press or letters to the IBA).

As an independent film-maker Loach (and Kestral II, the producers) had the task of securing the economic package, and were concerned to act 'in good faith' towards the French who were (through Jack Lang) both the most positive of their backers and potentially the best cinema market. Consequently, Loach encouraged Griffiths to accept a French actress.

The issue of Jacob Drittcmann's history was more fundamental, because their debate was premised on deep differences in notions of how to represent the 'real'. The differences between Loach's empiricist tendency ('authoritative sources') and Griffiths' realist position ('interpret reality, not simply reflect it') flowed through to disagreements over the script and the handling of actors.

For Griffiths, '*Fatherland* is a high style critical realism punctuated by possibly expressionist dreams'.[21] As in *Judgement Over The Dead*, the dreams (which Klaus has of his father) are partly socio-psychological ('they attest the pressure under which people like Drittemann operate – the unfinished business of the psyche, of the materials of the inner life that get so flattened and bleached out in social living in the DDR'[22]); partly sociological ('a lot of people that I talked to both in East and West Berlin have Wall dreams'[23]); partly ideological ('they say something about Klaus' history as a young Pioneer . . . about the authoritarian nature of life, of the way you are shaped by that as a child to accept or to resist – in Klaus' case . . . he's been shaped to resist'[24]).

But the dreams are also anti-naturalist – and as such represent Griffiths' main debt to Kundera: 'a sense of the past as dream; as dreamable. Plus a formal transilience and a narrative indirectness not previously deployed in the writing I'd done.'[25]

> It's a very non-naturalistic way of progressing the narrative, to cut to something and then to explain it later. . . . The dreams also shift time around. . . . Because in a sense what I want to do is posit the co-presence of both the past and the future in the present.[26]

The dreams are central to Griffiths' project of re-interpreting the myths of history as a constituent of present politics, and on behalf of a potential future one. As such, the precision of the script, and carefully directed acting, are crucial. In the original script of *Fatherland* there is a scene that Loach cut for budgetary reasons. In it Klaus encounters on the ferry to England a 'deck dense with lumpen khakied forms' of drunken British soldiers. One massive Scot speaks 'from the depths of his whiskeyed stupor':

> 'A'll fait any fucka here, awrait? Krauts, frogs, tulips, wops, wogs, the fuckin' lot o'ye.' . . . (He fixes on Drittemann, who stares back at him.) 'What're you? Fuck'n Kraut're ye? Shoulda fuck'n bombed

youse lot te fuck in the last lot, that's what we shoulda done. . . .
We'll fuck'n show ye . . . (stabs a finger at the ribbon on his chest)
Falklands. Falklands. See it. S'just the start that, eh?'[27]

The scene is important to Griffiths' text, because it marks a transition
point, not only from Europe to Britain (hence tying together the myths
of *Fatherland* and *The Last Place On Earth*), but also from the political and
sociological *grounding* of the play (the anti-stereotyped depiction of East
Germany contrasted with capitalist West Berlin) to the 'spy genre'
action of the second half. As such it *positions* Britain ('Fortress Britain')
both historically (the Second World War) and concurrently (the Falklands War) in relation to the 'European rottenness' that the play is
about. It also, Griffiths insists, 'takes you forward to the kids in Zurich
at the end'.[28]

Griffiths' realist method is very clear in this scene. He had actually
encountered this Scottish soldier, 'atrociously drunk and ferociously
aggressive' on a train trip from West Berlin to Rotterdam. The man
fixed Griffiths in the eye and said, 'You want a fait?':

> That was his first words, and those are the words that I use in
> *Fatherland*. But then I don't reproduce what happened. I actually
> take this guy on. . . . It seems to me that it works very much as a
> soldier in a Shakespeare history play would work. . . . He is disgorging
> out of his stupor a whole set of attitudes that have been very carefully
> fostered, a whole recrudescence of feelings about Britishness and
> about the rest of the world, which is *so* important to place on the trip
> towards what I call by caption Fortress Britain. It's not naturalism.
> You can't go for a soldier and hope that he's going to reproduce that
> if you shoot long enough. That is a construct.[29]

This theme of 'Britishness and the rest of the world' is then followed
through in Griffiths' text into a different class location (less desperate
and violent, more casually controlled) when the Cambridge landlady
tells Klaus and Emma: 'All sorts we get here, all shapes and sizes,
Japanese, Americans, Germans, a lot of French, it's the colleges you
know, the buildings, that'll be three pounds eighty . . . .'[30] As Griffiths
sees it, the precise dialogue of minor characters is as important as the
major ones': 'the landlady . . . gives a flavour and a texture of contemporary Britain, a kind of mindless, minimal, but nevertheless important,
racism'.[31]

However, Griffiths suspected Loach would use a non-actor in the
part, and that the lines might be changed to what an *actual* Cambridge
landlady had to say.

If she's a landlady that you've brought in to do the job, you may get some very interesting things, but you may not get the things that the text requires at that point. In all these ways I'm trying to distinguish between my sort of writing and naturalism. Film acting is minimal acting, but . . . it has to be *acting* for me, not . . . what naturalists are looking for, which is *being*.[32]

This rejection of naturalism raised central problems about method and form between Loach and Griffiths. Usually in the room-set there is Loach, his cameraman and one or two actors, with the sound man (as well as 'observers' like myself) firmly outside a closed door. There are seldom rehearsals, since for Loach

trying to capture a kind of spontaneous reaction is part of telling the truth. . . . A rehearsed, premeditated performance is, by and large, not true. The camera can see the lie.[33]

The 'true' performance for Loach is where the director confines himself to 'saying the minimum'.

Usually what the actors do is right if you've cast them right; what they do instinctively is right. And if what they do instinctively isn't right, then you've made a fault in the casting. So the less you say, usually the better you are.[34]

Ken Loach dismisses as 'propaganda' the view that he doesn't like to work with actors; but when he does use actors, he likes, on his own account, to find people who are 'most appropriate to the parts . . . as near as we can get to a genuine first-hand experience'.[35] Many of the characters in *Fatherland* – West German politician, record company executive, East German *émigré liedermacher*, journalists, etc. – were played by people who were these things in real life. Hence, rather than rehearsing the actors, Loach rehearses *off* them: 'It's all a question of me asking "what would you do here? And what did you do yesterday?"'[36]

Gerulf Pannach, who played Klaus Drittemann, and has had very similar experiences to him both in East Germany and in West Berlin, explained his experience of Loach's directing method:

He gives the actors a lot of room to create . . . the part through themselves. . . . He is very, very quiet, without stress, a man relaxing for the other people. . . . And in this way it's possible . . . that real situations are created. . . . I had an interview yesterday with a woman journalist from London. She was at the press conference in the film, and she asked me a question then that she asked me again yesterday. She forgot she had, but I remembered it. . . . The camera is like a window in his work. The camera, or the audience later, looks through a window to see what happens.[37]

For Loach, this is 'working at ground level', and he is deeply suspicious about 'generalizations' about 'isms' (like naturalism) which he finds 'sterile' and 'unhelpful' in thinking about his work. He feels especially let down by screen theorists on the Left, 'the people that you felt you were entitled to support from',[38] and speaks angrily of a board of screen theory luminaries at the BFI who refused money for a Jim Allen film:

It was about . . . relating nuclear weapons to the problems of unemployment . . . pointing out that actually they're part of the same economic system. . . . Because . . . I know a lot of people who were active CND who had no time for the miners' strike. . . . It was all to do with a theatre troupe; a very bold thing for Jim Allen to write. . . . Took it along to the BFI and these . . . people . . . sat back in their chairs and talked about 'seventies realism'. They had an image of what Jim Allen's writing was like and superimposed that on the script.[39]

The example indicates a different form of censorship from that of the commercial TV sector, from a different institution (state funded), with a brief to aid independent film-makers. Academic discourse ('seventies realism') was establishing its surveillant power.

Trevor Griffiths would sympathize with Loach's anger on this occasion. But in the case of *Fatherland*, Loach was not looking for money from a 'theory dominated' BFI board. He was working with a successful practitioner who was *also* a theorist. Loach pleaded with Griffiths not to mistake what theorists had written about their work for reality; but in fact there *were* basic differences between them which, though certainly theoretical, worked through to the most intimate details of directing method. For Griffiths the characters in the play are 'in an important sense, the language they use: complex, charged, resonant, particular, this language rather than another',[40] and so the precision of the script is important. He told Loach at their first meeting, 'This is a piece of very high style. It's not like grainy naturalism. It's a very sharply structured piece, faceted, and very precise.'[41] Loach argued that any particular dialogue 'is not sacred. Dialogue, it seems to me, is a part of behaviour and not something on to which behaviour is added.'[42] So, sometimes 'particular phrases turn out differently, but propelled by a strength of feeling which makes it the best take'.[43]

The differences were indeed, as Griffiths saw, those of theory, of views on recording history, of representing reality, and, to an extent, differences between naturalism and realism. Griffiths summed up the problems that two people were having who sincerely believed they were committed to the same politics:

> I think critical realism accepts that it is a convention, a literary convention, or a filmic convention; and naturalism on the whole doesn't allow its practitioners that degree of reflexivity and self-consciousness about what they're doing. . . . They actually believe, I think, that reality . . . is an unproblematical concept, that somehow your job as an artist is to set up a window on the real world, and allow the audience to see the real world through that window that you've introduced into their lives. Now, I suppose that nobody actually practises naturalism quite that way. I mean, they'd be crazy if they did. But that passes for theory quite often, when you push people. Whereas I think what I do is construct scenes which are fictions. . . . *Performance*, the deployment of performative skills in the realisation of the meanings and values of the text, is absolutely key to my work. My texts cannot be done by non-actors.[44]

Where, then, Ken Loach was interested in 'being', Trevor Griffiths was concerned with fiction, construction, reflexivity, and genre. Where Loach's references were to documentary (he told Griffiths that had Klaus Drittemann been English they could have used the folk singer from *Which Side Are You On?* to play him), Griffiths' references were to genres familiar to a European audience. He described the second half of the film as a 'road movie', and made reference to Tanner, Wenders and Fassbinder. But, typically, his notion was to politicize these directors and genres; while in turn, they might give him, formally, the required 'coolness'. It was in this way that he would 'show forth' the anti-epic tendency of the Kundera text.

> I don't think any of them has sought to present a picture of Europe which is . . . specifically and concretely political. . . . European film . . . over the last ten years . . . hasn't really had *matter*. . . . But it's given us new ways of imaging and seeing society. I find it a very cool and very attractive way of trying to deal with the problems of *where* to struggle . . . inside Western European societies now. . . . I think we need coolness. . . . I don't *want* to write a European epic in which there is the ancient battleground of right and wrong, because I think it gets more and more difficult to grasp. If the enemy is the state itself, and if its means of oppressing you are locked away, secreted in surveillance places like Menworth Hill, it's inordinately difficult to find a way of imaging that, of presenting that as evidential material

for an audience. I think you have to do it very coolly. You can't do it naturalistically.[45]

In *Fatherland* Griffiths didn't appropriate a single genre as in *Country*. He 'made usable' (as a matter of 'narrative indirectness') a *mélange* of European genres for a film about the 'rottenness of Europe' for a European TV audience. As with *Country*, though, these genres were critiqued in a reflexive way to 'dig into that terrain' whose myths he wanted to expose.

He planned the first part of the film to be in black and white; but the relationships (unlike the stereotype of East Germany) would be in 'vibrant colour'. This black and white section would then bleed into colour through the device of the blue light on the police car waiting to greet Drittemann as he crosses over into West Berlin. Then 'progressively throughout the film the colour became more and more chaotic, and exhausting, febrile, so that we did get the real temperature of Western Europe, it's unhealthiness. But I think that's probably too much for Ken. . . . And I know he's not shot the key bridge image of the police car.'[46]

Perhaps the clearest indication of the transformations between Kundera's, Griffiths', and Loach's texts is in the narrativization of the love-making scenes. In Kundera's 'Devil's Laughter',

> everything ends in great erotic scenes. I have the feeling that a scene of physical love generates an extremely sharp light which suddenly reveals the essence of characters and sums up their life situation.[47]

Thus, in the final section of the novel, Jan, about to make love to a married woman, becomes aware of the absurdity of their position, as each lifts their legs (out of trousers and pantyhose) high in the air, one after the other.

> the absurdity of two people standing face to face, kicking their legs in the air in a mad rush. . . . In fact, he was only a hair's breadth away from bursting out laughing. But he knew that if he did, they would not be able to make love. . . . There was only a fraction of an inch separating intercourse from laughter; and he was terrified of overstepping it: there was only a fraction of an inch separating him from the border, and across the border things no longer had any meaning.[48]

That foregrounded margin of 'nonsense' is the mark of Kundera's aesthetic resistance.

In Griffiths' text, as I said earlier, the contrast of the Klaus/Marita and Klaus/Lucy lovemaking is between the comradeship of 'Actually

Existing Socialism' and the commoditized eroticism of the West. Klaus and Marita make love not as a memory of their former marriage, but as a sign of the future – an 'actually existing' comradeship which counters both the Russian-dominated communism of the Eastern bloc (Klaus has been gaoled for distributing 'Defend Red Prague' leaflets) and the 'You're free to speak your mind, Herr Drittemann' hypocrisies of the West German news conference voices that overlay their sexuality. As with *The Last Place On Earth*, Griffiths is both grounding his images historically and sociologically *and* insisting on the existing seeds of social transformation.

Ken Loach had warned Griffiths from the beginning that he was 'bound to disappoint' him in the lovemaking scenes. In fact, Loach shot the lovemaking scenes (omitting intimate details of the Marita/Klaus sequence), but edited them out of the final print. This was not because they were 'no good' (in fact the Klaus/Lucy sequence conveyed all the violence and commoditization of the 'trustless fuck' that Griffiths had written). They were omitted on the grounds of naturalistic plausibility – significantly on the advice of his actors.

> They didn't work terribly well. . . . It made the new husband of his former wife in East Germany appear a bit of a dolt; and the man who was playing him had that sense too. . . . And the love scene with Lucy in West Berlin . . . made Klaus into a kind of random stud, which wasn't the character that emerged in the rest of the film.[49]

Loach and theory

Ken Loach is the last director that could be accused of lacking empathy (in the sense of 'mutual knowledge') with his subjects. Arguably, a central feature of his 'naturalist' method is in fact making discursive the practical consciousness of working-class miners, and in *Fatherland* playing between author Griffiths' discursive view of East European corruption and the practical experience of Gerulf Pannach, a *liedermacher* who has recently come from there. To the extent, then, that the notion of practical consciousness and its importance for left-wing theory has been underestimated, so too has Ken Loach.

On the other hand, Griffiths also engages with actual miners and dissidents in the writing process; and one of his worries working with Ken Loach was precisely the *lack* of engagement over theoretical issues during collaboration. 'It's only common sense, really' is one of Loach's more familiar comments under pressure of interview. The methodological (analytical, artistic) distinction between 'mutual knowledge' and 'common sense' is blurred much more readily by Loach than Griffiths; and

Loach's caution over 'unsubtle' devices of style (such as Griffiths' wish for a transition from black and white to colour) that draw attention overtly to political statement also suggests a tendency to avoid engaging with genre. Whereas Griffiths saw the Scottish soldier scene on the boat as an essential distancing device which historicized and politicized the 'road movie', Loach worried at its lack of fit with the enclosed boarding-house dialogue scenes that followed, and instead inserted a scene where police check cars for militant pickets on the motorway near Cambridge (as 'an immediate statement about conflict, authoritarianism and interfering with civil liberties'). For Loach the Scottish soldier scene was not adequately 'embedded in the film – particularly at that stage in the film where the main point is the narrative thrust of it. You can't take time off from that.' Loach was clearly concerned with embedding context seamlessly within the audience-gripping flow of the narrative.

> It's usually better if all the descriptive stuff comes early on and then the narrative gets a grip and drives you on to the end. My feeling is it's the wrong point in the film for a discursive sequence that isn't part of the main thrust of the story, and the main thrust of the story keeps you in rooms with two people talking to each other for most of it. . . . They don't engage, by and large, with society. . . . That was the problem I found really with the last third of the film.[50]

For Loach the 'embedding' of 'social context' came more familiarly from reference to police 'authoritarianism and interfering with civil liberties' in other texts of his own (*Days of Hope, Which Side Are You On?*) than from Griffiths' play with European genres.

Again, whereas for Griffiths the boat scene as Loach actually shot it was wrong because it lost the Falklands' reconstruction of British imperial myth, for Loach it was wrong on naturalistic grounds:

> because she wouldn't try and unwrap the cheese in the air. . . . Now we wanted to be outside in order to see you're on a boat. But you wouldn't mess with the paper in that wind. . . . So it's a mistake. . . . I don't believe it. . . . That's not a common sense thing to do.[51]

For all Ken Loach's often justified criticism of the 'rhetoric of the further education man', what he ultimately seems to lack is a theory of his own professional (as against his political) practice. He is much happier talking about 'practical' than theoretical problems of form as in this interview when I asked about his method and naturalism:

> When he's unwrapping the cheese on the bed, whereabouts is the camera in relation to him . . . in order to get it in the frame . . . ? How

far back in the corner of the room can you get, so that you can get both her and the doorway . . . in the frame? Do you put on a wider lens which makes the room look wrong? I mean, that's what you're actually battling with in the room, when everybody else is sitting outside.[52]

Sitting outside in this instance, and consciously excluded by Loach for the sake of naturalism of performance, were both Trevor Griffiths and the author of this book. In this very particular area of his production practice, Ken Loach discourages 'mutual knowledge', and so perhaps encourages what he calls 'caricature' of his 'common sense', both by Trevor Griffiths and the further education man.

7 Industry/performance: drama as 'strategic penetration'

In the many myriad structures of television, there does seem to be a constantly shifting point which you can actually plug into with something that is not totally down-the-line establishment oriented. . . . It means that somewhere in there there is somebody . . . who will pick up and maintain an involvement and interest in new and exciting work. That point moved away from BBC London . . . to Pebble Mill where there was quite a lot of very good activity, including *Boys From The Blackstuff*, and since then Channel 4 has seemed to be where the action was.

John McGrath[1]

As critic Michael Selig says, 'Over the last ten years of media criticism, it has become increasingly obvious that the commercial mass media are riddled with conflicts and contradictions at a number of levels – not only in programme content but also in the organization of corporate production, in the nature of the viewing experience, and in the media's social and political functions.'[2] Continuing the emphasis of the last two chapters on the constraints and 'strategic penetration' of radical authorship (which elaborated on issues of naturalism and drama as social event raised in Chapter 4), in this chapter I will examine contradictions at the various levels Selig describes: forms of content, social use and industrial organization, each taken as potential sites of resistance to dominant modes. In particular I will elaborate on the third issue raised in Chapter 4: the relations between theatrical and television values of practice – as seen from the production end.

Forms of content

Two conventions of classical narratives set especially important limits on expressing alternative viewpoints. First, to delineate good and evil as individual character traits limits the possible exposition of social conditions and processes. . . . Production relations and social relations in general cannot be depicted as the determining factor in individual or collective suffering. . . . Second, to employ a 'closed' narrative form, whereby all problems and contradictions become resolved by the end of the story, is to deny the ongoing, dialectical nature of social conflict.[3]

As we have seen, Ken Loach's *Days of Hope*, while not being questioned by left-wing theorists for its attempt to present an anti-individuating viewpoint, has been faulted by critics like MacCabe for its closed narrative form. The Loach/Allen narrative, MacCabe argues, states 'a contradiction which it has already resolved' in favour of a Marxist reading. A genuinely radical text would 'produce a contradiction which remains unresolved and is thus left for the reader to resolve and act out'.[4]

I will take up problems in MacCabe's notion of 'reading' the text in a later chapter. Here I will take it up at the production level through the work of John McGrath, since he has both been credited by left-wing critics for avoiding the narrative traps MacCabe ascribes to Loach, and has recently (in *Blood Red Roses*) stepped back from the overt reflexivity these critics valued. Colin McArthur, for instance, praised McGrath's *The Cheviot, The Stag and the Black, Black Oil* for both avoiding 'the autonomy and continuity of the individual consciousness'[5] and for its narrational strategies:

In the course of *The Cheviot, The Stag and the Black, Black Oil*, a particular player may fulfil the roles of narrator, singer, scene-shifter, nineteenth-century land speculator, twentieth-century property speculator, and Texas oil man. Crucially, the processes of giving direct pleasure to the spectators (largely through songs and sketches) and the requirements of political reflection take precedence over the display of actorial virtuosity.[6]

Though having a traditional narrative reliance on 'dramatic climaxes and crescendi' *within* its generic mix of humorous sketches, songs, historical reconstruction and drama, *The Cheviot* both emphasized key concepts 'such as mode of production, uneven development, colonialism and imperialism'[7] and challenged the transparency effect of naturalistic drama.

McGrath told me that after some uncertainty over *The Cheviot* as to how to make a touring theatre play into television,

I decided that the way to do it would be to use the theatrical presentation as a kind of alienating device – as a consciously Brechtian thing . . . to enable television . . . to carry polemic in drama, to be able to advance an argument through the theatrical presentation, and yet use the documentary and the drama reconstruction, the powers of television . . . to *show* the world – but in a *context* which was polemical.[8]

As such, *The Cheviot* (carrying both 'alienating' and 'showing forth' forms of presentation) developed out of McGrath's previous TV work. This background was unusual for a drama writer in combining the opportunity to 'try out endless different styles' (in a 'dramatized quotes' book review programme he did with Dennis Potter) with the 'gritty' documentary tradition of *Z Cars*, which he wrote for in its early days.

These were the personal and material conditions of production behind the generic mix of *The Cheviot*; though the influence of a particular kind of theatre – McGrath's touring 7:84 company – was also crucial. In its 7:84 version, *Cheviot*'s

form (of the ceilidh) was an adaptation of the traditional form of entertainment of the Highlands, the music was what the people like, and the songs, in Gaelic and English, went to the root of suppressed popular feeling. This show played for many months round small towns and villages in the north of Scotland, the Hebrides, the Orkneys, then into Glasgow Citizens Theatre.[9]

The touring mix of remote rural communities and cities was as important as the mix of genres since, in going back to the roots of popular pleasures, McGrath was drawing on traditional Gaelic culture, and challenging a colonial imposition of forms as well as subject matter.[10] For this reason (similar to Griffiths' emphasis on 'primitive' cultures), the 'remote communities in the Outer Hebrides . . . are very important, and not to be under-estimated, or written off by David Edgar as "peasants"'.[11]

Despite his criticism of playwright David Edgar here, McGrath at this stage was closer to Edgar's view of appropriate forms of popular radical drama than to Trevor Griffiths'. In an article in *Theatre Quarterly* in 1979, Edgar, while agreeing with Griffiths' positive distinction between realism and naturalism, criticized his attempt to use it as a workable strategy.

Many revolutionary artists have felt . . . that realism is an inadequate artistic tool in periods of heightened class struggle.[12]

Edgar agreed with Brecht that realism was more 'appropriate to an earlier phase of the class struggle'.[13] What was now needed was the exposure of capitalism 'in a much bolder and more aggressive fashion'.[14] Edgar argued that socialist theatre workers in Britain responded to the increased militancy of the early 1970s 'by rejecting the social realism . . . that had dominated radical theatre for 15 years', aware that

> in the television age, the masses are so swamped by naturalism, and, therefore by individualist assumptions, that the superficially similar techniques of realism are incapable of countering individualist ideology. The realist picture of life, with its accurate representation of observable behaviour, is open to constant misinterpretation, however 'typical' the characters, and however 'total' the underlying social context may be.[15]

As Edgar sees it, the only way to avoid this appropriation of realism is some form of agit-prop, where:

> The capitalist, for obvious example, is shown as a Victorian, top-hatted archetype because the makers of the piece of theatre believe that, despite all the surface changes in the appearance, style, and attitudes of the employing class, the fundamental reality is still that of heartless exploitation. There is no danger of misinterpreting the actions of the capitalist in terms of his individual psychology.[16]

Edgar admits that pure agit-prop, 'is not suited to the tasks of a period of class retreat'.[17] But, he argues, Trevor Griffiths' 'move into the enemy territory', working 'with the popular imagination . . . shaped by naturalism',[18] is not the way ahead, on three counts.

First, the 'inherent problem with television as an agent of radical ideas is that its massive audience . . . is confronted in the atomized, a-collective arena of the family living room, the place where people are at their least critical'.[19] The privatized audience is likely 'to take an individual, personalized (and therefore psychological rather than social) view of the behaviour demonstrated to them'.[20] This problem is exacerbated by format scheduling which inevitably 'has the effect of dulling the audience's response to challenging material by placing it within a predictable and familiar framework of regular programme slots'.[21]

Second, Griffiths' choice of a form 'which demands that the audience identify uncritically with its central character', will tend to direct an audience to draw on its *generic* 'experiential baggage' and 'take an individual-psychological view of events if . . . given any opportunity. Griffiths [in *Bill Brand*] in fact gave the audience ample opportunity to judge his central character's actions psychologically by giving him a broken marriage and a feminist mistress.'[22]

Third, Griffiths' attempts to 'counter the surface with the essence' are altogether too 'light' as devices to counter

> the barrage of programmes surrounding *Brand* which use the *same* form to present an *opposite* view about human behaviour. (On commercial television, the problems of 'strategic penetration' are even more acute, as the experience is itself strategically penetrated back by raw capitalist propaganda at 20 minute intervals.)[23]

In contrast, Edgar argues for new forms which, while not distancing audiences in a Brechtian way, still provoke them into thought 'by the very surprise and shock of the images'.

> There was . . . nothing in the whole of *Bill Brand* to compare with the climax of the second act of Griffiths' stage play *Comedians*, where the white-faced, football-scarfed, totally unfunny stand-up comic Gethin Price screams at two upper-class dummies he is terrorizing: 'There's people'd call this envy, you know. It's not. It's hate.'[24]

Here, Griffiths is using a familiar form (the stand-up comic) to disorient the audience's dramatic experience and deny generic expectations. 'Gethin Price's turn in *Comedians* depends completely on its denial of the basic principle of the form; Price is aggressively and deliberately *un*funny.'[25]

As Edgar sees it, attempts to work through other popular-cultural strategies have been most successful when employing forms 'actually peripheral to the urban British working class',[26] for audiences who are themselves equally marginal, as in the rural Scottish highlands. He thought '7:84 Scotland's use of the ceilidh form in *The Cheviot, the Stag and the Black, Black Oil* succeeded precisely because it drew on a rural folk-form, and, indeed, was directed at audiences in the rural highlands of Scotland.'[27] But, for the mass, urbanized TV audience, Edgar puts his hopes in the 'techniques of shock and disruption' which 'serve the same function today as Brecht's methods performed 40 years ago: they pre-empt the degeneration of realism into naturalism, and preserve a genuine dynamic between the surface and essence of society'.[28]

I have argued that Trevor Griffiths *regularly* (and not only in *Comedians*) attempts to deny the expectations of generic form. So Edgar seriously underestimates Griffiths' engagement with the politics of genre. And further, John McGrath himself found the need to work more closely *through* naturalism as a result of changing political circumstances in the late 1970s and the 1980s.

Blood Red Roses was a new engagement with naturalism. McGrath (making Lukacs' distinction between narrative realism and documentary naturalism) denies that his new engagement with naturalism is in any way a step back.

The purpose of wanting narrative, wanting to open up that closed world of television naturalism, is to be able to allow in what that excludes – reference to the movement of history and to the *changes* of economic realities. Simply by having a time-scale of 34 years, of being able to move the characters through that period in short scenes, and to be able to show the effect of time and the outside world on them, seems to me to be achieving what I was really interested in breaking with television naturalism for in the first place, but without the kinds of signals and signposts that the other shows had.[29]

McGrath's is an anti-formalist reflexivity (he says now that Raymond Williams 'quite correctly chastised' him for the over-formalistic emphasis of his earlier article 'Against Naturalism'[30]); or at least, like both Edgar and Griffiths, his is a *strategic* engagement with form, whether naturalist or avant-garde. Like Edgar, too, McGrath argues that different forms are needed in periods of class retreat.

I wrote the play . . . in the form it was in as a response to a changed political situation, and a changed relationship with the audience. Whereas through the '70s – up to about '77/'78 – there had been a sense that the work we were doing was expressing a kind of near-revolutionary upsurge of political optimism in the country, and certainly that amongst our audiences we were saying things that they wanted to hear when we said 'things will change', suddenly through the Callaghan dog-days of '78, beginning of '79, and then into the appalling debacle of Thatcher being elected in May '79, the mood of the country changed totally. . . . Because Thatcher and the whole right-wing ideology was mounting a huge attack on the whole concept of class, I wrote a play called *Swings and Roundabouts*, which was about how a class operates in Scotland *in detail*, in tiny, minute real/natural-istic detail, in order to counter what was a huge propaganda exercise.[31]

McGrath still rejects 'pure naturalism'.

Why I call *Swings and Roundabouts* closer to television naturalism is because first of all the action takes place over the course of one night – it's in real time and there's a small number of characters and the dramatic action concerns the relationships developing between those characters. . . . You create a little closed world, and you explore relationships and individuals. . . . But in naturalism proper it becomes almost a fetish to get the psychological nuance correct. . . . In *Blood*

Red Roses . . . psychology is more compressed. . . . It's a moving, changing part of a whole lot of other things that are moving and changing as well. . . . There is a context for psychological realities in a narrative play – or what I would now call a realist play; whereas in a television naturalistic play the psychological realities *become* the play, and the context of economical, political and social realities – and particularly class and gender conflicts – are able to be swallowed up by that psychological reality. . . . What you can't see is . . . that larger dialectic of society . . . how the changes in that will . . . heavily influence the consciousness of the next generation, or indeed of the *same* people in twenty years time.[32]

Realism for McGrath includes setting up a sense of historical process, as against a position of being trapped within a structure. Because of this realist position, McGrath would argue that there *is* a formal innovation in *Blood Red Roses*.

That's the way that time is treated in the three programmes. . . . I've not seen a lot of television that covers 34 years in one person's life. There's something like it in *Roots* – the American mini-series which started off the whole mini-series popularity.[33]

Hence, like Griffiths, McGrath is specifically challenging – disorienting – a popular television form.

Because *Roots* had a terrific impact, precisely because it showed the movement of history of the black people of America, it interested me as a form – the mini-series. . . . It seemed to me right for television that this saga should be told over three or four weeks of different episodes, precisely because it opens up that whole time-span. . . . So I think that the formal innovation, though deeply concealed, is one of using time to break down the naturalistic carapace of television drama.[34]

Blood Red Roses consciously addresses the kinds of problems Selig raises for classical narrative: its *realist* narrative determinedly addresses economic and social relations; and, far from resolving all problems and contradictions, and denying the 'ongoing, dialectical nature of social conflict', McGrath's piece ends in failure, while directly emphasizing the movements of history.

Blood Red Roses embraces that Gramscian pessimism of the intellect and optimism of the will. It shows that we have to face up to a series of setbacks and defeats in the life of Bessie and in the life of the working class in this country. But it also shows that Bessie is not alone; secondly, that there are millions of people mobilising in union activity and so on; thirdly, the music that I put on the last section is from . . . a Chilean group who have been exiled from their country for 13 years and are still able to write very optimistic music. If they can be optimistic, we've got to be because we've got no excuse for not being. *Blood Red Roses* is both optimistic in terms of seeing through solidarity a way forward; and it's pessimistic in the sense that it sees the difficulties faced by working-class struggle in the '80s very clearly and faces up to them.[35]

Days of Hope, too, of course, ends in failure, and Loach was criticized by MacCabe because of it, and because of the prioritization of 'visual epistemology': 'In *Days of Hope* institutions have no reality over and above their ability to produce individuals who are betrayers. Instead of an analysis of the Labour Party or the TUC we are treated to the *sight* of the perfidy of a Wedgwood or a Thomas'.[36] Where the past is *seen* as a fixed and immutable finality (as individual 'betrayal'), rather than *analysed* institutionally in its relevance to the present, MacCabe argues, we have a 'mythical history' proposing the visible truth of unchanging working-class experience. I have already disagreed with MacCabe's assessment of Loach; in the case of McGrath, *Blood Red Roses* is focused on betrayal – but it is betrayal not by individuals but collectivities (of women by men, of rank-and-file by union leaders), these in relation to both state betrayals (at the level of multinational corporations) and private betrayals (at the level of the domestic household). The 'optimism of the will' is not, I would argue, based on the 'primacy of the visual' but on a (properly) utopic hypothesis of collectivism; and the 'pessimism of intellect' depends on an analysis of the betrayals of collectivism, not by individuals but by the frequently conservative daily routines of institutions and households.

Viewing experience and social use

Although it is a mistake to regard viewers as passively determined by the media, alternative interpretations of programmes are limited, as Selig says, by

the viewing of media products within a context of leisure. . . . The production and dissemination of media products remains dominated by the social and economic elite. As such, the elite can maintain a distinction between the media's social function as leisure and bourgeois Art's function as culture.[37]

This is also, as we have seen, David Edgar's point. By constructing the area of popular leisure as 'distraction from work', as 'just entertainment', capitalism has constructed a new and important area of profit-making supposedly separate from (and ameliorating) the world of work. At the same time, it has displaced much of television's questioning of society's ethical nature to 'serious' minority programming and the world of 'Art'. 'Art' and 'entertainment' are the two sides of the 'different and exclusive uses which have characterized the mass media'[38] – different in their concern with overtly questioning the status quo, arguably more or less exclusive in their address to different classes.

However, the fact that John McGrath actually got his opening (and important ingredients of his form) from working *in* high-culture Arts programmes, might make us pause before making a too simplistic separation of 'Art' and 'Entertainment' genres of television. If we look at the programming on the four available British TV channels on 11 December 1986, when the second part of *Blood Red Roses* went out – ITV's current affairs 'This Week' and 'News at Ten', BBC 2's current affairs '40 Minutes', and BBC 1's 'Question Time' and a half-hour play – it is arguable that McGrath's mini-series would have appeared the most 'entertaining' choice for many viewers. Certainly, in even reviewing series like *Blood Red Roses* and *The Last Place On Earth*, newspaper critics in the 'mass' dailies assume a broad following for these shows among their readers.

By co-opting the popular forms of mini-series and action-drama, McGrath and Griffiths were challenging the ghettoizing of programmes (and whole TV channels like PBS in the US, BBC 2 in Britain, and the ABC in Australia). By engaging in this 'strategic penetration', Griffiths is also challenging the 'Art/Entertainment' dichotomy as between 'Theatre' and television.

> I simply cannot understand socialist playwrights who do not devote most of their time to television. That they can write for the Royal Court and the National Theatre, and only that, seems to me to be a wilful self-delusion about the nature of theatre in a bourgeois culture now.[39]

It is this commitment of Griffiths which has led to David Edgar's criticism that it is equally a 'wilful self-delusion' for Griffiths to think that the controllers of television would ever allow a *Bill Brand* to go out for every *Sweeney* it aired. In response to the argument that avant-garde and socialist theatre has not built up a mass following in the working class, Edgar replies,

What it *has* done is to create substantial support among the socialist movement (by which I mean members of revolutionary parties, and non-aligned supporters of various Marxist organisations, causes and campaigns) . . . appropriately in the sense that the subject matter can speak directly to an audience that does not consist in the majority of manual workers . . . ; authoritatively in that the plays draw on the direct experience of those who create them; and controversially in that sexual politics is an area of theory and practice on which socialists have tended to be at best woolly and at worst downright reactionary.[40]

John McGrath, with his touring 7:84 groups in Scotland and England, has also challenged Griffiths' distinction between television and theatre as between the 'terraces' and 'covered stands'. In a Cambridge lecture, McGrath argued that 'It is possible to make a theatre of the terraces.'[41] Between 1968 and 1975, with the upsurge of working-class militancy,

A new, hard-working and enterprising kind of theatre emerged, not from nowhere, but from a fusion of many past traditions and experiences – like those of Joan Littlewood, the Unity theatres, the Workers Theatre Movement of the 30's, the political theatre of Brecht, Piscator, O'Casey, Odets and many others. . . . A theatre emerging from such a fusion *had* to be a theatre of the terraces, *had* to and *did* play to, and help mobilize, large popular audiences, did contribute to a depth of cultural meaning to the working-class movement, and indeed continues to do so, but under changed conditions.[42]

While recognizing the political significance of TV drama, McGrath emphasizes the importance for writers of keeping their feet in popular theatre. 'The theatre, particularly if it is as close to its audience as I think it should be, will feed you back more than it takes. An ongoing trusting relationship with an audience . . . particularly a popular audience, will give strength and courage, and new ways of seeing things, and a fresh imagination, and endless facts and information, and a constantly developing, tested-out theoretical level, and a whole lot of human kindness, generosity and solidarity, to writer and theatre company alike.'[43]

On the one hand, audiences in working men's and trades council clubs *can* handle complex ideas: 'if an idea, no matter how complex, can be seen to be a necessary weapon in a struggle, a popular audience will *want* to know about it'.[44] McGrath has described the strategies used by 7:84 Scotland to bring political material to, on the face of it, unpromising venues. Subsequently, '*because* we had taken *The Game's A Bogey* round and built audiences who knew and enjoyed our work, and who trusted us, we were able in the next shows to develop, to push the style in all kinds of directions, to make increasingly complex statements'.[45] On the other hand, touring with a play has the advantage over television in establishing a forum where analysis is tested out near to the coal face. It was to meet this difference between touring theatre and television that McGrath made a film version of *Blood Red Roses*. Taking it around film theatres allowed him to engage with Edgar's 'activists'.

A lot of people have found it who've been involved in trade union or political activity, or who would like to be; a lot of women activists have come to see it, and the level of discussion has been one of really people wanting to support the film, wanting to know why more of this kind of stuff isn't shown on television and made for television.[46]

Whether it is Loach debating his work at trades halls, McGrath touring *Blood Red Roses* with 7:84, or Griffiths debating *Oi For England* with audiences of skin-heads around England,[47] the radical theatre/TV intervention in popular culture crucially engages an active and working audience, refusing the dominant culture's commoditization of drama as 'entertainment', and insisting on its social use and effectivity.

Organization of production

Each show must somehow integrate itself into television's continuous and seamless commercial flow. . . . The desire to maximize profits through minimizing production costs manifests itself in 'industrial' methods of production; this encourages repeating protagonists . . . in which 'good' (i.e. the central character) continually triumphs over 'evil'. . . . Further, the settings of most programmes reproduce a middle-class, consumerist lifestyle which echoes those promises of social and personal utopia offered by the commercials' images of commodity gratification.[48]

I looked at 'spaces for resistance' in this segmented television flow of drama and commercials in Chapter 1. Here I will examine the problem from the point of view of the director or writer positioned inside 'industrial methods of production'. Even in top-rating series with a decidedly working-class orientation like the British *EastEnders* (as one of its writers complained at a Cambridge forum), there is still the psychological 'pseudo-science' of habituated naturalism, blunting creativity and political penetration. The institutional spaces for political and critical engagement *are* there, but, as McGrath said, they shift from place to place over time. Troy Kennedy-Martin spoke of the 'ebbs and flows' in this regard across different departments at the BBC.

For fifteen or twenty years (after the early *Z-Cars*) . . . the Series department really was a popular drama department which happened to do series; and by 'popular' it meant it's not 'political' and probably without content. The first serious *series*, like *Pennies from Heaven* and *Law and Order* were actually done by the Plays department. . . . Later, *within* the Series department, Jonathan Powell had his little 'Classics' division, which was really there to do worthy classics, but eventually he began to do things like *Tinker, Tailor* and say 'That's a classic'. So he began to move and redefine his department. . . . Through Powell's leadership . . . you get things like *The Singing Detective* . . . to counter *EastEnders*. . . . There's a little bit more content, and a more political edge to some of it.[49]

Another space for innovation at the BBC was at Pebble Mill, as Michael Wearing explained:

Boys from the Blackstuff came out of Birmingham. . . . In Birmingham we did plays *and* short series . . . and in our minds the ideal was that there was no qualitative distinction between the two.[50]

Kennedy-Martin's and Wearing's examples suggest that though traditional distinctions between 'serious' (single plays, theatre) and 'mass' (series, television) certainly do exist, personal and organizational factors change over time, and with them the spaces for 'strategic penetration'. As John McGrath told frustrated writers at Cambridge in 1986, the 'constantly shifting point' for innovation had moved on again.

I would say that about 80% of the independent drama producers producing for Channel 4 are refugees from the BBC, who have set up their own companies to escape its oppressive structure. . . . But there's a problem here, because if you want to get a play or show on to Channel 4, you've got to become a capitalist and an entrepreneur and . . . get into hassles as an employer sometimes *against* trade unionists in order to make shows which are vaguely socialist or on the Left.[51]

In discussions of this kind, the same names recur: Jonathan Powell, David Rose, Michael Wearing, Kenneth Trodd: the few 'television Diaghilevs', as Wearing calls them, in contrast to executive producers who have no drama experience, and spend their time 'feeding broad notions of what the channels require for the air time. . . . That's why we see so much . . . "dross".'[52]

But few though they are, the system must (McGrath insists) throw up these 'Diaghilevs' who commission the Potters, Kennedy-Martins and Bleasdales.

> It's the old classic contradiction of capitalism really. In order to run at all efficiently, television, like any other large capitalist enterprise, has to bring in the brightest people . . . who contain amongst them . . . some people who are bright enough to see what's going on in capitalism. . . . I think this is what happens in almost every sphere – there are contradictions. The Arts Council is not a monolith. It is full of people – very bright, intelligent people, and so some of them will support a lot of what we're trying to do.[53]

Nevertheless, John McGrath's experience confirmed the broad thrust of Selig's point about 'middle-class' production.

> The broad mass of the decision-makers in television drama do not wish really to know about me, or any kind of Left-wing, or socialist, or even working-class drama in television, unless it's *EastEnders*. The small sections of those people who do want people like myself and Trevor Griffiths to remain constant and true to ourselves and to what we're trying to say in turn alienate the others more and more, because the latter keep expecting us to swing into their camp slowly, since, after all, we're getting older and by now should be backtracking and coming over to at least an SDP position. . . . And at the moment the groups of supportive people are getting smaller . . . so it becomes a bit more difficult.[54]

In addition McGrath points to the differences in organizational space available to *different* radical dramatists.

> If you become a superstar writer like Potter or Griffiths or Bleasdale, then I suppose it's a bit easier to get through the larger institutions like the big commercial 5 or the BBC. For me, I don't think I'll ever be a superstar writer for television in that sense, and I'm happy to make what I want to do for Channel 4 as an independent. There is space there, and without Channel 4 it would not exist at all – but it's not easy.[55]

It is even less easy for younger writers without a visible signature. McGrath at least had the advantage of starting his career at a time when there were more obvious openings. As Michael Wearing sees it:

> It's crucial that facilities exist for people like Troy Kennedy-Martin and John McGrath when they are young and unknown – like Alan

Bleasdale was in the mid-70s when I first knew him. At that time there was a technique in television of the 30-minute play. . . . This was . . . a form where television could actually afford, as it saw it, the risk of a new writer. . . . But I don't know where the new writing is getting a look in now.[56]

One point of access for new writers is the popular series. Kennedy-Martin and McGrath both gained early writing experience with *Z-Cars*; nowadays there is more space for writers in soaps. There, of course, 'industrial methods of production' are most intense, and (as the *EastEnders* writer said) the possibilities for innovation even more limited. But they are not completely closed off; and even here writers often draw on 'theatre' in determining their values of practice.[57]

Obviously, the *kind* of intervention (and its attendant problems) varies according to the kind of organizational space that is being worked in: as an independent working for Channel 4, as a 'two-hours a week' producer of commercial soap opera, or a 'quality' writer on BBC 2. I will conclude Part 2 with discussion of radical agency positioned in each of these three organizational spaces – McGrath's *Blood Red Roses*, Bleasdale's *The Boys From The Blackstuff*, and JNP (Sydney)'s *A Country Practice* – all of which dealt with the 'problem' of unemployment, and, as such, offered the potential for a structural examination of a major social contradiction.

Signs of unemployment

In the last few chapters there has been an emphasis on 'named' writers and directors: Trevor Griffiths, Ken Loach, Troy Kennedy-Martin, Alan Bleasdale, John McGrath. Yet, TV drama is very much a collective effort and even where a small independent production team has a close-knit political relationship there will be disagreements. There will always be creative inputs from actors, editors and other personnel. McGrath describes *Blood Red Roses* as 'a kind of growing process in the theatre', as he made changes to the text in response to audience comment and the contribution of actors. Furthermore, 'the television version changed in rehearsal a bit, not a lot in shooting, but a great deal in the course of editing.'[58]

In the scene where Bessie is talking to other women in a new factory job after changing her name, as shot the narrative ended with Bessie asking if there was a trade union in the factory.

This indicated . . . the way that the disfranchising of the workers has gone on in the smaller factories through the country. . . . The two editors were absolutely adamant that that line was not necessary;

that what you wanted to see in that scene was not that she was going to go back and start trade union activity – which was me making my kind of point – but that she was happy just to be involved in an exchange with these women, that she was enjoying coming back to a different kind of life. And so that little bit got cut out.[59]

Similarly, a small section was cut out of the 'Unemployment – A Health Hazard' block of *A Country Practice* at a meeting of producer, script editor and editor. In this case the cut lines referred to the ruthless workings of the free-enterprise system. In the *Blood Red Roses* example, the editors were bringing the text back to the personal experience of unemployment (and Bessie's short lived work euphoria) against McGrath's broader point that the overall drama should deal emotionally with exemplary victory and 'large defeat'. McGrath's editing decision had to find a balance between, on the one hand, the mini-series' 'need' for the personal and experiential, and, on the other, the risk of psychologism and naturalism. In the case of *A Country Practice*, the producer and script editor were bringing the text back to the Australian Medical Association's original suggestion that the episode expose the experiential aspects of 'unemployment as a health hazard' (the bad diet, the growing lethargy and hopelessness, the high suicide rate). This was at the expense of a more radical producer's desire to indicate 'the need for some kind of structural change'. Here the editing 'balance' was between the assumed analytical capacity of a 'quality' audience and 'preaching, to a majority'.[60]

These minor (but politically resonant) cuts in the narratives of *Blood Red Roses* and *A Country Practice* indicate two important theoretical points about 'strategic penetration' in the TV industry. First, as Keir Elam has argued, any dramatic performance is 'a density of semiotic practices . . . a *multiplication* of communicational factors'.[61] So that at any one point in the communication process potentially conflicting signs compete for audience attention: the dramatist as 'pre-text', the director who chooses the 'transmitters' and the forms their signals take; the actors, set and costume designers, stage manager, sound and music composers. In Chapter 5, for instance, I discussed actor Martin Shaw as 'transmitter' of meanings in *The Last Place On Earth*.

Secondly, as I have argued elsewhere in analysing 'Unemployment – A Health Hazard', in television this semiotic density is bedded in a routinized *process* of professional practice.

We have here the sense of a dramatic text as performed, as 'spoken' by multiple voices, and not only . . . in front of the television cameras, but in a series of 'theatrical' spaces from forward planning meetings, through plotting meetings, script editing meetings, rehearsals, studio, audio and video editing, through to the producers' edit. . . . Each of these performances in some way transforms or transcodifies earlier ones, and they do so according to a hierarchical range of professional values and practices – each of them a 'source' of information, to use Elam's term, and also perhaps a system insofar as directing, acting, set design, musical scoring, etc., each has its own selection and combination rules constructed across a complex of technical, dramatic, and cultural discourses. . . . It is a power situation in which each performer is spoken by a range of industrial, generic, formal, and cultural discourses, each perhaps with its own space for contradiction and drama.[62]

The value of the notion of 'semiotic thickness' in this organizational context is that it allows us to think systematically about a TV text as the site of contestation and struggle *within and between* professional practices, rather than as a simple mechanism for the flow of dominant (or radical) ideology. To take an example of a case where the 'thickness' of performance worked against the radical intention of the writer, Poole and Wyver describe Trevor Griffiths' problems with the 'Art' coding of set design and costumes in his TV version of *Sons and Lovers*. Here, because of the typical concern of a 'quality' series for 'materialism of detail' (historical/photographic exactitude, which, in fact, Griffiths argues, is a posed and middle-class view of the working class) over 'the materialism of forces' ('where money is short, exploitation rife and life crushingly hard'), 'at least 25 per cent of the historical reality, the "truth" you were aiming at, simply drains away'.[63]

Differences of class view are fundamental here, but they are mediated through the accepted professional conventions of programme research, photography, set design and costuming. As Poole and Wyver say, even the 'opening title sequence, featuring a soft-focus watercolour being painted, directs us towards an interpretation of Lawrence's autobiographical hero, Paul Morel, as a study in sensibility'[64] rather than the precise (historical and geographical) class and gender study that Griffiths intended.

Millington and Nelson (on *The Boys From The Blackstuff*)[65] and Tulloch and Moran (on *A Country Practice*)[66] have begun to describe the similar and systematic ways in which different kinds of TV drama serial establish hierarchies of working perspective to deal with conflicts of critical assumption and professional practice. But there will also be significant differences, which depend on the different blends of what Caughie calls 'controller' and 'creative' discourse in the different production spaces. We can begin to look at these by focusing on the different degrees of 'interference' with radical intentions in the three unemployment dramas, and the channels through which they were conveyed.

Blood Red Roses

With *Blood Red Roses*, John McGrath (as writer and director) had the least direct interference. But then, many quirks and ambiguities within the capitalist industry had to collude before he could work at all. *Blood Red Roses*, McGrath says, depended on a series of contradictions: the state-funded Arts Council's support for the original 7:84 Scotland's touring version of the radical play; the existence of Channel 4 (and McGrath setting up as a 'capitalist and entrepreneur', encouraged by Jeremy Isaacs who wanted more Scottish input to the Channel); the transnational production house for *Dallas*, Lorrimar, putting money into radical drama (presumably for tax reasons) during the brief tenure in London of an executive who 'had an intelligent interest in drama' (and chose to explain the series' worrying politics to his company as 'the struggle of the individual' rather than 'against multinationals').[67] In this context, the main pressure to change things came from the kind of audience, actor and other professional involvement that McGrath preferred. He had, however, no control over the (lack of) international distribution of *Blood Red Roses* (which is another reason why he was keen to have a cinema version).

'Unemployment – A Health Hazard'

Producer–writer Michael Brindley at JNP, Sydney, encountered the most interference, but was still able to achieve a trade-off situation at the script-editing stage. Some of the more radical lines that Brindley protected at the script-editing stage against the executive producer were lost after the studio recording. But, as Brindley himself said, these were primarily the result of the director's *shooting style*, so that in the end he was glad the lines were cut. The scene in question was between the chronically unemployed (but skilled) Hodge, the plumber, Bob, who has given him some work (and whom he has now undercut), and the conservative, retrenched older man, Des.

> When it got to Hodge's lines about free enterprise, director Mandy Smith cut to a close-up of Hodge and had him speak those lines with a fair amount of venom. Now that was certainly never my intention – it suggested to the audience that there was some kind of personal

malice from Hodge towards Bob Hatfield. . . . I would . . . have kept
it on . . . a three-shot with Des slightly background. . . . Then I would
have got Hodge to play it in a very matter-of-fact manner, in a way
that suggested – as it were as a subtext – 'Look Bob, there's nothing
personal about this. This is the way the system is set up. The way
things are, if I'm going to survive, I have to screw you.' . . . My
intention was that Des in particular . . . would be distinctly uncom-
fortable by what he had just witnessed and would realize something
about his own case, because he had given thirty years to a company
and they had just thrown him out the window when they didn't need
him.[68]

It was this *personal* aggression from Hodge towards Bob Hatfield that
most worried the producer. As a very conservative character with 'a
heart of gold', Hatfield's regular conversion to liberal causes is a major
narrative agent in *A Country Practice*'s project of 'trying to change
people's attitudes in some minor way'.[69] Had the scene been shot as
Brindley wanted, it is probable that it would not have been cut; and it
is significant that the producer said she would have left it in *as shot* had
it been screening on the ABC.

The example well illustrates the process of the script as performed in
a *succession* of professional spaces. Lines which survived the more overt
political intervention of the script-editing stage were lost later, where
they encountered a new

range of systems of interpretation (including, in this case, camera
style, gestural style, the professional association of close-ups with
personal expressivity, the negotiation of differing political and formal
intentions through this professional discourse, the relationship of
editing decisions to notions of audience and genre, etc.).[70]

In particular, it was the director's and actors' tendency to naturalism of
performance (creating, as McGrath says, 'a little closed world' where
'you explore relationships and individuals') intersecting with perceptions
of the *organizational space* of the series (conceived in terms of narrative,
genre and audience) which defeated Brindley's radical intentions.

The Boys From The Blackstuff

Alan Bleasdale's space for 'strategic penetration' on BBC 2 was greater
than Brindley's, less than McGrath's. On the one hand, it is clear that
the 'script-led' style of 'quality' drama production gave Bleasdale greater
control and a more powerful voice during editing than Brindley. Director

Philip Saville deferred to him over important editing decisions, and producer Michael Wearing, while having the power to make final decisions generally took a background role because dealing with an 'author'.

On the other hand, just because a performance text *is* semiotically dense, there are various levels at which the director can counter the political intentions of the writer. *The Boys From The Blackstuff* music composer Ilona Sekacz spoke of Saville's request for 'a slightly more feminine aspect to the music. . . . He wanted just in general terms the idea of something softening the heavy political dialogue.'[71] Saville was able to insert a stronger female presence into the series; though not necessarily of the kind that feminists would argue for, and not without opposition.

> Saville . . . saw the need to emphasize Angie's femininity by dressing her in a skirt and high heels, even if this conflicted with images of real working-class women. His efforts to glamorize Angie were finally resisted at the insistence of the designer and Julie Walters; a uni-sex outfit of bomber jacket, jeans and sneakers was adopted instead: Julie Walters: 'When you're in the trenches you don't wear a dress and high heels.'[72]

Saville's disagreement (as 'a wealthy Southerner of cosmopolitan outlook') with Liverpool-based, mainly working-class actors led to some tensions in production, Julie Walters noting that the director 'didn't know those people like we did . . . didn't know about working-class people'.[73] However, Saville's quite productive relationship with Bleasdale also underlines the interesting formal complexity of politics and genre. As Michael Wearing observed, Bleasdale himself was working away from the realist/naturalist forms that underpinned Walters' objections. Millington and Nelson point to ways in which Saville's interest in the surreal as 'another dimension of the real'[74] extended the tendencies in Bleasdale towards the comic grotesque; and Wearing also, in asking for the transfer of the blackly comic pub scene to the final episode, had a similar effect.

> It seemed to me like *the* final Hogarthian statement you could possibly make. . . . I somehow had the notion that we needed an objectifying, almost alienating device which counterpoints the sense of the real life-force in George and what his life had stood for.[75]

It was the *actors* (particularly Peter Kerrigan who had worked with Jim Allen and Ken Loach) who insisted in pulling the text back towards critical realism. Kerrigan argued with Bleasdale, drawing on his own labour activist experience.

> I had the script of 'George's Last Ride' and the ride wasn't in it – rather the route was there, but the content wasn't and I gave him the 'I was a bull on the docks. . . . I worked from six in the morning till eleven at night carrying 2-cwts of bag-ash and every bone on your back was rubbed to the flesh.' And if you didn't do it you weren't on the next shift. It was little things like that that would have explained the hardness of the man . . . a hardness that had been forged in him because he'd been through more traumatic times than Chrissie and Yosser in the Thirties.[76]

As Bleasdale describes it:

> Peter said that he thought it was a very black view of the labour movement, of socialism and the state of the nation. And I said, 'Yes, actually I do believe the prospects with all three parties are pretty black at the moment.' . . . I said that as a slightly non-committed but passionate socialist. . . . And Peter said, 'There should be some hope – I can't believe there's no hope!' And I said if *you* believe that I'll put that in – so that is Peter![77]

It was this mix of actors', writer's, director's and producer's signatures, working often collaboratively, sometimes in tension, that gave *The Boys From The Blackstuff* its particular grotesque/realist form (see Chapter 11). As Elam notes, the semantic ambiguity of performance derives not only from the potential for contestation between different production codes and practices at any one moment, but also from 'the *discontinuity* of its various levels. . . . Not all the contributory systems will be operative at every point in the performance: each message and signal will at times fall to a zero level.'[78] In 'George's Last Ride', actor Peter Kerrigan's critical realist discourse (of hope) literally fell to zero with George's death. George's funeral was marked by a growing movement into the grotesque. This was carried by a variety of signifiers, in particular implausible action (as George's wife falls into the grave), music and dress.

The aesthetic complexity of the way this works, stretching the narrative across a combination of continuity, counterpointing and contradiction, is nicely illustrated by Millington and Nelson's description of the way in which Saville's directorial emphasis on characters' hands operated in the performed text.

> The idea of establishing a sense of unity and communion in a family group in visual physical terms arose spontaneously out of the

director's observing Jean Heywood's use of hands to project emotion.
. . . The director's focusing on tactile communication in the shooting
of the family scenes of this episode stood in marked contrast with the
barriers being set up between people elsewhere in the series. The use
of hands and tactile business also added a new layer of irony to the
behaviour of 'Shakehands' in the pub scene, as he created chaos by
using the symbolic gesture of friendship to achieve physical domination
over his victims.[79]

Here an ideolectal feature of a particular actor's performance was
used, initially, to conflict with a camera style and set design that
emphasized the physical barriers between the unemployed and their
world. Later, it was used in contrast to the blackly comic camaraderie
of the pub, where 'Shakehands' heart of gold' performance operates as
a grotesque version of ACP's Bob Hatfield. Nothing could represent the
ambivalent potency of this *un*-working class better (and at the same
time generate a formal play between realism and grotesque) than the
tyranny of those hands, as 'Shakehands' punishes the nearest and most
visible oppressors.

Innovation, 'quality' and the audience

The matter of 'strategic penetration' is (both practically and theoretically)
a difficult one. But current theorists are right to emphasize its importance.
As Jane Feuer has argued,

> Given the structure of the American broadcasting industry . . . a
> child could come to the conclusion that innovative programmes are
> not likely to emerge from it. But such a simplistic conclusion is
> misleading, even in the industry's own terms. For just as the system
> demands the repetition of previously successful formulas, it also
> reproduces itself on the basis of constant novelty and innovation.[80]

Kerr, Feuer and other authors of the *MTM: 'Quality' Television*
collection have traced the shifting cultural, economic, institutional and
legislative environment that moved MTM's 'quality' image from situation
comedy to social issues (*Lou Grant*), and then (under focused economic
and political attack)[81] to *Hill Street Blues*, indicating the precariousness
of 'spaces for contradiction' based on the implied liberalism of an up-
market audience. At MTM, 'quality' (as conscious inter-textuality and
self-reflexivity) was primarily a signature of house 'style-as-authorship'
in the networks' fight to capture an affluent, young audience moving
over to cable. The same is true, according to Hayward, of *Moonlighting*,

where 'Instead of dreams of radical, analytically deconstructive television the media mutation of the late Eighties has followed hot on the prophecy of theory and witnessed an eclectic pillaging of once esoteric formal devices, pressing them into forms of popular cultural *bricolage* glacially unconcerned with niceties of radical schools or purist debates.'[82] Seen this way, 'strategic penetration' (or 'Fitting MTM into the cracks of the system') comes to seem like capitalist recuperation. Anti-naturalist devices, as Hayward says, are 'intended to delight their audiences rather than estrange them'.[83]

As Feuer notes, 'This does not mean that the MTM style lacks progressive elements, only that, as with all forms of artistic production under capitalism, the progressive elements may be recuperable to an ideology of "quality".'[84] Scheduling is crucial here, since, as Selig also notes, it can confine progressive TV drama only to the 'quality' audience of 'liberal, sophisticated, upwardly mobile professionals', and miss out on the 'mass' audience altogether. Alan Bleasdale was conscious of this when he attacked BBC 2's decision to screen *The Boys From The Blackstuff* on Fridays after 10.00 p.m. At that time, he complained, 'the only people watching [would] be *Guardian* readers, chess players and people tied to chairs'.[85] He insisted that this 'will be a popular, big city, people's show, and believe me, even the boys with Giros, with only enough money for two shandies and a long walk between two pubs, go out of a Friday night. They are my audience, they are the people I am writing for, and I'm going to miss them.'[86] In the last resort, 'strategic penetration', as radical theorists and practitioners alike are aware, is all about the 'mass' audience.

In this chapter I have examined the meeting point of theatrical and television values of practice, as it were, from the inside, via the experience (and theory) of radical dramatists who move between stage and television. In particular I have looked at this in relation to problems concerning naturalist and reflexive form, problems concerning the construction of leisure as a 'balance' between 'Art' and entertainment, and problems concerning the various institutional spaces for dramatists working within industrial methods of production.

This chapter completes my analysis of 'authored' drama, in which I have elaborated (in Chapters 5, 6 and 7) on the issues of drama as social event, naturalism and television and theatre raised by Caughie (Chapter 4). In the next two chapters I will return to popular series/serials and consider the matter of audiences.

Part Three

Reading drama: audience use, exchange and play

8 'Use and exchange': delivering audiences

> Our main task in this business is to deliver an audience. . . . Now the best way to ensure that . . . is to try and attract as broad a demographic response as you can. Looking at *A Country Practice*, we divide our audience into three categories in age group: the 18's and under, the 18 to 50, and the 50 plus. It's generally true of the industry that if you can get a third of the audience into each of those categories, you're doing very well. A lot of programmes don't manage that balance, and they fail. . . . What we're interested in is what the political parties are interested in: the swinging voters. . . . We give the committed audience enough to keep them happy, and we concentrate on the swinging audience, the 18's and under. They're the kids who are very volatile in their likes and dislikes, who respond to peer pressure. . . . All of the attacks from the other commercial networks on *A Country Practice* are aimed at that young audience.
>
> James Davern[1]

In each chapter so far, I have wanted to emphasize both the controlling, comodifying qualities of TV drama and its 'spaces for resistance'. Despite my emphasis on production in the last few chapters, inevitably each chapter so far has raised questions of reception as well. But 'audiences' have been understood in different ways according to different frames of knowledgeability. First, there are broadcasters' understanding of their audiences. Television production, to be popular, must appeal to many different kinds of viewer at the same time. Consequently, a sense of aggregating audiences is at all times in the minds of producers of commercial TV drama as much as collecting different kinds of voters is in the minds of politicians. Left-wing producers and dramatists like Michael Brindley (Chapter 1), Trevor Griffiths (Chapters 3, 5, 6), and John McGrath (Chapter 7) work on the back of these 'mass' definitions of audience, trying to achieve a 'demystified' public – an audience able and willing to promote social change. As well as these broadcasters' definitions of audience, there are, secondly, notions of the audience 'inscribed' in the text and subject to manipulation by 'dominant ideology'. This 'audience in the text'[2] has often been drawn on by left-wing theorists to explain how the media have deprived us of our potential for 'dreaming'. But this kind of text- (or genre-)centred analysis can also argue that TV drama opens up 'spaces for resistance' among audiences – as in the discussion of soap opera (Chapter 1) and science fiction (Chapter 2).

Thirdly, there is the definition of audience carried by other media forms, like newspapers, or by pressure groups, like Mary Whitehouse's National Viewers' and Listeners' Association which from time to time make TV drama a 'social event' (as we saw with Griffiths' *The Last Place On Earth* in Chapter 5). Like schools (another 'apparatus for the superintendence of reading'[3]) these 'cultural operators' establish 'appropriate' (and often conservative) standards of sensibility – that mix of aesthetic and moral judgement which establishes what is 'good' for the public. But as with the 'producers' audience' and the 'audience in the text', the analysis of these 'cultural operators' (which position audiences within 'reading formations') can point to 'resistances' to 'dominant readings' – as in the *City Limits* discussion of *The Last Place On Earth* and also in the discussion of fanzines. So, for instance, Henry Jenkins III writes that Lorrah's writing in *Star Trek* fanzines 'represents a painstaking effort to construct a feminist utopia'[4] out of the narrative closures of a 'male' genre.

Fourthly, there are the meanings brought to the text by the audiences themselves in the process of 'going on' with their daily routines. It is in this area that ethnographic audience work has recently become popular, again pointing to 'resistances' to 'dominant' readings. In the following two chapters I want to approach an ethnography of audience, as I did earlier with production. But I will be looking at the other three areas of audience definition as well.

Again, the emphasis will be on the sense of tension between viewer 'passivity' and audience agency which continues to define the agenda of critical audience research in each of these areas. As Robert Dunn summarizes the current debate:

> In Baudrillard's conception, social control is inherent in the very logic of signification. For him the commodity system reproduces itself every time we consume the code (e.g. the messages of television advertising and entertainment). Here Baudrillard . . . is claiming that the reproduction of meaning is the 'order of power'. . . . By

addressing the spectator in a psychological mode, however, television discourse opens itself up to structures of desire *in the audience itself*. . . . While seeking to channel desire in socially preferred ways, the media cannot avoid reproducing the prevailing utopian elements of individual and collective life within the audience (love, esteem, sexuality, family, community, material security). Whether and to what extent these meanings are decoded in hegemonically prescribed ways continues to remain an open question . . . which can be settled only by theoretical and empirical investigation.[5]

I agree with Dunn that both theoretical and empirical audience research is needed to see whether Baudrillard's theory of simulacra or any other theory of control as commodification is quite as all-powerful in producing the 'passive' spectator as has often been claimed. Inevitably this will require a shift from the notion of audiences as Baudrillard's 'masses' (conceived as *commodities* to be exchanged between programmers and advertisers) to one where audience members are considered as social subjects with their own practical and discursive history, as *agents* in the making of meaning. In this chapter I will begin to make that shift: starting with the perception among broadcasters of 'delivering' audiences to advertisers, and moving on to the notion of audience *use* of the text.

Selling the audience

It is a commonplace of the TV industry that the purpose of commercial television is not to deliver programming to people but rather to deliver audiences to advertisers. However, just why some programmes do deliver a mass audience is difficult to predict. In terms of audience demographics James Davern feels he does know.

> The *A-Team*'s target audience is the under-18 male, and they get them. *A Country Practice* doesn't get them because the under-18 male . . . likes to see the guns go off and the bombs explode. . . . It's the under-18 females that we're looking at primarily, because we find that what pleases the under-18 female can usually be broadened to encompass the 18 to 50's and the 50's and over.[6]

What Davern's comments reveal is, first, the emphasis on *overall* ratings and second, the emphasis on *demographic breakdown* of the ratings, according to age and gender. But none of this explains *why* different demographic groups like a particular show; although producers always have their hunches and professional rules of thumb, such as Davern's feeling that the targeted under-18 female audience likes 'more romance'. The furthest that the industry goes with systematic research into audience 'liking' is with 'Q' (qualitative) ratings; and with audience 'tracking'. The 'Q' figure (for a programme or a personality) is the percentage of people who *know* the show and vote it 'excellent' (on a five-point scale). 'Anything above 15 per cent you know you've really something good going for you.'[7]

In association with the 'Q' figures, there are the specially commissioned 'tracking' studies:

> If a programme is slipping in the ratings, we'll try and find out why. . . . Just going through the phone book . . . we isolate the past viewers who don't watch now to find out why. Future viewing intentions – that's very important, to see if they're going to go back to the programme.[8]

With *A Country Practice*, despite ordinary 'Q' ratings for the first episode, tracking tests

> indicated a build-up of interest as people watch more and more of it. As a result of that research, the Channel started it off in the non-rating period, which paid off.[9]

Similarly, with the early months of *EastEnders*, as David Buckingham describes: 'Although *EastEnders* appeared to be losing the ratings battle, the dramatic rise in its appreciation indices suggested that it was building up a loyal following which would provide a firm basis for future growth.'[10]

Tracking research can also be commissioned to find reasons for audience likes and dislikes in very specific instances.

> We had a little slip in the ratings of *A Country Practice* at one point of time. . . . Although *A Country Practice* dealt with controversial issues from the beginning, it was always aimed at family viewing, and at the start, when we were first testing, everybody was saying, 'Oh, because it's a programme I can watch with my children. I know I'm not going to be embarrassed by anything in there.' At this point in time, they'd given Vicky the vet a lover who was a married man, and the audience started to object to it. That was the reason for the slipping, and the tracking study brought it out. So poor old Vicky lost her lover.[11]

As well as appealing to the under-18 female, then, *A Country Practice* *must* go on appealing to the family audience (*and* to the over-55 female group where it gets its highest 'Q' rating). Norma Regent's tracking research for Channel 7 probably influenced Jim Davern's later refusal (despite continuous in-house pressure) to cover incest as an 'issue'. As script editor/producer Forrest Redlich put it:

> The block in my mind is this little blonde girl in a pink dressing gown. She's on the floor of the family loungeroom and she's watching *A Country Practice*, about a nice, supportive rural community. Then we introduce incest. I can picture her taking it in, then looking at her father. Who knows what effect it could have on her? . . . We know the story could help a child in trouble who has no one to turn to. But it could undermine the whole family structure for others. It's such a black, ugly topic and it's really 10 p.m. material, not 7.30 family viewing time.[12]

'Quality' audiences

In Australia, *A Country Practice* is regarded as a 'quality soap', but it still must deliver big audiences across the full demographic range to stay on air. In the USA, in contrast, 'quality' shows may keep going on a smaller but more 'up-market' audience range. As Michael Pollan explains:

> *Hill Street Blues* attracts such large numbers of the young adults (18 to 49 year-olds) for whom advertisers pay a premium, that the show is worth more than a Top Ten hit with lesser demographics. Advertisers pay $15 per thousand for the prime consumer that *Hill Street* attracts (compared to less than $4 per thousand for the general viewer).[13]

Not only did *Hill Street Blues* attract the all-important 18–49-year-old, urban, high-income and well-educated audience that was threatening to defect to cable and pay-TV, but a 1982 Nielsen survey indicated that whereas most prime-time programmes were rated lower in cable households, *Hill Street Blues* actually rated better there. So it made sense for Thorn-EMI to choose the show for its first advertisements for video software on US network television; and, Paul Kerr observes, 'Mercedes-Benz – a rare presence in prime-time – became a regular *Hill Street* advertiser in 1983.'[14] 'Quality' product was chasing 'quality' shows for 'quality' audiences. As Kerr notes, *Hill Street*, 'for all its relatively low status in the overall ratings, actually rates first among men of all prime-time programmes in the crucial consumer category of 18–49 year-olds'.[15]

All of this (the limited case of 'tracking' research apart) is still little more than counting heads. Provided they are the *right* heads – viewing in the right places with the right disposable income – programmers can count fewer of them and remain on air. But exactly *why* people find 'quality' in *Hill Street Blues* or *A Country Practice* remains something of a professional mystery. Very general intuitions about 'relevance' in terms of the 'mood' of the era (as in the view that *'Hill Street'*s "post-liberal shading to neo-conservative" politics seemed to fit the mood of the decade'[16]), or general notions of what different genders like (as in Davern's 'girls tend more towards romance, interpersonal relationships, warmth, mutual support'[17]) are made to work hard in the absence of more sophisticated measures.

Audience 'uses'

Nevertheless, there is an important convergence in views about audience pleasure between practitioners like Davern and an early (but still current) social scientific approach to audience 'gratifications'. Davern points out that 'both males and females in that under-18 age group like subject matter which provokes thought and discussion. The gutters of the world are full of producers who thought their audience was stupid.'[18] And 'uses and gratifications' theorists McQuail, Blumler and Brown argue against the view prevalent in traditional social scientific theory that pleasure among 'mass' audiences is simply a matter of escapist diversion.

Work in the 'uses and gratifications' tradition was the first to take seriously popular television leisure as a socially involving and significant activity, in an attempt to find quantifiable ways of measuring the main satisfactions of audience content. For quiz shows, for instance, McQuail *et al.* found four 'clusters' of gratification response: self-rating appeal, basis for social interaction, excitement, and educational appeal. Extension of this method to other genres 'yielded a total of nineteen clusters';[19] including escape from the constraints of routine: '*The Saint* helps you escape from the boredom of everyday life'; emotional release: 'Sometimes *The Dales* makes me want to cry'; companionship: 'The characters in *The Dales* have become like close friends to me'; personal reference: '*The Dales* sometimes brings back memories of certain people I used to know'; and value reinforcement: 'It's nice to know there are families like the Dales around today.'[20] McQuail *et al.* also discovered that most television genres could serve most of these appeals, to different degrees for different people.

What these examples indicate is the *use* of popular television in people's daily interactions. Respondents said, for instance, 'The people in *The Dales* sometimes have problems that are like my own' and 'It sometimes helps me to understand my own life', responses replicated in recent work on *Dallas* by Ien Ang, and indicating again that very different kinds of show, set in very different eras and social milieux can produce similar pleasures.

However, the 'uses and gratifications' approach to television reception has properly been criticized on a number of counts. First, as Stuart Hall has argued, the emphasis in 'uses and gratifications' theory on diverse needs being met in diverse (generic) ways for different individuals ignores the fact that the encoding of messages (within the class, gender, and institutional structures of society) ensures that some meanings are 'structured in dominance'.[21] Even soap opera, which frequently contains an 'open' mix of official and alternative discourses, encourages – as David Buckingham says of *EastEnders* – 'viewers to organise its moral and ideological universe in certain ways, and only makes available a *limited* range of perspectives'.[22]

The second criticism, that the approach is too atomistic and psychologistic, flows on from the first in the emphasis given to structural contradiction and sub-cultural difference. Morley notes the need to link 'differential interpretations back to the socio-economic structure of society, showing how members of different groups and classes, sharing different 'culture codes', will interpret a given message differently, not just at the personal, idiosyncratic level, but in a way ' "systematically related" to their socio-economic position'.[23]

To be fair to McQuail *et al.*, there *is* a sociological emphasis in their work, and some attempt to analyse class and sub-cultural responses. For instance, the 'basis for social interaction' appeal was strong among those 'with a large extended family' who used 'gossip as a coin of exchange',[24] whereas the highest-scoring group for escapist or compensatory 'excitement' consisted of 'working-class viewers who had measured low on an index of acts of sociability and who were late-born children of large families'.[25]

As these examples suggest, though, the desire to quantify tended to a mere listing of sociological variables as indicators of difference, rather than relating to a sense of social structure as a site of contradiction, process and agency. From this *latter* perspective the ('Personal Identity') response (to the news) of 'It helps me to realise my life is not so bad after all', would be explained very differently. Bernard Sharratt, for instance, relates the popularity of genres concerned with violence, horror and terror (such as news and melodrama) on the one hand to the structural insecurity and sense of acute vulnerability among the working class at a time of economic recession, and on the other hand to the fact that, in the equally insecure world of televison 'fact' and fiction, there is more control, even if only in escaping from it.

> The escape and fantasy . . . may essentially have been not so much an escape *into* its world as an escape back from its world into the familiar world which, however insecure, irrational and hostile . . . was then experienced by comparison as not as horrific and risk-laden as it might be. . . . After coming out of melodrama, it is the *normal* world which is made to seem more attractive. . . . That endorsement of 'normality' is at the root of conformism, of acquiescence, of ideology.[26]

Similarly, Sharratt would explain the 'self-rating' appeal of quiz shows to working-class audiences ('I can compare myself with the experts', 'I laugh at the contestant's mistakes', etc.) very differently from McQuail *et al.* Given the lack of *structural* social knowledge about how the system operates, and therefore about the causes of their economic insecurity and political impotence, working-class audiences can derive pleasure in an apparently more intimate expertise, which Sharratt calls 'pseudo-knowledge':

> The use of close-ups, the familiar faces of newscasters and actors, the sense of acquaintanceship with characters derived from regularly watching a long-running series, the personal interviews, the chat shows, indeed the whole notion of a 'television personality'. . . . But the kind of knowledge that television offers is often moulded in precisely the form of 'knowing' *personalities*. . . . What is offered in these forms of presentation is a peculiar form of mystified demystification: history is seen as made by actual men (and even, occasionally, women) but history (and art and science) is thereby reduced to biography and anecdote. *I, Claudius* and *Panorama* link hands.[27]

Sharratt's argument clearly relates closely to McArthur's about television history, 'fact' and 'great men'; and also to my earlier discussion about layers of 'knowledgeability' (theoretical, discursive and practical). Like McQuail *et al.*, Sharratt sees different TV genres performing the same needs, but here relates questions of audience pleasure (like expertise, intimacy, escape, etc.) to determining ideological meanings that the works convey. The *relationship* of the real world of social violence with the comfortable intimacy of the family living room is itself a source of pleasure: 'the streets of *Kojak*'s New York or *The Sweeney*'s London, the creepy terrors of Transylvanian castles, the napalmed villagers of Viet-

Nam, all *enhance* the reassuring, solid presence of the surrounding sitting room'.[28]

As Sharratt argues, it is possible to see why

> this structure of experience should be a particularly seductive one for an audience largely composed of people whose normal existence is . . . rather precariously maintained, while the dangers threatening it (illness, unemployment, inexorable price rises) are both frighteningly real and yet invisible, lurking in an apparently different world that yet can intersect unexpectedly, inexplicably and disastrously with the familiar domestic world of everyday experience. To survive without neurotic anxiety one has then either to believe that the reality of those threats . . . is a nightmare we can switch off when we wish – or one has to analyse, understand and defeat the sources of those threats.[29]

As we have seen earlier, it is precisely representations of *how* to understand and defeat those threats which are marginalized or forced into the ambiguities, cracks and fissures of television production. Meanwhile (as we saw in Chapter 1) some audiences neither switch off nor analyse but rather *negotiate* with the 'dangers threatening normal existence' (such as illness) by way of their favourite TV dramas.

Conditions of reception

Sharratt calls for a new approach combining an emphasis on conditions of production (focusing on lack of 'fit', and therefore spaces for resistance to dominant ideologies) with an emphasis on *conditions* of reception which would be both individual and group/class oriented. This approach would be both empirical in examining the particular television experience of audiences and theoretical in placing this within class and gender structures.

> Part of my concern is to understand the experiences and aspirations not of the 'class' as a whole but rather of the individuals and families who comprise the 'audience'. . . . As we . . . switch on the television we enter into relationships with others and with ourselves that cannot easily be mapped onto the relations of production and consumption that constitute the specifically economic and political identity of a class. In the disharmony between the collective strengths of a class and the individual position of the members of a class, one of the functions of 'popular' art may perhaps be located.[30]

David Morley's work has been important in this new stress on

conditions of reception. Like Sharratt, Morley both accepts the notion
of a dominant cultural order which reduces the number of possible
interpretations, and argues for 'breaks' and discontinuities in this 'order of
things'. Spaces for resistance to dominant ideologies operate both at the
'sender' end of the communication circuit and at the 'receiver' end.
Because of its complexity of production practices, a television work
must always remain polysemic despite its quest for a preferred meaning.
This is not, Morley insists, to fall back on the democratic (individualistic)
pluralism of uses and gratifications theory, for a television work is a
structured polysemy. But nor is it to assert (as much screen theory has
done) the automatic positioning of the audience member in the text so
as to simply reproduce the dominant ideology. A text works within a
field of pre-existing social representations, and to locate the production
of the subject entirely on the side of signification is to 'ignore the social
construction of the subject outside the text'.[31] Hence Morley attacks
the 'unjustifiable conflation of the reader of the text with the social
subject';[32] and the consequent over-emphasis on avant-garde texts that
destabilize this relationship, which has been the project of so much
screen theory and underpinned MacCabe's attack on Ken Loach's
work.

Also, like Sharratt, Morley criticizes the sociologism of approaches
which attempt to 'derive decoding directly from social class position'.[33]
Any audience member in fact inhabits a variety of cultural codes and
discourses, so that the 'meaning of the text will be constructed differently
according to the discourses (knowledges, prejudices, resistances, etc.)
brought to bear on the text by the reader and the crucial factor in the
encounter of audience/subject and text will be the range of discourses
at the disposal of the audience'.[34] The audience 'subject', then, exists
'only as the articulation of the multiplicity of particular subjectivities
borne by an individual (as legal subject, familial subject, etc.), and it is
the nature of this differential and contradictory positioning within the
field of ideological discourse which provides the theoretical basis for the
differential reading of texts'.[35]

Having said this, though, there is a tendency in Morley's *Nationwide*
work to reduce decoding to a single, homogeneous meaning within any
one class or occupational group. He admits that he ignores 'contradictory
positions within the same group';[36] but nor does he take account of the
role of the interviewer in situating audience interpretation, and, as
Wren-Lewis has pointed out, ignores the effect of group dynamics in
the interview situation in moving towards a unified interpretive position.[37]

This is not to say that group dynamics (*and* positions of interpretive
power such as the interviewer wields) are not *normal* aspects of television

reception: Messaris has indicated the degree to which parent/child interaction in front of the television screen determines the latter's perception of reality and behavioural learning through imitation;[38] Tulloch and Moran have looked at the normative power of 'teacher talk' in discussing television in school;[39] Palmer has pointed to the ways in which children act out favourite television shows in the playground, with boys relegating lower-status persons (girls or younger boys) to the role of baddies.[40] What *is* important is that the micro-levels of power in the audience reception situation are taken account of, as well as the macro-level of ideology and social stratification.

A valuable example of this kind of analysis is Hodge and Tripp's *Children and Television*, which examined children's responses to the *Fangface* cartoon, and was video-recorded to enable analysis of visual as well as verbal interaction. As the authors point out, the cartoon 'had a sexist bias that is fairly typical for the media: 1 female out of 5 main characters, playing a minor, largely passive role'.[41] The interviewer pitched the discussion at some points to examine sex roles.

Int: Let's take say, the girl, Kim (Stephen looks across to Kristie. Adrian and Craig exchange glances, and smile).

What sort of a person do you think she was?

Adrian: Hmm. A smart person. (Grins) She think she . . . she thought she knew all the answers, nearly.[42]

For Hodge and Tripp, Adrian's interpretation of the passive cartoon character Kim as 'knowing all the answers' is not 'wrong', since in fact it is directed at his classmate Kristie who is 'aberrant' (as a girl) in the large number of utterances she makes, and the numerous eye-glances she receives from boys. By focusing on non-verbal indicators (smiles, sideways glances, eyelines) rather than overt statement, Hodge and Tripp argue that the boys in the group establish a 'male common meaning', ascribing the 'smart person' put-down to Kristie, not Kim.

> The primary effect of the TV show, here, is not as a direct influence – a version of the world which is uncritically repeated by its passive victims. What it does is to provide the pre-text for a struggle in which Kristie is briefly and very lightly punished for breaking sexist ideological norms.[43]

As Hodge and Tripp point out, 'we can never directly study what children actually think about TV. All we can know is the meanings that they produce in specific circumstances';[44] and their research situation was clearly not a 'typical' viewing situation. But then *all* 'conditions of reception' are in a sense unique textual situations, since playground games, discussions in the family room during and after programmes, interviews in classrooms are all reconstructions of the TV work, with significant selections and omissions, and are all located within *some* system of power (of parents and children, husbands and wives, peer-group opinion leaders, unfamiliar interviewers, etc.). So, as Hodge and Tripp also say, 'though the precise interview-situation may be atypical and artificial, its underlying type is not. These interviews are typical of exchanges where there is an asymmetry of power.'[45] There is no audience situation 'uncontaminated' by social discourse and power.

So, for instance, Tulloch and Moran (analysing the failure of a class of boys from professional middle-class homes to interpret the episode in *A Country Practice*, 'Unemployment – A Health Hazard', in terms of its intended challenge to the dole scrounger myth) discussed the way in which not simply the boys' class background but also the 'teacher-talk' of the interviewer (as well as the 'educational' signature of the show which the popular press circulated prior to transmission) conspired to 'call up' a dominant response based on the official school discourse. The boys adhered to school values about qualifications leading to employment, which led to a contradiction with the episode's particular educational aim, since these boys still despised the young unemployed as 'dole bludgers'. In another kind of audience text, such as an anonymous questionnaire, a more macho interest in action and car crashes could emerge as a significant reading from the same boys. And, in another mode again, the fan letter, a much more intimate 'revelation' relationship with the star as authority figure could appear.[46] Clearly, the nature of the *vehicle* of audience communication helps determine meanings.

Yet even here, in this most intimate of media communication forms, the fan letter, there is a direct *negotiation* with figures in power. In some letters, for instance, viewers, arguing from their own experience that 'marriage is damned hard work', insisted that their favourite character should remain married, and there was the sense that

> their investment – of time and emotions – makes the programme in so many ways *their* show. They feel this entitles them to say what should or should not happen. These fans are insisting explicitly (by the threat of withdrawing their viewing) as well as implicitly (in the courtliness of their compliments) on their right to have a say.[47]

In each of these cases, certain textual virtualities are privileged and *made to mean* by the interpellation of discourses other than those 'preferred' in the work. The sign 'unemployment' was activated according to socially located discourses, as was the sign 'marriage' addressed by the fan letter. Girls from migrant backgrounds with unemployed, unskilled parents interpreted the unemployment story very differently from the boys, by way of the previous week's episode, 'A Touch of Class' which focused on exploitation and industrial injury among migrant piece-workers. They were 'making meanings' here *both* inter-textually *and* via their parents' recent experience – another example of audiences negotiating with the 'dangers threatening normal existence'.

As Morley says, audience analysis 'must aim to lay bare the structural factors which determine the relative power of different discursive formations in the struggle over the necessary multi-accentuality of the sign – for it is in this struggle over the construction and interpretation of signs that meaning . . . is produced'.[48] But in *The 'Nationwide' Audience* he does not go nearly far enough in moving between the 'class as a whole' and the 'individuals and families who comprise the audience' that Sharratt calls for.

In his later work, Morley has tried to build on the 'uses and gratifications' approach, while taking the family rather than the individual as the dynamic unit of consumption. In particular, he is concerned with differential power within the household in controlling the TV set, the VCR, and its software. Television has become both a focus for household interaction (often 'allowing' closer than usual physical contact) *and* a site where patterns of decision-making and dominance within the family are determined (children may be denied their favourite programme until they have tidied their rooms).

There are also clear gender distinctions in the use of television viewing. Men tend to be more engrossed in their TV watching than women, seeing it as a legitimate relaxation time at the end of the workday. For women, television watching is a more social activity 'involving ongoing conversation, and usually the performance of at least one other domestic activity (ironing, etc.) at the same time'.[49] For women, the home is seldom simply a sphere of leisure. Their domestic managerial function continues (child care, domestic chores, etc.) through their viewing, and only rarely (when all the family is out of the house) will they, rather guiltily, 'indulge' themselves. Women

accept the terms of a masculine hegemony which defines their preferences as having a low status. Having accepted these terms, they then find it hard to argue for their preferences in a conflict (because, by definition, what their husbands want is more prestigious).[50]

Because it tends to be the men who control the automatic control device, who select viewing, and who prefer the family to watch (in silence) 'factual' programmes, even the watching of favourite TV dramas is often a privilege that the wife and children must negotiate for. As Morley says, many women respond in 'the classically feminine way of dealing with conflict – in this case over programme choice – by avoiding it, and "rescheduling" the programme (often with someone's help in relation to the video) to a point where it can be watched more pleasantly'.[51]

This development in Morley's work is useful in incorporating aspects of a 'uses and gratifications' approach within an analysis of gender power: and in analysing the way this power is mediated by the different relationship of work to leisure between men and women. There is, however, still a tendency in this work to a categorical analysis: gender positions act as deep structures determining cultural practices (with some impressionistic examples of intervening class variables). Moreover, Morley's recent emphasis has taken him right away from the analysis of 'the audience in the text', preferred meanings, and questions of textual openness and closure.

'Open' and 'closed' performances

Marco de Marinis' work in the semiotics of theatre performance has tried to address this question of the 'opening' of texts and audience response. The audience operates in conditions of 'controlled relative autonomy',[52] and the degree to which control occurs varies across kinds of text. 'Closed' performances anticipate 'a very precise receiver' and demand 'well-defined types of "competence" (encyclopaedic, ideological, etc.) for their "correct" reception'.[53] This kind of performance is close to Elliott *et al.*'s 'closed' category where the weekly cop show reproduces the 'common sense' values of the state's orthodox discourse. But it also includes the kind of work which draws for central meanings on the encyclopaedic knowledge of fans, like for instance long-running science fiction series.[54]

In contrast to closed performances, Marinis differentiates two 'open' kinds.

> Those making a point of addressing themselves to a receiver which is neither too precise, nor too clearly defined in terms of their encyclopaedic, intertextual or ideological competence.[55]

Because of its need to aggregate different audiences, television must promote 'open' texts of this kind. Despite its 'encyclopaedic' appeal to a small body of fans, *Doctor Who* must draw on a range of audience competences and pleasures to catch its 'bedrock' and 'bonus' viewers.[56] Similarly, although soap operas do rely on the fan's 'encyclopaedic' knowledge for a great deal of their pleasure and discrimination, as we saw in Chapter 1 they are also more 'open' in Marinis' sense, in allowing increasing space for the inscription of many different audience groups. Marinis notes that this kind of 'open' text 'leads to a real increase in the number of "authorised" spectators and in the types of reception allowed for and compatible with the Performance text':[57]

> those avant-garde or experimental Performance texts whose 'openness' (their highly indeterminate make-up and loose fixing of reading strategies) . . . requires an audience to possess a range of encyclopaedic, intertextual and ideological competence which is anything but standard. In this sense, we can agree with Eco that, in reality, there is nothing more closed than an 'open' work.[58]

This distinction which Marinis makes between the popular 'open' text that encourages an increase in the number of authorized spectator positions, and the avant-garde and self-reflexive text which radically reduces its range of audiences, is paralleled in television studies by Fiske's distinction between the 'writerly' text by an avant-garde author, which 'shocks the reader into recognition of the text's discursive structure and will require the reader to learn new discursive competencies',[59] and the 'producerly' text which 'relies on discursive competencies that the viewer already possesses'.[60]

The *popular* 'open' text can be considered as challenging the closure of official discourses in two particular ways: in the formal space it leaves the audience; and in its projection, as Lovell puts it of the 'utopian and oppositional elements of popular culture'.[61] I will deal with each of these in turn: first with what Marinis calls the manipulation of the physical performance/audience relationship; secondly with Lovell's consideration of 'good sense' and the 'refusals' of the dominated.

Performance and audience

Ellis has pointed out that a defining quality of television, in contrast to film, is its segmentation, its flow of short segments – thirty-second news items, commercials and short sequences of drama,[62] allowing, as we have seen, for a contestation as well as flow of perspectives. In addition, whereas in the cinema audiences are relatively imprisoned within a dark auditorium in a voyeuristic relationship with the narrative, people often do other things while attending to television. Hobson found housewives working in the kitchen listening to the soundtrack (or keeping an eye on a black and white TV), and popping into the living room to see particularly significant moments of their favourite soaps 'in colour'. Palmer talks of school children doing their homework during the 'boring' parts of television drama, and, when they hear the music build up, they look up, watch, and then do a bit more homework. And in Chapter 1 I discussed the 'decentred', interruptible relationship between women homemakers and daytime soaps. According to their different contexts (kitchen, living room, playground, classroom, etc.) TV audiences see different performances.

At this point, the Morley-type 'uses' of TV approach can be brought into contact with theories of television closure. For instance, Fiske argues that TV has therefore to adopt strategies to attract the viewer's attention, which leads to specific characteristics of the medium. 'One is its direct address – its ability to appear to speak to the viewer in his/her domestic surroundings and to engage in a form of conversation. This produces in its turn, a kind of indirect address, a closeness and access-ibility of the television image . . . almost a friendliness or intimacy. . . . Its forms are those of interpersonal gossip.'[63] It is precisely this sense of intimacy, coupled with 'inside knowledge' about major political, sporting and showbiz celebrities which Sharratt suspects as 'pseudo-knowledge':

> Since the people who actually control our society are not known personally to many of us, and since the systematic nature of that control is itself difficult to grasp, it may become important to assert an expertise and quasi-acquaintanceship in areas which at least masquerade as important.[64]

Johnson, as we saw in Chapter 2, argues that this sense of intimacy gave women a kind of pseudo-authority within the economics of the home. Other writers, though, are more positive about aspects of TV intimacy, arguing that 'gossip' among women watching soaps (as well as between them *and* the soaps) is part of an 'exchange of mutuality among equals' that is central to the management of domestic politics.[65]

Because a television audience's reception is selective, it relies on sound, Ellis argues, to cope with differential attention – and Palmer's example shows how sound can 'hail' the audience. Marinis examines other interpolating devices amidst the semiotic density of theatrical performance, which are relevant to television as well. It is 'absolutely essential that the audience discard and even drastically eliminate some of the mass of stimuli to which they are exposed both successively and simultaneously by the performance'.[66] Performance texts have modes of 'making perceptible' and 'generating coherence' by way of attentive focalization. For instance, in *A Country Practice*, an unusually fore-grounded and apparently arbitrary close-up of Simon's abandoned dessert (which blurred the two-shot of Vicky and her father talking about the possibility of a city marriage beyond it) drew on fans' 'encyclopaedic' knowledge. Because Vicky, who disliked cooking, had specially made this dessert for Simon, many fans at that moment 'knew

Simon and Vicky would get engaged', despite her talk of getting married to a city man. Here the close-up worked against the narrative and dialogue in which Simon was discomfited. But other viewers, less 'competent' in knowledge about Vicky's views on entertaining, and on Vicky's preference in men (which was the opposite of a sophisticated city one), are likely to have passed over this focalizing device with minimal attention.

The example also draws attention to another significant way in which performance focuses an audience's attention. Marinis emphasizes the importance of novelty and surprise in attracting selective attention. This 'abandoned dessert' incident was certainly a surprise for fans who 'knew' Vicky. But Marinis also emphasizes that experiments on visual perception show that it is 'precisely by playing upon the dialectic of novel/known, strange/familiar, complex/simple, unexpected/predictable, odd/consistent' that the audience's attention is aroused. Pleasure resides in the 'unbroken dialectic between the frustration and satisfaction of expectations'.[67]

Sameness, surprise and resistance

This dialectic of sameness and surprise (familiar enough in soaps, and, as we saw in Chapter 2, central to the function of TV drama as myth) is an integral part of 'addressing the spectator in a psychological mode'. My audience research also suggests its relationship with audience pleasure. Jenetta McNamara, a Cambridge housekeeper, explained her pleasure in *Sons and Daughters* very much in these terms. By and large, she enjoyed the regularity of prediction: 'I feel I know what's going to happen in each episode, but I like to watch it just to prove myself right.'[68] However, she emphasized her particular pleasure when Patricia (the 'bitch' who is 'always on top in the programme') tries to get a job and is turned down. 'Because . . . it was really funny seeing her in the same position as me.'

> I liked that. It really sort of shocked me that she didn't get a job, because usually, in most soap operas, the stories are so predictable you know exactly what's going to happen. But this time I was wrong.[69]

Jenetta's comments also indicate that while Marinis' psychological research emphasis is useful in drawing attention to some of the attention focusing devices of soaps, sociological factors (in this case, female, working-class unemployment) *mobilize* the sameness/surprise space of soaps for resistance. Jenetta especially enjoyed the unpredictable outcome of Patricia failing to get a job because she viewed her as a 'top' person.

Jenetta 'enjoyed seeing the rich suffer', especially in situations where she herself had succeeded.

Jenetta's pleasures cannot, though, be categorically related to her class position. Other factors, such as her satisfaction in having 'made it' from a Lancashire industrial suburb factory to running a Cambridge University hostel where she has some degree of responsibility and control over her day, are important too. Significantly, though she also 'likes to see the rich suffer' in *Dallas*, she enjoys *Upstairs, Downstairs* (a drama series about servants and their masters) *because* 'I've always been in domestic servitude', and she *doesn't* like to see the rich there suffer 'because they're sort of really good to the staff. You know, sort of what Great Britain was all about, I suppose.'[70]

The 'unexpected/predictable' play of performance is here embedded in a complex mix of subjectivities, determined by (sometimes contradictory) class, gender, occupational and institutional patterning. This will include Jenetta's own generic competence as a soap viewer. As Bennett and Woollacott argue, 'it is the reader's foreknowledge – culturally derived from . . . her experience of similar narrative types – that, in the end, all will be well which renders this troubling excitation securely enjoyable'.[71]

Jenetta brings this mixture of subjectivities to soaps which are *themselves* contradictory in the possibilities they offer for subject positions. As Lovell argues, *popular* programmes must

> provide the use-values which the audience seeks in such entertainment. Some of the pleasures of entertainment will be readily mobilised for domination. Others may be more intractable. Among the latter will be those expressing the hopes and aspirations of the dominated which are thwarted under capitalism and patriarchy. To be sure, these will be deeply embedded alongside the contradictory sensibilities of domination, rather in the manner in which 'good sense' exists within 'common sense'. But their expression and development in however contradictory a manner within popular culture ensures that they remain alive and available for different mobilisations and articulations.[72]

The dialectic Lovell is exposing here goes beyond the continuity/surprise aspect of performance and individual perception, to sociological questions of control and resistance. As Lovell says, commonsense thinking is 'a mishmash of received notions, truisms, reflections on experience, etc.';[73] that combination, for instance, of unemployment experience with inherited definitions of being part of the British heritage and the sense of 'fair' domestic servitude we noted in Jenetta. But within common sense, as Gramsci recognized, there is a substratum of 'good sense', a space where lived experience (Jenetta's desire for the rich to suffer) cannot ever be wholly appropriated for dominance. There are, Lovell argues, 'unrecuperable elements in the experience of the dominated', and because of this 'the hopes, fears and aspirations of those who are oppressed within the structures of class and sex domination of contemporary society will find partial, confused and contradictory expression in such forms as common sense'.[74]

So as well as having exchange value (the 'delivery' of audiences to advertisers that James Davern talks about), popular television drama must (*pace* Baudrillard) have a *use* value ('the repository of useful attributes which the purchaser of the commodity gains access to and uses'[75]) if it is to give pleasure. And we have, Lovell insists, 'absolutely no theoretical grounds for supposing that the use-values consumed are identical, or even commensurate with, the ideological requirements of capitalism. . . . We are therefore likely to find subversive, or at least unassimilable, elements within popular entertainment – what Dyer has called "utopias".'[76] This is a very different contextualization of television drama's 'use' value (in its pairing with the *economic* determinants of the industry) from that of McQuail *et al.* (where 'use' was paired with the more psychologistically considered 'gratifications').

My argument has been that, to understand *why* audiences like what they do, while it is necessary to avoid the individualistic/psychologistic tendencies of uses and gratifications theory, it is still necessary to consider conditions of reception, in terms of the experiences and aspirations of individuals and their families in front of the screen. While Morley is right to consider the contradictory positioning of the audience (as a result of both 'fissures' within the work *and* the viewer's multiplicity of subjectivities), it is important to understand the micro-levels of meaning construction (as *always* a power negotiation, even in the intimacy of fan letters), as well as the broader implications of class, gender and ethnicity. Indeed, it is important to examine the way these latter are *negotiated* (as in the Hodge and Tripp example) by way of the former.

For instance, in managing the personal sphere, and constructing a set of emotionally mutual relationships with others who are doing the same, women soap viewers are playing with and *mobilizing* the specific features of television as a communication vehicle that I have considered: intimacy, gossip, focalization, the tension between unexpected and predictable; as well as the broader cultural aspects of 'common sense' and 'good sense'. They are indeed being 'delivered' as part of James Davern's commodity exchange with advertisers, as Johnson would argue; but they are also using the show for 'qualities' of their own. It's 'use value' for them is in establishing patterns of solidarity with other women, and a cultural space different from that of men.

9 Sub-culture and reading formation: regimes of watching

Structures of feeling. . . . We are talking about characteristic elements of impulse, restraint and tone; specifically affective elements of consciousness and relationships: not feeling against thought, but thought as felt and feeling as thought: practical consciousness of a present kind, in a living and inter-relating continuity.

Raymond Williams[1]

Really, I build my life around television. . . . *Dallas* is really soapbox . . . all wonderful dresses and glamorous girls. Believe me, I like *Dallas* . . . and *Dynasty*. . . . But I prefer the Australian ones. . . . I wouldn't miss *Sons and Daughters* if I could help it, because the story holds me. It always ends on a note that you are wondering where the next programme's going. . . . That makes a person want to switch it on. *A Country Practice* I like *very* much. . . . It's just sort of natural, down-to-earth everyday life . . . and its scenery is nice. . . . And there's no swearing. . . . It's clean. There is no rape or anything. I think that's refreshing. . . . I don't like *EastEnders* because it's *so* down to earth. . . . Life is very drab, anyway for me. . . . People listening, like myself, like to be uplifted a bit.

Pensioner, Bournemouth[2]

In this chapter I will be considering audiences as socially situated viewers. Fiske's summary of current theories of audience 'pleasure and play' is a useful starting point to demarcate the area covered here, particularly in its implications for my main theme of resistance and control. Fiske distinguishes between: (i) psychoanalytical work (drawing on Lacan and especially influential in screen theory) which focused on 'the audience in the text', and emphasized the power (and pleasure) of male voyeurism in subjecting women to the masculine 'look' of the spectator and the masculine agency of the hero; (ii) the Barthesian notion of '*plaisir*', which is the type of sub-cultural pleasure 'experienced by more liberal or even radical viewers of *Hill Street Blues* or *Cagney and Lacey* . . . in confirming their social identity as one that opposes or at least interrogates dominant social values';[3] and (iii) 'the form of pleasure as *jouissance* whose roots seem to lie primarily in ideological evasion'[4] and whose radical act is in replacing cultural myth by the personal/ erotic.

Though Fiske refers to the *socially controlling* power of male voyeurism and desire in television (as in the fragmentation and fetishization of the female body in TV cosmetic advertisements) and the *personally liberating* power of *jouissance* in the 'body and its sensualities' (as in the 'intensity' of soap opera close-ups), his main concern is with the *socially resistant plaisir* of sub-cultural identity. Similarly, it is the way in which socially controlling discourses are engaged with by sub-cultural ones that is my emphasis here; and just because ideological discourses are activated in daily routines of viewing among Sharratt's 'individuals and families who comprise the "audience"', we need to examine how any TV drama, as a polysemic complex of meanings, relates to viewers' daily rituals (including their patterns of generic expectation as members of 'reading formations'). So I will be focusing on the interweaving of 'common sense' and 'good sense' as texts are made by sub-cultures, other media works (like magazines and fanzines), and regimes of watching. I will be examining 'reading' as producing the text out of social experience and an inter-textual horizon of expectations.

Sub-cultures, texts and the production of subject positions

Sub-cultures 'are the meaning systems and modes of expression developed by groups in particular parts of the social structure in the course of their collective attempt to come to terms with the contradictions in their shared social situation'.[5] A definitional feature of sub-cultural analysis within sociology has been its distinguishing of the practices and values of certain social groups from those of the 'dominant', 'parent' or 'official' culture. Indeed, the very distinction between 'orthodox', 'alternative' and 'oppositional' positions which Elliott *et al.* apply to production, derives initially from work by Parkin,[6] Hall[7] and others on sub-cultures.

Hebdige, for instance, has argued that US popular culture provides a space for working-class audiences to find meanings opposing the dominant values of British élite culture.[8] Brown speaks of women's 'resistant pleasures' in the 'relationship between the dominant patriarchal ideology and the "wild zone" of . . . feminine discourse' in soaps.[9] And Fiske, introducing his reading of Madonna, argues that 'Exploring the strategies by which subordinate subcultures make their own meanings in resistance to the dominant is currently one of the most productive strands of cultural studies.'[10]

In this debate, critics looking for 'the subversive appeals of certain types of glamorous commercial programming to oppressed groups'[11] define sub-cultures actively; as in Hall *et al.*'s 'certain activities, values, certain uses of material artefacts, territorial spaces, etc., which significantly differentiate them from the wider culture'.[12] The emphasis on those subversive *uses* of artefacts and spaces by oppressed groups contrasts with the more 'objective' approach of Liebes and Katz to the *Dallas* audience in the USA, Israel and Japan, where the focus is on 'critical' and 'referential' readings by different ethnic groups.

Although Liebes and Katz point to differences between Americans, for whom 'the programme has no moral',[13] Russian Israelis who focus on its ideological nature as 'part of a consciousness industry speaking to the illiterate',[14] and Japanese who 'reject the program as an example of glossy American packaging of a corrupt and degenerating society',[15] because Liebes and Katz have no interest in the power dimensions of class, gender, age, religion and ethnicity, the differences they detect are read off as a somewhat transparent expression of dominant cultural differences. There is no emphasis on *sub*-cultural struggles to activate meanings in the context of a dominant culture. So there is no analysis of the class nature of the US response (unlike Seiter *et al.*'s *Dallas* study); or of the presumably quite complex negotiation of the *Dallas* text by Russian Jews who have rejected the USSR while still despising 'rotten capitalism'.

An area of 'sub-cultural' study which *has* focused centrally on the use of 'material artefacts and territorial spaces' to challenge dominant values is that of the child audience. Children, like the old, are a social group with little power in society. Yet, no more than the elderly, are they simply the passive dupes of television 'effects'. Palmer draws attention to the various ways that children actively engage with the TV: cognitive (as children draw on their experience to understand content); physical and environmental (as children construct living spaces around the set, people them with their pets, dance, play with the TV buttons, etc., while monitoring the screen); and interactive (as children comment on and discuss TV programmes with their families, and re-make and act out sequences of their favourite soaps in the playground).[16]

Palmer describes different kinds of interaction in relation to the same show according to different viewing partners; and examines the way in which participation in playground games of *Prisoner* and *Sons and Daughters* confirms the solidarity of friendship groups. Yet, as we have seen from Hodge and Tripp's analysis, TV shows can also be used as a matter of gender conflict and divisiveness among children, who may make 'texts' out of a TV work as a matter of *power* struggle.

A number of researchers have considered children's use of television drama not so much as a gender struggle between boys and girls (as in the Hodge/Tripp example), but a sub-cultural negotiation of power between children and the school itself. Curthoys and Docker argue that *Prisoner* (an Australian soap about life in a women's prison) is very popular with children mainly because of 'its portrayal of a situation not so very different from that of school: the ethic about not dobbing, or lagging, the ingenious strategies for circumventing formal authority, the informal networks of knowledge and relationships, the getting of things in and out of the institution that are not supposed to be there, the use of humour, cheek and wit to resist authority and rules'.[17] Palmer records children's inclusion of 'the real bad' teachers in *Prisoner* games; as for instance, they convert the school library on rainy days into the prison laundry.

> The library carried a bonus in the form of a book trolley which was transformed into the laundry trolley for their role play. The laundry trolley features in many of the scenes where prisoners plan their moves against the wardens.[18]

As children in the playground transfer the name 'vinegar tits' from the hated warder in *Prisoner* to a disliked schoolteacher, they are bringing what David Lusted has called the 'power to play'[19] out of the children's spaces of relative autonomy (the playground, the school gates where they talk, the toilets and bike sheds where they smoke) into the 'official' world of the library and classroom. And the struggle that is waged there is often more than one of age, but also of class and culture.

As Hodge and Tripp point out, because the values of working-class students are often 'inappropriate to the essentially middle-class way in which academic learning takes place', they come into conflict with school learning.[20] Television is mobilized as part of this class conflict. Action drama is appropriated by boys in its *difference* from the intellectual world of the teachers. As Connell has pointed out, it is hardly surprising that teenage boys grasp 'with considerable fervour the social practices that confirm physical masculinity'.[21] Smoking, swearing, sexual bravado, driving fast cars and action drama have an appeal to working-class boys who are doubly deprived. They are deprived in class terms. And they are at an age when 'the body lets the developing male down',[22] because they are learning to assume dominance in a patriarchal culture, yet are still relatively weak in the very (physical) qualities which that culture values. So their 'pretensions to masculine force and competence' are challenged by peers, controlled by parents and devalued by teachers.[23] More generally, the pleasure young people find in voyeuristically contemplating the sexual 'secrets' which soap opera reveals may well derive, as Buckingham notes of *EastEnders*, in the drama's empowering of children to talk about aspects of adult behaviour normally kept hidden, and which 'they are normally forbidden to talk about'.[24]

There are two ways in which this kind of 'cultural capital' is deemed inappropriate in the world of school. First, it lies well outside the school's formal curriculum (and even outside the more 'general knowledge' or 'informal curriculum' that is sanctioned if not taught by teachers – such as the information that comes from TV quiz shows). For girls, the ability to repeat character parts from the previous night's soaps in playground games gives particular pleasure because, as Palmer says, it is 'a means of rewarding in the playground a sphere of learning and experience that was not often valued or considered "legitimate" knowledge for classroom discussions'.[25] In contrast, Hodge and Tripp point out, the middle-class child, with a cultural knowledge derived from BBC/ABC news and current affairs shows 'will have a basis for interaction with the teacher denied to the other child'.[26] There is a knowing complicity at work here, where the middle-class child (who probably *also* watches *Prisoner* and *Cop Shop*) adapts to the *hidden curriculum* of the school; whereas the others' emphasis on action, sexuality and the physical may well lead to resistance to the school's ordered norms of deference and hard work for exams. So, secondly, working-class, unlike middle-class children, less readily internalize norms of not only what to learn but also *how* to learn.

This mutual knowledge about how to learn leads to a further complicity between middle-class boys and their *interviewer* when it comes to discussing TV in the classroom; as Tulloch and Moran note:

> The interviewer asked them questions and regulated appropriate discussion behaviour (defined as listening quietly, taking turns to answer, etc., just like the teacher). When we listened to the tapes, we noticed that even in the most detailed of linguistic acts (like attracting students' attention, checking understanding of what had just been said, focusing discussion, and controlling the number of people talking at one time or in sequence) the interviewer talked just like their teacher. . . . In its very *form* our interviewer's talk supported the school's hidden curriculum, with which these boys were so familiar. Not surprisingly, a major discourse, controlling many of the boys' interpretations . . . was the formal curriculum one ('taking exams is the

path to successful employment') supported by the hidden curriculum ('appropriate behaviour in school is the way to gain qualifications').[27]

However, girls of the same age, but from working-class, migrant backgrounds, faced with the same interviewer and the same questions, never once raised school study as a way to avoid the desperate unemployment of their own parents. Significantly, for many of them the favourite TV show was *Prisoner*, 'because I go along with the inmates', and 'because it shows you what will happen if you were in there'.[28] They engaged with their young female interviewer not so much as 'teacher', but as mutual 'fan' and friend.

For these girls at least, the 'them/us' parallels which Hodge and Tripp draw between the represented world of prisons and the known world of school may well hold. They argue that *Prisoner*, by revealing that each set of decision-makers in the institution is responsible to another power group higher up the line, potentially draws students' attention to the hidden curriculum of the school. School principals (like prison governors) follow orders too. 'The political economy of the school, and by analogy, society, is thus exposed by dramatisation.'[29] Similarly, Curthoys and Docker ask of *Prisoner*, 'Do adults as well as children, then, see in the programme the drama of power in different contexts, in the family, the school, the workplace – of how power is desired, and how it is resisted?'[30]

As Tulloch and Moran found, for *some* school students (migrant working-class girls, not white Australian middle-class boys), the intertextual linking of 'exploitation' scenarios from *A Country Practice* and *Prisoner*, blended with their own experience of oppression, may well provide an insight into the political economy of school, work, and society generally. For others, like the fifteen-year-old boy quoted below, fantasizing his own preferred scenario for *A Country Practice*, the determining 'structure of experience' seems closer to that adolescent moment of male weakness that Connell describes.

A mad trucky comes through the town and Franky tries to stop him but gets killed so then they call in Mad Max to help get rid of the trucky. As he chases him the truck driver drops a bomb and blows the town sky high. But Vicky and Simon escape and go to another valley and get down to repopulating the country and then they call it Bowen Valley.[31]

Certainly there is sub-cultural resistance here, but rather than the class/ethnicity/gender-exploited resistance of the girls, this is resistance in a moment of *transition* to the dominance of patriarchy, as this boy resists in turn the authority of the (female) interviewer-as-teacher, the comfortable 'family viewing' authority of Wandin Valley, and, indeed, the authority of the series' producers who specifically *don't* make their show for the teenage boy who 'likes to see the guns go off and the bombs explode'.

There is, then, no more than a *potential* discourse of resistance within *Prisoner*, providing children with 'a set of cultural categories complete with connotations, value systems and ideological inflection with which to think through their . . . powerlessness'.[32] Migrant girls in Sydney identified with the 'strong woman inmate' image, which is so different from the weakness of their mothers, oppressed by industrial accidents and building society summonses. Probably boys who articulate their powerlessness through *Prisoner* do it in very different ways from these girls. Still, the potential *is* there in the text; *Prisoner* does differ from other TV dramas in definitions of masculinity and femininity. As Curthoys and Docker point out,

> Images of female strength are not uncommon in television drama; indeed they have proved extremely popular in characters such as the *Bionic Woman, Wonderwoman* . . . *The Avengers*. But in all these cases, suggestions of female strength and capability are intertwined with emphases on conventional female beauty. In *Prisoner* . . . the women are not in the least glamorised. . . . Their faces . . . are signs of hardship, suffering, hard experiences, alternately soft and hard, happy and depressed, angry or bored.[33]

Valuing traditional authority as well as resisting it, *Prisoner* plays between 'common sense' and 'good sense' – the 'good sense' of lived experience for instance of Australian ex-prisoner, Sandra Wilson:

> Interest in women's prisons has been stirred by the television programme *Prisoner*, and many people ask 'are there any Veras or Megs or Beas?' From my experience inside I can affirm that there are.[34]

Emphasizing the polysemic possibilities of a work in terms of the ambiguities of 'good' and 'common sense' helps avoid the tendency in work by Docker and Windschuttle to a kind of left-wing populism which ascribes 'progressivism' according to popular experience and simple resistance to authority. For Windschuttle soaps are:

> well placed to perform popular culture's traditional functions of moral support and the confirmation of community values: human ingenuity and courage can overcome malevolence; loyalty and persistence will eventually win out; justice, even at the personal level, is worth

fighting for. In an unequal society, the preservation of such values is essential if any sort of social change is to be won from below. Even in soap operas . . . such as *Prisoner* . . . ubiquitous themes still emerge in the problems of people living together in confined spaces. . . .[35]

This is similar to Zipes' argument (Chapter 2) about Utopian elements in popular culture. The point is, though, that these 'ubiquitous themes' are processed differently in different class, gender, ethnic and age formations. Resistance to the authority of school (and 'teacher-talk') can have quite complex social ramifications, which are by no means entirely progressive. Tulloch found that children from affluent middle-class backgrounds were quite capable of sending up (rather than colluding with) the teacher-talk of their interviewer, especially when he was a 'soft' male, introducing into their classroom TV content (soap opera) which many of the students (adopting the high culture values of their social background) overtly despised. In this case it was quite conservative prejudices of class, gender and reading formation which conspired to provoke a 'resistance' reading of *A Country Practice*.[36] Similarly, the 'masculine claims to authority and personal space' which Kessler *et al.*[37] describe in the resistance of working-class boys to, in this case, the feminist discourse of their teacher, can hardly be described as progressive.

There is a tendency in some analyses of *Prisoner* towards a categorical use of 'class', rather than to examine the way in which it is complicated by other discursive positions, such as gender, age, institution, family, etc. Kessler *et al.* point out that what is apparently the *same* resistance within the classroom to the same teacher by boys and girls of the same class is in fact significantly different in terms of gender politics, since 'while resistance among boys confirms and even exaggerates their masculinity, the same behaviour among girls violates conventional femininity. . . . The school resistance of young women like this is a genuine challenge to their subordination as women.'[38] So gender positioning will impinge on class 'readings'.

In examining *Prisoner* and the school-age audience, we need to remember Willis' analysis of working-class lads' quite precise awareness of the school's authority structure *coupled with* a less precise understanding of the wider social structure; and remember, too, that what may be 'subversive' of *school* authority among boys may simply reproduce the *patriarchal* exploitation of females. As I have argued elsewhere, in the high culture sending up of both soap opera and interviewer mentioned above, the resistance to teacher-talk generated 'another asymmetry of power — between those who dislike (mainly boys) and those who like (mainly girls) the show'.[39] In this situation the girls were more or less silenced, and withdrew (via glances, giggles and whispers among themselves) into their own solidarity group. There has been a tendency in 'populist' audience work to ignore these complexities of agency.

In this context the potential of *Prisoner* (or any other 'progressive' text) to generate *out of* the precise knowledge of the school's power system a broader sociological understanding is important, but never conclusive. Yet Giddens is right to argue that Willis' 'lads" 'partial penetration' of their life experiences (while being functional in general for the reproduction of capitalist wage labour) may nevertheless 'be potentially radicalizing for the individuals involved, in which case it could lead to disruptive rather than cohesive consequences for the wider social system'.[40] In certain circumstances television drama can radicalize that 'partial penetration' in ways quite different from the 'half-formed picture' I discussed in Chapter 2 (as I will show in relation to *The Boys From The Blackstuff* in Chapter 11). But, in other cases, boys' experience of their own confrontations with the police can be re-incorporated within the 'mythology' of the East End underworld, as Buckingham found in his audience study of *EastEnders*. Boys praised *The Bill* as a more accurate representation of East End life than *EastEnders* because it enabled them to make sense of their own experience of living in that working-class environment – via the myth of the underworld – as more 'glamorous'. Here quite conventional notions of the glamour of big-time crime completed the 'half-formed picture' of the boys' experiences.

The point I am making here is that the important relationship is between the polysemy of the television work (rather than any *inherent* progressiveness) and the familial, institutional, age, gender, class and ethnic complexities of particular sub-cultural practices, experiences and needs. As with Willis' school, so with TV drama,

> making one's *own* sense out of *their* preferred sense is an act of opposition.[41]

But the 'act of opposition' of male teenagers via *Prisoner*, *The Bill*, or *A Country Practice* is of a very different order in terms of gender politics from that, for instance, of gays who have made *Dynasty* into a cult show.

> The programme's emphasis on high style, high fashion and its portrayal of interpersonal relations as competitive point scoring are all readily inserted by a gay subculture into the discourse of camp. . . . For this subculture, [Joan Collins'] style of dress with its broad shoulders and sometimes severe lines combines with her interpersonal

aggression to deny traditional distinctions between masculinity and femininity.[42]

Male teenagers may well be reproducing structures of patriarchal dominance, class superiority, or both; the gay sub-culture is undermining the very categories of difference on which that superiority rests. What is common to the television drama usage of all the social groups I have discussed – the elderly and their 'ordinary, everyday' soaps, children and *Prisoner*, middle-class boys, migrant working-class girls and *A Country Practice*, gays and *Dynasty* – is the adoption of characters, relationships, images and styles which are significant in relation to their practical consciousness. In each case the pleasures ('*plaisir*') include those of establishing the solidarity of the group – often as a community of the underprivileged. Seldom is this sense of community as a group apart so clear-cut or *discursive* as in Hebdige's account of punk and other music sub-cultures (though it approaches this in gays' appropriation of *Dynasty* style), where the composed articulation of dress, music, language and lifestyle is a direct challenge to the semiotics of 'normality'.[43] Much more often, as a mix of 'common' and 'good sense', the sense of community expresses a 'structure of feeling' deriving from the practical consciousness and the lived experience of exploitation that Lovell describes.

Structures of feeling and practical consciousness

Embedded as it is in routine practices (of, for instance, the migrant girls' solidarity group mentioned above), this active relationship of text and audience cannot simply be a matter of transmitting ideology in the strict sense of *ideas*. As Lovell says, there are, in addition, aesthetic and emotional effects which are often much richer than the fairly common-place ideas to be 'extracted from even the most progressive and complex work'.[44]

To develop a vocabulary for these audience effects, Lovell draws on Raymond Williams' use of 'structures of feeling'. As affective elements of practical consciousness ('characteristic elements of impulse, restraint and tone'), Williams distinguishes 'structure of feeling' from the 'more formal concepts of "world view" or "ideology"' with which it is in 'tension'.[45]

> The tension is as often an unease, a stress, a displacement, a latency: the moment of conscious comparison not yet come, often not even coming.[46]

Neither contained within official consciousness, nor within an oppositional or alternative world view, practical consciousness may include 'a
kind of feeling and thinking which is indeed social and material, but . . .
in an embryonic phase before it can become fully articulate and defined
exchange'.[47]

'Structure of feeling' is close (in terms of emotional and social
involvement) to Sharratt's 'structure of experience'. But Williams here
is dealing with authors rather than audiences: for instance, with Dickens'
or Mrs Gaskell's response to working-class poverty and debt prior to
the development in Western society of an alternative (Marxist) world
view. 'Structure of feeling' is 'specifically related to the evidence of forms
and conventions – semantic figures – which, in art and literature, are often
among the very first indications that such a new structure is forming
. . . as the articulation (often the only fully available articulation) of
structures of feeling which are much more widely experienced'.[48]

This 'authorial' definition seems unnecessarily restrictive, and
ignores the power of sub-cultures to redefine the text in reading it, by
themselves re-working 'forms and conventions'. Henry Jenkins, for
instance, points to female fans transforming *Star Trek* 'into women's
culture, shifting it from science fiction into romance, bringing to the
surface the unwritten feminine "countertext"', and forcing it 'to
respond to their needs and to gratify their desires'.[49] The 'eroticization'
of the *Star Trek* text is in this case conscious, at the level of form,
convention and discourse as articulated in fan magazines; in other
cases, as in Lovell's example of *Coronation Street*, it is more embryonic, at
the level of practical consciousness. 'One source of pleasure for the
middle-aged housewives watching *Coronation Street*, who, themselves, in
this role, are stereotypically desexualized within an ageist and sexist
culture, must surely be its sexualization of the middle-aged, the
ordinary, the housewife.'[50]

Here again we have the notion of pleasure in the context of the lived
experience and exploitation of a social group; in this case of women
who have spent a lifetime trapped in home routines that service a
husband's career. But (like Williams) Lovell rightly wants to go beyond
'audience-as-sub-culture' analysis to examine the way in which 'formal
and aesthetic properties of the work' relate to 'structures of feeling'.[51]
For instance, in the case of *Coronation Street*, long-established conventions
of the soap opera form (like strong, middle-aged women characters)
offer 'to its women viewers certain structures of feeling . . . which are
only partially recognised in the normative patriarchal order'.[52] To
retain their dramatic interest, these women characters must remain
independent to the degree that the *normal* order of things in soaps 'is

precisely that of broken marriages, temporary liaisons', reversing patri-archal norms of lasting romantic love.[53]

What other restraints, Lovell asks, 'over and above the structure of feeling itself, determine and limit the properties of those formal struc-tures?'[54] In the case of the female *Star Trek* fans, what inherited forms and conventions are *available* for establishing 'counter-texts'? In addition to 'structure of feeling', Lovell wants to identify 'structure of sensibility', which would allow us to raise questions about the historically based class and gender properties of aesthetic form, how they are established and maintained, and how (as in the *Star Trek* fanzine example) they may be used to subvert dominant generic forms. In particular she points to 'factors such as monopolies on education and cultural history' as of obvious importance.[55] In Chapter 2 I began to examine 'the historically based class and gender properties of aesthetic form' in terms of genre and ideology. In this chapter I will mainly examine 'structure of sensibility' as it relates to audiences, in the sense of monopolies (and alternatives) of cultural definition: as *reading formation*.

Reading formation and inter-textuality: structuring sensibility

The most useful elaborated analysis of the relation of 'monopolies of cultural definition' to audiences has been the notion of 'reading forma-tion'. Bennett and Woollacott define reading formation as 'the inter-textual relations which prevail in a particular context, thereby activating a given body of texts by ordering the relations between them in a specific way such that their reading is always–already cued in specific directions from such relations'.[56] An example of this was discussed in Chapter 3, where I looked at ways in which academic definitions of 'history' texts circulate, so activating (for both TV producers and audiences) regulatory patterns for making and reading TV drama. Again, in Chapter 1 I noted Robert Allen's argument that soap opera viewers are always 'tainted' with the effect of previous viewings and readings; in particular soaps are 'always-already-read' via the supervisory discourse of 'high culture' institutions such as university literature departments, schools, and 'serious' newspapers and magazines.

Reading formations are, Bennett and Woollacott point out, 'the product of definite social and ideological relations of reading composed, in the main, of those apparatuses – schools, the press, critical reviews, fanzines – within and between which the socially dominant forms for the superintendence of reading are both constructed and contested'.[57] Recent work in the cognitive aspect of television reception indicates that 'individuals bring with them to each new situation pre-established expectancies and plans (i.e. schema) which are based on previous experience'.[58] What the concept of 'reading formation' adds to this cognitive approach is the claim that these schema have material social supports (like schools, universities, etc.) with much greater regulatory power than the 'mother's discourse' that Allen describes.

Nevertheless, as the *Coronation Street* and *Star Trek* examples suggest, that 'mother's discourse' is never negligible. It has its own 'cultural operators' (like fanzines, inherited 'romance' forms, etc.) which establish their own schema. Cultural operators, as Bennett and Woollacott note, *contest* as well as construct dominant reception patterns. Literary critical reviews and fanzines, for instance, are situated very differently in the system of cultural stratification. So, on the one hand, analysis of monopolies of cultural definition can emphasize the 'dominant', top-down quality of reading formations – as in the case of the 'Boys' Own' reading formation (Chapter 5) supported by English schools, newspapers, films, comics and other popular cultural forms. But, on the other hand, there is the bottom-up 'guerilla activity' of using culturally *devalued* reading formations to subvert culturally dominant ones – as in the *Star Trek* fanzine example.

Supervisory discourses

In the history of discursive struggle around the status of soap opera (often between 'high culture' males and 'low culture' females) Allen points to two types of academic discourse – aesthetic and sociological – which have had exceptional regulatory power in devaluing it as a genre. Traditional aesthetics presumed a definable aesthetic object with temporal and spatial boundaries that were fixed and known; yet soap opera as a narrative form is predicated on the impossibility of closure, and lacks dramatic unity. Traditional criticism has erected a pantheon of 'great works' related to the personal vision of individual artists and 'figure in the carpet' level of difficulty; yet soap operas are marked by authorial anonymity, 'short-cut pleasures', and collective 'factory' production.[59]

Together these 'lacks' in popular culture generally, and soap opera in particular, constituted (within aesthetic discourse) the notion of 'escapism' and 'diversion' from properly fulfilling experience – from 'authentic' sensibility. Regular circulation of this discourse over some forty years prepared the critical ground well for those current newspaper critics whose style, as Curthoys and Docker note, 'likes to reveal the critic's wit and verbal play at the expense of contemptible popular offerings'.[60] *Prisoner*, for this kind of critic, is 'a slickly made tear jerker', 'an insult to the intelligence – nothing but nasty people behaving nastily in a nasty situation'.[61] How different then, Curthoys and Docker note, 'must *Macbeth* and *King Lear* be – nothing but nice people behaving nicely in nice situations?'[62]

In addition, from the early 1940s, social scientific discourse has suggested that soap opera enjoyment needed to be explained as some kind of social, psychological or educational lack on the part of its (mainly female) listeners. The social scientific scenario of the housewife as passive victim (of the advertisers and profit makers hidden behind the soaps), has been central to what Ien Ang calls the 'ideology of mass culture',[63] and this has blended in interesting (sometimes radical, always dismissive) ways with the conservatism of aesthetic discourse. Together these discourses have done much to define (in both class and gender terms), 'official' structures of sensibility, the notions of what true 'feeling' *is*, and how it properly relates to aesthetic form. In doing so, they have privileged certain ('High Art') notions of cultural competence, and defined others out of existence – in the eyes at least, of many school teachers, university teachers and 'serious' newspaper critics.

Reading as poaching

Recently a 'populist' school of media critics has begun to challenge the 'high culture' presumptions of 'official' reading formations. Keith Windschuttle, for instance, argues that soap operas are more 'authentic' than other genres in relating closely to the daily experience of ordinary people. This argument relating soaps to the daily routines of the audience is an important one (which will be elaborated in the next section). But it doesn't address Lovell's question about the historically based class and gender properties of aesthetic form – for instance, the fact that the soap opera form was, as Allen says, 'a solution to an advertising problem': how to use daytime radio to attract the largest possible audience of women. The solution (as we saw in Chapter 2) was to inscribe in the text the managerial 'woman-as-mum' – the *privileged* consumer. Clearly this 'woman as household manager' reading position is an integral *part* of the 'daily experience of ordinary people' who watch soap opera. Similarly, as Bennett and Woollacott say, women fans of James Bond do not have an existence that is clearly separable from the orders of inter-textuality (romance novels, soap operas, magazines) which mark their formation as readers. Thus interpretations of James Bond films by men were 'to a certain extent formed by the generic expectations of the imperialist spy thriller, while the parameters of romantic fiction and the image of the Byronic hero provided one inter-textual focus for women readers'.[64]

In other words, women readers of James Bond (or of *Star Trek*) carry to the reading of those texts their cultural (inter-textual) experience as readers. The 'reading formations and institutional apparatuses which organize and reorganize the social and ideological relations of reading'[65] are by no means only those of 'official' culture. Bennett and Woollacott suggest that romance narratives, emphasizing female narcissism and phallic castration, provide a competence in reading the 'wounded' Byronic hero through the 'dog-days' Bond of the novels; and that 'a reading competence in soap opera' may further enhance the caring subjectivity of the romance reader (her pleasure in 'the partial destruction of the hero's power') by way of the 'maternal understanding subject'.[66] Similarly, Jenkins argues, in the case of *Star Trek* fans, 'Women, con-fronting a genre "by, for and about men of action", choose to read it instead as a type of women's fiction. In constructing their own stories about the series characters, they turn frequently to the more familiar and comfortable formulas of the soap, the romance, and the feminist coming-of-age novel. . . . Kirk's story becomes Uhura's story and Chapel's and Amanda's, as well as the story of the women who weave their own personal experiences into the lives of the characters.'[67]

Readers are, Jenkins adds, bricoleurs in Levi-Strauss' sense: they 'draw upon materials not of their making, materials already at hand in their cultural environment, yet make those raw materials work for them'.[68] It is this *'objet trouvé'* quality of certain inherited forms and conventions (as in women's romance and soap opera) which (to use Lovell's word) 'offer' structures of feeling which are 'not yet fully articulate and defined exchange'.[69]

Those 'materials already at hand' are not, of course, always commercial media forms like the romance or soap opera. They may indeed be articulated ideologically through specialized (academic, 'super-cultural') texts, as in feminist discourse. Fiske, for instance, comments that 'women have told me how much they enjoyed *Charlie's Angels* when it appeared on their screens in the 1970s, and that their pleasure in seeing women taking active, controlling roles was so great that it overrode the incorporating devices that worked to recuperate the feminist elements in its context back into patriarchy'.[70] Here the circulating potency of alternative or oppositional feminist texts provided both producers (par-tially) and female audiences with different ideological frames to bear on the programme. Similarly, some feminists watching the Australian version of *The Last Place On Earth*, and faced – like the *Star Trek* fans – with a genre, as they saw it, 'by, for and about men of action', simply stopped viewing the series. Griffiths' text was re-worked but – unlike the *Star Trek* case – only to be closed off.

My point here is that 'readers as bricoleurs' make texts work by way of *other* materials (reading formations) already at hand. Both academic and commercial discourses establish 'top-down' regulatory reading patterns. But both academic and commercial discourses are also susceptible to what Michel de Certeau calls reading as 'poaching', as readers, like nomads, poach 'their way across fields they did not write'.[71] For example, the earliest Bond novels were critically legitimated by 'academic' reviews which 'both addressed and sought to produce a "knowing reader"' who, 'knowing' that Fleming was writing 'tongue-in-cheek', would supposedly not be adversely affected by the novels' racism and sexism, but 'would appreciate their purely formal role in parodying, by means of excess, the earlier imperialist spy-thrillers of such writers as John Buchan and Cyril McNeile'.[72] So here a 'high culture' reading position (established via literary reviews) was promoted to challenge a 'naive', 'Boys' Own' reading of Bond. Later this 'quality' signature provided by critical reviews was replaced by a different supervisory discourse emphasizing the more popular action-adventure genre. But in fact *both* the academic ('parody') supervisory discourse *and* the more commercial 'action-adventure' one were, according to Bennett and Woollacott, challenged in many women's 'readings and pleasures' via 'patterns of subjectivity established in "women's fiction"'.[73] As this Bond example suggests, readers are in fact 'poachers' in relation to the supervisory discourses which seek to control them; and they do it by way of *other* (often commercial) reading formations. The polysemy of any television drama opens it out to a range of reading formations, in which *other* popular media works (like magazines, fanzines and publicity) as well as 'academic' and 'ideological' theses act as important aids to socially coherent reading.

The effect is frequently subversive, though not necessarily radical. In *The Last Place On Earth* example, the conservative features of a 'Boys' Own' reading formation contested Griffiths' radical intention through a whole range of production, circulation and reception practices. But in the case of James Bond, women's formation as readers of romance arguably had a more progressive effect, working *against* the 'Boys' Own' readings of the imperialist spy thriller. So a women's reading formation, as we saw in Chapter 2, which in itself often works conservatively to reproduce the myth of women's 'natural' domesticity, was here operating to challenge patriarchal definitions of gender and sexuality.

This *inter*-textual function of media texts (where one popular television work is organized, re-organized, circulated and given a shifting range of inflections in other, often printed works) can usefully be examined diachronically and synchronically. Bennett and Woollacott, for example, have examined the production of 'James Bond'; first as 'culturally knowing' parodies of the spy-thriller genre for a small metropolitan intelligentsia; then in the early 1960s in films and vastly popular paperback books valorizing a modern technological élite at the expense of establishment traditions (with the accent now on new sexually 'liberated', 'meritocratic' mores, rather than on the 1950s 'nationalistic' interpretation of spying); and later, by the 1980s, with a particular focus on parents of pre-adolescent children, the Bond imagery now used 'to advertise instant-whip ice creams and peanuts'.[74] In this 'Bond' trajectory, criticism (as carried in magazines and fanzines) and publicity (as carried, for example, by best-selling dust-covers, TV promos, etc.) have been important in shifting dominant interpretations, and films have also acted back on the reading of 'earlier' novels.

Bennett and Woollacott's theoretical interest is less, however, in the periodic re-organization of the 'Bond' text, than in breaking analytically with the *identity* of the text at any one moment, and in re-inserting it within an inter-textual web of 'cultural operators' (fanzines, interviews with stars, advertising spin-offs, etc.). So, as well as analysing shifts of meaning diachronically through time, it is important to realize that *at any one time* there are *competing* commercial (and academic) discourses, which situate popular television drama in their own ways, ostensibly for different audiences, but with the possibility always open for any one reader to be positioned in a contestive field of reading formations. Consequently, we are faced, in the case of any one 'text', with a complex relationship between a *range* of inter-texts and a *differentiated* cluster of audiences.

Tulloch and Moran,[75] for instance, examine the way in which actors in *A Country Practice* are made into stars by women's magazines, TV guides, afternoon newspapers, fanzines and the production house's own publicity. *Woman's Day* situates the stars in terms of a home/celebrity discourse which relates directly to the *economy* of the magazine in aggregating an audience of both home-makers and the 'single, glamorous, consuming, liberated woman'. *TV Week* appropriates stars of *A Country Practice* for the 'here-and-now' of this week's ratings by way of the 'guilty secrets' discourse of conventional soaps (which ACP has itself rejected). The production house's own publicity emphasizes the 'issues' aspect of its stars and storylines, generating an image of 'educational but entertaining' which relates directly to the show's *generic* self-image (as neither 'too downer' nor 'too soapy') and to its *institutional* location (on the 'commercial ABC'). In relation to *EastEnders*, Buckingham argues that the merchandising spin-offs from the show (emphasizing 'its embodiment of the solid, homely respectability of British family life'[76]) and the in-house promotion ('the association with royalty, and with "official" – and somewhat nostalgic – definitions of national identity'[77]) work against 'the rather more subversive elements of working-class culture which are present'[78] in the serial.

The discursive *proliferation* of soaps like *EastEnders* and *A Country Practice* by way of a widening range of material and institutional operators (as the shows become more popular) makes it unlikely that any audience member encounters the text in a 'pure' form, within a single reading formation. Rather, the different discursive fields in which the texts circulate carry with them to the viewing of the TV show their own accumulated weight of readings. Many of these are 'commercial'; but for children at least, the appropriation of *A Country Practice* by schools for the examination of social issues (teenage glue-sniffing, needle-sharing, etc.) resonates with the accumulated 'wisdoms' of official school discourse.

Some discourses, such as the academic/aesthetic and the commercial, do seem to have (in Robert Allen's terms discussed in Chapter 1) a special regulatory power. *A Country Practice*'s own 'educating but entertaining' series ('issues')/serial ('soap') trajectory, for example, weaves between 'high culture'/academic and commercial/entertainment discourse. Still, at any one time, there is never *one* commercial (or academic) discourse but rather a range of discourses establishing cultural definitions and regulating consumption. And, as we saw with the example of *A Country Practice* in Chapter 1, the appropriation of 'academic' or 'high culture' positions by individual production workers can lead to the insertion in the text of more radical reading positions.

Since TV drama producers, critics and audiences are *all* situated within reading formations, these are, as I argued in the case of *The Last Place On Earth*, historically concrete, shaping texts 'from the inside out'.[79] In his writing of the screenplay, Trevor Griffiths resisted the 'Boys' Own' reading formation which he discerned behind the social criticism within Huntford's original book, but it also *resisted him* via press previews, performance styles (as in the case of Martin Shaw), production practices (as in director's cuts, editing and camera style), transmission practices (which reduced the text in Australia to an epic encounter between a 'dreamer dominated by his wife' and a ruthless professional), and British audience formations (as in the case of Mr Tulloch). Because of the continuing salience of a 'Boys' Own' reading formation in the practice of actors, critics, and audiences, the text and readers of *The Last Place On Earth* were, in Bennett and Woollacott's phrase, 'being co-produced within a reading formation'.[80] In the USA the problem was a different one, since, as Griffiths discovered, much of the audience wasn't aware that Scott didn't win and was not part of a British 'Boys' Own' reading formation. Consequently the 'who wins' generic hermeneutic of action-adventure stories (rather than the 'Boys' Own' 'England expects . . . ' narrative) impacted more strongly.

It is in this complex sense that the 'intra-textual . . . is always the product of a definite set of inter-textual relations'[81] – both for 'producers' and for 'audiences'. Texts are social sites for 'a series of bids and counter-bids to determine which system of inter-textual co-ordinates should be granted an effective social role in organising reading practices'[82] – and, I would add, production practices. The play between generic expectation and 'excess', specific institutional practices, the semiotic density of performance and audience positioning that I have described in various parts of this book, all engage with 'texts' via this contest of reading formations.

Regimes of watching

There is a sense in which theories of 'reading formation', despite their criticism of screen theory for constructing the passive viewer, *still* deprive the audience of agency. Women may counter-read the action-adventure of James Bond as romance, but they are still positioned (in this analysis) fairly passively *within* that reading formation. Yet the exchange of meanings between regulatory (generic and inter-textual) discourses and audiences generally takes place within particular viewers' daily routines.

As we saw in Chapter 2, soap opera has contributed to a process of structuring the day which extends that of the sphere of industrial production, positioning women as privileged consumers. But, as Seiter *et al.* say, this '*general* function of soap operas as clocking device' (where many women feel guilty if they 'put their feet up' rather than doing the ironing while daytime soaps are on) needs to be related to '*particular* ways in which the program is incorporated into *specific* structures of everyday life, which depend on the social context of the viewer'.[83] Here, I take the view that television drama texts are defined as much by the regime of watching as by their conditions of performance, production and circulation, and have effect as part of the domestic routine.

The relationship of 'reading' to these routines may be ambiguous and contestative, as Radway shows in her analysis of women's romances. But it can also be confirming, as we saw in Chapter 1 in the way in which medical soaps (and books) worked and gave pleasure within the 'care' routine of the elderly. Another example of the way in which soaps routinely function in a *confirmatory* way frequently came up in my interviews at Bournemouth, where Australian soaps signified a 'decent' culture, sometimes in contrast to the 'glamorized Americans', sometimes to the 'rough' English of *EastEnders*. 'The American ones are glamorised, but it's a family. . . . I don't care for *EastEnders*. . . . It's "rough", shall we say. I think it lets a nation down a type like *EastEnders*.'

> You get to know the families or the people and its all clean – you know, no jumping in and out of bed. It's like knowing another family, if you understand me. And if you live alone, it's something to look forward to, seeing this family come along, or this set of actors and actresses who become part of you in a way.

Many of the elderly ladies in Bournemouth watched Scottish, Australian, English and US soap operas through the afternoon and evening; they argued that their flats and facilities were so designed as to give them little else to do. Other old people in the same units were more selective in their TV watching, and so placed soaps differently.

I have described elsewhere[84] some of the relations between age, gender, physical disability and routines of viewing, arguing for instance that even in the case of 'high culture' elderly people who normally reject TV drama as 'pretty grotty really', it is possible to get hooked. There are at least two reasons for this. The first has to do with the enormous shared knowledge that regular soap viewers build up on a daily basis, and with the paradigmatic complexity of the soap text; the second, with the interaction between this textual sense of mutuality and the viewer's daily experience.

Dorothy Hobson discovered in her audience study of *Crossroads*, that 'viewers possess a level of knowledge about the storylines, the sets and the characters which few professional critics would be able to match'.[85] This knowledge is then drawn on to establish patterns of discrimination (systems of similarity and difference) between characters and repeated events that a 'naive' reader trained in the values of traditional literary criticism often finds stereotyped and banal. Robert Allen points out that the high degree of narrative redundancy, where the one event is rehearsed many times (or reappears thinly disguised as a new event), is not just a device to keep non-daily viewers up with narrative developments, nor just used to stretch subplots out to help fill up the voracious time demands of daily soaps, but

> invokes a paradigmatic network. It makes a difference that Lucy chose to confide in Debbie about her plight because Debbie was once married to Rick. Debbie's telling Chris of Lucy's revelation is read

against the background of Debbie's inability to conceive a child and Chris' recurrent infidelity, and so forth. . . . To the experienced reader . . . soap operas' distinctive networks of character relationships open up major sources of signifying potential that are simply unreadable to the naive reader.[86]

In his study of *EastEnders*, David Buckingham distinguishes the narrative processes of retension ('whereby viewers are given cues which invite them to recall past events'[87]), protension ('whereby viewers are given cues which invite them to . . . speculate about coming events'[88]), and lateral reference (via the parallel strands of soap opera). Thus, a particular scene he describes is 'rich in such references – to the Den/Angie/Jan triangle, to Ian and Wicksy's rivalry, to Michelle's past relationship with Den, and to Nick Cotton's attempts to blackmail Kath. In each case, we are implicitly invited both to recall past events and to speculate about future developments'[89] via the process of lateral reference. *EastEnders*, Buckingham argues, is even richer than soaps like *Coronation Street* and *Brookside* in its interwoven storylines, thus inviting viewers to '"work harder" at reading the text' and so contributing to the audience's 'sensation of narrative pace'.[90] The audience's 'work' (and pleasure) here depends on its knowledge of the tangled network of relationships in which characters are involved. 'Den Watts, for example, has simultaneously been the father of Sharon, the husband of Angie, the lover of Jan, the best friend of Pete, the father of Michelle's baby Vicky, the business rival of Naima, the employer of Pauline, Ethel, Lofty (Michelle's husband), Wicksy (Pete's son) and Pat (Wicksy's mother). Developments in any one of these relationships are therefore bound to have implications for others, and the effects of major dramatic incidents will reverberate throughout the different levels of the narrative.'[91]

It is this process of retension, protension and lateral reference in soap opera which appears to the uninitiated as narrative repetitiveness and syntagmatic redundancy. The 'naive' viewer who wants television to connect very directly with 'the real world' (like some of the 'high culture' elderly I met in Bournemouth), then complains that soap opera 'isn't getting you any further, is it?' However, sometimes particular physical and routine experiences (such as disability among the elderly) can lead to 'naive' 'high culture' critics becoming fans. So, Miss Herring (in Bournemouth), who generally scoffed at soap opera, got locked into the radio serial, *The Archers*. 'I used to stand up on calipers to eat my lunch at the sink . . . because it was not wasting time doing two things at once, and I used to have the wireless on while I was doing that. . . . But I did get so that I wanted to put it on the next day to see what happened.' As a result of her disability and daily routine Miss Herring was *shifting* her positioning within reading formations.

'You like to know', one woman told Dorothy Hobson, 'what's going to happen next', and Hobson points out that the reason for this desired combination of suspense and habit (often carried by the soap's concluding freeze-frame as in *Sons and Daughters*) is also related to the viewer's own social experience.

> Sometimes women need habits and routines to get them through the day. . . . When she was talking about how she spent her time during the day this woman told me that she often looked out of the window of her ninth-storey flat and counted cars as they travelled along the main road below. If you are so isolated that you resort to counting cars, the importance of a television serial to 'look forward to.' . . . does not seem strange.[92]

At other times, as Hobson also points out, the 'habit' of watching is less isolated, but rather a precious social and cultural space carved out of the frantic routine of an over-demanding family.

This, as Susan Kippax has shown, is as true of middle-class (but unwaged) women who enjoy high-culture forms like theatre, opera and concerts as it is of female fans of soap opera. One woman told her that 'to go and immerse myself in a concert or to go to a movie or something is all mine . . . it's my input and I build on my own character and memories of everything through that'.[93] Kippax adds, 'In this world which is hers (and it is not something she shares to any great extent with her husband) she gains an identity, a sense of self, in which she can recognize herself as an intelligent and autonomous being.'[94]

Yet, as Kippax notes, in seeking identity in the arts, women 'appropriate the dominant structures', accept *men*'s definitions of what counts as art, 'belittle their own knowledge and their own skills', and don't see 'art forms which derive from the domestic realm . . . as part of the arts'.[95] So 'women's experiences *as women* are denied'.[96] This positioning in dominant reading formations was true to some extent of Miss Herring too. Deprived by what she called the 'nicely private' girls' education of the cultural competences which, she believed, would have allowed her to enjoy 'intellectual' documentaries, she felt she was 'missing out' on things now, and was half-embarrassed by liking *The Archers*.

This structure of feeling, combining desire for a separate cultural space with what Kippax describes as 'only a *self*-recognized worthiness, and one that is accepted in a timid and unconfident manner'[97] is only too familiar to women soap viewers. There, too, the domestic threat to this precious space is moral and intellectual as well as physical, as husbands dismiss soaps' combination of habit and expectation with the put-down of 'What's happening to Vera in the next episode?' But one probable difference between opera and soap opera is that as well as being a social space carved *out* of daily routine, soaps' pregnancies, abortions, affairs, work problems, etc., are also *interwoven with it*. Hobson describes a 'What happened to Jill in *Crossroads* last night?' conversation, as four pensioners sat near her with their sandwiches and flasks of coffee, discussing their own families' problems, slipping into 'What about Emily's trouble with Arthur?' in *Crossroads*, and then back to their own children and grandchildren.[98]

Similarly, Tulloch describes a conversation about *A Country Practice* overheard on a commuter train which revealed, as in Hobson's example, the way in which 'wanting to know what happened next' is interwoven with – often related to – personal experience; and how this personal experience frequently represents areas of hardship in women's lives.

> Some of these hardships appear minor ones: a sister's frustration at being unable to control her own name in the company of a group of young men. Other hardships are spoken of by way of a common sense discourse that naturalises them, such as women's 'inevitable' fear of controlling the video. . . . Other areas of hardship, though – to do with difficult pregnancies, to do with exploitation at work – *are* recognised.[99]

The hardships that soap opera women face as they are exploited, made pregnant and abandoned (or grind on with their chores while their husbands take lovers) are played out, empathized with, and the characters' reactions criticized.

> I thought when Jill was going through this drunken phase . . . after this other fella ditched her, I thought was pathetic actually. Because she's been through it all before. It's about time she. . . . It's part of life. We could all turn to the bottle but you just don't, do you, in real life, you know. Some do, I agree some do, and I suppose that is what they are trying to get over. . . . [100]

Here, soaps are 'precisely a way of understanding and coping with problems which are recognized as "shared" by other women, both in the programme and in "real life"'.[101] Hobson recounts the response of one elderly woman viewer of *Crossroads*, to a storyline of a woman's frigidity on honeymoon:

> We used to say we were frightened of our husbands putting their trousers on the bedrail. You know, we had no pill, we had nothing. I

mean, I'm speaking perfectly open to you, we were terrified really, if the man got anything out of it it's right, but you were too frightened to let yourself go, and that's just it.[102]

This is a tale of repressed emotions, which is shared here with a sympathetic woman interviewer, but shared more regularly with the women on the screen and with other women viewers. This precious social space of drama – containing a reality at least as potent and significant as the men's newsworld of politics and violence – is the space of gossip and memory. Mary Ellen Brown talks of gossip as 'a hallmark of membership' of women's oral culture. As they slip easily in and out of gossip (about their own family and friends, about the soap characters, and about fan magazines' 'insights' into the actors who play the soap characters), women 'test the boundaries between fiction and life'.

Women are not put down, objectified, or devalued in women's gossip. Neither are they in the soaps. I would suggest that one prevailing pleasure that women find in soaps is validation of their own kind of talk. Women, in the relationship they establish through gossip *about* the soaps and in the affective pleasure of communal watching practices, establish a solidarity among themselves which operates as a threat to dominant representational systems.[103]

'What's happening to Vera in the next episode' is indeed *made* in this discourse to be more important than the closed narratives (*silently* received) of their husbands' news and current affairs. Fiske makes the point about gossip and oral culture (still, he insists, a crucial part of industrialized culture) that it is responsive to its immediate community. It resists the centralization and ideological control that goes with men's quiet reception of 'masculine' narrative forms, 'and it promotes cultural diversity'.[104]

This is particularly the case with gender relations. Women are very clear about the value of gossip, and often recognize their *husbands'* impoverishment when it comes to television watching.

In watching men tend to not wish to be caught out in emotions. I mentioned watching *Hill Street Blues*. . . . And last time I remember marvelling at a person working in the conditions these men supposedly work in with the boss – having an office like Grand Central Station but the size of a postage stamp – and thought: 'Well, that does appeal to men'. The point was that everybody kept their emotions so under tabs constantly, whereas here it's all very much discussed.[105]

In this way women deny their husbands' put-down that soaps are 'unrealistic'. In effect they are arguing for another level of reality, at the emotional and psychological level, which their repressed men have been socialized not to see or feel. Gossip ('women's talk') is a making discursive of women's daily routines and emotions. It is, as Brown says, 'feminine discourse' – as distinguished from the more theoretical and 'supercultural' 'feminist discourse which presupposes an involvement with the politics of the Women's Movement'.[106]

Ien Ang discovered the same emphasis on emotional reality in her female *Dallas* audience. One respondent complained of *Dallas* being 'pretty far outside reality' in so far as 'a whole family is living in the one house' and 'the family relationships are so weirdly involved'; but felt it was also real in having 'a semblance of humanity . . . recognizable people, recognizable relations and situations in it'.[107] Another viewer wrote:

> Do you know why I like watching it? I think it's because those problems and intrigues, the big and little pleasures and troubles occur in our own lives too. . . . In real life too I know a horror like J.R., but he's just an ordinary builder. That's why I see so many aspects and phases of life, of your own life, in it. Yes, it's really ordinary daily problems more than anything that occur in it and that you recognize.[108]

As Ang says,

> in order to be able to experience *Dallas* as 'taken from life' these letter-writers seem to abstract from the denotative level of the text. The concrete living circumstances . . . are rather regarded as symbolic representations of more general living experiences: rows, intrigues, problems, happiness and misery. . . . In other words, at a connotative level they ascribe mainly emotional meaning to *Dallas*. In this sense the realism of *Dallas* can be called an 'emotional realism'.[109]

Ang criticizes both empiricist and screen theory approaches to audiences for being (like these women's husbands) too dominated by a cognitive-rationalistic idea; and in doing so she brings us back to notions of 'good sense' and 'use value' by way of 'structure of feeling'. Empiricist and screen theory positions, Ang argues, are:

> based on the assumption that a realistic text offers *knowledge* of the 'objective' social reality. According to the empiricist realists a text is realistic (and therefore good) if it supplies 'adequate knowledge' of reality, while in the second conception a classic-realist text is bad

because it only creates an illusion of knowledge. But the realism experience of the *Dallas* fans quoted bears no relation to this cognitive level – it is situated at the emotional level: what is recognized as real is not knowledge of the world, but a subjective experience of the world: a 'structure of feeling'.[110]

When, in other words, Miss Herring slipped for a while from 'sort of trying to understand' 'intellectual' documentaries to the 'see what happened next' world of soap opera, she was moving from one site on which to negotiate her exploitation as a women (the school/documentary world of cognitive and formal knowledge where 'I am basically extremely ignorant') to another, at the level of emotional reality. In both terrains she was *negotiating* with the difficulties women face, resisting them; as were the women who criticized Jill in *Crossroads*, and the older lady who recalled her youthful frigidity.

The world of soap *articulates* (in the same way as the nineteenth-century literary texts Williams analyses) a particular structure of feeling. It establishes (like romance) a particular (gendered) reading formation; but this is a reading formation constantly negotiated between inter-textuality and daily social experience. Ang says: 'This structure of feeling can be called the *tragic* structure of feeling; tragic because of the idea that happiness can never last for ever but, quite the contrary, is precarious. In the tragic structure of feeling emotional ups and downs occupy a central place.'[111] As those *Crossroads* fans put it, 'It's part of life. We could all turn to the bottle but you just don't, do you, in real life. . . . Some do, I agree some do.'

If, in the real world of domesticity these women cannot do a lot to change their condition, then at least in the world of *Dallas*, as one viewer put it, 'you know all along that everything will turn out all right'.[112] Ang adds 'The "flight" into a fictional fantasy world is not so much a denial of reality as playing with it. A game that enables one to place the limits of the fictional and the real under discussion, to make them fluid. And in that game an imaginary participation in the fictional world is experienced as pleasurable.'[113] This is a very different under-standing of the relationship between text and social experience than we saw in Fiske's analysis of *Doctor Who* in Chapter 2. At least here, in the soap form, there is a chance to draw on one's own 'good sense' to impact on the world of 'natural' hierarchies.

Ang addresses Sharratt's fear that the disharmony between the col-lective strengths of class or gender and the individual position of television viewers indicates popular culture's conservative function. She argues that, despite the conservative implications (for women) of

soap opera content, 'fiction and fantasy . . . function by making life in
the present pleasurable, or at least livable, but this does not by any
means exclude radical political activity or consciousness'.[114] Shows like
Dallas, Ang argues, don't necessarily enforce on women an identification
with the tragic and masochistic positions of Sue Ellen and Pamela. To
view it that way is for critics to overpoliticize pleasure.

> A feeling of discomfort . . . always underlies, and is essential for any
> political struggle for a better future. . . . But it is impossible to live
> solely with a feeling of discomfort. We cannot wait until the distant
> Utopia is finally achieved: here and now we must be able to enjoy life
> – if only to survive. . . . Life must be experienced as being worth the
> effort, not just because a prospect exists for a better future, but also
> because the present itself is a potential source of pleasure. One
> dimension of life in which the distance between a (pleasurable)
> absent and an (unpleasurable) present can be eradicated is that of
> fantasy. . . . At the level of fantasy we can occupy those positions
> without having to experience their actual consequences.[115]

In an interesting variation on this argument about the ideological
ambivalence of soap opera as melodrama, Jane Feuer has argued that
whereas 1970s sitcoms (like *All in the Family* and *The Mary Tyler Moore
Show*) 'dealt with liberal "messages" within a narrative form (the
episodic series sitcom) limited by its own conservatism', soaps as
'prime-time serials reverse this, bearing what appears to be a right-
wing ideology by means of a potentially progressive narrative form'.[116]
Like Lovell, Feuer argues that formal devices typical of TV soap opera
(the exaggerated end-of-scene, locked gaze close-ups accompanied by
bursts of dramatic music, the 'intensifying technique' of fast zoom-ins,
the often contrived defeat of marital happiness and demystification of
romantic love) generate an 'excess' which the conservative storyline
cannot finally contain. Unlike the liberal sitcoms, prime-time soaps 'can
never *resolve* contradictions by containing them within the family, since the
family is the very site of economic struggle and moral corruption'.[117]
   Liebes and Katz's research on Japanese response to *Dallas* indicates
that it was precisely the show's intra-family conflict which was seen in
Japan to be representative of 'a corrupt and degenerating society'.[118]
This example, however, reinforces Feuer's recognition that the 'especially
active role for the spectator' which the continuing melodramatic serial
seems to offer is not *necessarily* (as Ang seems to imply) 'a salutary or
progressive stance'.[119] As Michael Pollan argues, '*Dallas, Dynasty* and
Falcon Crest give us the satisfaction of feeling superior to them: we can
look down on their skewed values and perverted family lives from the

high ground of middle-class respectability'[120] – whether in the US or in Japan.

Whether or not, of course, particular women *do* separate the conservative tendencies of *Dallas*' content from the 'radical' possibilities of its pleasures is an empirical question. Certainly, my own research found plenty of cases where women's pleasures related quite directly to matters of content as matters of middle-class morality, as Pollan predicts. For instance, 77-year-old (British Raj born and educated) Mabel Tulloch in Bournemouth spoke of her preference for the Australian *A Country Practice* over English and American soaps:

> I'm not keen on *Dallas*, and *Dynasty* I don't bother to watch at all. . . . *A Country Practice* strikes me as being a more normal life, a home life, the sort of life we can imagine ourselves living, rather than the American big money thing. And I don't watch *Coronation Street*. . . . I got sick of some of the slummy atmospheres. I like the middle type story, like *A Country Practice* and *Crossroads*. . . . Middle-class sorts of shows.[121]

In contrast, Seiter *et al.* found that the experience of working-class women 'clearly conflicts in substantial ways with the soap opera's representation of "a woman's problems" . . . as upper or middle class'.[122] Yet, at the same time (and this at least seems to support Ang's point) such class norms were, as well as being criticized, also validated as part of a necessary escapism of the viewer into a very different lifestyle. Perhaps, as with Jenetta McNamara at Cambridge, their 'escapist' pleasure was in seeing the more powerful classes suffer.

Others again, as Ang found in Holland, could get around their political values by adopting a 'high culture' position and *liking Dallas*. '*Dallas* is just so tremendously exaggerated, it has nothing to do with capitalists any more, it's just sheer artistry to make up such nonsense.'[123] Ang notes that the pleasure in *Dallas* here is in mocking it.

> According to Michel Foucault commentary is a type of discourse that has the aim of dominating the object. . . . Thus *Dallas* too is 'dominated' by the mocking commentary of these viewers. . . . 'At first we watched out of pure curiosity, now because we're hooked on it. Mostly we watch with a group of people and we laugh, scream and roar. . . . ' Commenting on *Dallas* has here become a ritual. . . . Ironizing viewers . . . do not take the text as it presents itself, but invert its preferred meaning through their ironic commentary.[124]

Ang's example of the 'ironic' reader usefully contextualizes Liebes and Katz's 'metalinguistic' reading, both in terms of cultural struggle and daily routine (in so far as these viewers keep a daily notice board of *Dallas* events). It also should draw our attention to the important distinction Annette Kuhn has made between theories of the textually inscribed 'spectator' and the actual 'social audience' in her attempt to reconcile 'text' and 'audience' theories.[125] If Ang and Feuer are right, the soap genre constructs the active female 'spectator' in the space between a 'tragic' structure of feeling and the liberating 'play' or 'excess' of the form. However, this particular discursive field is itself dominated in the case of the ironic reader by a high culture discourse which appropriates those self-same generic traits, and accents them by way of mockery. Behind this ironic commentary there lie, of course, other texts, contained in a supervisory 'artistic' discourse that establishes its own reading formation. It is in this dynamic interplay between text, inter-texts and the socially situated viewer (actively positioned in both routine and discourse) that 'meaning' is generated.

Performer/spectator/audience

At different moments of the text/audience cycle different daily routines operate, with different effects; but they are always inter-textual. Tulloch and Moran, for instance, describe another 'ironic' response to some of the generic features of TV soaps that Feuer pinpoints; but this time in *production*, where the editor of *A Country Practice* laughingly avoided going out on a zoom-in close-up as being 'too *Sons and Daughters*'.[126] Here a different set of discourses – determined by channel competition and house-style – positioned the ironic response. But the '*quality* at two hours a week' daily routine of this editor and other production workers still operates, as with Ang's ironic readers, by way of inter-textual relations. Producers of TV drama, *in the moment of production*, are themselves inscribing supervisory discourses as 'readers' of other texts: readers of 'quality' texts (as mediated by the production practices and values of BBC-style 'responsible drama'); and readers of 'just melodrama' (as conveyed by the 'ordinary soap' practices of other commercial programmes).

The 'spectator' inscribed by the *A Country Practice* team thus has its own discursive ambiguity. It is situated in the drama (as well as in many of the secondary media texts that re-organize it[127]) between 'quality' and 'melodrama', 'education' and 'entertainment' in a tension which can be made to work in different ways by different members of the production team. So, for one radical producer, the emotional appeal of soaps is a deliberate lure to hook a popular audience:

Obviously a huge percentage of the audience tunes in to those. So . . . that . . . to begin with you present the stereotype. By doing that you hope to engage the audience's interest, and then for the next two hours you steadily undermine that stereotype.[128]

But, on a commercial channel, the audience must *stay* hooked. Consequently, if the series strand in *A Country Practice* (where 'issues' are narrated) isn't 'working', the show 'reaches into soap opera'. Another producer describes how a precisely defined demographic 'spectator' (the under-18 female viewer, who is thought to like the animal strands) is called up to rescue the show.

Way back we had a story that didn't work at all. . . . So in desperation we killed Marta's horse. . . . Now all that anyone ever remembers about that block was that the horse died. When in doubt, throw Fatso the wombat in. It's always on the serial strand that you punch it up.[129]

Whether it is this inscribed under-18 female 'spectator' of *A Country Practice* or Ang's ironic 'social audience' for *Dallas*, both are constructed *inter-textually*: the ironic audience's mocking commentary is spoken from within the 'academic' discursive field of high culture; the under-18 spectator is positioned by way of a mix of commercial perceptions of *typical* genres (for under-18 females, under-18 males, etc.) and *appropriate* forms (for this channel ambivalently placed between 'education' and 'entertainment').

My conclusion, then, is that while it is useful to think of generic form as mediating between conditions of production and consumption, 'exchange' and 'use', 'product' and 'pleasure', we should not think of that form as more distinct than audiences are from commercial, aesthetic/academic and other reading formations. If the ironic audience can be thought of as *performing* the soap text by way of high culture discourse, we also need to think of the text as being performed by a socialist producer/ script editor at the script-editing stage (see Chapter 1), or by 'commercial ABC' channel executives at the commissioning stage, or by *Woman's Day* as part of its home/glamour economy, or by schoolgirls using the show to confirm their solidarity within friendship groups.

If we think of each of these performers (at the channel, in the studio, at the production office, at the women's magazine, at home, in the playground) *attempting to inscribe spectator positions* according to their own formation as social audiences, then we can begin to examine those 'discourses possessing greater constitutive authority at specific moments than others'.[130] We will be examining the politics of textual agency and contestation without bracketing out structures of power.

Much of the work on television audiences discussed in this chapter has implicitly addressed what MacCabe described as 'certain formalist tendencies' in his own work and in theories of spectator inscription generally. Fiske, for instance, argues that television's popularity as an institution of entertainment *depends* upon 'its meanings being capable of being inflected in a number of different ways'[131] by different audiences; and he rightly rejects MacCabe's denial of 'the ability and freedom of the viewer to bring extra-textual experience and attitudes to bear upon the reading of the programme'.[132]

Fiske's distinction between the financial economy of television (where programmes are exchanged between producers and distributors, and audiences are exchanged between programmers and advertisers – both as material commodities) and the cultural economy of television (where the commodity 'audience' becomes sub-cultural 'audiences' – a shift 'from a commodity to a producer . . . of meanings and pleasures'[133]) is a useful one in helping us think about structure, agency and power. Central to Fiske's thesis is the argument that 'the power of audiences-as-producers in the cultural economy is considerable. . . . This power derives from the fact that meanings do not circulate in the cultural economy in the way that wealth does in the financial. They are harder to possess (and thus to exclude others from possessing).'[134] In the cultural economy, texts are not 'containers of meaning' transmitted to consumers as 'the end point of a linear economic transaction'.[135] They are, rather, '*provokers* of meaning and pleasure',[136] giving audiences a semiotic power across 'a huge multiplicity of points and forms of resistance'.[137]

Yet because Fiske continues to accept the power of 'visual epistemology' – even in the cultural economy – he does not seriously consider those 'points and forms of resistance' within the media industry itself where precisely those dominant myths of empiricism and naturalism have been challenged. Unlike radical practitioners such as Griffiths and McGrath, he makes no sustained distinction between naturalism and realism; indeed he is cautious about accepting 'the notion of the real' at all, even though his view that the 'unequal distribution of power in society is the central structuring principle in understanding the relationship of any one group to others, or to the social system as a whole'[138] is clearly a realist one.

So although Fiske's *own* text is a bid to establish reading positions in terms of this 'central structuring principle', realist *television texts* which do the same (by way of engaging with reading formations established within popular genres) are still criticized for denying sub-ordinate groups 'the means of articulating and understanding their subordination by denying them a discourse with which to speak and think their opposition'.[139] Hence Fiske does not give the same positive weight to agency within production as he does within the audience.

It seems curious that while he accepts that 'extra-textual experience' among women shaped by the women's movement brings a 'different ideological frame to bear' on cop shows, when oppositional *producers* bring a different ideological frame to bear on action-adventure genres and mini-series, they somehow remain trapped within hegemonic myth and discourse. The belief in the 'omniscience' of visual epistemology remains strong, even among media theorists who challenge the 'omniscience' of the text over audiences.

The point is that MacCabe's non-contradictory 'unity of position' never exists, either in textual producers (themselves formed inter-textually and ideologically as social audiences) or readers. The assumption that a left-wing textual 'omniscience' meshes without ambiguity or contradiction with the social experience of even the more radicalized members of the working class (let alone the conservative working class that voted for Thatcher) ignores the problem of the different layers of 'knowledgeability' that I have described, and the (not always coherent) relations between them. Radicals in theory are frequently less radical in daily routines: as John McGrath points out, it was some of the most radicalized working-class males who routinely expected their wives to have 'the tea on the table'; who often put pressure on their actor wives in the 7:84 company to give up touring for the same reason; and who criticized McGrath's *representation* of these problems in *Blood Red Roses* as 'against the working class'.

Blood Red Roses worked inter-textually in a bid to free the signs of 'strong' Scottish womanhood (as sexually 'pure', rural working-class, waiting-on-the-man 'femininity' represented in traditional Scottish TV drama) from conventional reading formations; but it also articulated (as a process of discussion and negotiation between McGrath and his actors) the contradictions of class and gender in their own routine (professional and domestic) activities. In that sense *Blood Red Roses* 'played' parodically (as Bessie sets her union-leader husband's tea on the table) with real life power structures in a similar way to school students who (as Fiske says) satirically re-enact TV shows in the playground to critically reformulate the power structures that control them.

Particularly as McGrath, Griffiths *et al.* work increasingly towards a collective production process, the distinction between production and audience textual 'play' becomes less meaningful. One should recall that not only were the contradictions between professional and daily domestic experiences of 7:84 actors re-presented in *Blood Red Roses*, but that the real life 'Bessie McGuigan' was audience member for the theatre performance of the work, and her response helped reformulate the television production – which McGrath then circulated as *film* in order further to negotiate between audience and text. Left-wing dramas (of the Loach, McGrath varieties) always exist as a product of theoretical and experiential negotiation between 'authors' and 'audiences'. In that *collective* sense they articulate experience; and as Fiske says himself, 'to articulate one's experience is a necessary prerequisite for developing the will to change it'.[140]

Part Four

Conclusion: comedies of 'myth' and 'resistance'

10 Comic order and disorder: residual and emergent cultures

Cosmic terror is the heritage of man's ancient impotence in the presence of nature. Folk culture did not know this fear and overcame it through laughter, through lending a bodily substance to nature and the cosmos; for this folk culture was always based on the indestructible confidence in the might and final victory of man. Official culture, on the contrary, often used and even cultivated this fear in order to humiliate and oppress man.

Mikhail Bakhtin[1]

I might have concluded this book with the following analysis from the *Guardian* of the 'Cold War' interests of Capitol Cities (controllers of the ABC network). It 'explains' the production of the right-wing mini-series *Amerika*:

William Spencer is also a director of United Technologies ($3.9 billions in military contracts in 1985); M. Cabell Woodward is vice-chairman of ITT ($1.5 bns in Pentagon contracts); Frank Cary doubles in on the IBM board ($1.5 bn from defence); Alan Greenspan is with Alcoa (weapons use a whole lot of aluminium products). Not forgetting Capitol Cities longtime legal council, board member until 1980, shareholder still to the tune of $7 million or so – William Casey, just retired as director of the CIA.[2]

To have ended like that would have been to emphasize the top-down power of 'official culture'; the extent to which, as Trevor Griffiths says, 'one's field of action is prescribed by party, or by history, or by the tradition of doing things in certain ways'. That power of social control has certainly been one of the main themes of this book.

Yet it is important – politically as well as theoretically – to remember that the institutional predictability of life is '"made to happen" by social actors'.[3] A great deal of current media research takes seriously

Giddens' caution that the 'top-down' view of social structure is only a methodological procedure in sociology, not an ontological reality. Indeed, to close with the sense that 'Cold War' control of TV drama *is* some kind of immutable reality would be to add one's own categorizing and 'surveillant' power as academic to that of TV's controllers.

Instead, I have chosen for the last chapters an account of the comic in TV drama, because comedy's quality to control *and* subvert re-emphasizes both the major themes of this book. In particular I will end with a discussion of Trevor Griffiths' *Comedians* and Alan Bleasdale's *The Boys From The Blackstuff* because, rather than emphasizing a sur-veillant consciousness, Griffiths and Bleasdale, in their different ways, have drawn deeply on the comic 'marauding behaviour' and practical consciousness of England's working class and unemployed.

I want to use comedy as a concluding case study to bring together the theoretical issues I have discussed through the book. So my discussion of TV comedy will draw on the separation and nexus of TV genres; on myth and dreaming; on genre, 'normality' and the unspeakable; on history and critically realist forms; on authorship as 'strategic penetra-tion', drama as social event; on production ideology and 'density' of performance; on text and inter-text, structure of feeling and the socially situated viewer; and, above all, on social order and human agency. TV comedy, as I have said, partakes centrally of myth and liberation; and *The Boys From The Blackstuff* and *Comedians* articulate clearly the dangers *and* hopes of 'laughing in adversity'.

Television comedy

> The comedy of illogical and incompatible discourses, 'crazy' comedy, and the comedy of incompatible social codes . . . 'social' comedy, are derived from the same impulse. The mechanics of situation comedy are, then, to organize disruption in terms of discourse.
>
> Albert Moran[4]

A number of critics have pointed to a distinction between two major types of comedy: the comedy of formal disruption (which 'aware of language', disorders and recombines it), and the comedy of social disruption (which disturbs the empirically given social-discursive order). Lovell argues that though the 'Ellis/Neale distinction between comedies of formal disruption and social comedy tends to favour the radical potential of the former, the conservative nature of the latter',[5] in fact there are various kinds of comedy of social disruption offering different tendencies in terms of 'subversion' or 'incorporation'.

In this latter area, Lovell distinguishes between (i) comedies of social realism (*Yes Minister*) where comedy is generated through the exposure of contradictions between the normative and typical social orders, (ii) naturalistic comedies which depend on role reversal (*George and Mildred*); and (iii) farce, where (as in *Fawlty Towers*), 'Nothing happens which exceeds the bounds of possibility, but its fictional world is governed only by Murphy's Law – if it can happen, then sooner or later it will.'[6]

> The stronger the referencing of social reality, the less 'subversive' sitcoms tend to be. This is not because this form of comedy is immune to subversion, but because the conventions of realism invite the audience to take its action and characters as typical. Radical criticism within this form is potentially more damaging, and this may be why it is realist forms which have usually provoked controversy and censorship. At the other end, precisely because the conventions in play invite us to see character and action as exceptional, there can be greater licence.[7]

This doesn't necessarily mean that farcical sitcoms are more radical politically; and Lovell is likewise sceptical about comedies of formal disruption, 'which can easily degenerate into the rather tiresome and predictable frolics of the Pythons'.[8] Kristin Thompson, too, denies that 'smashing language' is necessarily progressive. She relates *Monty Python*'s generic parodies and 'separation of coded elements' to Brecht's criticism of surrealism as an art that does not 'return from alienation', and which is 'paralysed from the social point of view'.[9] *Monty Python* and other comedic works which subvert conventional TV language 'may expose and parody social codes but stop at the level of amusement'.[10] In contrast, Thompson argues, a reflexive film by Godard is not 'simply a satire of existing conventions of Hollywood romances'.[11] It returns from alienation to interrogate the social order. It is not, in Trevor Griffiths' phrase, 'terminal art'.

> To see the world as absurd is also to see it as incapable of change, as hopeless. The film-maker accepts political responsibility by returning from alienation.[12]

Several critics have extended this argument about the reflexivity of comedy. Dana Polan examines self-reflexive devices in cartoons, distinguishing between (i) formal reflexivity, which he argues is a *typical*, non-threatening component of (high culture) art and (ii) political reflexivity, the 'sense of the changing and changeable nature of the world'.[13] Commenting implicitly on the MacCabe debate about textual contradiction, Polan argues:

The conventional work of art does not banish contradiction; rather it works by divorcing contradiction from its social causes. . . . *Mary Hartmann, Mary Hartmann* . . . represents the triumph of contradiction: a show which attacks the consumer world is sponsored to sell the very sort of products its content disdains. . . . Shows like *Mary Hartmann, Mary Hartmann* have made pessimism, discontent, and irony marketable.[14]

Commenting on *Moonlighting*, Philip Hayward points to the *commodification* of reflexivity as part of a ratings battle between the ABC and NBC in the United States. *Moonlighting*

not only achieved best overall viewing figures, analysis also showed that it also attracted a large proportion of the high income bracket 25–50-year-old audience (a section of the television audience particularly attractive to advertisers); and proved so popular that it acted as an *anchor* for the rest of the channel over the evening (pulling viewers to ABC). But this success was not without its pressures – the particular sort of audience that the show appealed to was notoriously fickle, not having the strong programme allegiances of other age and class groups. So in order to maintain an audience for the show it had to keep introducing new tricks and surprises into the basic format. The area it successfully identified and exploited was the media literacy of its viewers, the conversance of its audience with the conventions of both established television genres and contemporary and vintage Hollywood cinema. Drawing on this the series self-consciously played with these conventions in a way that its (largely college-educated audience) would both recognise as witty and clever and recognise as being premised on their own conversance. In clear contradiction to perceptions of American television and its *production line* basis as innately conservative, the series prioritised experimentation, innovation and above all surprise as key elements of its appeal.[15]

Similarly, Jane Feuer points out that reflexivity and parody in the MTM-style sitcom is aimed at delivering 'quality' (high culture) audiences to advertisers, rather than being politically subversive. In contrast the non-MTM sitcom *Buffalo Bill* was 'both "quality TV" and "radical TV"' because it directed 'its satire *at* television as an institution' and refused the 'typical MTM pattern whereby family harmony is restored by the end of each episode'.[16]

As Polan rightly argues, the *realist* Brecht has been overlaid (and virtually occluded) by the formalist, reflexive Brecht of screen theory. Brecht's realism 'is a social quality . . . a form of knowledge. . . . The political artwork embodies a difference between the way things are and the way they can be.'[17] *Pleasure* in Brecht depends on the spectator's new recognition that 'the world can be remade'.[18] This is also the position of Trevor Griffiths' Eddie Waters in *Comedians*: 'a true joke, a *comedian's* joke . . . has to *liberate* the will and the desire, has to *change the situation*'.

The emphasis of most of these critics tends to be on the tension between the 'supercultural' (critical realist) and 'common sense' domains of comedy. But there are other comedies that draw on the domain of *non*-sense (of carnivalesque reversal, parody and the bodily refusals of the oppressed). In this and the next chapter I will look at both kinds of comedy, by focusing on the politics and pleasures of television sitcom and the grotesque.

Sitcom and social disruption

Ted: [to Greta] Where's the wog?
Greta: In the lounge, having a beer.
Ted: Bludging my beer in usual migrant fashion, I suppose.
Greta: Dad, surely he can have one of your beers?
Ted: Yes, sure he can have one of my beers – as long as I can leave it in the bottle when I shove it down his throat. [Going into the lounge-room] Money on the fridge, wog, money on the fridge.

Kingswood Country[19]

The relationship between genre and audience expectation is an integral one. Steve Neale notes that 'the existence of genres means that the spectator . . . will always know . . . that everything will cohere, that any threat or danger in the narrative process itself will always be contained'.[20] This is what Feuer calls the 'ritual' or mythical level of genre, genre as repeated 'exchange between industry and audience, an exchange through which a culture speaks to itself'.[21] Given this tendency to a culturally expected re-ordering, the *specificity* of any particular genre (as Woollacott points out) lies not in its exclusivity of elements but in their combination.

It is possible to suggest that all genres play with a disturbance, process and closure within the narrative, although in different ways. In so doing, genres construct particular temporal sequences.[22]

So, in the detective genre, closure is achieved through finally bringing together the time of the criminal act and the time of its investigation. In the thriller and the crime series, there is a multiplying of phallic threats (from the villain, from women, from the hero's institution), each threat setting up its own tasks and temporal sequence that have to be performed before the narrative can satisfactorily close. In science fiction there is a narrative tension between Romantic and 'scientific' discourses, setting up alternative temporal domains (evolution/atavism, structure/chaos), which a long-term series like *Doctor Who* will from time to time actualize as parallel worlds within the same diegesis.[23]

In situation comedy there is again narrative tension as two or more discourses contend, and here the alternative temporal domains are frequently generational. Woollacott gives the example of *Steptoe and Son*, where constant threats from 'outside' (offers and attractions which promise to lure Harold away from his exploited working relationship with his father) must be contained each week with wit and humour for the 'situation' to remain the same. But in contrast to the syntagmatic progression of other genres, in sitcom the temporal orders frequently remain separate; in *Steptoe and Son* 'the disturbance from the "outside" does not lead to an obvious resolution in which either Harold takes the offer and leaves or rejects the offer and stays, but to Harold's inability to take the offer and his remaining without acceptance'.[24]

> In situation comedies . . . the contradictions and resistances of bringing together . . . the two discourses, has to be accomplished with economy and wit, with conscious and overt fictional manipulation.[25]

In *Family Ties*, in one episode the narrative takes up the issue of teenagers and drugs. Alex takes drugs to help him revise, and as a result falls asleep and misses the exams. Some of our pleasure here may be in anticipating this, so that, as Woollacott says, the 'comedy stems from the timing and economy' with which the narrative resolves this 'anticipation of the inevitable'.[26] But as well as this narrative 'circularity', there is a different temporal aspect to an audience's pleasure, based on generational difference. The drug 'problem' is inscribed as yet another incident in the male chauvinist careerism of Alex (his use – and over-use – of stimulants during exams). But it is *also* situated in terms of Alex's parents' background as Sixties quasi-hippies who had lived with the drug culture. Here the social 'message' is not simply introduced and expelled weekly in order to get on with the next social problem, as it would be in an 'issues'-oriented soap like *A Country Practice*. It works as part of the *ongoing* clash of cultures (marked as a clash of time periods, of generations): between, in this case, the 'radical/permissive' Sixties and the more hard-nosed survivalism of the Eighties. Thus, whereas anti-consensual values tend to be introduced at the narrative margins of soaps, and whereas conflicting notions of community (as between the residual moral values and new multicultural diversity in

EastEnders) tend to merge,[27] opposed cultural values (*both* potentially normative for differentially situated audiences – as here between Sixties and Eighties viewers) are structurally central to sitcom. As Alex's father talks nostalgically of his (past) drug-culture, Alex falls asleep and misses the exams for which the speed was needed in the first place. Here opposed cultures (of leisure and work) are inscribed in terms of different eras, with different temporal rhythms.

Sitcom's unresolved generational tension, motivated each week by a 'threat' (Alex's speed) or 'offer' (Harold's job) from outside the close-knit 'situation', means that the genre is particularly well-placed to negotiate historical positions alternative to 'official' discourse. Moran shows how inter-cultural conflict in Australian sitcoms is mapped across a generational gap, the 'official' new Australianness (of multi-culturalism) facing the only too typical 'naive, insensitive, prejudiced, chauvinist' values of an older Australian 'digger' generation[28] (as in the humorous interaction of the xenophobic Ted of *Kingswood Country* and his Italian son-in-law, Bruno, cited at the head of this section).

As Moran points out, Australian sitcom is difficult to export, and sitcom everywhere concerns itself with specific national inflections – hence the shift from Alf Garnett's preoccupation with the monarchy and British politics to Archie Bunker's references to Vietnam and the counter-culture, when *Till Death Us Do Part* became *All In The Family* for the US market. Nevertheless, there are overarching continuities. The racially prejudiced, irascible father faced by married daughter and son-in-law (who have different values to the older generation) is a familiar sitcom situation. More recently, as cultural values swing to the right, the converse generational pattern has emerged: the liberal-minded, educated professional parents (of *Family Ties*, *The Cosby Show*) now facing the growth traumas of their often more conservatively minded children. Here it is the liberal discourse rather than the 'digger' chauvinism which is earmarked as 'time-past'; but it continues experientially within the growth patterns of the family, enabling a humorous engagement with stereotypes: of racism (*The Cosby Show*) and sexism (*Family Ties*).

This alternation of stereotyped generational patterns is an important way in which sitcom negotiates consent in its audience. As Woollacott argues, important re-workings of stereotypes of blacks, women and homosexuals take place across a range of sitcom texts:

> regardless of whether a series like *Butterflies* truly 'subverts' or 'in-corporates', it does move its viewers on to a different set of ideological coordinates in relation to extra-marital sex on the woman's part.[29]

A 'generation gap' example of this is discussed by Serafina Bathrick, in tracing the Jewish mother/daughter (Ida/Rhoda) relationship through the *Mary Tyler Moore Show* and its spin-off, *Rhoda*. As the comedy breaks through its *own* 'gags about fat and age' to a conciliation based on Ida's recognition of a new generation's norms about marriage and mothering, 'utopian aspects of feminism' emerge.

> It is not that all family relationships are hopelessly entrenched or that we can only sit back and laugh at the status quo. It is also that alternatives surface in these woman-oriented comedies, and . . . the possibilities for new relationships among women seem to emerge, even within families, when there are possibilities for relationships between women and work.[30]

Bathrick's 'Utopian' example suggests one way in which sitcom may challenge its own mythical function whereby 'a culture speaks to itself'. In addition, Woollacott suggests that sitcom can, as part of television's segmented flow, articulate 'different and potentially oppositional ideological discourses'[31] *in relation to other genres*. *Till Death Us Do Part*, for instance, used sitcom's outside/inside tension to play against 'law and order' articulations which were becoming familiar (for reasons I analysed in Chapter 2) in cop series.

> Garnett's suggestion that 'we've got to start shooting a few people' may sound more reminiscent of the solution that is found in most episodes of *The Professionals*, but it is also a conclusion that we are supposed to laugh at rather than applaud. Moreover while *Till Death Us Do Part* was relatively unusual amongst the popular situation comedies of its period in its direct concern with political issues, it was also organised like many other situation comedies to pull the right-wing views of the inimitable Alf Garnett into a family narrative, playing off his position outside a liberal consensus against his position within the family. . . . The crime series, however, tended to place those same problems and characters as threatening to and outside the parameters of the family, class and 'normal' sexuality.[32]

At certain historical moments, Woollacott argues, particular TV fictions enter 'a place in the public arena above and beyond their immediate textual base'.[33] The public outcry surrounding *Till Death Us Do Part* in fact made it a *social event*, providing a nexus through which ideologies could be 'actively reorganised, shifting the subjectivities at their core',[34] at the same time that 'law and order' dramas like *The Sweeney* and *The Professionals* worked to stabilize existing subjectivities. It is in this area of generic contestation 'that it is possible to establish in historical rather than formal terms the subversive or incorporate qualities of situation comedies'.[35]

Alternatively, we could argue, sitcoms which 'pull "deviance" into the "universal" problems of family, sexuality and class'[36] are not working *oppositionally* to crime series, but are (in Silverstone's sense) marking boundaries between common sense, normality and the unspeakable. Jim Bee suggests that the norm of 'correct' (familial) socialization in sitcom 'is assumed as the position of the text from which deviancy will be recognised and found amusing'.[37] In particular, the familiar mapping of the disjunction of normative and typical social orders across *generational* opposition displaces structural contradiction by 'natural' ones (where change is a matter of age and biography) in ways similar to the police series (Chapter 2). Bee argues that in British sitcom 'each type of deviance is given as a biological/psychological problem for social-isation',[38] with the 'wayward' (male, working-class) rogue representing 'fun' in relation to the duller norm of middle-class married women. 'Sitcom accepts monogamy as natural and inevitable and plays with the strains and sacrifices required "naturally" of men.'[39]

A major difference between sitcom and soap series, as Eaton notes, is the narrative imperviousness of the family in the former. Whereas in soaps the narrative unfolding traces the growth and break-up of family ties, in sitcoms,

> If a structural change has to take place it happens before the series begins, or between series . . . thus the change from *Man About the House* to *George and Mildred*, where two characters from the former show now constitute their individual family unit outside the parameters of *Man About the House*.[40]

In the Australian sitcom *Mother and Son* (precariously balanced between 'whether Maggie Beare is suffering from the beginnings of senile dementia . . . or whether she is merely a shockingly manipulative old bag'[41]), the exasperation and pathos may sometimes, as one TV critic[42] says, seem 'only too real' for comfortable comedy, but Maggie can never end up in an institution. The family stays together. The 'only too real' discursive tension of sitcom is *contained* by the family.

There are arguments, then, for both mythical and resistant functions of sitcom. On the one hand, the mapping of outside disruption across alternative social orders/generations in sitcom questions the 'normalcy' of any one social typification. We may (as Lovell says of social realist sitcom) 'laugh at the ideal, because it is so far from what we are shown as "real", and laugh in turn at this "real" because it is so far from the ideal',[43] but the Utopian can still be figured and predicted at certain key dramatic moments (as in the Ida/Rhoda example). On the other hand, however, the family group itself is privileged *as* ideal in its ability to tolerate difference through laughter. Profoundly opposed social and philosophical positions are incorporated within the generational demo-cracy of the family, usually as problems of socialization 'which are "typical", "natural" and not excessive'.[44] Hence, Eaton argues, the family 'is a sufficiently stable situation, settled enough to be able to bear repetition and to deal with the onslaughts of the outside in a recognizable, characteristic way'.[45] The fact that the 'situation' generally does not change for the family within sitcoms, means that, ultimately, cosmic disorder is held at bay. This is strengthened by the mode of address of television itself: what Ellis calls the distracted glance of 'the family in here' at the television which sets up for them 'the world out there'. Ellis argues (similarly to Sharratt) that 'TV confirms the normality and safety of the viewer's presumed domestic situation. The viewer delegates the activity of investigatory looking to TV itself.'[46] Whereas genres representing violence (news, action-drama, etc.) confirm the 'normality of the domestic' in their very difference from it, sitcom celebrates that all-tolerant normality itself.

It is probably this generic 'tolerance' that enables the sitcom to remain popular over a longer period of time than westerns, spy thrillers and police series. Whereas shifts in dominant articulating principles in society (such as the 'law and order' movement, feminism, etc.) are, as Woollacott says, 'registered in the area of popular fiction by the increased popularity of appropriate genre articulations',[47] within sitcom these shifts are both marked and resisted by way of the ideal/typical articula-tion of different social orders. What Raymond Williams calls 'residual' (e.g. the chauvinist digger) as well as 'emergent' (e.g. feminist) world views are continuously at play in sitcom allowing the one show to aggregate quite different audiences, and the genre to remain popular through major shifts in social values.

The discussion of sitcom 'order' and 'disorder' so far has been theoretical. Can empirical audience analysis throw any further light on this?

Sitcom audiences

Archie on sex:

> Archie: Look, I know you'se kids go by what you call this new mortality – skirts up to here, hot pants up even further, see-through blouses, movies with people in bed, sometimes three, four o' them.

Mike: But Archie, people's bodies – the fact that they go to bed – they make love – it's part of life!

Archie: So's throwing up! But I ain't paying three bucks to see it.

Archie on homosexuals:

Archie: I never said that a man wears glasses is a queer. A man that wears glasses is a four-eyes. A man that's a fag is a queer.

All In The Family[48]

Lovell argues that comedy in social realist sitcom stems from the gap between the socially ideal and the socially typical. But what is 'ideal' and what is 'typical' within the one sitcom will, of course, vary for differently situated viewers. Quantitative research on the reception of *All In The Family* has drawn attention to the marked 'personality' (as well as gender and race) differences in reading the programme.

Wilhoit and de Bock's analysis of *All In The Family*'s reception in Holland (a country undergoing 'serious contemporary concerns' similar to those portrayed in the show, like resentment against racial minority groups, a growing urban youth counter-culture, and changing relationships within the family) confirms that very different audiences find the same sitcom funny. 'The two major characters of *All In The Family* . . . appear to have sharply divergent images among the Dutch audience, with the two having only humour and harmlessness in common.'[49]

Other quantitative research points to the enjoyment of different *kinds* of humour according to gender, race and 'personality'. Surlin and Tate's analysis of the show's reception in 'prejudiced' rural communities in the US and Canada notes that 'US males found "Archie on sex" [see above] most humorous; Canadian females found "Archie on religion" least humorous'.[50] *Within* the male category, 'high authoritarian' men tended to find Archie's 'homosexual' jokes un-funny. Surlin and Tate comment: 'This indicates that normative sexually-oriented humour should appeal to both high and low authoritarian individuals. It is perceived deviant sexual behaviour which the more closed-minded person cannot accept.'[51] Another way of putting it is that homosexuality is as 'unspeakable' (at least for certain audiences) in sitcom as traditionally it has been in soap opera, whereas 'normal' sexuality is not – which perhaps supports Jim Bee's point.

Brigham and Giesbrecht point out in their study of *All In The Family* and racial attitudes, that 'liking for, or agreement with, Archie was *not* related significantly to liking for the programme as a whole'.[52] In fact, a variety of strategies were available to provide different pleasures in the show. 'Persons high on parental authoritarianism or lifestyle intolerance were more likely to view the programme as just entertainment, devoid of serious intent';[53] whereas 'Blacks who most enjoyed the programme tended to see its overall effect as more beneficial and felt less agreement with Archie and his views.'[54] Further, 'all the white samples agreed, to a considerably greater extent than did the blacks, that Archie is more prejudiced than the typical white person'.[55] What seems clear from Brigham and Giesbrecht's findings is that there was a sufficiently focused divergence (as between Archie's and Mike's values) in the one show for *white* viewers with very different values to enjoy it. In contrast, black viewers tended to enjoy *All In The Family* if they felt that the programme as a whole allowed the 'ideal' aspects to emerge via Mike's values. University blacks, who enjoyed the programme less, also tended to see it as more 'harmful' in its effect on whites. Cultural differences among whites, then, seem to account for different pleasures (related to different character generations), whereas blacks only enjoyed the show if they felt it was 'on their side'.

This quantitative 'uses and gratifications' research on *All In The Family* suffers from the problems I pointed out earlier; particularly in its tendency to psychologistic categories ('high authoritarian individuals', 'closed-minded persons') rather than to relate systematically sub-cultural differences in reading (for instance, as between members of a black university and a black church group) to socio-economic position. Nevertheless, there are useful pointers here to the way in which differently positioned viewers mobilize the *segmented* nature of TV sitcom ('heterosexual' joke *sequences* for instance eliciting more general support among men than 'homosexual' ones; while enjoyment among blacks was 'consistently related to evaluation of specific aspects of the programme'[56]); as well as examples of the way that different *audiences* establish narrative 'causality'. For instance, 'Persons who were highly ethnocentric or intolerant of divergent lifestyles were less willing than persons low on these factors to say Archie was usually responsible for trouble in the Bunker family. . . . Only panelists who were highly intolerant of other lifestyles were more likely to see Mike as generally initiating the bickering in the series.'[57]

This 'segmented' reading of sitcom, tied together by the *viewer*'s construction of the narrative, can lead to a very different relationship between sitcoms like *Till Death Us Do Part* and police series than the 'contradictory' one that Woollacott suggests. In my elderly audience it was quite possible for a viewer to like *Till Death Us Do Part* and identify with Alf Garnett's ideals despite the series' generally anti-'law and order' thrust. For this elderly, male, working-class viewer the 'ideal' resides in Alf's traditional values, a residual quality lingering on in the contemporary period which he sees as 'typical' for its radical rejection of white supremacy, conservatism and monarchy.

In his reading, *Till Death Us Do Part* and *The Sweeney* were not opposed ideologically, but contained a nostalgic retreat to a conservative working-class, Cockney environment of the past.

Mr Gilroy: I liked *Till Death Us Do Part*.

Mrs Gilroy: That's all the old Cockney and the language and all that.

Mr Gilroy: I agreed with him. . . . I used to like *The Sweeney* – and *Minder*.

Mrs Gilroy: There again, that's all filmed where he lived – Notting Hill Gate. He says 'Look, I know that road, know that shed, know that yard'. . . .

Mr Gilroy: Yeah it was all old Cockney, you see. . . . And it's funny as well as exciting. . . . I know what they're doing, like second nature sort of thing. . . . And I could go there blindfolded. . . . I wish I'd never come to Bournemouth. I don't like it here. . . .

Mrs Gilroy: There's no people like him here. . . . All the rest are, to him, toffee-nosed. But they're nearly all widows, and they've got pensions as well as old-aged pensions.[58]

For Mr Gilroy, age and class differences were interwoven complexly with his pleasures. The Cockney London of 'bad language', used-car yards and sharp practices (as in *Minder*) were a deeply felt part of his own working-class past as a barrow boy and bookie, distinguishing him from the 'toffee-nosed' elderly widows of Bournemouth. But other values also distinguished him from the young. Like Alf Garnett, Mr Gilroy and his Cockney friend Mr Savage rejected 'young people's' shows ('that's not music, that's just noise'); and they lost their early interest in the Cockney *EastEnders* because 'too noisy' and introducing 'punk' styles and values.

The elderly are not a targeted audience group. It is the 'yuppy' young professionals, with high disposable incomes and 'high culture' values, who are the 'quality' audiences that 'quality' sitcoms are delivering to advertisers by way of a new kind of 'quality' signature. As Feuer points out, the sitcom 'relevance' drive (*All In The Family*) and 'quality' drive (*The Mary Tyler Moore Show*) were part of the US networks' new orientation to 'quality' demographics, at the expense of 'rural' sitcoms (*The Beverly Hillbillies*) and westerns (*Gunsmoke*) largely watched by the elderly.

The elderly (and, I suspect, other underprivileged groups) must carve their pleasure as a kind of guerilla activity out of the segmented nature of television, weaving together another temporal zone out of genres as different (or even apparently opposed) as *Name That Tune*,[59] *Minder* and *Till Death Us Do Part*. So although, as I said earlier, popular genres separate connected parts of the social order, and although they also negotiate social change differently by way of their specificities of narrative/temporal organization, they can also (via their very segmentation) be re-connected (as in Mr Gilroy's case) by *other* maps of place, time, language and value.

Sitcom in particular, because of the genre's usually unresolved narrative opposition of opposed (generational) cultures, *centres* this kind of mapping exercise. In *The Sweeney* and *Minder* Mr Gilroy retraced his former environment of Notting Hill Gate. But in *Till Death Us Do Part* he retraced far more: his old cultural milieu *and* its displacement by the present. Again, as in the case of certain soaps, sitcom connected the 'ordinary, everyday' (and, more centrally than in soaps, its past) with the world 'outside'.

Residual and emergent cultures

Sitcom values *both* traditional familial *and* new 'independent' relationships. Like other genres, sitcom needs to be analysed in terms both of myth and resistance. On the one hand, Bathrick sees the Mary Tyler Moore sitcoms as actively working with feminism, replacing the 'romantic' male lead and the traditional family Utopia with 'the mutual exchange that has always characterised the daily lives of women'.[60] This mutual exchange has displaced the 'managerial', 'consumerist' and domestically ghettoized woman of early soap opera.

> These three shared lives . . . provided an alternative to family life. . . . They also questioned consumer values and the place of woman as buyer and believer in the myths of transformation. And above all, these women affirmed the interdependence and compatibility of a daily life that combined home and work. Thus Mary, Phyllis and Rhoda formed a familial group, sustained by what is most necessary to modern life: community and critique.[61]

Feuer also sees a progressive potential here:

> the MTM family . . . represents a positive alternative to the nuclear family that had for so long dominated representations of the family on American television. . . . The work family . . . gives us a vision of

that merger of work and love that Freud said was the ideal of mental, and that many would also see as the ideal of political, health. MTM shows us this ideal over and over again within what in reality are the most oppressive institutional contexts: the hospital, the police precinct, the TV station. . . . For women especially, the alternatives presented were ideal ones, not depictions of the reality of work but images of a liberated existence that could be taken as a goal to strive towards.[62]

So, Feuer argues for the female sitcom audience (as Ang does for the soap audience and Radway for the romance reader), that MTM product provides a progressive Utopian fantasy from which to interrogate the banal reality of daily domesticity.

On the other hand, Bathrick points to the historically regressive, patriarchal representation of Mary's role among the newsmen at work, her 'True Woman' status denying 'her role as producer in that context';[63] and for Feuer, the 'MTM work family is clearly a response to the breakdown of the nuclear family inside and outside the television institution'.[64] In particular, Bathrick notes of MTM product, 'the ideology of the nineteenth-century True Woman who was worshipped as she was assigned the role of family maintenance-expert'[65] is re-directed from the domestic family to the new professional work-family, as capitalism re-orders its economic relations (with up to 43 per cent of women in the workforce by 1970). In an important sense, this *making-familial* of the world of female professional work is extremely conservative, valuing stasis over change. Feuer points to the anti-unionism of *WKRP in Cincinnati* where 'the message is clear: the work family does not need to organise because it is already a democratic institution; all problems can be resolved within the family structure'. In this case the union represents the outside 'threat' into 'an already Utopian situation'.[66]

This ambiguating relationship of woman's 'independence' and 'work' with a traditional 'True Woman' familial paradigm well suits a television economy which has to aggregate audiences, and so attract the professional 'liberated' woman without losing the traditional audience that values motherhood and domesticity. As Feuer points out, MTM sitcoms were *both* 'modernist' in their appeal to a 'sophisticated' audience *and* 'warm, humane comedies' for a mass audience. To this degree MTM sitcom worked to pull together not only 'mass' and 'quality' audiences, but (in terms of its female viewers) different *generations* of mothers and daughters.

It is its emphasis on aggregating audiences (familiar enough in popular television, but here marked by its mapping across the narrative *irresolution* of generational conflicts) that allows sitcom to play on fantasies and Utopias relating to such different structures of feeling as our elderly

Cockneys', US blacks', and Feuer's female viewers'. It is perhaps helpful at this point to recall Raymond Williams' contention that 'myth' must *always contain* 'dreaming': 'no dominant culture ever in reality includes or exhausts all human practice, human energy, and human intention'.[67] There is always 'practical consciousness, in specific relationships, specific skills, specific perceptions' which any dominant social order neglects, represses, or only partially incorporates.[68]

On the one hand, there is residual culture, including 'certain experience, meanings and values' which, though still active in the cultural process, is 'lived and practised on the basis of the residue . . . of some previous social and cultural institution or formation'.[69] The daily routines of the Gilroys and Savages, as lived through the language, the practices and the locations of *Till Death Us Do Part*, *The Sweeney* and *Minder*, were residual in Williams' sense.

On the other hand, there is emergent culture, 'new meanings and values, new practices, new relationships . . . continually being created' and difficult to distinguish as between 'those which are really elements of some new phase of the dominant culture . . . and those which are substantially alternative or oppositional to it'.[70] The Mary Tyler Moore world of feminism and domesticity and the 'anti-racist'/'anti-authority' world of *Till Death Us Do Part/All In The Family* are emergent in this complex sense – *both* incorporated *and* alternative. My point here, in examining the nexus of sitcom's narrative tension, audience aggregation and structures of feeling, is that 'official' culture is open to challenge from both residual and emergent politics and pleasures. As Lovell says, even where alternative ideas are recuperated in sitcom, 'then the dominant ideology no longer comprises only the "ideas of the ruling class"'.[71]

11 'Marauding behaviour': parody, carnival and the grotesque

Part of the [radio] quiz show I do . . . the question we had was, 'What were the famous words that Lord Nelson said to Hardy as he lay dying on the deck of HMS Victory?'. And the answer: 'Gissa job, Hardy, I can do that.' You know, it folds you up. . . . [Yosser's] just part of Liverpool folklore now.

Billy Butler[1]

'Gissa job, Hardy' is a parodic play on 'official' history ('Kiss me, Hardy'), and as such is part of an emergent structure of feeling among the permanently unemployed in northern England under Thatcher. It is an example of that 'marauding' and 'guerilla' activity I described earlier, which uses the segmented nature of television for its own purposes. Butler's radio respondent took Yosser's 'Gissa job' catchphrase out of the TV series (then current), *The Boys From The Blackstuff*, and conjoined it in an unexpected way with the 'famous last words' of Lord Nelson. Since Nelson's words (like Scott's diaries) are part of a 'Boys' Own', 'England expects . . . ' reading formation, one effect of this was to render received history as folklore, so fracturing 'common sense' tradition. The 'England expects . . . ' of the Nelson–Scott–Churchill official history had been inverted to '*We*, the unemployed, expect . . . '.

That élite Nelson–Scott–Churchill history is open to parody precisely because it takes its hierarchy so seriously. 'Parody', Susan Stewart argues, 'can only survive so long as there is common sense, so long as there is a discourse which takes itself seriously';[2] and common sense, as we have seen, 'takes itself seriously' at different levels of knowledgeability. I have discussed earlier Trevor Griffiths' authorial engagement with the 'common sense' of British historiography. Proverbs and 'famous words' are different examples of common sense working discursively. As with the traditional Liverpool response to hardship of 'If you don't laugh, you'll cry', they are 'conventional wisdoms' which help *order* sense by giving it a popular history. Proverbs and sayings are circulating and manageable 'texts' of common sense, part of its enabling power to 'understand' the world.

Truisms ('You know what I mean', 'If you don't laugh, you'll cry'), proverbs ('An apple a day . . . ', 'A stitch in time . . . '), and famous sayings ('Kiss me, Hardy', 'England expects . . . ') all work to confirm mutual knowledge. They establish, as Stewart says, a baseline of coherence for discourse. They are 'what everybody knows' and so can be left unsaid except at moments of ritualized and phatic interaction. Generally, they represent the unarticulated world knowledge upon which 'more important' discourse ('talking for a purpose') is based.

> To make apparent what is unnecessary to the situation, what does not need to be articulated, would be to invert this hierarchy and disintegrate the boundaries of the situation – to disintegrate the very basis of 'shared understanding' upon which the situation is constructed. Disaster would result since attention would be dispersed away from any purpose at hand, and the consequent failure to 'go on' would undermine all confidence in the viability of the given social construction of reality.[3]

Parody and 'nonsense' threaten common sense with precisely this kind of disaster. As Silverstone argues, the world of 'common sense' is threatened from two directions: the 'super-cultural' (or esoteric) and the nonsensical. On the one hand, there are those 'esoteric' discourses which *interrogate* the naturalism of common sense philosophically: socialism, feminism, the Griffiths-style critical realism that I discussed in Chapters 3–7. On the other hand, there are the 'nonsense' positions which *dismember* common sense by reversing or recombining its ordering and baseline categories, 'according to some "contra-sensible" principle'.[4] If the trick of super-cultural discourse is to turn 'mutual knowledge' into 'common sense' (see Introduction), the trick of nonsense is to disintegrate common sense into 'play'.

So, 'An apple a day keeps the fingers sticky' is, as Stewart says, parodic play in the sense that the metaphorical power of the proverb is inverted into messy literalism. Its 'common sense' is fractured. In contrast, *Doctor Who*'s 'An apple a day keeps the . . . Oh never mind!' (as the Doctor hands a psychotically militaristic colonist an apple in 'Kinda') is 'esoteric' social satire rather than nonsense. Satire, unlike nonsense, takes itself seriously: as in this *Doctor Who* narrative, which (drawing inter-textually on Le Guin's *The Word For World Is Forest*) supports an environmentalist discourse of trees and fresh apples against intergalactic imperialism.

Moreover, at the production and audience levels, 'Kinda' is not nonsense either, because it is part of a new hierarchical *re-ordering*. Firstly, it is a new producer's discourse in rejecting his predecessor's 'slapstick nonsense' for 'wit' ('An apple a day keeps the . . . Doctor away') and a faster-paced, action-oriented, US-style product.[5] Secondly, it is an audience re-ordering too. Long-term fans had strongly disliked the 'Fawlty Towers in Space' comic inflection of the Graham Williams/ Douglas Adams era which often ignored programme continuity. 'Kinda' helped return the show to the 'integrity and coherence' of its mythography.[6] Nonsense challenges *any* tradition 'as having integrity and coherence through time',[7] whereas the 'Kinda' joke worked to tie together the series as institution (the fans' history) with the series as product (the US market) by way of eliminating its temporally parodic ('Seventies') signature.

In contrast, 'Gissa job, Hardy' is parodic nonsense in signifying itself *as* play. It has 'fun' by 'showing the infinite connectability of all things and the arbitrariness of most connections'.[8] The reversal of the heroic 'England expects . . .' tradition to one of collective working-class demand is achieved by way of displaying the arbitrariness (the *textuality*) of 'famous words'.

This kind of 'fun with textuality' is a feature of 'meta'-fictional TV forms. For instance, the zany British sitcom, *The Young Ones*, overtly drew attention to itself as television construction by referring to the camera, the set, the acting, and so on. More subtly, it used the genre's familiar *generational* conflict to 'make strange' not only the comfortable and cosy 'borrowed text' (Cliff Richard's bland 'Fifties' hit record), but also each generation of media-stereotyped 'young ones' thereafter. By unexpectedly conjoining in time this series of ten-year stereotypes ('Fifties', 'Sixties', 'Seventies', 'Eighties'), sitcom's organizing principle (of unresolved and contending generational discourse) was itself parodied.

Similarly, in a long 'unfolding' text like *Doctor Who*, while early elements of the show may exist as an encyclopaedic, intensive, ordering mythography for the fans and production team, they are, for that very reason, prime targets for parody. During the 1970s, actor Tom Baker's demystifying of the naturalistic implausibility of Daleks as 'ball-bearing, pepper pot' monsters, drew narrative attention to a problem which directors had tried to hide by lighting, camera angle and editing for over a decade. As Baker 'played' with the series' foundational attempts at horror, he was inverting reflexively a central common-sense wisdom of the show: the belief that 'behind-the-sofa' fear was a bedrock element of its success. Producer Nathan-Turner's 'apple a day' used a safer version of the comic to step back from these dangerously parodic ('slapstick', 'send-up') excesses of his predecessor. But in that earlier era of the show (with Douglas Adams as script editor) the very ground rules of popular SF (as anthropocentric future history) were shaken up, and revealed as arbitrary constructions.[9]

Nonsense, as Stewart says, is 'the outer space of the intertextual universe', emphasizing the 'mechanics of the composability that is textuality' and emphasizing the arbitrariness of beginnings, middles and ends. So, in *The Singing Detective*, Dennis Potter drew on the popular genre of detective fiction to parody the beginnings, middles and ends of 'authored' drama, with its stress on social and psychological 'depth'. In particular, *The Singing Detective* emphasized the arbitrariness of looking for a text's 'source' in authorial, generic, physical or psychological determinants. The supposed 'real' source of the text in childhood trauma (the author's mother's affair and his teacher's cruelty), physical sickness (identical to Potter's own), economic systems (Hollywood and professional plagiarism), or inter-textual 'influence' (the language style and subject matter of Raymond Chandler) were each denied in turn, as they were fractured and re-combined according to 'contra-sensible' principles. These various 'sources' interwove, overlaid and displaced each other in constructing the narrative, so denying the status of 'real' determinant to any one strand, or the status of derived 'fantasy' to any other.

Both the *Doctor Who* and *The Singing Detective* examples are parodic because they open up the closures (of 'common sense') that 'text' places on experience. John Fiske argues that *Doctor Who* confirms our social experience as believable through our 'easy' and uncontradictory reading of the text. Yet a problem I have with his analysis is that the particular text he chooses to discuss ('Creature From The Pit') is from the Douglas Adams era, consciously foregrounding its own textuality via language play, parodic acting style and over-the-top stereotyping.

Whether this kind of 'meta-fiction' which parodies generic form is *socially* subversive, however, is a matter of debate, and brings us back to the question of 'returning from alienation' discussed in the last chapter. The 'Kiss me Hardy'/'Gissa job Hardy' example of Liverpool humour is parodic in Stewart's sense, since it substitutes 'elements within a dimension of a given text in such a way' (here relying on sound similarity) 'that the resulting text stands in an . . . incongruous relation to the borrowed text'.[10] But it is *also* socially subversive, in so far as it is the discourse of the unemployed. It is part, as Butler says, of their resistant folk culture. When the same demand ('Gissa job – we can do that – gissa job') is chanted at the Liverpool goalkeeper as he makes a save, professional and social hierarchies are being challenged.

Carnival and TV drama

Bakhtin has argued that folk culture can parody both generic form *and* social hierarchy, so challenging conventions and systems which 'control us through our fear of infinity'.[11] This folk culture is collective and interactive in Zipes' sense. But in contrast to 'the Utopian image of a better life for themselves'[12] which Zipes sees as a use value embedded in folk art, Bakhtin finds parody and 'nonsense' there. Folk art (such as the medieval grotesque and the carnival) *inverted* the controlling religious symbols of official culture (e.g. a dying ass bequeathed his parts to the Pope as a parody of saintly relics). Or it simply pissed on them.

> Dung and urine lend a bodily character to matter, to the world, to the cosmic elements, which becomes closer, more intimate, more easily grasped, for this is the matter, the elemental force, born from the body itself. It transforms cosmic terror into a gay carnival monster.[13]

Though certainly parodic, neither the 'meta-SF' *Doctor Who* nor *The Singing Detective* examples seem cases of Bakhtin's folk resistance, any more than the 'culturally knowing' James Bond parodies of spy thrillers were (Chapter 9). Each, after all, relied on the intellectual reflexivity of known 'authors' (Ian Fleming, Douglas Adams, Dennis Potter); and each could easily be appropriated (like MTM 'meta' sitcom) as part of the 'quality' and 'Art' signature of the TV or 'Literary' institution (in the case of Adams and Potter, the BBC). Nevertheless, the folk struggle that Bakhtin describes does continue, according to a number of critics, in popular television.

Fiske, for instance, draws on Bakhtin's emphasis on the *bodily character* of resistance in seeing the *A-Team*'s BA as 'a carnivalesque figure: he is an inverted adult, an honorary child . . . excessive . . . all body and verges on the grotesque'.[14] Tulloch and Alvarado draw on Bakhtin's emphasis on the *clowning reversal* of established hierarchies to argue that *Doctor Who*'s Trickster figure in 'Kinda' 'opens up the perspective of disorder', so extending the series' 'tradition of the grotesque'.[15] In each case the parody is re-appropriated: in *Doctor Who* by the action-adventure marketing of the series; in *The A-Team* by a patriarchal construction of 'masculinity'. Nevertheless, Fiske argues, contradictions are generated in *The A-Team* 'between the social and the physical. . . . Those to whom BA offers an articulation of their sense of social subordination may well find oppositional or resisting pleasures in the impossibility of ever subordinating totally such a powerful and intransigent figure.'[16]

Fiske also suggests that other popular TV genres (wrestling, music video) centre 'on the role of the signifier, on the body',[17] thus contradicting 'meaning' with physical sensation. As such, they oppose ideology's 'sense' with the 'non-sense' (*'jouissance'*) of popular pleasure. Though the Rabelaisian licence that Bakhtin describes of indulging 'to excess in the bodily pleasures of eating, drinking and sexuality'[18] is seldom granted by broadcast television, 'the parody, the travesty is still there. The Madonna look parodies consumerism, the *Miami Vice* look turns style into spectacle . . . [that] "scandalous" place where pleasure rules in opposition to the work ethic of traditional capitalism.'[19]

Apart from Fiske, Brown and Barwick have made the most extended claim for the carnivalesque in popular television, arguing that 'Bakhtin's description of carnival's relation to the Church is analogous to the position of soap operas in relation to dominant cultural forms such as "serious" books and night-time television.'[20] This is similar to Potter's use of popular detective fiction to parody 'serious' authorship. But in the case of soap opera it is grounded in the daily gossip of audiences, not in what TV critics call the 'intelligent television' of authors.

> It is particularly clearly relevant in relation to the soap's use of women's talk, which . . . potentially mocks the speech of dominant discourse. . . . In dominant discourse, talking for a purpose is acceptable, but talking for pleasure is not. Men's public purposeful talk (preaching, politics) is revered, but women's private talk is denigrated as purposeless and malicious. . . . Gossip is feared . . . as dangerous to the dominant culture. . . . Through talk, women may understand . . . the workings of dominant ideology and official culture (and sometimes laugh at it).[21]

Brown and Barwick argue that just as the 'temporary suspension of hierarchical rank in Medieval carnival led to the creation of a marketplace speech and gesture that was "frank and free" and assumed no distance between those who came in contact with each other',[22] so the 'egalitarian' and phatic contact of women's gossip about soap opera establishes 'a network of fans that cuts across class and social hierarchies'.[23] Carnival laughter, Bakhtin says, is 'the laughter of all the people . . . it is directed at all and everyone, including the carnival's participants'.[24] Similarly, Brown and Barwick argue, women soap fans laugh at themselves as they *knowingly* blur distinctions between their own world, the soap opera world and the fan magazines' world of soap stars. Laughing at themselves rather than ridiculing others, these women's laughter 'corresponds to Bakhtin's description of carnivalesque laughter as free from the necessity of putting down another person'.[25]

Though Fiske, and Brown and Barwick, point to textual characteristics of the carnivalesque in popular drama ('Close-ups of people at the peak of emotional conflict expose this agonistic body to scrutiny in much the same way that a grotesque image reveals too much, defying dominant rules of propriety about how much emotion it is acceptable to show'[26]), the brunt of their emphasis is on the agency of audiences (as subcultures) in appropriating and mobilizing contradictions – as in *The A-Team* and soap opera. Whereas Douglas Adams' 'meta' science fiction is an authorial critique of popular television, these are audience *celebrations* of it.

Throughout this book my emphasis has been on the agency of television workers (as well as audiences) in mobilizing 'spaces for resistance'. Is there space for authorship which is *also* a folk resistance, in Bakhtin's sense? I will end this chapter with some analysis of comedy, the carnivalesque and parody in the work of two socialist authors: Trevor Griffiths and Alan Bleasdale. The difference between both of them and Douglas Adams is in their relationship with a popular audience. *Their* mobilization of popular culture (and its mobilization of them) will be examined before I return, at the end, to audiences.

Authors and the 'unsayable': *Comedians*

Bakhtin's distinction between a *controlling* comedy ('putting another down for its source of humour') and the humour of liberation and excess is the focus of Trevor Griffiths' television play, *Comedians*. In it Griffiths addresses the politics of comedy in popular culture.

> Many popular activities are genuine sites of resistance to other forms of activity and one of the great battles to be fought popularly at the moment is to seek to find those activities which genuinely summate a working-class life, as against those which are commercially imposed and clearly manipulative.[27]

In *Comedians* Bakhtin's conflict between 'official' and 'liberating' medieval humour is transferred to the recent history and culture of the working class. Griffiths contrasts the 'democratic' comedy of the 'Lancashire Lad', Eddie Waters (who always refused the 'big time' of national success to stay in the face-to-face contact of working-class clubs) with the 'commercial' comedy of Bert Challenor. Once a comic, Challenor is now an impressario with considerable power to make or break comedians' careers, while claiming to represent 'what the people want'. As Waters says of Challenor's Comedy Artists and Managers Federation, 'They wanted to control entry into the game. I told 'em no comedian worth his salt could ever "federate" with a manager.'

Challenor's preferred humour is simple:

> I'm not looking for philosophers, I'm looking for comics . . . who see
> what people want and give it to 'em. . . . We're not missionaries,
> we're suppliers of laughter.

In fact, this 'simple' humour draws on the sexist and racist 'putting
another down' which, as Griffiths is well aware, exists as deeply as any
folk resistance in working-class culture. But, as in *The Last Place On
Earth*, in addition to exposing myths of control, Griffiths insists that
there are other things growing in that culture, 'plants to do with
democracy, to do with equality, to do with commonness and fraternity'.[28]

Waters' sense of commonness and fraternity is displayed in his career
(which now includes giving up evenings to train the young working-
class comics who are about to audition before Challenor), and in his
understanding of comedy itself. For Eddie Waters, Challenor's comedy
is the humour of hate; his slick commercial success is bought at the
expense of the Irish, Jews, Negroes, women, workers, the insane and all
other 'defectives'. Waters tells his class of comics:

> Do we fear other people so much that we must mark their pain with
> laughter and our own with tears. People deserve respect because
> they're *people*. . . . A joke that feeds on ignorance starves an audience.
> Most comics *feed* prejudice and fear and blinkered vision, but the
> best ones . . . illuminate them, make them clearer to see, easier to
> deal with. . . . A joke releases tension, says the unsayable. But a true
> joke, a *comedian*'s joke, has to do more than release tension. It has to
> *liberate* the will and the desire, has to *change the situation*.

Waters' 'liberating' power of humour is utopic. As Challenor says, it is
a 'philosopher's' comedy, and it is based on Griffiths' realist perception
of the need to 'illuminate' prejudice, exploitation and fear in order to
change them. In *Comedians* Griffiths appropriates sitcom's generational
conflict to reverse its often too easy identification of 'prejudice' with the
old and outmoded. It is not the ageing Alf Garnett or the 'old Australian
digger' but the young comics who perform the sexist and racist jokes in
front of Challenor. So it is the *Jewish* comic who puts down feminism;
and it is an *Irish* comic who raises laughs with his put-down of idle
blacks, grasping Jews and gossiping women:

> There was this coloured fellow on his way to work [Pause]. Don't
> you think that's funny. There was this very honest Jew [Pause]
> Doesn't say a lot my wife – talks all the time, but doesn't say a lot.

The terrible irony here is that it is comics from oppressed groups who themselves continue to circulate the truisms, proverbs and 'famous sayings' of their oppression.

But in addition to this contrast between 'mythic' and 'liberating' humour, Griffiths also contrasts an older with a current working-class culture, as Eddie Waters' club comedian tradition is swept aside by the hard 'football terraces' performance of his favourite pupil, Gethin Price. In his act in front of Challenor, Price is deliberately unfunny, drawing on the mime/monologue style of the Swiss clown Grock as he addresses two dummies in evening dress. Earlier, Price had viciously parodied Waters' criticism of the 'comedy of hate'. Now the dummies put Price's own sexist and racist jokes in parenthesis, representing at once Challenor's put-down that 'all audiences are thick collectively, but it's a bad comic who lets them know it', and at the same time (as Price forces the dummies to rock with laughter to his quips) the 'ignorance that starves an audience'.

Price's act, as Poole and Wyver say, is anti-naturalistic.[29] But its reflexivity is not 'artistic' or at the *expense* of popular culture. What contextualizes Price's humour is not a particular 'style' of European avant-garde comedy (intended to appeal to the 'encyclopaedic' knowledge of a 'high culture' audience), but the violent youth culture of the English working class. Price *does* let the audience 'know it'. His challenge (addressed directly to the television viewer) of 'Don't you worry, you're not going to keep us down for long. We're going to come right back up there where we can get at you' is accompanied by his use of 'borrowed texts': the chant of Manchester United soccer fans and the Kung-fu actions of Bruce Lee. The linkage of forms of working-class oral tradition and Kung-fu movie (both popular 'cultural competences' of a hard urban youth environment[30]) here break through Griffiths' text as the 'unsayable' of his own socialist discourse.

Yet Price's popular culture (like Waters' before him) is *grounded* in the experience of exploitation. As he tells Waters,

> You've forgotten what it's like. 'Nobody hit harder than Eddie Waters' – that's what they used to say, didn't they? That's because you were still in touch with what made you – the hunger, filth, diphtheria, unemployment, means test, pay-clubs, bed bugs, head lice – was all that truth beautiful? Truth was a fist you hit with – now it's like cow-flop. . . . Nothing's changed. . . . We're still caged, still exploited, prodded and pulled at, milked, fattened, slaughtered, cut up and fed out. We still don't belong to ourselves. Nothing's changed Mr Waters. It's just you've forgotten. That's all – and you stopped laughing, didn't you? In three months here you've not said a single funny thing. Maybe you lost the right.

Waters replies that he had stopped being funny when he visited concentration camps where Jews had been recently exterminated, and shortly afterwards heard a German audience 'laugh easily' at Jewish jokes. 'I didn't laugh. . . . I discovered there were no jokes left. Every joke was a little pellet of Final Solution.' For Waters those death chambers, those jokes were 'the logic of our world extended. . . . I had an erection in that place. Something in me *loved* it too. We've got to dig deeper than hate.'

Griffiths would not agree with Baudrillard that the 'same process of forgetting, of liquidation, of extermination, the same annihilation of memories and of history . . . the same absorption without trace, the same black hole as Auschwitz'[31] is an inevitable feature of television representation. Rather, *Comedians* is itself 'strategic penetration' of popular television, while also reminding us that the resistant world of carnival, oral culture and fandom has *the potential of hate* as well as laughter. Both are deep-laid seeds in an ambivalent working-class culture of liberation *and* oppression.

Griffiths dramatizes this ambivalence across his familiar oppositions of reformism and revolution, 'soft' and 'hard', radical speech versus 'unsayable' action and violence. As a parodist, Gethin Price '*smashes* the categories and says NO – I stand in no line, I refuse my consent'[32] – including consent to the categories of his author. Griffiths admits that the Price character 'forced its way into the text'. In an important sense, the 'unsayable' Price puts into question Griffiths' 'surveillant' power as socialist theorist, as well as his practice as a successful writer who – like Eddie Waters – is separated from his working-class roots. For Griffiths Price's hardness is

> frightening because it's full of passion and it's full of a sense of injustice and . . . will not be . . . enormously selective in its targets. And a great many people, liberal humanists like Eddie Waters, will be discovered to be objective enemies of that energy and that potential and will not be treated kindly. . . . And who knows, *I* might be one of those people whom 'truth hits like a fist'.[33]

Gethin Price – in his silence, his mime, his violence – in fact smashes the categories of both 'official' and 'oppositional' discourse. His voice is that of an oral youth culture forcing itself into Griffiths' text, and parodying Waters' sense of comedy as well as his educated, philosophical, 'super-cultural' understanding of the world. As such, Poole and Wyver argue, it affirms a new 'potential for self liberation' in Griffiths' work which 'can be seen to reflect the beginnings of fundamental changes in political understanding by certain sections of the Left – particularly the advent of "autonomous" struggles'.[34]

Yet, in another sense, Price *is* recuperated by his author. His *reasoned* demand of Waters to remember the hunger, filth, diphtheria and bed bugs of his class is still a socialist discourse; and it relates inter-textually to both the Norwegian socialist's speech in *The Last Place On Earth* and to a very similar speech by Trofimov to Lopakhin in Griffiths' version of Chekhov's *The Cherry Orchard*. To this degree, in subordinating various television genres ('action-adventure', 'comedy', 'classic drama', etc.) to his familiar dialectic of 'soft' and 'hard', 'reason' and 'violence', Griffiths is clearly in authorial control, refusing (as he says of his *Cherry Orchard*) to 'celebrate a pessimism'.[35] The soccer-terrace violence of Price and the revolutionary violence of Trofimov are both blows at television's 'naturalism without politics', which for Griffiths represents 'the plight of the middle classes'.[36] But as a member of that middle class, Griffiths is reflexively aware of the 'unsayable' beyond the *other* boundary of common sense from his socialism. In *Comedians* the 'philosophic' and the 'unsayable' contest across the barren ground of Challenor's 'common sense'.

Realism and grotesque: *The Boys From The Blackstuff*

Alan Bleasdale, whose work also engages with the loss of belief in unified class struggle during the 1970s, has frequently been accused of the pessimism that Griffiths refuses to celebrate. A number of critics have suggested that Bleasdale's *The Boys From The Blackstuff* ends in profound despair, as 'the Boys' shuffle off in the shadow of the modern god of profitability, the multinational sugar company. David Lusted, for instance, argues that the series 'returns its successfully aroused and problematised working-class audience to an apoliticised consciousness'.[37]

But Lusted is here emphasizing only the 'super-cultural' challenge to common sense in the text. In that respect he is right. The socialist character, Snowy, is killed off in episode one; and his militant father, George Malone (with final words 'I cannot *believe* there is no hope') dies early in the last episode, leaving Chrissie scurrying back and forwards, a tiny environmentally trapped figure as the camera pulls up and away to reveal the wasted dockland setting. Lusted says, 'All that is left is the "world going mad" . . . "an absurd black farce" that corresponds to the cynical humour "the Boys" use as their strength and only defence against the material oppression visualised in the landscape of urban decay.'[38] To what extent, then, does the difference between Bleasdale's and Griffiths' authorial control equate with that between the avant-gardist 'world as absurd' and the 'return from alienation' I discussed earlier?

If *The Boys From The Blackstuff* does create a 'political absence' for the characters, it doesn't necessarily leave one for the viewer. Lusted's criticism does nothing to explain the sense of strength (and even activism) that the series clearly provided for many of its audience. Two unemployed Liverpudlians had this to say:

> Although the series was very pessimistic towards the end . . . it's made me more resolved to say, get off the floor and fight back. . . . [39]

> . . . what the series has done is . . . explain unemployment to ourselves. There's a lot of humour in the series, a lot of tragedy. Someone once said, your life in Liverpool was a tragedy played as if it were a comedy. Well, the trouble with that is that we tend to put a brave face on things if we can manage it, so we don't talk to each other about the problems we, as unemployed people, have. But since the series has been on, people have been saying, yes I've been through that, I've thought like that, and it isn't just a question of individual characters. All of us have been, at some time or another, as desperate as Yosser, or feeling stripped of dignity as Chrissie. At times, maybe, we felt as optimistic as George, but it's like all the characters were facets of us put together; the kind of life all of us have, and that's a great achievement to make. He's given us words to communicate with each other about our own experiences. [40]

Early in the series, Angie accuses Chrissie of escapism into the truisms and proverbs of Liverpool humour: 'I've heard enough of that – if you don't laugh, you'll cry – I've heard it for years – this stupid, soddin' city's full of it. . . . Why don't you fight back, you bastard. Fight back.' The humour that she is rejecting is the kind of 'bounded knowledgeability' of Chrissie telling the accusing unemployment sniffers to let him know when they are coming next time and 'I'll bake a cake'; or of Loggo asking the unemployment clerk to hurry along 'or I'll miss me golf lessons'. Director Philip Saville found ample evidence of this Scouse humour in auditioning for the show. 'One of the things . . . was their immediate desire to tell you a joke. I interviewed something around 400 people all with the same line. The tenor of a joke is based on someone's misery, someone's bad luck and it's often anti-women.' [41]

This is Eddie Waters' 'comedy of hate', often self-dismissive, against which the series 'fights back'. In the last 'absurd black farce' of the pub scene, there is (for all the individual jokes and put downs) a *folk* refusal, a collective parody of the economics of unemployment. The profit/

commodity-oriented society is momentarily overturned in a final gesture of ludicrously conspicuous consumption as recently retrenched workers lavishly spend their final wages in a series of redundancy parties.

The figure of 'Shakehands' is both parodic and pivotal in these scenes. He lumbers about the pub in search of hurts to resolve at a bodily level, where he is able to use his working-man's strength to some effect against the petty persecutors of the poor and deranged. Youths slip speed into the beer slops that the bar assistant drinks; 'Shakehands' punishes them for their laughter with his crushing grip. His name, 'Shakehands', itself represents working-class mutuality and solidarity, so reproducing (grotesquely) the 'good man' image of George Malone – but at a bodily, non-discursive level. Names are important, as Chrissie demonstrates when insisting on Malone's 'local' name of George, against the Catholic Church's baptized name of Patrick. At the funeral service, he halts the soaring, rhetorical flights of the priest with his own class's discourse: 'I'm sorry Father, that's not on . . . George Malone was a good man – the best man I ever knew.'

For George Malone is not simply an industrial activist who dies; he is also one of Eddie Waters' figures of 'commonness and fraternity'. Above all, he is the discursive consciousness of unemployment, to whom the class-broken men (like Yosser) come to talk and listen. George's memories, like Alf Garnett's, are generational and aged, inviting a nostalgic, 'residual' audience identification. But like Eddie Waters' memories, they are also witness to a lifetime of discursive struggle against the economic order, and are Utopian dreams of the future as well. 'They say that memories live longer than dreams, but my dreams, those dreams of long ago, they still give me hope and faith in my class. I can't believe that there's no hope, can't.'

Unlike sitcom, the generational dreams are *listened* to, sought after, and taken up, but in skewed, often parodic ways which comment more on the system than the characters who carry them: in Yosser's manic love for his kids; in 'Shakehands'' 'That's not nice. . . . He's my friend'; and in Chrissie as the 'common man', who, for Bleasdale is 'the pivot of the series'.

> He's the bloke who . . . has a few pints, comes home, plays with the kids, has a reasonably solid relationship with his wife. And everything's gonna be OK, until forces that he has no control over take him over, and he's shipwrecked; his points of reference are lost. But I think by the end of the series . . . you see a development in him. . . . I think hope is personified by the character of Chrissie.[42]

That 'hope' lies in the developing scope of Chrissie's consciousness.

In the final episode, the priest's soaring oration against cosmic terror ('men's public, purposeful talk – preaching, politics') is reduced (as in carnival) to bodily functions as he vomits drunkenly at the wake. Chrissie and Loggo stop for a moment to watch, before going off for those 'few pints' in a pub scene where the entire economic system is reduced to black comedy as the unemployed conspicuously consume with their fellows.

As Philip Thomson puts it, grotesque humour is never *simply* liberating: the grotesque is that condition where both 'the comic aspect of the abnormal and the fearful and disgusting are felt equally'.[43] So, as in Griffiths' *Comedians*, there is 'laughter and horror, mirth and revulsion, simultaneously'.[44] The final pub scene in *The Boys From The Blackstuff is* both fearful (the social decay, the head-butting) and funny. And the figure of Yosser – (like Gethin Price) with his shift between naturalistic and expressionistic make-up, his slightly overdone, almost monster-like pallor – has a comparable effect, comical yet disturbing at the same time.

Many viewers will remember the manically comic absurdity of Yosser's bricklaying; but they also recall the 'Gissa Job' desperation for his children that underlies it. Equally audiences remember the interweaving of zany working-class togetherness with despair, both in the scenes of Yosser with his children and in the grotesque pub scene, a structure of feeling that offsets the simple negative of the conclusion.

In particular, we should remember that a TV drama like *The Boys From The Blackstuff* inserts itself within (and reactivates inter-textually) earlier representations and existing patterns of humour in popular culture. It engages, as *social event*, with pleasures of already established reading formations. Radio disc jockey Billy Butler described how *Blackstuff*'s 'all encompassing impact: from humour to fear' reached the heartland of Liverpool's cultural resistance: Anfield.

> To be part of Liverpool folklore, you exist at football matches. . . .
> Every time someone scored a goal, it was 'We can do that, gissa job, we can do that. . . . ' The Liverpool goalie . . . every time he makes a save, the Kop chants, 'We can do that Bruce, we can do that. . . .'[45]

Whereas soccer chants break through into *Comedians*, *The Boys From The Blackstuff* broke through into the greater audience of soccer chants. Through it, the audience for Liverpool's greatest success at a time of economic desperation – the champion football club – spoke of working-class skills and demands. And it did so as part of a *familiarly* discursive Liverpudlian humour. This interweaving of different forms of folk culture in a pleasurable resistance should be remembered when football and television are all too readily described as 'bread and circus' vehicles of social control.[46] They are that too; but in them Gramsci's 'optimism of the will' continues.

John McGrath has detailed the history of this Liverpool articulation more precisely,[47] through radio comedy, popular music and theatre, adding:

> the most important feature of *Boys From The Blackstuff* has been its public pronouncement of a widespread private grief – and its reference back of that private grief to public events and political decisions. Simply by speaking that sorrow out loud, it has done a great deal for those bearing it. When the Kop at Anfield shouts 'Give Us A Job', and the demands for the plays to be repeated are almost universal – and the standard of artistic achievement in all areas of the work is so high – then we can once again be proud of what television drama in this country can achieve.[48]

It is in its working with emotions (to set against a more cognitive politics), in its referencing of private griefs to public events, that *The Boys From The Blackstuff* seems to succeed so well with an audience. Indeed, its formal structure is to set the super-cultural (socialist) message in counterpoint with the grotesque, across the naturalistic wasteland of 'common sense' unemployment. Producer Michael Wearing says that he re-sited the pub scene as an 'alienating device which counterpoints . . . George and what his life had stood for'.[49] My argument is that the counterpointing is not simply of an (ageing) optimism against a bleak pessimism. In the era of Thatcher and loss of direction in the working-class movement (represented by the attitude of George's surviving sons: 'They don't care about anything that hasn't got tits or comes out of a barrel'), grotesque comedy is one way of keeping emotions, passions and pleasures strong.

Blackstuff: production

Bakhtin argued that parody and carnival serve to subvert hierarchy in two ways: formally and socially. Literary parody undermined the hierarchy of styles maintained by orthodox practices; carnival inverted the social hierarchy maintained by official culture. Arguably, *The Boys From The Blackstuff* does both, so that George's last 'I can't *believe* there is no hope' is not only a refusal of social hierarchy, but also (in its narrative counterpointing by increasing signs of the grotesque) a parodic engagement with the naturalist tradition of Loach's *Days of Hope*. Ten years after the more positive relationship between *Days of Hope* and a

victorious miners' strike against Toryism, *The Boys From The Blackstuff*
worked out of an oppositional TV culture that owed a great deal to Ken
Loach and Jim Allen, but more to defeats in the Labour movement. In
Days of Hope it is the young who challenge (in their reformist or
revolutionary ways) the common sense of their elders. In *Blackstuff* it is
the old who stand for hope, in the face of the *dead* revolutionary Snowy,
and the *continuing* reformism of their other sons.

Yet this reversal of the *Days of Hope* narrative is never a simple
pessimism; formally the quest for popular strength continues by way of
Blackstuff's parodic *engagement* with naturalism. In this, both historical
and professional production conditions played a hand. Michael Wearing
points out that the long production delays around the series allowed
historical events – monetarism, wild-fire unemployment, 'race' riots in
the major cities – to bite deep, so that it 'became clear that no way
could we make a "funny" Liverpool programme about all this'.[50]
Certainly, the actors were deeply committed. Tom Georgeson:

> It moved me that I'd been part of something that made a statement
> for a lot of people who would otherwise have felt very alone in the
> sort of world that Mrs Thatcher is making us live in now, where she
> wants the working people frightened and desolate. . . . I'm not in the
> business to be a star; I'm in the business to try and help people . . . to
> live.[51]

On the other hand, there was the class distance of the director; as
well as his professional history of combating TV naturalism through
generic parodies like *Gangsters*. Millington and Nelson are convincing in
their description of the way in which the Saville 'style' complemented
the Bleasdale 'interruptus' technique of black comedy shock to 'dislocate
the viewer from habitual modes of perception'.[52] In conjunction with
Bleasdale's own grotesque materialism, Saville's 'distance' and 'style'
forged a new and more dynamic realism out of the lost optimism of
Days of Hope.

Dennis Potter has argued that

> The best naturalist or realist drama, of the Garnett–Loach–Allen
> school for instance, breaks out of [television's] cosy habit by the
> vigour, clarity, originality and depth of its perceptions of a more
> comprehensive reality. The best non-naturalist drama, in its very
> structure, disorientates the viewer smack in the middle of the
> orientation process which television perpetually uses. . . . It shows
> the frame in the picture when most television is showing the picture
> in the frame.[53]

The Boys From The Blackstuff blends both, as in Saville's most remarkable stylistic conceit, where George, on his last ride, remembers the popular culture of the past; and his account of an old violinist precedes that soaring fiddle on the soundtrack, accompanied by a camera that tilts and pans through 360 degrees, finally to cover the skylights of the decaying warehouse. Here, the self-conscious anti-naturalism actually *counters* the pessimism of current facticity with the optimism of history-as-memory. It juxtaposes urban decay with soaring light and music in a fitting prelude to George's 'I can't *believe* there is no hope'. In those moments of memory, the *emotional* pleasures of working-class habits, culture and solidarity may outweigh our analysis of their temporary defeat. Moments like these are unorthodox in the play's generally naturalistic narratives: but they are *repeated* unorthodoxies, systematic interruptions which grow more recognizable for an audience as the series develops.[54]

I am talking here of an imputed audience. What an actual audience does with *The Boys From The Blackstuff* (and what *other* inscriptions of meaning are determined within its field of inter-textual relations) may be another matter. Bleasdale himself had a clear notion of the audience he was aiming at, as we saw earlier; while BBC 2 (by transmitting it in the Sunday evening Arts slot) revealed, as Millington and Nelson say, 'certain in-house perceptions of the nature of the series in terms of "serious" drama'.[55]

Blackstuff: inter-text and audience

The *Radio Times* set its own agenda in its preview, emphasizing 'the affable masculinity of Bleasdale and the fact that "he has no party political axe to grind"'.[56] However, unlike Griffiths' experience with *The Last Place On Earth*, the BBC press release carried an interpretation close to Bleasdale's own: 'that the current economic order of our society is a black farce entailing an incalculable human cost'.[57] This by and large set the agenda for press reviews of the show, though there were the expected political inflections (the *Daily Mail*, concerned about dole scrounging, emphasized the 'fiddles' by the unemployed and DOE staff), as well as familiar 'high culture' interpretations. Thus the *Financial Times* did with the series what 'Lit. Crit.' aesthetics had earlier done to Zola:[58] 'It has been said *Boys From The Blackstuff* is about unemployment. . . . *Boys From The Blackstuff* is about the human condition.'[59]

There was little recognition in the quality press of a possible tension between the realism and black comedy of the series[60] due, I would argue, to a ready-made formula in our dominant literary-critical tradition (of which the 'Chekhovian' mood is a notable example) of a 'laughter through tears' sense of the comically futile struggles of the 'human condition'.[61] In addition there is the central emphasis in the series on the search for personal identity which, as Millington and Nelson say, is familiar to 'an essentially bourgeois-liberal dramatic tradition stretching at least from Shakespeare's *King Lear* to Arthur Miller's *Death of a Salesman*'.[62] As Lusted argues, the series' emphasis on the 'crucially formative role of work in the combination of individual and social identity', and its 'formal marks of the "literary" . . . is easily received by the middle-class audience which constitutes the literary culture'.[63]

Yet it seems that none of these media agendas and critical discourses deterred positive working-class interpretations. Some letters to Bleasdale consciously *contrasted Blackstuff* (as an oppositional representation of class) to the predominantly middle-class focus of standard television. One Irish correspondent wrote: 'Never before have I seen my family, my friends and acquaintances, my class, the people I know and live among and love and often despair of, portrayed on the screen with such realism, sensitivity and affection: our hopes, our aspirations, our frailties and contradictions.'[64]

The words are close to Terry Lovell's own comments on the pleasures in solidarity formation of popular TV. As some letter writers make clear, the series acts to articulate these feelings; and a particular sub-cultural sense of identity with the series came from the Liverpool area, where people wrote out of 'love of Liverpool and the anger at what is happening to it'.[65] But that sense of making 'me feel for a while that I'm not totally alone'[66] extended also to middle-class viewers, like the trainee probation officer from Norwich who criticized social work theory by way of her own ethnographic/sociological discourse.

> We should be trying to understand people through sharing their 'meanings' – the meaning they attribute to their everyday worlds, not imposing academic theories upon them. . . . Far too many of the social workers and probation officers I know . . . simply fall back on their 'authority', their formal role, and impose an irrelevant middle-class morality on them.[67]

So, on the one hand Yosser's phrases were appropriated and recirculated by advertising agencies; but on the other they became part of political struggle: the striking Waterworkers' placards, 'We are the boys from the wetstuff', the Resident Association's 'Gissa decent house', the Anfield chant, 'We can do that, gissa job', the *Time Out* review of *The Last Place On Earth* headed 'The Boys From The White Stuff'.

The Boys From The Blackstuff was massively popular for an 'Art' series (a total of 30 million viewers watched its BBC 1 second showing), highly visible, and – to use Trevor Griffiths' term – 'usable'. As such it broke clear of the reflexivity of both the 'avant-garde intellectuals' and the 'upwardly mobile professionals' that Feuer discusses in relation to MTM sitcom. Its formal inventiveness had more to do with two other things.

First, as Lusted has well argued, it has 'integrated in a unique way the political, social and cultural histories . . . of the working class' which are usually separated across the separate genres of news/documentary, naturalist drama and music hall.[68] *Blackstuff*, for instance, goes beyond soap opera in placing the home in the context of work (or not-work).

> The effect of this is to disturb, 'make strange', the conventional connections between the home/not-home and work/not-work spaces, promising alternative possibilities for social relations that cross the dominant divisions along gender and wage-labour lines among men/women, waged labour/non-waged labour, domestic labour/unemployed labour both within the text and among the audiences. This is a major shift in the politics of working-class representation and a considerable achievement.[69]

Second, there is the counterpointing of critical realist and grotesque modes that I have discussed above. Certainly, like any text, *The Boys From The Blackstuff* is polysemic. Lusted points to Yosser's appeal to 'the working-class male audience for its combination of signs of masculine power, loyalty and swift justice; the maternal audience for its gentleness and dedication to the family ideal; and the middle-class audience in general (for whom Yosser is a tragic victim) to arouse the social conscience'.[70] Some feminists (but not others) are angered by *The Boys From The Blackstuff*'s 'male-dependent' representation of women;[71] and one radical social worker in Manchester disagreed with the trainee probationary officer from Norwich in finding the profession's treatment of Yosser the 'weakest part of the best TV drama series ever. . . . We would have helped Yosser keep his children'.[72]

But Lusted's conclusion from all this polysemic possibility, that 'after brilliantly constructing the space to speak, it forgot what it needed to say',[73] is denied by many viewers who emphasized that *The Boys From The Blackstuff* enabled the unemployed to communicate among themselves what hitherto they had only felt unclearly and individually. My argument is that the combination of realism and the grotesque potentially fused a bleak representation of the capitalist present with a continuing history of folk humour and resistance, a new combination of Gramsci's 'pessimism of the intellect, optimism of the will'.

The Boys From The Blackstuff's 'alienating' shocks made discursive an historical situation where a class's practical consciousness of how to 'go on' – Chrissie's 'few pints, playing with the kids, reasonably solid relationship with his wife' – no longer made 'common' sense. As Giddens notes, knowledgeability is deeply embedded in practical consciousness, and is only given discursive form when individuals are questioned by others about why they acted as they did. *The Boys From The Blackstuff* does that questioning, and, as audience responses indicated, encouraged viewers to be discursive in their turn. As Richard Paterson says of the series, 'Common sense understandings contain some elements of good sense which can be drawn out if a framework is provided. The melodramatic representation of the plight of male characters in the community focused both a personal and a political sense of anger, previously unexpressed.'[74]

It is not only religious and official culture which wards off ontological insecurity. Routine – the placing of the world in time-space sequences of practical consciousness – does that too.[75] And it is not only religious and official culture which *Blackstuff* parodies, but routine as well, particularly as Paterson argues, male routine[76] – including the 'if you don't laugh, you'll cry' truisms and 'sayings' of Liverpool humour.

In its parody, *The Boys From The Blackstuff* points *both* to humour's arbitrary textuality *and* to its contextuality (in 'Scouse' wit, as a passive response to oppression). The play with genre and inter-textuality that the series is noted for is more than the 'camp' amusement that appeals to the media conversance of the tertiary educated.[77] It returns from alienation, but in a spirit of carnival rather than in the control of social theory. Among many unemployed the 'alienating' shocks of *The Boys From The Blackstuff* built up a sense of solidarity, out of a structure of feeling where cognitive strategies had, for the moment, lost their way.

Notes

Introduction

1 Brandt 1981: 35.
2 ibid., p.35.
3 ibid., p.20.
4 ibid., p.3.
5 ibid., p.23.
6 ibid., p.32.
7 ibid., p.30.
8 ibid., p.16.
9 ibid., p.19.
10 ibid., p.25.
11 ibid., p.235.
12 ibid., p.30.
13 ibid., p.21.
14 ibid., p.32.
15 ibid., p.35.
16 Buckingham 1987: 29.
17 ibid.
18 Troy Kennedy Martin, St John's College, Cambridge, October 1986.
19 Fiske 1988: 15.
20 John Caughie in Bennett *et al.* 1981: 328.
21 Brandt 1981: 26.
22 Fiske 1988: 183.
23 ibid., p.228.
24 ibid., p.254.
25 ibid., p.262.
26 ibid., p.260.
27 ibid., p.230.
28 Fiske 1982: 93
29 ibid., pp. xiii-xiv.
30 ibid., p. xiv.
31 Hartley 1982: 30
32 Fiske 1982: 94–5

33 ibid., p.111.
34 Brandt 1981: 20.
35 ibid., p.30.
36 O'Sullivan *et al.* 1983: 148.
37 ibid., p.147.
38 Fiske 1988: 33.
39 O'Sullivan *et al.* 1983: 60.
40 ibid.
41 Giddens 1986: 535, 541.
42 Giddens 1987: 87.
43 ibid., p.88.
44 ibid.
45 Fiske 1988: 35.
46 ibid., p.55.
47 Roland Barthes 1973: 42.
48 Fiske 1988: 36.
49 ibid., p.41.
50 For a discussion of empiricism and sense experience, see Terry Lovell 1981: 12.
51 McLennan 1984: 124.
52 Giddens 1987: 91.
53 James 1987: 91.
54 ibid., p.102.
55 Giddens 1984: 535.
56 O'Sullivan *et al.* 1983: 233.
57 Fiske 1982: 93.
58 Giddens 1979: 250.
59 Giddens 1984: 4.
60 ibid., pp.5, 6.
61 Giddens 1986: 536.
62 Giddens 1984: 7.
63 Radway 1984: 96–7.
64 Giddens 1984: 284.
65 ibid., p.336.
66 ibid., p.289.
67 Ken Loach, Australian Broadcasting Corporation radio interview, December 1986.
68 Lovell 1981: 95.
69 Trevor Griffiths, South Bank Show, 1984.
70 ibid.
71 ibid.
72 ibid.
73 Giddens 1984: 285.
74 Giddens 1987: 107.
75 Giddens 1986: 544
76 Giddens 1981: 4.
77 Janet Wolff 1981: 136.
78 Fiske 1988: 314

79 Giddens 1987: 65.
80 Radway 1984: 221.
81 Rethinking the Audience: New Tendencies in Television Research Symposium, in Blaubeuren, West Germany, February 17–20, 1987.
82 Morley 1987: 25.
83 ibid., p.47.
84 Radway 1984: 6.
85 ibid., p.218.
86 Tulloch and Moran 1986: Introduction.
87 Anderson 1987: 167.
88 Radway 1984: 221.
89 ibid., p.220.
90 Kaplan 1986: 164–5.
91 ibid., p.11.
92 Lindlof and Meyer in Lindlof 1987: 7–12.
93 For a definition of structure within a theory of social agency, see Giddens 1984: ch.1. To talk as Giddens does of a 'bounded situation' in the context of the reproduction of social structures is to adopt an epistemologically realist position: 'real' here in Giddens' sense, as that *structurally stable* order of relationships which, at any one point in time and space, we, and others like us 'in connected and similar contexts, accept . . . as such – not necessarily in their discursive consciousness but in the practical consciousness incorporated in what they do' (Giddens 1984: 331).
94 Ang 1987: 20.
95 ibid.
96 Hobson 1982.
97 Radway 1984: 220.
98 Walkerdine in Burgin *et al.* 1986: 191.
99 ibid., p.192.
100 ibid., p.168.
101 Kaplan 1986: 143
102 ibid.
103 Walkerdine 1986: p.187.
104 An exception is Poole and Wyver 1984.
105 Williams, Spring 1977: 73.
106 ibid.
107 Radway 1984: 212.
108 Williams 1977: 73–4.
109 Dyer *et al.* 1981: 6.
110 Lovell in Dyer *et al.* 1981: 52.
111 Mellor in Pawling (ed.) 1984: 46–7.
112 Hebdige, Spring 1987: 70.
113 See Ang's criticism of Morley (1987).
114 Connell 1983: 36.
115 James 1987: 93.
116 Kaplan 1986: 144–5.
117 ibid., p.164.
118 ibid.

119 Wright 1975: 137.
120 In the preface to the British edition of her book, Radway acknowledges
this problem: 'Were I conducting this study today, I would want to
compare the meaning and significance of the romance as it is inserted in
the day-to-day existence of both writers and readers. . . . The recuperation
is clearly important, but again I feel that we must not allow it to blind us
to the fact that the romance *is* being changed and struggled over by the
women who write them.' *'Reading the Romance'*, MS, pp.17, 26.
121 Fiske 1988: 16.
122 ibid., p.19.
123 James 1987: 105.
124 Loach's comments were originally a tailpiece to Chapter 6 but were
omitted because of publisher's requirements for a shorter book. I would be
happy to pass them on to anybody interested to read them.

1 'Soft' news: the space of TV drama

1 Dennis Potter in Self 1984: 1.
2 Allen 1985: 10.
3 *Sydney Morning Herald* 1986: 1, 16, 11–17.
4 Peter Luck, ibid., p.1.
5 ibid., p.25.
6 Elliott, Murdock and Schlesinger April 1983: 174.
7 For a discussion of the continuous serial, the episodic series, the sequential
series and the episodic serial, see Tulloch and Alvarado 1983: ix-xi.
8 Elliott *et al.* 1983: 163.
9 ibid.
10 ibid.
11 ibid.
12 ibid., p.164. On this point, see also Drummond, Autumn 1976: 24.
13 Elliott *et al.* 1983: 164.
14 ibid., p.172.
15 ibid., p.164.
16 ibid.
17 ibid., p.161.
18 See for instance, the debate about *Days of Hope* in Bennett *et al.* 1981: 285–
352.
19 Modleski 1982: 93.
20 Fiske 1988: 222.
21 ibid., p.182.
22 Buckingham 1987: 100.
23 ibid., p.103.
24 ibid., p.111.
25 ibid.
26 ibid., p.112.
27 Fiske 1988: 199.
28 ibid., p.213.

29 ibid., p.211.
30 Tulloch and Moran 1986: 195.
31 ibid., p.198.
32 ibid., pp.200–1.
33 ibid., p.200.
34 Barthes 1967: 63.
35 Hayward 1988: 185, 186.
36 Barthes 1967: 63.
37 See, for instance, David Morley on the gendered relations of TV genres: Summer 1981: 1–14.
38 See Tulloch and Moran 1986: ch.15.
39 Brunsdon 1981: 32–7.
40 Interviews at John Pound's house, Bournemouth, November 1985.
41 Hartley 1982: 80.
42 Tulloch and Moran 1986: 236.
43 Hartley 1982: 39.
44 ibid., p.139.
45 Windschuttle 1984: 189.
46 ibid., p.188.
47 Hartley 1982: 115.
48 Modleski 1982: 88.
49 ibid., p.90.
50 For an extension of this discussion which takes up the issue of observer/'other' relations that I raised in the Introduction, see Tulloch 'Approaching the Audience: the Elderly' in Seiter, Warth, Kreutzner and Borchers 1989 (forthcoming).
51 ibid., p.92.
52 ibid., p.93.
53 Ang 1987: 72.
54 ibid., p.81.
55 Seiter, Kreutzner and Borchers 1987: 28.
56 Elliott *et al.* 1983: 161.
57 Ellis 1982: 112.
58 Fiske 1988: 103.
59 *b & t advertising marketing and media weekly*, 13 April 1984: 28.
60 Allen 1985: 128.
61 Fiske 1988: 104.
62 ibid.
63 ibid., p.102.
64 ibid.
65 ibid., p.100.
66 ibid.
67 ibid., p.101.
68 ibid.
69 Budd, Craig and Steinman, in Gurevitch and Levy (eds) 1985: 297.
70 Sandy Flitterman, 'The Real Soap Operas: TV Commercials', in E. Ann Kaplan (ed.) 1983: 87.
71 ibid.

72 ibid., p.95.
73 Allen 1985: 153.
74 Kellner 1981: vol. 10, no. 1, p.42.
75 ibid., p.174.
76 ibid.
77 Williamson 1978: 47.
78 King and Rowse, *Framework* 22/23: 42.
79 Tulloch in J. Tulloch and G. Turner (eds) 1987: 136.
80 Hartley in Masterman 1984: 123.
81 ibid., p.126.
82 ibid., p.125.
83 ibid: 'endless talk of self-discovery and personal relationships; endless looking for affection, love or esteem from others'.
84 ibid., p.127.
85 Fiske 1988: 258–9, 261, 262.
86 ibid., pp.257–8.
87 ibid., p.258.
88 ibid.
89 Tulloch in Tulloch and Turner 1989: 125, 126.
90 Wickham 1987: 158.

2 Genre and myth: 'a half-formed picture'

1 Sally Potter speaking at the Sydney Film Festival, July 1985.
2 Zipes 1979: 95.
3 Fiske 1982: 93.
4 Counihan, June 1982: 197.
5 ibid., p.199.
6 Johnson (forthcoming): MS p.39.
7 ibid., p.43.
8 ibid.
9 ibid., p.44.
10 Nightingale in M.E. Brown (ed.) (forthcoming).
11 ibid., p.51.
12 Nightingale in Brown (forthcoming), MS pp.14–15.
13 Johnson (forthcoming).
14 ibid., p.31.
15 ibid., p.35.
16 Allen 1985: 156.
17 For discussion of realist theory and generative mechanisms, see Chapter 3; also Allen 1985: 7, 100, 176.
18 Mellor 1984: 31.
19 Dorfman 1983: 115.
20 ibid., pp.111–12.
21 ibid., pp.115–17.
22 Eco 1979: 107–24.
23 Radway 1984: 17, 208.
24 Dunn 1986: 50, 52.

25 Barthes 1973: 117 ff.
26 Silverstone 1981: 3.
27 ibid., pp.42–4.
28 Fiske 1988: 106.
29 ibid., p.71.
30 Dorfman 1983: 118.
31 Wright 1975: 27.
32 Silverstone 1981: 194.
33 ibid., p.192.
34 ibid., p.67.
35 Radway 1984: 74, 75.
36 Silverstone 1981: 159.
37 Tulloch and Alvarado 1983: ch.3, and later this chapter.
38 Tulloch and Moran 1986: 68.
39 Giddens distinguishes between the repetitive, 'day-to-day' flow of daily life, the irreversible 'being toward death' of biological life, and the 'longue durée' (long-term existence) of institutional life – see Giddens 1984: 35 ff.
40 Silverstone 1981: 180.
41 ibid., pp.179–80.
42 Goodlad extracted in Tulloch 1977: 120.
43 Silverstone 1981: 180.
44 ibid.
45 Tulloch 1981: ch.10, 11.
46 Silverstone 1981: 113.
47 Hurd, Autumn 1976: 47.
48 Fiske 1988: 114.
49 Hurd 1976: 48.
50 Dennington and Tulloch, Autumn 1976: 38.
51 Hurd 1976: 49–50.
52 Westergaard in Hurd 1976: 39.
53 Hurd 1976: 52.
54 Clarke in Bennett *et al.* 1986: 219–32.
55 Ross 1987: 322.
56 Donald in Alvarado and Stewart 1985: 123.
57 For an excellent analysis of 'Country Boy' see Drummond, Autumn 1976: 15–35.
58 Caswell 1984: xi–xviii.
59 Donald 1985: 127.
60 ibid.
61 For a discussion of traditional theories of narrative, see Fiske 1988: ch.8, and Tulloch 1982: ch.6, 7.
62 Neale 1980:20; see also discussions of Neale's work in Clarke 1986: 227, and Bennett and Woollacott 1987: 95–6.
63 Clarke 1986: 231–2.
64 Fiske 1987: 222.
65 Bennett and Woollacott 1987: 98.
66 ibid., pp.110, 113.
67 ibid., p.115.

68 ibid., p.280.
69 Tulloch and Alvarado 1983: 99–100.
70 Bennett and Woollacott 1987: 280.
71 ibid., p.281.
72 ibid.
73 ibid., p.282.
74 ibid., p.173.
75 ibid , p.4.
76 ibid., p.5.
77 Skirrow in Alvarado and Stewart 1985: 177.
78 Winterbottom in Alvarado and Stewart 1985: 159.
79 Fiske 1983: 84.
80 ibid., p.73.
81 ibid., p.88.
82 ibid., p.96.
83 ibid., p.99.
84 Fiske 1988: p.228.
85 ibid.
86 ibid., p.229.
87 ibid.
88 ibid., p.260.
89 'To begin to resemble the other, to take on their appearance, is to seduce them since it is to make them enter the realm of metamorphosis despite themselves.' (Baudrillard 1984: 15)
90 Fiske 1988: 260.
91 Kellner 1987: 138.
92 Fiske 1988: 230.
93 ibid., pp.216, 219.
94 Fiske 1982: 95.
95 Fiske 1983: 99.
96 Tulloch and Alvarado 1983: 110.
97 ibid., p.122. See also Tulloch 1980.
98 Tulloch and Alvarado 1983: 126.
99 For a similar analysis of the SF *audience*, see Mellor 1984: 37 ff.
100 Tulloch and Alvarado 1983: 128–9.
101 ibid., p.141.
102 To the extent that leading fans commented that 'The Sun Makers' was 'heavily laced with left-wing propaganda': see Tulloch and Alvarado 1983: 149.
103 ibid., p.58.
104 ibid.
105 ibid.
106 Donald 1985: 129.
107 ibid., p.134.
108 Bennett and Woollacott 1987: 131.
109 ibid., p.135.
110 ibid., p.136.
111 ibid., p.137.

112 Tulloch and Alvarado 1983: 131.
113 Zipes 1979: 4–5.
114 ibid., pp.6–7.
115 ibid., p.5.
116 ibid., p.14.
117 ibid., p.17.
118 ibid., pp.94–5
119 ibid., p.99.
120 ibid., p.125.
121 ibid., pp.122–3.
122 ibid.
123 Trevor Griffiths, interviewed by Misha Glenny, 1985, in *Judgement Over The Dead*, p.xvi.

3 'Reperceiving the world': making history

1 South Bank Show, London Weekend Television, 1984.
2 Caughie in Bennett, Boyd-Bowman, Mercer and Woollacott 1981: 328.
3 Lawson, December 1983: 97.
4 See, for instance, Allen 1985: ch.1.
5 Caughie 1981: 328.
6 Lawson 1983: 98.
7 ibid.
8 ibid.
9 ibid., p.99.
10 Cunningham, December 1983: 83.
11 Crofts and Craik, December 1983: 92.
12 Cunningham 1983: 86.
13 ibid., p.84.
14 Crofts and Craik 1983: 94.
15 Cunningham 1983: 85.
16 Cunningham 1989: 43, 44.
17 ibid.
18 ibid.
19 On *Days of Hope* see Bennett in Bennett *et al.* 1981: 303.
20 *Sydney Morning Herald*, 27 January 1988: 1.
21 McArthur 1978: 40.
22 ibid.
23 Interviewed in Cambridge, November 1985.
24 Huntford 1985: 118.
25 ibid., p.119.
26 Interview with Misha Glenny, 1985, pp.41–2 (Griffiths typescript).
27 ibid., p.36.
28 ibid., p.42.
29 McArthur 1978: 45.
30 ibid.
31 As in the lecture by the gentlemanly mine owner, Pritchard, to the arrested miners about the British tradition of peaceful and gradual reform, while the

soldiers who will put down the working-class struggle indulge in bayonet practice in the background.

32 McArthur 1978: 27.
33 ibid., p.28.
34 Together with legalistic discourses attacking feudalism from a position of bourgeois individualism, and new aesthetic perspectives emerging with the Renaissance.
35 ibid., p.5.
36 ibid.
37 ibid., p.8.
38 Huntford 1985: 272.
39 ibid., p.188.
40 McArthur 1978: 28.
41 Interview with John Tulloch, November 1985.
42 Lovell 1981: 18.
43 McLennan 1981: 30.
44 ibid., pp.31–2.
45 Interview with Misha Glenny, 1985, pp.44–5.
46 Cited in McArthur 1978: 13.
47 South Bank Show, 1984.
48 Interview with Misha Glenny, 1985, p.12.
49 ibid., p.25.
50 ibid., p.48.
51 ibid.
52 In the original Griffiths' text of *Judgement Over The Dead*, this scene is preceded by one where Scott tells a young naval lieutenant sent to bring him to the Admiral, 'In future, you will knock and *wait* when approaching a senior officer's quarters, is that understood?'
53 ibid., p.31.
54 ibid., pp.46–7.
55 ibid., p.47.
56 ibid., pp.31, 36.
57 See Lukacs 1969.
58 Interview with Misha Glenny, 1985, p.37.
59 ibid.
60 McArthur 1978: 34.
61 Interview with Misha Glenny, 1985, p.45.
62 Interview with Nicole Boireau, May 1985, pp.45, 52–3 (Griffiths' typecopy).
63 Interview with Misha Glenny, 1985, p.47.
64 Interview with Boireau, p.54.
65 See Lukács, 1969: ch.2.
66 Griffiths, *Fatherland*, First Draft (May 1984).
67 ibid.
68 ibid.
69 Interview with John Tulloch (1985).
70 ibid.
71 ibid.

72 *Fatherland*, First Draft.
73 Interview with John Tulloch.
74 ibid.
75 Interview with Misha Glenny, 1985, p.12.
76 Interview with John Tulloch.
77 ibid.
78 ibid.
79 ibid.
80 ibid.
81 ibid.
82 ibid.
83 ibid.
84 ibid.
85 Interview with Misha Glenny, 1985, p.48.
86 McArthur 1978: 8.
87 Interview with Misha Glenny, 1985, p.41.
88 ibid.
89 Kellner 1987: 143.
90 ibid.
91 ibid.

4 'Serious drama': the dangerous mesh of empathy

1 Wolff, Ryan, McGuigan and McKiernan in Barker *et al.* 1976: 143.
2 Grant 1987: 24.
3 ibid.
4 Cited in Caughie 1981: 337.
5 ibid., p.338.
6 ibid., p.339.
7 ibid.
8 ibid.
9 Williams, Fall 1977–Winter 1978: 5.
10 ibid.
11 For a discussion of Regan as 'existential' hero, see Drummond 1976: 25–6.
12 Williams, Spring 1977: 69.
13 ibid., p.70.
14 ibid., p.71.
15 ibid., p.72.
16 ibid., p.63.
17 Caughie 1981: 335.
18 Raymond Williams, Foreword to John McGrath 1981.
19 Caughie 1981: 332.
20 Interview with Misha Glenny, 1985, p.4.
21 Caughie 1981: 333.
22 ibid., pp.341–2.
23 For MacCabe's notion of classic-realist text (which collapses together the
     naturalist/realist distinction of Williams/Lukacs) see 'Realism and the
     Cinema: Notes on some Brechtian Theses', '*Days of Hope*: A Response to

Colin McArthur', and 'Memory, Phantasy, Identity: *Days of Hope* and the
Politics of the Past', in Bennett *et al.*, *Popular Television and Film* (1981),
pp.216–35, 314–18 (the first two originally published in *Screen*; the third in
Edinburgh Magazine).
24 MacCabe 1981: 308.
25 ibid., p.312.
26 Dunn 1986: 53.
27 MacCabe 1981: 316.
28 Cited in Dunn 1986: 53.
29 Kellner 1987: 128.
30 Baudrillard 1984: 17.
31 ibid., p.22.
32 ibid., pp. 23, 24.
33 ibid., p.18.
34 ibid.
35 Kellner 1987: 143.
36 Caughie 1981: 342.
37 ibid., pp.343–4.
38 Interview with John Tulloch, November 1985.
39 ibid.
40 Caughie 1981: 346.
41 ibid., p.351.
42 Interview with John Tulloch, November 1985.
43 Zielinski, Winter 1980: 91.
44 ibid., p.92.
45 ibid., p.93.
46 Markovits and Hayden, Winter 1980: 78.
47 Caughie 1981: 349.

5 TV drama as social event: text and inter-text

1 Interview with Misha Glenny, pp.1–2.
2 Tania Wollen in Alvarado and Stewart 1985: 170–1.
3 ibid., p.167.
4 ibid., p.171.
5 ibid., p.166.
6 ibid., p.164.
7 ibid., p.160.
8 ibid., p.161.
9 Interview with Misha Glenny, p.2.
10 ibid., p.6.
11 ibid., p.10.
12 ibid., p.20.
13 Interview with John Tulloch, November 1985.
14 Keir Elam 1986: 12.
15 ibid., pp.8 ff.
16 ibid., p. 12
17 ibid., p.18.

18 ibid., p.23.
19 Huntford 1985: 391.
20 ibid., p.370.
21 ibid., p.476.
22 ibid., p.523.
23 ibid., p.543.
24 ibid., p.524.
25 ibid., p.543.
26 Griffiths 1986: 305.
27 ibid.
28 Huntford 1985: 542.
29 ibid., p.189.
30 ibid., p.526.
31 For a succinct discussion of levels and voices of narration, see Rimmon-Kenan 1983: ch.7.
32 Huntford 1985: 507.
33 ibid., p.527.
34 ibid., p.524.
35 For a theoretical discussion of degree of perceptibility and reliability of narratorial voice, see Rimmon-Kenan 1983: 96–103.
36 Huntford 1985: 488.
37 ibid., p.519.
38 ibid., p.520.
39 ibid., p.521.
40 ibid.
41 ibid.
42 ibid., pp. 520–1.
43 ibid., pp.372, 308.
44 ibid., p.386.
45 ibid., p.479.
46 ibid., pp.528–9.
47 ibid., p.156.
48 Griffiths 1986: 5–6.
49 ibid., p.96.
50 ibid., p.25.
51 ibid., p.99.
52 ibid., p.68.
53 ibid., p.59.
54 ibid., pp.64–5.
55 ibid., p.68.
56 ibid., p.82.
57 ibid., p.159.
58 ibid.
59 ibid., p.199.
60 ibid., p.196.
61 ibid.
62 ibid., pp.288–9
63 ibid., p.289.

64 ibid., p.290.
65 ibid., p.291.
66 Cited in *The Times*, 11 February 1985, p.12.
67 ibid.
68 *The Listener*, 14 February 1985.
69 Huntford 1985: 522.
70 Elam 1986: 23.
71 ibid., p.25.
72 See Elam 1986: 27.
73 Huntford 1985: 522.
74 Elam 1986: 29.
75 See McArthur 1978: 22.
76 For a discussion of 'secondary' and 'tertiary' media texts, see Fiske 1988: ch.7.
77 Interview with Misha Glenny, 1985, p.28.
78 Letter to Sir Gordon Hobday, 15 May 1984.
79 Interview with Misha Glenny, 1985, pp.29–30.
80 ibid., pp.30–2.
81 Interview with John Tulloch, November 1985.
82 Letter to Sir Gordon Hobday, 30 January 1985.
83 ibid.
84 ibid.
85 Interview with Misha Glenny, 1985, p.35.
86 *The Observer*, 10 March 1985.
87 ibid.
88 ibid.
89 *The Observer*, 24 February 1985.
90 The *Sunday Express*, 17 February 1985.
91 Interview with Misha Glenny, 1985, p.30.
92 The *Sunday Express*, 17 February 1985.
93 ibid.
94 ibid.
95 *The Daily Telegraph*, 8 February 1985.
96 *The Observer*, 17 February 1985.
97 *The Observer*, 24 February 1985.
98 ibid.
99 ibid.
100 *Media Week*, 15 February 1985.
101 *The Listener*, 14 February 1985, p.27.
102 *City Limits*, 15–21 February 1985, p.15.
103 ibid.
104 Peter Luck, The *Sydney Morning Herald* 'The Guide', 27 July–2 August 1987, p.6; Robin Oliver, 'The Guide', 20–7 July 1987; Richard Coleman, The *Sydney Morning Herald*, 25 July 1987, p.42.
105 Coleman 1987: 47.
106 Baudrillard 1984: 19.
107 Interview in Bournemouth, November 1985.
108 *The Times*, 18 February 1985.

109 Interview in Bournemouth, November 1985.
110 ibid.

6 Authored drama: 'not just naturalism'

1 Interview with John Tulloch, November 1985.
2 Poole and Wyver 1984: 152–3.
3 ibid., p.162.
4 South Bank Show, 1984.
5 For an analysis of *Chekhov*'s 'specific historicity and precise sociological imagination', see Tulloch 1980.
6 Interview with John Tulloch.
7 Kundera 1983: 233.
8 Kundera 1983: interviewed by Philip Roth in Kundera 1983: 235.
9 Kundera 1983: 187.
10 Milan Kundera, interviewed by Philip Roth in Kundera 1983: 235.
11 ibid., p.237.
12 Kundera 1983: 61.
13 ibid., p.206.
14 Griffiths 1987: 53.
15 Interview with John Tulloch.
16 Trevor Griffiths 1987: 77.
17 Interview with John Tulloch, November 1985.
18 ibid.
19 Letter from Ken Loach to Trevor Griffiths, January 1985.
20 Letter from Trevor Griffiths to Ken Loach, 30 January 1985.
21 ibid.
22 Interview with John Tulloch, November 1985.
23 ibid.
24 ibid.
25 Letter to John Tulloch, (undated) 1988.
26 Interview with John Tulloch, November 1985.
27 *Fatherland*, First Draft.
28 Interview with John Tulloch, November 1985.
29 ibid.
30 *Fatherland*, First Draft.
31 Interview with John Tulloch, November 1985.
32 ibid.
33 Interview with John Tulloch, November 1985.
34 ibid.
35 ibid.
36 ibid.
37 Gerulf Pannach, interview with John Tulloch, November 1985.
38 Ken Loach, interview with John Tulloch, November 1985.
39 ibid.
40 Interview with John Tulloch, November 1985.
41 ibid.
42 Letter from Ken Loach to Trevor Griffiths, 1 February 1985.

43 ibid.
44 Interview with John Tulloch, November 1985.
45 ibid.
46 ibid.
47 Milan Kundera, interviewed by Philip Roth in Kundera 1983: 236.
48 Kundera 1983: 214.
49 Ken Loach, interview with John Tulloch, December 1986.
50 ibid.
51 ibid.
52 ibid.

7 Industry/performance: drama as 'strategic penetration'

 1 John McGrath, St Johns College, Cambridge, October 1986.
 2 Selig 1985: 19.
 3 ibid.
 4 Colin MacCabe in Bennett *et al.* 1981: 312.
 5 Colin McArthur 1978: 52.
 6 ibid.
 7 ibid.
 8 Interview with John Tulloch, November 1986.
 9 McGrath 1981: 121–2.
10 McGrath's 1987 *There Is A Happy Land* continued this work; a TV history of
    the Gaelic-speaking areas of Scotland from 2000 years ago to the present,
    'showing how they have been treated by the central power in Scotland, then
    by the central power in London, and increasingly by the central power in
    Washington . . . and their language and culture constantly pushed to the
    fringes and under threat – told through the songs that were created by the
    events of that history'.
11 McGrath 1981: 122.
12 Edgar, Winter 1979: 26.
13 ibid., p.27.
14 ibid.
15 ibid.
16 ibid.
17 ibid., p.28.
18 ibid., p.30.
19 ibid.
20 ibid.
21 ibid.
22 ibid.
23 ibid., pp.30–1.
24 ibid., p.31.
25 ibid., p.32.
26 ibid., p.29.
27 ibid.
28 ibid., p.32.
29 ibid.

30 McGrath, Spring 1977: 100–5.
31 Interview with John Tulloch, November 1986.
32 ibid.
33 ibid.
34 ibid.
35 ibid.
36 MacCabe in Bennett *et al.* 1981: 318.
37 Selig 1985: 21.
38 ibid.
39 Cited in Edgar 1979: 29.
40 ibid., pp.32–3.
41 ibid., p.103.
42 ibid., pp.103–4.
43 ibid., p.116.
44 ibid., p.95.
45 ibid., p.77.
46 Interview with John Tulloch, November 1986.
47 See Poole and Wyver 1984: 175–9.
48 Selig 1985: 20.
49 Troy Kennedy-Martin, St John's College, Cambridge, October 1986.
50 Michael Wearing, St John's College, Cambridge, October 1986.
51 John McGrath, Cambridge, October 1986.
52 Wearing, Cambridge, 1986.
53 McGrath, Cambridge, 1986.
54 Interview with John Tulloch, November 1986.
55 Interview with John Tulloch, November 1986.
56 Michael Wearing, Cambridge, 1986.
57 For instance, *A Country Practice* writer, Tony Morphett: 'It's characteristic of *Country Practice* that there's always a heavy and light side to it, and obviously the medical story – the life and death story – tends to be the heavier side, and then you do have the comedy side, very often with Bob, Cookie and Esme. But this is a very long-standing tradition of drama anyway. You know, apart from, say, *Twelfth Night*, the Shakespearean plays with the best comedy in them, the funniest comedy in them, tend to be the tragedies.'
58 Interview with John Tulloch, November 1986.
59 ibid.
60 See John Tulloch, December 1986: 90–108.
61 Elam 1980: 37.
62 Tulloch 1986: 93–4.
63 Cited in Poole and Wyver 1984: 145.
64 ibid., p.143.
65 Millington and Nelson 1986.
66 Tulloch and Moran 1986.
67 John McGrath, Cambridge, 1986.
68 Cited in Tulloch 1986: 107.
69 See Tulloch and Moran 1986: ch.11.
70 Tulloch 1986: 108.
71 Millington and Nelson 1986: 146.

72 ibid., p.87.
73 ibid., p.95.
74 ibid., p.120.
75 ibid., p.61.
76 ibid., p.64.
77 ibid.
78 Elam 1980: 45.
79 Millington and Nelson 1986: 132.
80 Feuer in Feuer *et al.* 1984: 24–5.
81 Kerr in Feuer *et al.* 1984: 132–47.
82 Hayward 1988: 185.
83 ibid.
84 Feuer 1984: 56.
85 Cited in Millington and Nelson 1986: 150.
86 ibid.

8 'Use and exchange': delivering audiences

1 James Davern, Executive Producer of *A Country Practice*, paper at Australian Teachers of Media Conference, 1986.
2 David Buckingham makes the useful distinction between 'creating the audience' (producers' understanding of the audience they are looking for), 'the audience in the text' (the inscribing of the audience via narrative and other strategies), 'between the text and the audience' (the inter-textual role of newspapers, magazines and other 'secondary' texts in generating meaning), and 'popular television and its audience' (empirical study of the actual audience of popular TV shows) – see Buckingham (1987).
3 See Bennett and Woollacott 1986: p.65.
4 Jenkins III (unpublished), p.17.
5 Dunn 1986: pp.57, 58.
6 Davern (1986).
7 Interview with Norma Regent by Kerrell Duck, 1986.
8 ibid.
9 ibid.
10 Buckingham 1987: 21.
11 ibid.
12 Redlich 1984: 1.
13 Cited in Feuer, Kerr and Bahimagi 1984: 26.
14 Feuer *et al.* 1984: 157.
15 ibid.
16 ibid., p.26.
17 Davern (1986).
18 ibid.
19 McQuail, Blumler and Brown in McQuail (ed.) 1972: 153.
20 ibid.
21 For instance, for causal chains of explanation of strikes and unions, see Philo, Beharrel and Hewitt 1977: 8; also Downing (cited in Morley 1980: 13), and Morley 1981.

22 ibid., p.174.
23 Morley 1980: 15.
24 McQuail *et al.* 1972: 152.
25 ibid.
26 Sharratt in Bradby, James and Sharratt 1980: 280.
27 ibid., pp.284–5
28 ibid., p.285.
29 ibid., p.286.
30 ibid., p.276.
31 See Morley 1980: ch.7.
32 ibid., p.159.
33 ibid., ch.3.
34 ibid., p.18.
35 ibid., p.161.
36 ibid., ch.4.
37 Wren-Lewis in *Media, Culture and Society*, V5 N2, April 1983: 195.
38 Messaris in Gumpert and Cathcart 1986: 519–36.
39 Tulloch and Moran 1986: ch.16.
40 Palmer 1986b: 106. See also Palmer 1986a.
41 Hodge and Tripp 1986: 151.
42 ibid., pp. 151–2.
43 ibid., p.153.
44 Hodge and Tripp, Report to the sponsors, TV W7, Perth, undated: ch. 5, p.14.
45 ibid.
46 Tulloch and Moran 1986: ch. 14, 16.
47 ibid., p.234.
48 Morley 1980: 156.
49 Morley 1986: 150.
50 ibid., p.161.
51 ibid., p.160.
52 Marco de Marinis 1986.
53 ibid., p.7.
54 In the case of *Doctor Who* most producers have been careful to ensure continuity in terms of the minutiae (as well as broader themes) of the show's history, often dropping in references to twenty-year-old details that long-term fans would pick up and enjoy. In contrast, other producers (like Graham Williams – see Chapter 2) looked for a bonus audience with a different encyclopaedic knowledge (such as that of 'classic' film buffs), often at the expense of the show's own continuity, and to the intense irritation of the fans: see Tulloch and Alvarado 1983: 65–7.
55 de Marinis 1986: 7.
56 See Tulloch and Alvarado 1983: 149.
57 de Marinis 1986: 9.
58 ibid., pp.8–9.
59 Fiske 1985: 95.
60 ibid.
61 ibid.

62 Ellis 1982.
63 Fiske 1985: 21.
64 Sharratt 1980: 283.
65 See Brunsdon 1981: 32–7.
66 de Marinis 1986: 14.
67 ibid., p.24.
68 Interview at Cambridge, November 1985.
69 ibid.
70 ibid.
71 Bennett and Woollacott 1987: 94.
72 Lovell 1981: 49.
73 ibid., p.43.
74 ibid., p.48.
75 ibid., p.47.
76 ibid., pp.48–9.

9 Sub-culture and reading formation: regimes of watching

 1 Williams 1977: 132.
 2 Interview in Bournemouth, November 1985.
 3 Fiske 1986: 228.
 4 ibid.
 5 Murdock, quoted in Morley 1980: 14.
 6 Parkin 1973.
 7 Hall 1973.
 8 Cited in Morley 1987: 22.
 9 Brown 1987: 10.
10 Fiske in Allen (ed.) 1987: 270.
11 Morley 1987: 22.
12 Hall and Jefferson (eds) 1976: 14.
13 Liebes and Katz 1987: 24.
14 ibid.
15 ibid., p.25.
16 Palmer 1986b.
17 Curthoys and Docker 1984: 27–8.
18 Palmer 1986b: 111.
19 David Lusted, address to Australian Teachers of Media Conference, Sydney 1984.
20 Hodge and Tripp 1986: ch.6, p.25.
21 Connell 1983: 29.
22 ibid.
23 ibid.
24 Buckingham 1987: 164.
25 Palmer 1986b: 108.
26 Hodge and Tripp 1986: ch.6, p.29.
27 Tulloch and Moran 1986: 262.
28 ibid., p.271.
29 Hodge and Tripp 1986: ch.6, p.45.

30 Curthoys and Docker 1984: 30.
31 Tulloch and Moran 1986: 257.
32 Fiske 1985: 8.
33 Curthoys and Docker, 1984: 16–17.
34 ibid., p.22.
35 Windschuttle 1984: 187.
36 Tulloch, 'Formal Curriculum: St Ives High School' (unpublished).
37 Kessler, Ashenden, Connell and Dowsett 1985: 34–48.
38 ibid., p.38.
39 Tulloch, 'Formal Curriculum' (unpublished).
40 Giddens 1984: 296.
41 Cited in Giddens 1984: 290.
42 Fiske 1985: 9.
43 Hebdige 1979.
44 Lovell 1981: 46.
45 Williams 1977: 132.
46 ibid., p.130.
47 ibid., p.131.
48 Lovell 1981: 45.
49 Jenkins 1987: 19.
50 Lovell 1981: 52.
51 ibid., p.45.
52 ibid., p.50.
53 ibid.
54 ibid., p.45.
55 ibid.
56 Bennett and Woollacott 1987: 64.
57 ibid., pp.64–5.
58 Gunter in Kent (ed.) 1983: 62.
59 Allen 1985: 12.
60 Curthoys and Docker, 1989: 65–6.
61 ibid., p.66
62 ibid.
63 Ang 1987: ch.3.
64 Bennett and Woollacott 1987: 167.
65 ibid., p.267.
66 ibid., pp.227–9.
67 Jenkins 1987: 15, 19.
68 ibid., p.2.
69 Williams 1977: 131.
70 Fiske 1985: 39.
71 de Certeau 1984: 174.
72 Bennett and Woollacott 1987: 23.
73 ibid., p.220.
74 Bennett and Woollacott 1987: ch.2.
75 Tulloch and Moran 1986: ch.13.
76 Buckingham 1987: 122.
77 ibid., p.123.

78 ibid., p.122.
79 See Bennett and Woollacott 1987: 263.
80 ibid., p.64.
81 ibid., p.263.
82 ibid., p.60.
83 ibid., p.18.
84 Tulloch in Seiter *et al.* 1989.
85 Hobson 1982: 126.
86 Allen 1985: 71.
87 Buckingham 1987: 50.
88 ibid.
89 ibid.
90 ibid., p.54.
91 ibid., p.55.
92 Hobson 1982: 116–17.
93 Kippax 1988: 13.
94 ibid.
95 ibid., p.19.
96 ibid.
97 ibid., p.16.
98 ibid., p.125.
99 Tulloch, paper at Blaubeuren Symposium, Germany, February 1987.
100 Hobson 1982: 130.
101 ibid., p.131.
102 ibid., p.135.
103 Brown 1987: 22.
104 Fiske 1986: 78.
105 Tulloch and Moran 1986: 246–7.
106 Brown 1987: 3.
107 Ang 1987: 42.
108 ibid., p.43.
109 ibid., pp.44–5.
110 ibid., p.45.
111 ibid., p.47.
112 ibid., p.49.
113 ibid.
114 ibid., p.135.
115 ibid., pp.133–4.
116 Feuer 1984: 16.
117 ibid.
118 Liebes and Katz 1987: 25.
119 Feuer 1984: 15.
120 Cited in Feuer, p.14.
121 Interview in Bournemouth, November 1985.
122 Seiter *et al.* 1987: 28.
123 Ang 1987: 96.
124 ibid., p.97.
125 Kuhn 1984: 18–28.

126 Tulloch and Moran 1986: 9.
127 ibid.; see ch.11, 13, 16.
128 ibid., pp.181–2.
129 Tulloch 1986: 97.
130 Kuhn 1984: 27.
131 Fiske 1986: 66.
132 ibid., p.39.
133 ibid., p.312.
134 ibid., p.313.
135 ibid.
136 ibid.
137 ibid., p.316.
138 ibid., p.16.
139 ibid., p.44.
140 ibid., p.71.

10 Comic order and disorder: residual and emergent cultures

1 Cited in Thompson 1982: 43.
2 From an American 'radical magazine' cited in the *Guardian*, 23 February 1987.
3 Giddens 1984: 285.
4 Moran 1985: 182.
5 Lovell 1982; Neale 1980; Ellis 1975.
6 Lovell 1982: 23.
7 ibid., p.30.
8 ibid., p.29.
9 Cited in Thompson 1982: 30.
10 ibid.
11 ibid., p.31.
12 ibid.
13 Polan 1978: 30.
14 ibid.
15 Hayward 1988.
16 Feuer in Feuer *et al.* 1984: 54.
17 Polan 1978: 31.
18 ibid.
19 Cited in Moran 1985: 186.
20 Neale 1980: 28.
21 Fiske 1988: 110–11.
22 Woollacott in Bennett, Mercer and Woollacott (eds), 1986: 199.
23 As in 'Inferno' where the hubris of scientific exploration is played across alternative worlds of democracy and military dictatorship, each containing the same characters, but ending in the one case in the Earth's destruction and in the other by its saving (as its scientific madness is contained).
24 Woollacott 1986: 200.
25 ibid.
26 ibid., p.202.

27 See Buckingham 1987: 91.
28 Cited in Moran 1985: 186.
29 Woollacott 1986: 213.
30 Bathrick in Feuer *et al.* 1984: 115–16.
31 Woollacott 1986: 213.
32 ibid., p.216.
33 ibid., p.217.
34 ibid.
35 ibid.
36 ibid.
37 Bee 1986: 12.
38 ibid., p.26.
39 ibid.
40 ibid., p.36.
41 Simonds 1988: 5.
42 ibid.
43 Lovell 1982: 24.
44 Bee 1986: 25.
45 Eaton 1981: 36.
46 Ellis 1982: 167.
47 Woollacott 1986: 214.
48 Cited in Surlin and Tate 1976: 63.
49 Wilhoit and de Bock 1976: 80.
50 Surlin and Tate 1976: 65.
51 ibid., p.67.
52 Brigham and Giesbrecht 1976: 74.
53 Wilhoit and de Bock 1976: 82.
54 Brigham and Giesbrecht 1976: 55.
55 ibid., p.72.
56 ibid., p.74.
57 Wilhoit and de Bock 1976: 80.
58 Interview in Bournemouth, November 1986.
59 For further discussion, see Tulloch in Seiter *et al.* (forthcoming).
60 ibid., p.122.
61 ibid., p.130.
62 Feuer 1984: 58.
63 Bathrick 1984: 130.
64 Feuer 1984: 57.
65 Bathrick 1984: 100.
66 ibid., p.58.
67 Williams 1977: 125.
68 ibid.
69 ibid., p.122.
70 ibid., p.123.
71 Lovell 1982: 28.

11 'Marauding behaviour': parody, carnival and the grotesque

1 Cited in *Boys From The Blackstuff* 1984: 54.
2 Cited in Thompson 1982: 36.
3 ibid., pp.32–3.
4 ibid., p.35.
5 See Tulloch and Alvarado 1983: ch.4 5, 6.
6 ibid., pp.65–7.
7 Susan Stewart, cited in Thompson 1982: 31.
8 ibid., p.35.
9 See Tulloch and Alvarado 1983: ch.4.
10 Susan Stewart, cited in Thompson 1982: 36.
11 Cited in Thompson 1982: 43.
12 Zipes 1979: 7.
13 Cited in Thompson 1982: 43.
14 Fiske 1988: 242.
15 Tulloch and Alvarado 1983: 276.
16 Fiske 1988: pp.212, 222–3.
17 ibid., p.240.
18 ibid., p.246.
19 ibid., pp.264, 260.
20 Brown and Barwick (unpublished), p.6.
21 ibid., pp.6, 7.
22 ibid., p.11.
23 ibid., pp.12–13.
24 Cited in Brown and Barwick, p.16.
25 ibid., p.18.
26 ibid., p.19.
27 Cited in Poole and Wyver 1984: 106–7.
28 Interview with Misha Glenny, p.41.
29 Poole and Wyver 1984: 101.
30 See Cohen and Robbins, *Knuckle Sandwich* (Harmondsworth: Penguin, 1979). Cohen and Robbins argue that working-class oral traditions provide urban youth with the 'cultural competence' to appropriate Kung-fu movies, hence their popularity.
31 Baudrillard 1984: 23.
32 Cited in Poole and Wyver 1984: 112.
33 ibid., p.113.
34 ibid.
35 ibid., p.151.
36 ibid., p.153.
37 Lusted, 'What's Left of Blackstuff? Political Meaning for a Popular Audience', in *Boys From The Blackstuff*, British Film Institute Dossier, p.47.
38 ibid., p.46.
39 Cited in Archer, p.49.
40 ibid.
41 Cited in Millington and Nelson 1986: 132.
42 ibid., p.170.

43 Cited in Thompson 1982: 18.
44 ibid.
45 Archer 1984: 54.
46 Umberto Eco, for instance, argues that Bakhtin's theory of carnival is false: 'If it were true, it would be impossible to explain why power . . . has always used circuses to keep the crowds quiet; . . . why humour is suspect but circus is innocent; why today's mass media, undoubtedly instruments of social control . . . are based mainly upon the funny, the ludicrous, that is, upon a continuous carnivalization of life. . . . Bakhtin was right in seeing the manifestation of a profound drive towards liberation and subversion in Medieval carnival. The hyper-Bakhtinian ideology of carnival as *actual* liberation may, however, be wrong.' (Umberto Eco, 'The frames of comic "freedom"', in Umberto Eco, V.V. Ivanov, Monica Rector, *Carnival!*, Berlin: Mouton, 1984, p.3.) It is, obviously, the 'profound drive' rather than 'actual liberation' which reveals itself in the relation between Liverpool unemployed and *The Boys From the Blackstuff*, especially in its critique *of* 'the funny' which 'reminds us of the existence of the rule' (Eco, p.6); of the fact that 'scouse' humour sanctions the economic order by recognizing its own impotence. It is in its challenge to this reading formation, its sense of 'drive' *and* solidarity, which, I believe, places *Blackstuff* outside Eco's distinction between comedy, media carnival and humour. Humour, which Eco values most, is also (in its 'sense of superiority, but with a shade of tenderness', p.8), the most individualistic, patronizing and 'Chekhovian' (in the 'classless'/'Art' appropriation of that term).
47 John McGrath, 'The Boys are Back', in *Boys From The Blackstuff* Dossier, p.64.
48 ibid.
49 Cited in Millington and Nelson 1986: 61.
50 ibid.
51 Cited in Millington and Nelson 1986: 95.
52 ibid., p.134.
53 Cited in Millington and Nelson 1986: 20.
54 See Millington and Nelson 1986: 62.
55 ibid., p.154.
56 ibid.
57 ibid., p.155.
58 For instance, L.W. Tancock: 'A work of art must have some fundamental human truth; it must not merely make a number of puppets dance to a political tune. . . . Zola is not merely concerned with demonstrating some theory of his about trades unions or socialism, but with universal human nature', Introduction to Emile Zola, *Germinal* (Harmondsworth: Penguin, 1954), p.13.
59 Cited in Millington and Nelson 1986: 159.
60 See Millington and Nelson 1986: 161.
61 See Tulloch, 'Chekhov Abroad: Western Criticism', in Clyman (ed.) 1985: 188 ff.
62 Millington and Nelson 1986: 171.
63 Lusted 1984: 44.

64 Cited in Millington and Nelson 1986: 164.
65 ibid., p.163.
66 ibid.
67 ibid.
68 Lusted 1984: 42.
69 ibid., p.44.
70 ibid., p.41.
71 See Smith pp.39–40.
72 Interview with Derek Clifford, October 1986.
73 Lusted 1984: 47.
74 Paterson in Curran, Smith and Wingate 1987: 223.
75 See Anthony Giddens 1984: 50, 60–4.
76 Paterson 1987: 218–30.
77 Cf. Colin McArthur on the inter-textual play with genres in commercials: 'being appropriated by the camp sensibility, by which is meant a sensibility which appropriates art in a hermetically sealed kind of way, to produce meanings and pleasures which have no point of purchase on the wider social and political life of the society'; in Masterman 1984: 66. See also Hayward (1988).

Bibliography

Allen, Robert C. (1985) *Speaking of Soap Operas*, Chapel Hill: University of North Carolina.

Allen, Robert C. (ed.) (1987) *Channels of Discourse*, Chapel Hill: University of North Carolina.

Alvarado, M. and Stewart, J. (1985) *Made for Television: Euston Films Limited*, London: British Film Institute.

Anderson, James A. (1987) 'Commentary on qualitative research and mediated communication in the family', in Thomas R. Lindlof (ed.) *Natural Audiences: Qualitative Research of Media Uses and Effects*, Norwood: Ablex.

Ang, Ien (1987) 'Wanted: audiences: on the politics of empirical audience studies', Blaubeuren Symposium.

Archer, John (1984) 'The "Did You See . . . ?" interviews', in *Boys From The Blackstuff* Dossier.

Barker, Francis *et al.* (eds) (1976) *Literature, Society and the Sociology of Literature*, Colchester: University of Essex.

Barthes, Roland (1967) *Elements of Semiology*, London: Cape.

Barthes, Roland (1973) *Mythologies*, St Albans: Paladin.

Bathrick, Serafina (1984) '*The Mary Tyler Moore Show*: Woman at home and at work', in Feuer *et al.*

Baudrillard, Jean (1984) *The Evil Demon of Images*, Sydney: Power Institute Publications.

Bee, Jim (1986) 'The discourse of British domestic sitcom', paper presented to the 1986 International Television Studies Conference, University of London Institute of Education.

Bennett, Tony (1981) 'The *Days of Hope* debate: Introduction', in Bennett *et al.*

Bennett, Tony and Woollacott, Janet (1987) *Bond and Beyond*, Basingstoke: Macmillan.

Bennett, Tony; Mercer, Colin; and Woollacott, Janet (eds) (1986) *Popular Culture and Social Relations*, Milton Keynes: Open University Press.

Bennett, Tony; Boyd-Bowman, Susan; Mercer, Colin; and Woollacott, Janet (1981) *Popular Television and Film*, London: British Film Institute.

Boys From The Blackstuff (1984), British Film Institute Dossier 20.

Bradby, David; James, Louis; and Sharratt, Bernard (1980) *Performance and Politics in Popular Drama*, Cambridge: Cambridge University Press.

Brandt, George W. (ed.) (1981) *British Television Drama*, Cambridge: Cambridge University Press.

Brigham, John C. and Giesbrecht, Linda W. (1976) '"All in the Family": radical attitudes', *Journal of Communication*. Autumn.

Brown, Mary Ellen (1987) 'The politics of soaps: pleasure and feminine empowerment', *Australian Journal of Cultural Studies*, V4 N2.

Brown, Mary Ellen and Barwick, Linda (unpublished) 'Motley moments: soap opera, carnival and the power of the utterance'.

Brunsdon, Charlotte (1981) '"Crossroads" – notes on soap opera', *Screen*, V22 N4.

b & t advertising marketing and media weekly, 13 April 1984.

Buckingham, D. (1987) *Public Secrets: EastEnders and its Audience*, London: British Film Institute.

Budd, M.; Craig, S.; and Steinman, C. (1985) 'Fantasy Island: marketplace of desire', in M. Gurevitch and M. Levy (eds), *Mass Communication Review Yearbook*, V5, Beverly Hills: Sage.

Burgin, Victor; Donald, James; and Kaplan, Cora (1986) *Formations of Fantasy*, London: Methuen.

Caswell, Robert (1984) *Scales of Justice*, Sydney: Currency.

Caughie, John (1981) 'Progressive television and documentary drama', in Tony Bennett, Susan Boyd-Bowman, Colin Mercer and Janet Woollacott, *Popular Television and Film*, London: British Film Institute.

Clarke, Alan (1986) ' "This is not the boy scouts": Television police series and definitions of law and order', in T. Bennett *et al.*, *Popular Culture and Social Relations*, Milton Keynes: Open University.

Clyman, Toby W. (ed.) (1985) *A Chekhov Companion*, Westport: Greenwood.

Cohen, P. and Robbins, D. (1979) *Knuckle Sandwich*, Harmondsworth: Penguin.

Coleman, Richard (1987) Television review, *Sydney Morning Herald*, 25 July.

Connell, R.W. (1983) *Which Way Is Up? Essays on Class, Sex and Culture*, Sydney: Allen & Unwin.

Counihan, Mick (1982) 'The formation of a broadcasting audience: Australian radio in the twenties', *Meanjin* V41 N2. June.

Crofts, Stephen and Craik, Jennifer (1983) 'Constructing the political in *The Dismissal*', *Australian Journal of Cultural Studies*, V1 N2. December.

Cunningham, Stuart (1983) '*The Dismissal* and Australian television', *Australian Journal of Cultural Studies*, V1 N2. December.

Cunningham, Stuart (1989) 'Textual innovation in the Australian historical mini-series', in J. Tulloch and G. Turner (eds), *Australian Television: Meanings and Pleasures*, Sydney: Allen & Unwin.

Curran, James; Smith, Anthony; and Wingate, Pauline (1987) *Impacts and Influences: Essays on Media Power in the Twentieth Century*, London: Methuen.

Curthoys, Ann and Docker, John (1984) Paper at Australian Communications Association Conference.

Curthoys, Ann and Docker, John (1989) 'In praise of *Prisoner*', in J. Tulloch and G. Turner (eds), *Australian Television: Meanings and Pleasures*, Sydney: Allen & Unwin.

Davern, James (1986) 'The "A Country Practice" audience', paper at Australian Teachers of Media Conference.

de Certeau, Michael (1984) *The Practice of Everyday Life*, Berkeley: University of California Press.

de Marinis, Marco (1986) 'Dramaturgy of the audience', paper at Australian Drama Studies Association Conference.

Dennington, John and Tulloch, John (1976) 'Cops, consensus and ideology', *Screen Education*, N20. Autumn.

Donald, James (1985) 'Anxious moments: The Sweeney in 1975', in M. Alvarado and J. Stewart, *Made for Television: Euston Films Limited*, London: British Film Institute.

Dorfman, Ariel (1983) *The Empire's Old Clothes*, London: Pluto.

Drummond, Phillip (1976) 'Structural and narrative constraints and strategies in "The Sweeney"', *Screen Education*, N20. Autumn.

Dunn, Robert (1986) 'Television consumption and the commodity form', in *Theory, Culture and Society*, V3 N1.

Dyer, Richard *et al.* (1981) *Coronation Street*, London: British Film Institute.

Eaton, M. (1981) 'Television situation comedy', in Bennett *et al.*

Eco, Umberto (1979) 'The myth of superman', in U. Eco, *The Role of the Reader: Explorations in the Semiotics of Texts*, Bloomington: Indiana University Press.

Eco, Umberto (1984) 'The frames of comic "freedom"', in Umberto Eco, V. V. Ivanov, Monica Rector, *Carnival!*, Berlin: Mouton.

Eco, Umberto; Ivanov, V.V.; and Rector, Monica (1984) *Carnival!*, Berlin: Mouton.

Edgar, David (1979) 'Ten years of political theatre, 1968–78', *Theatre Quarterly*. Winter.

Elam, Keir (1980) *The Semiotics of Theatre and Drama*, London: Methuen.

Elam, Keir (1986) 'Text appeal and the analysis paralysis: towards a processual poetics of dramatic production', paper written for the Australasian Drama Association Conference, Sydney University.

Elliott, Philip; Murdock, Graham; and Schlesinger, Philip (1983) '"Terrorism" and the state: a case study of the discourses of television', *Media, Culture and Society*, V5 N2. April.

Ellis, John (1975) 'Made in Ealing' in *Screen*, V16 N1.

Ellis, John (1982) *Visible Fictions*, London: Routledge & Kegan Paul.

Feuer, Jane (1984) 'Melodrama, serial form and television today', *Screen*, V25 N1.

Feuer, Jane (1984) 'MTM Enterprises: an overview', in Feuer *et al.*

Feuer, Jane (1984) 'The MTM style', in Feuer *et al.*

Feuer, Jane; Kerr, Paul; and Bahimagi, Tise (1984) *MTM: 'Quality Television'*, London: British Film Institute.

Fiske, John (1982) *Introduction to Communication Studies*, London: Methuen.

Fiske, John (1983) 'Doctor Who: ideology and the reading of a popular narrative text', *Australian Journal of Screen Theory*, Nos 13–14.

Fiske, John (1985) 'Television, culture and communication', paper at the Australian Communications Conference.

Fiske, John (1987) 'British cultural studies and television', in R. Allen (ed.) *Channels of Discourse*, Chapel Hill: University of North Carolina.

Fiske, John (1988) *Television Culture: Popular Pleasures and Politics*, London: Methuen.

Flitterman, Sandy (1983) 'The real soap operas: TV commercials', in E. Ann Kaplan (ed.) *Regarding Television: Critical Approaches – An Anthology*, Los Angeles: American Film Institute.

Giddens, Anthony (1979) *Central Problems in Social Theory: Action, Structure and Contradiction*, London: Macmillan.

Giddens, Anthony (1981) *A Contemporary Critique of Historical Materialism*, V1, London: Macmillan.

Giddens, Anthony (1984) *The Constitution of Society*, Cambridge: Polity Press.

Giddens, Anthony (1986) 'Action, subjectivity, and the constitution of meaning', *Social Research*, V53 N3 Autumn.

Giddens, Anthony (1987) *Social Theory and Modern Sociology*, Cambridge: Polity Press.

Goodlad, J. S. R. (1977) *The Sociology of Popular Drama*, London: Heinemann, extracted in J. Tulloch, *Conflict and Control in the Cinema*, Basingstoke: Macmillan.

Grant, Steve (1987) 'No place like home', *Time Out* (March 25–April 1).

Griffiths, Trevor (May 1984) *Fatherland*, First Draft.

Griffiths, Trevor (1984) South Bank Show interview.

Griffiths, Trevor (1986) Interviewed by Misha Glenny, 1985, in *Judgement Over The Dead*, London: Verso.

Griffiths, Trevor (1987) *Fatherland*, London: Faber & Faber.

Griffiths, Trevor. Original script of *The Last Place On Earth*.

Gumpert, Gary and Cathcart, Robert (1986) *Inter/Media: Interpersonal Communication in a Media World*, New York: Oxford University Press.

Gunter, Barrie (1983) 'Children's interactions with television: new research perspectives and an eye on future developments', in Sally Kent (ed.), *TV and Children: Comprehension of Programs*, Melbourne: Monash University Education Faculty Research Monograph.

Gurevitch, M. and Levy, M. (eds) (1985) *Mass Communication Review Yearbook*, V5, Beverly Hills: Sage.

Hall, S. 'Encoding and decoding the TV message', cccs mimeo, University of Birmingham.

Hall, Stewart and Jefferson, Tony (eds) (1976) *Resistance Through Rituals: Youth Subcultures in Post-War Britain*, London: Hutchinson.

Hartley, John (1982) *Understanding News*, London: Methuen.

Hartley, John (1984) 'Out of bounds: the myth of marginality', in L. Masterman, *Television Mythologies: Stars, Shows and Signs*, London: Comedia.

Hayward, Philip (1988) 'How ABC capitalised on cultural logic: The Moonlighting Story', *Mediamatic* V2 N4.

Hebdige, Dick (1979) *Subculture: the Meaning of Style*, London: Methuen.

Hebdige, Dick (1987) 'The impossible object: towards a sociology of the sublime', *New Formations*, N1. Spring.

Hobson, Dorothy (1982) *Crossroads: The Drama of a Soap Opera*, London: Methuen.

Hodge, Robert and Tripp, David (1982) *The Active Eye: Children and Television*, Report to the sponsors of TVW7, Perth.

Hodge, Robert and Tripp, David (1986) *Children and Television: A Semiotic Approach*, Cambridge: Polity Press.

Huntford, Roland (1985) *The Last Place On Earth*, London: Pan.

Hurd, Geoff (1976) 'The Sweeney – contradiction and coherence', *Screen Education* N20. Autumn.

James, Paul (1987) 'Theory without practice: the work of Anthony Giddens', *Arena* 78.

Jenkins III, Henry (unpublished) *'Star Trek* "rerun, reread, rewritten"': fan fiction and women's culture'.

Johnson, Lesley (forthcoming) *The Unseen Voice: A Cultural Analysis of Radio Broadcasting in Australia, 1923–1939*, London: Methuen.

Kaplan, Cora (1986) *The Thorn Birds: fiction, fantasy, femininity*, in Victor Burgin, James Donald and Cora Kaplan, *Formations of Fantasy*, London: Methuen. pp. 164–5.

Kaplan, E. Ann (ed.) (1983) *Regarding Television: Critical Approaches – An Anthology*, Los Angeles: American Film Institute.

Kellner, Douglas (1987) 'Baudrillard, semiurgy and death', *Theory, Culture and Society*, V4.

Kellner, Douglas (1981) 'Network television and American society: introduction to a critical theory of television', *Theory and Society*, V10, No.1.

Kent, Sally (ed.) (1983) *TV and Children: Comprehension of Programs*, Melbourne: Monash University Education Faculty Research Monograph.

Kerr, Paul (1984) 'Drama at MTM: *Lou Grant* and *Hill Street Blues*', in Feuer *et al.*

Kessler, S.; Ashenden, D. J.; Connell, R.W.; and Dowsett, G. W. (1985) 'Gender relations in secondary schooling', *Sociology of Education*, V58.

King, Noel and Rowse, Tim (1980) '"Typical Aussies": television and populism in Australia', *Framework* 22/23.

Kippax, Susan (1988) 'Women as audience: the experience of unwaged women of the performing arts', *Media, Culture and Society*, V10.

Kuhn, Annette (1984) 'Women's genres', *Screen*, V25 N1.

Kundera, Milan (1983) *The Book of Laughter and Forgetting*, Harmondsworth: Penguin.

Lawson, Sylvia (1983) 'An audience for *The Dismissal*', *Australian Journal of Cultural Studies*, V1 N2. December.

Liebes, Tamar and Katz, Elihu (1987) 'On the critical ability of television viewers', Blaubeuren Symposium.

Lindlof, Thomas R. (ed.) (1987) *Natural Audiences: Qualitative Research of Media Uses and Effects*, Norwood: Ablex.

Lindlof, Thomas R. and Meyer, Timothy P. (1987) 'Mediated communication as ways of seeing, acting, and constructing culture: the tools and foundations of qualitative research', in Lindlof.

Loach, K. December 1986, Australian Broadcasting Corporation radio interview.

Lovell, Terry (1981) *Pictures of Reality: Aesthetics, Politics and Pleasure*, London: British Film Institute.

Lovell, Terry (1981) 'Ideology and Coronation Street', in Dyer *et al.*

Lovell, Terry (1982) 'A genre of social disruption?' in *Television Sitcom*, British Film Institute Dossier, London.

Lukács, Georg (1969) *The Historical Novel*, Harmondsworth: Peregrine.

Lusted, David (1984a) 'What's left of Blackstuff? Political meaning for a popular audience', in *Boys From The Blackstuff*, British Film Institute Dossier.

Lusted, David (1984b) Address to Australian Teachers of Media Conference, Sydney.

MacCabe, C. (1981) 'Memory, phantasy, identity: *Days of Hope* and the politics of the past', in Bennett *et al*.

Markovits, A. S. and Hayden, R. S. (1980) '"Holocaust" before and after the event: reactions in West Germany and Austria', *New German Critique*, N19. Winter.

Masterman, L. (1984) *Television Mythologies: Stars, Shows and Signs*, London: Comedia.

McArthur, Colin (1978) *Television and History*, London: British Film Institute.

McGrath, John (1977) 'TV drama: the case against naturalism', *Sight and Sound*, V46 N2. Spring.

McGrath, John (1981) *A Good Night Out: Popular Theatre: Audience, Class and Form*, London: Methuen.

McGrath, John (1984) 'The boys are back', in *Boys From The Blackstuff* Dossier.

McLennan, Gregor (1981) *Marxism and the Methodologies of History*, London: Verso.

McLennan, Gregor (1984) 'Critical or positive theory? A comment on the status of Anthony Giddens' social theory', *Theory, Culture and Society*, V2 N2.

McQuail, Denis (ed.) (1972) *Sociology of Mass Communications*, Harmondsworth: Penguin.

McQuail, Denis; Blumler, Jay; and Brown, J. R. (1972) 'The television audience: a revised perspective', in D. McQuail (ed.) *Sociology of Mass Communications*, Harmondsworth: Penguin.

Mellor, Adrian (1984) 'Science fiction and the crisis of the educated middle class', in C. Pawling (ed.) *Popular Fiction and Social Change*, London: Macmillan.

Messaris, Paul (1986) 'Parents, children and television', in Gary Gumpert and Robert Cathcart, *Inter/Media: Interpersonal Communication in a Media World*, New York: Oxford University Press.

Millington, Bob and Nelson, Robin (1986) *'Boys From The Blackstuff': The Making of TV Drama*, London: Comedia.

Modleski, Tania (1982) *Loving With A Vengeance: Mass-produced Fantasies for Women*, New York: Methuen.

Moran, Albert (1985) *Images and Industry: Television Drama Production in Australia*, Sydney: Currency.

Morley, David (1980) *The 'Nationwide' Audience: Structure and Decoding*, London: British Film Institute.

Morley, David (1981) 'The nationwide audience: a critical postscript', *Screen Education*, N39. Summer.

Morley, David (1986) *Family Television: Cultural Power and Domestic Leisure*, London: Comedia.

Morley, David (1987) 'Changing paradigms in audience studies', Blaubeuren Symposium.

Neale, Steve (1980) *Genre*, London: British Film Institute.

Nightingale, Virginia (forthcoming) 'Women as audiences', in M. E. Brown (ed.) *Television and Women's Culture*, Sydney: Currency.

O'Sullivan, Tim; Hartley, John; Saunders, Danny; and Fiske, John (1983) *Key Concepts in Communication*, London: Methuen.

Palmer, Patricia (1986a) *Girls and Television*, Sydney: Ministry of Education.

Palmer, Patricia (1986b) *The Lively Audience: A Study of Children around the TV Set*, Sydney: Allen & Unwin.

Parkin, F. (1973) *Class, Inequality and Political Order*, London: Paladin.

Paterson, Richard (1987) 'Restyling masculinity: the impact of "Boys from the Blackstuff" ', in James Curran, Anthony Smith and Pauline Wingate, *Impacts and Influences: Essays on Media Power in the Twentieth Century*, London: Methuen.

Pawling, C. (ed.) (1984) *Popular Fiction and Social Change*, London: Macmillan.

Philo, G.; Beharrel, P.; and Hewit, J. (1977) 'One-dimensional news – television and the control of "explanation" ', in P. Beharrel and G. Philo (eds) *Trade Unions and the Media*, London: Macmillan.

Polan, Dana (1978) 'Brecht and the politics of self-reflexive cinema', *Jump Cut*, N17.

Poole, Mike and Wyver, John (1984) *Powerplays: Trevor Griffiths in Television*, London: British Film Institute.

Potter, Sally (1985) Speech at the Sydney Film Festival, July.

Pound, John. Interviews at his house in Bournemouth, November 1985.

Radway, Janice (1984) *Reading the Romance: Women, Patriarchy, and Popular Literature*, Chapel Hill: University of North Carolina.

Radway, Janice. Preface to British edition of *Reading the Romance*, MS: 17, 26.

Redlich, Forrest (1984) 'Green Guide' in the *Age*, 11 October, Sydney.

Rethinking the Audience: New Tendencies in Television Research Symposium, in Blaubeuren, West Germany, 17–20 February, 1987.

Rimmon-Kenan, S. (1983) *Narrative Fiction: Contemporary Poetics*, London: Methuen.

Ross, Andrew (1987) 'Miami Vice: selling in', *Communication* V9.

Seiter, Ellen; Kreutzner, Gabriele; and Borchers, Hans (1987) '"Don't treat us like we're so stupid and naive": towards an ethnography of soap opera viewers', Blaubeuren Symposium.

Seiter, Ellen; Warth, Eve-Maria; Kreutzner, Gabriele; and Borchers, Hans (1989) *Remote Control*, London: Routledge.

Self, David (1984) *Television Drama: An Introduction*, London: Macmillan.

Selig, Michael (1985) 'Conflict and contradiction in the mass media', *Jump Cut*, N30.

Sharratt, Bernard (1980) 'The politics of the popular? – from melodrama to television', in David Bradby, Louis James and Bernard Sharratt, *Performance and Politics in Popular Drama*, Cambridge: Cambridge University Press.

Silverstone, R. (1981) *The Message of Television: Myth and Narrative in Contemporary Culture*, London: Heinemann.

Simonds, Diana (1988) 'Pink Guide' in the *Sydney Morning Herald* 1–17 February.

Skirrow, Gillian (1985) 'Widows', in Alvarado and Stewart.

Smith, Ruth (1984) 'A feminist view', in *Boys From The Blackstuff* Dossier.

Surlin, Stuart H. and Tate, Eugene D. (1976) '"All in the Family": Is Archie Funny?', *Journal of Communication*. Autumn.

Sydney Morning Herald, 27 January 1988.

Tancock, L. W. (1954) Introduction to Emile Zola, *Germinal*, Harmondsworth: Penguin.

Thompson, John O. (1982) *Monty Python: Complete and Utter Theory of the Grotesque*, London: British Film Institute.

Tulloch, John (ed.) (1977) *Conflict and Control in the Cinema*, Basingstoke: Macmillan.

Tulloch, John (1980) *Chekhov: A Structuralist Study*, Basingstoke: Macmillan.

Tulloch, John (1981) *Legends On The Screen: The Narrative Film in Australia 1919–1929*, Sydney: Currency.

Tulloch, John (1982) *Australian Cinema: Industry, Narrative and Meaning*, Sydney: Allen & Unwin.

Tulloch, John and Alvarado, Manuel (1983) *Doctor Who: The Unfolding Text*, Basingstoke: Macmillan.

Tulloch, John (1985) 'Chekhov abroad: western criticism', in Toby W. Clyman (ed.) *A Chekhov Companion*, Westport: Greenwood.

Tulloch, John (1986) 'Responsible soap: discourses of Australian TV drama', *East-West Film Journal*, V1 N1.

Tulloch, John and Moran, Albert (1986) *A Country Practice: 'Quality Soap'*, Sydney: Currency.

Tulloch, John (1987) Paper at Blaubeuren Symposium, Germany. February.

Tulloch, John and Turner, Graeme (1989) *Australian Television: Meanings and Pleasures*, Sydney: Allen & Unwin.

Tulloch, John (unpublished) 'Formal curriculum: St Ives High School'.

Tulloch, John (1989) 'Approaching the audience: the elderly', in Ellen Seiter, Eve-Maria Warth, Gabriele Kreutzner and Hans Borchers *Remote Control*, London: Routledge.

Walkerdine, Valerie (1986) *Video Replay: Families, Films and Fantasy*, in Burgin *et al.*

Westergaard, J. H. (1972) 'The myth of classlessness', in R. Blackburn, *Ideology and the Social Sciences*, London: Fontana.

Wickham, Gary (1987) 'Foucault, power, Left politics', *Arena* 78.

Wilhoit, G. Cleveland and de Bock, Harold (1976) '"All in the Family" in Holland', *Journal of Communication*. Autumn.

Williams, Raymond (1977) 'A lecture on realism', *Screen*. Spring.

Williams, Raymond (1977) 'Realism, naturalism and the alternatives', *Cine-Tracts*, V1 N3. Fall 1977 – Winter 1978.

Williams, Raymond (1977) *Marxism and Literature*, Oxford: Oxford University Press.

Williams, Raymond (1981) Foreword to John McGrath, *A Good Night Out: Popular Theatre: Audience, Class and Form*, London: Methuen.

Williamson, Judith (1978) *Decoding Advertisements*, London: Boyars.

Windschuttle, Keith (1984) *The Media*, Ringwood: Penguin.

Winterbottom, Michael (1985) 'In production: Minder', in Alvarado and Stewart.

Wolff, Janet (1981) *The Social Production of Art*, London: Macmillan.

Index of Programmes

Index of Names

Index of Concepts